D0936951

Jack Hylton

Jack Hylton

Pete Faint

2014

First Printing: 2014

ISBN 978-1-326-06139-5

Published by Pete Faint
pete@petefaint.com
www.petefaint.com

For more information, visit www.jackhylton.com

This book is dedicated to anyone who has ever threatened to write a book for over twenty years.

Keep plugging away...

Contents

Acknowledgements

Outside The Jack Hylton Music Rooms, Lancaster University.

Having been researching Jack Hylton for so long, there are many people who I need to thank for their time, going back to my MPhil studies of the late 1990s. Firstly to my tutor from that period, Professor Denis McCaldin, who was a constant source of encouragement during those years, not only a person of great knowledge on the subject but the sort of man who could guide a stupid person like myself to gain a rather serious qualification.

Denis introduced me to Jack Hylton Junior, who is not only now a very dear friend, but also the ultimate resource for most things within this book. I value our time together immensely, whether talking about his Dad or talking our usual nonsense.

Many other people have generously given their time to make this book what it is. Also at Lancaster at that time was Stella Birchall, who was always my first link to Denis McCaldin. Currently at Lancaster are Helen Clish and Liz Fawcett, who work in the Hylton Archive and have shown great patience over the years with my obscure questions and requirements. Dr. Lindsay Newman was in charge of restoration of the archive and gave her time willingly in the 90s to allow me to view the archive, despite it not at that time being suitable for such viewing.

Through Jack Junior, I contacted Lady Beverley McKay (Hylton's second wife) and Jackie Ward-Ramos (his eldest daughter). Beverley has sadly since passed away. I thank all the family for all their patience, information and reminiscences. I also fully respect the guarded way they approached their father's private life and I hope the whole family is happy with the book.

Peter Wallace, despite working in Brazil throughout my studies, suggested a number of possible leads over the internet, almost all of which were helpful. Chris Hayes, a former *Melody Maker* journalist was gracious in his reply, despite being very ill. Through him, I contacted Alasdair Fenton, to whom I owe a huge debt with his encyclopaedic knowledge of all things Hyltonian.

Thanks must also go to pianist Billy Munn (who remembered 1931 vividly), Avril Dankworth (for her kind words and the article written by her late husband Les Carew), Marion Freyther (who very kindly translated everything I asked, free of charge), Steve Race OBE (for enthusiasm and the contact of Avril Dankworth), Malcolm Drew (for his information on Hylton's early career, and photograph) and Dr. Stephen Walsh, at the University of Wales, Cardiff, for his thoughts on Stravinsky and *Mavra*.

The National Jazz Archive in Loughton is a valuable resource, and thanks are due firstly to Ken Jones (the former archivist) and to David Nathan (the current archivist) for their help and enthusiasm. Also I'd like to thank Anthony Holmes (who sourced a great deal of information on the Jack Hylton Music Maker juke boxes), and authors Brian Rust and Pamela Logan, (who both answered my queries kindly and swiftly) and Catherine Parsonage (who kindly donated her book to a fellow impoverished author!)

More recently, this book probably wouldn't have happened had it not been for the 50th anniversary concert at Lancaster University, which ran alongside this project. For that I have to thank Fiona Sinclair, who was enthusiastic and on-board with everything I threw at her at our initial rather noisy meeting in Manchester, and throughout the project, as was Chris Osborn at Lancaster University, who also helped with the project as a whole and the continuing Hylton legacy.

I'd also like to thank Marianne Aben, the current owner of Hylton's old home, Langsmeade House in Lower Milton, who had the wherewithal to write down the reminiscences of Rose Ilbury and then share them with me before Rose became too ill. Also to the Meredith family, who allowed me to run away to their holiday cottage in Wales, where I'm writing these very words in rural peace. There are also worthy mentions for my internet contacts; Paul Holdroyd, who kept me abreast of goings on through many years of me nearly losing interest; Andy Wint, for his help with information on Ennis Parkes; Andrew Rigby for his invaluable help with the early radio broadcasts of the Hylton band and Simon Vaughan for his information on Radiolympia.

Everything you'll read has previously been read by two wise academics, my very dear friends Mark Goggins and Su Briggs, and I owe them both a huge thanks for reading this and making all the rubbish bits good. I suspect if it wasn't for their help and advice, what you're about to read would probably be mostly gibberish. Also to another dear friend, Martin Kay, who did the final, rather thorough proof read. If there are any typos, we can blame Martin.

Finally, I would like to thank my wife Lucy, who has always been accepting of a little bit of Hylton in our life, but over the last year has been gracious in accepting how much time I have spent pouring over every detail of this man, and how our house has been taken over by Hylton 78's, LP's, pictures, files, folders, photocopies, books about dance bands, books about people associated with Hylton, and constant trips away to Lancaster or to my little 'writing sessions' in mysterious locations.

Foreword

Fade in, fade out – the scene changes. Todays frenzy is tomorrow's flop. This year's rave may well become next year's yawn. But though shows may fold, great showmen go on and on...And Jack Hylton was one of the greatest showmen of them all. He loved the footlights and the people who sang, danced and clowned in front of them. This was his world and he vastly enriched it by his shrewd judgement, his dour courage and his rare gift for creating stars. But there is also this to say about Jack. He was generous to those at the bottom of the bill and to those who could no longer make it. And for this we thank him – and salute him.

Donald Zec
The Stars Shine For Jack programme – 1965

Preface

Hylton with Joseph c.1955. Nicky, Hylton's chauffeur, would let Joseph out of the car first, so everyone would know Jack was on his way!
(Jack Hylton Archive)

A parson in a Lancashire chapel was interrogating his Sunday school on its general biblical knowledge, and, in particular, on Judas Iscariot: "Can you tell me", said he, "a famous biblical character whose initials were 'J.I.'?" A dear little urchin readily responded. "Yes", he said, brightly, "Jack 'ylton!"[1]

I'm often asked about my interest in Jack Hylton. To be honest it's become something of an obsession, rather than an interest. It first started in 1992 when I began my studies at Lancaster University. I was studying music, which meant a considerable amount of time spent in the Jack Hylton Music Rooms, which feature a huge smiling picture of Jack in its entrance hall. As a lover and player of jazz music in an otherwise mostly classical department I (with just a few friends) was something of a musical outsider. I was once told "you know about jazz, you must know about Jack Hylton". I didn't of course, but I decided that if I was the guy running the Music Society Big Band, rehearsing in a room named after a jazz musician then yes, I should know about him.

I assumed a trip to the library and a quick scan of one or other of his biographies would fill me in with anything I needed to know. What became clear was that there wasn't a biography of any description, not just in that library, not in any library. I did manage to find out that this chap was rather successful and a little further study made me realise that he was something more than that: the leader of the greatest show band Europe (or probably the world) experienced in the inter-war years. It also became clear that he also happened to be amongst the most important theatrical producers in Britain in the years following the dance band days, until his death.

For reasons that escape me now, I decided to take things a bit further and extend my studies and looked into possibly doing what I at that time called 'a degree in Jack Hylton'. The university in their infinite wisdom decided to give their funding to someone who wanted to write something about Mozart and someone who wanted to write something about 'cellos. At least that's the way I remember it.

Rather than leave things there, after a year in which I was supposed to see sense, I didn't see sense and paid for my own further study (for three years) and managed eventually to become a degree-wielding expert on Hylton. During this period it became clear that the university held an archive of some kind and the apocryphal story was that the entire contents of this archive had been rescued from the leaking loft at the Adelphi Theatre in London and placed in a disused toilet in the Geography department at Lancaster.

On closer inspection, it became obvious that all the toilets in the Geography department were in regular use and the slightly less exciting true story is that the archive was at that time being stored in a small storeroom in a residential block near the Jack Hylton Music Rooms.

I remember vividly being shown the archive by Professor Denis McCaldin shortly before I began my studies and being rather overwhelmed by it all. Even to this day my regular visits still overwhelm me but back then a floor to ceiling pile of boxes was rather over-facing. Also during that time the archive was moving into a rebuilt and expanded library and found its current home, in a temperature controlled (i.e. freezing cold) room within the Rare Books Archive, where it slowly began to be logged, sorted, displayed and cleaned up, making it slightly less over-facing than before.

Of course the archive has been the singular greatest resource one could ask for when writing a book of this nature. Hylton was a great hoarder and employed the services of a press cuttings agency, which cut out and stuck in enormous books almost every mention of his name in every newspaper in Europe from 1922 until long after his death in the late 1960s. From these one can almost put together a day-by-day log of Hylton's professional life. It's both fascinating and impossibly tedious, but without it I'd not have got anywhere near this.

What the archive doesn't tell you is much about Hylton's private life, and given what a lark it appears to have been, it's amazing it was kept out of the tabloids, which loved the salacious gossip then as they do now. Hylton must have had some kind of hold over the editors, or they were in it together! [2] A little deeper research is needed for that part of the story, but one can find out enough if one digs deep enough. I've not felt the need to be sordid or assume the rumours are facts, but an idea of how he led his life is certainly present here. Of course his son Jack Junior was a great source here and I don't apologise for keeping the odd story out of this book, for the sake of dignity. Suffice to say Hylton was a lively chap, and much loved.

I also make no excuse for the number of quotations within this book. A great deal of them are from Hylton himself; he wrote often for the newspapers and trade papers, especially through the 1930's and was interviewed often through the 1940s and 1950s. His words tell the story better than my words. Where other authors tell their own story, I have no problem regurgitating their words when they can tell better their personal experience of the man. If that leaves this book rather quotation heavy, then so be it.

I genuinely feel that the story is better told in the first person and I definitely wasn't there, so I'd rather the protagonists told the story in their own words. I hope you agree.

I really hope you enjoy what I've written. It's been a labour of love and I think it's a great story. I also really hope that, whilst reading this, you do what I did whilst writing it – listen to Hylton's music. Almost ever word you read has been accompanied by popular and less popular Hylton numbers, from the many available CDs on the market, to the rarer items which I have floating around, many of which are available for download on the Official Jack Hylton Website (www.jackhylton.com).

Yes, that's a plug for the website I've been running since 1999. On it is a great deal of information contained in these pages, plus many pictures, information on the CDs available to buy and that I've compiled, and plenty of links to music, video and other curiosities relating to Hylton which couldn't be contained within these pages. Please visit the site, please buy the CDs and please tell your friends to buy more copies of this book – being a Hylton scholar is little more than an excuse to lose money.

Chapter 1: 1892-1905

'Jack Hilton – Boy Soprano' (Jack Hylton Archive)

Jack Hylton's story begins in Bolton, in the northwest of England in the late nineteenth century. It ought to be a tale of great poverty, a shining example of the aching grimness of post-Industrial Revolution life in a stereotypical northern town, where the protagonists have little or no life to speak of, no money and no home of their own. Their son then drags himself away from this, to greatness in the 'big smoke'.

Jack Hylton

This is not a story I can tell, despite many of the mini-biographies that appear of Hylton on LP and CD sleeves trying to tell it. The life that Jack's parents George and Mary Hilton embarked on together in 1892 was not one of great riches or luxury, but this was a couple who were striving for something other than the mundanity of life in the cotton mills of Bolton.

Bolton is a mill town,[1] ten miles north of Manchester, close to the West Pennine Moors. Traditionally part of Lancashire, the Metropolitan Borough of Bolton (which encompasses Bolton itself along with several small nearby towns and villages) is now part of Greater Manchester. Bolton developed from parts of the parish of Bolton-le-Moors, which eventually developed into a small town. Flemish weavers settled in the 14th century (with another wave in the 17th century) and introduced the manufacture of woollen cloth. In the 19th century Bolton saw massive growth, in part due to this history of weaving but also due to developments in spinning technology led by local man Samuel Crompton's invention of the spinning mule in 1779. His first cotton mill opened in 1780. The industrial revolution was boom time for Bolton and the population rose from 5,339 in 1773 to 168,000 in 1851. The Manchester Bolton & Bury Canal was built in the 1790s and the Bolton and Leigh Railway (the first in Lancashire) was opened in 1830. This rapid growth and expansion (several hundred cotton mills appeared during this period) led to similar levels of poverty and degradation which were more famously noted in nearby Manchester. Improvements were made: streets were lit by gas in 1814; the Royal Infirmary opened in 1883; electricity was first generated in Bolton in 1894. Into this world came the Hilton and Greenhalgh families.

We know little about the formative years of Mary Greenhalgh or George Hilton, other than what we can glean from the public records. Both came from relatively humble beginnings. George's father Samuel Hilton (1829-1881) worked as a cotton weaver in Tonge-with-Haulgh, in Bolton, Lancashire, whilst Mary's father John Greenhalgh (1845-1896) was a woodworker in the Belmont area of Bolton. These two areas are close by, outside the centre of Bolton but still very much centred around the cotton trade, with mills situated in almost every township in the parish. John Greenhalgh married Elizabeth (born 1845) and together they had seven children, including Mary, who was born in 1870. Samuel Hilton married Nancy (born 1831) and together they had five children, the youngest of whom was George, born in 1871.

The cotton mills in which Samuel Hilton and his family worked were implausibly bleak places within which to live and work:

> Shoehorned into the mills even as toddlers, forced to work unbelievably long hours when trade demanded it, starved when boom turned into bust, on the scrapheap at 35 or 40 with nothing but the hated workhouse and then death to look forward to. That was the lot of many workers... Children as young as five were thrown into the mills, while others a little older worked 12, 13 or 14 hours a day in the grimmest and most dangerous conditions, and were beaten by overseers just to keep them awake towards the end of their back-breaking shifts.

> But grim or not, the conditions were sometimes preferable to those existing at home. Manchester and her cotton satellites became "frontier" towns, with long, sunless terraces of jerry-built houses thrown up piecemeal to accommodate the thousands of workers pouring in from the countryside, built with little regard to basic sanitation and none at all to comfort... With families crowded into these unhealthy hovels, sickness and disease were close neighbours and epidemics struck regularly. Cholera and typhoid were always on the prowl, and in the smoke-saturated air of the cotton towns, where the sun was never more than a dull orange glow through the smog, children were lucky to survive into adulthood.[2]

In this environment George Hilton and Mary Greenhalgh met. As the 1880s became the 1890s George was living at home with his parents and working as a yarn twister in a cotton mill, whilst Mary was living at home and working as a school teacher at Christ Church School in Ainsworth, Bolton:

> In my childhood I thought of her as severe. She had been a schoolteacher and never lost her school teaching ways.[3]

We know little else of their romance and early life together, except that when they married in April 1892, it was just three months before their first son was born:

> ...Then my father rose. 'There's nothing so wonderful about it [Jack's swift rise to fame] at all,' he said. 'What *is* remarkable is that if I hadn't met Mary' – that's mother – 'one wet Sunday afternoon in Bolton in 1891, there'd have been no success. What's more there'd have been no Jack Hylton!'[4]

They named him John Greenhalgh Hilton, taking Mary's maiden name as his middle name and taking the first name of her paternal Grandfather. He was born on July 2nd 1892 at 75 Division Street[5], Tum Fowle, in the village of Great Lever in Bolton. Recollections from Jack's cousin Fred suggest his mother was "knitting a pair of socks to earn a shilling the day he was born"[6]. Great Lever is now a humble suburb of Bolton, the largest town in Europe, and most of the cotton mills have either been demolished or turned into antiques centres or chic modern flats. The inevitable back-to-back terrace in which George and Mary lived is long gone.

So life began for John Greenhalgh Hilton in modest circumstances, in a house less than a mile from Burnden Park,[7] the home of Jack's beloved Bolton Wanderers Football Club, though they moved from there after just six months. The young family lived on George's modest wage from the cotton mill, but this was a future Hilton was unwilling to settle for. In Jack's own words "he believed life should be joyous"[8].

Along with working in the cotton mill, George was also something of an amateur entertainer. Later he would strongly encourage his eldest son to play the piano and sing and this passion for the entertainment industry clearly was a massive influence on the young John Hilton:

> My father, who was a good amateur singer, also fancied himself as a violin player. Before I was seven, however, I formed the conclusion that Pa's efforts on the fiddle were not up to concert level, and one day I had the impudence

to tell him that I hoped to do greater things in the musical line than ever he had managed to achieve.[9]

Jack aged three, with grandmother Elizabeth Greenhalgh. (Jack Hylton Archive)

George Hilton was an active trade unionist and an avid follower of Robert Blatchford's Clarion Movement. Blatchford was born in Maidstone, but after serving in the army began working as a journalist, eventually working for the *Morning Chronicle* in Manchester. Whilst there, he was taken to the slums of Ancoats and Hulme by Socialist Joe Waddington. Blatchford finally became a Socialist after reading *What is Socialism?*, written by Henry Hyndman and William Morris. Blatchford was not a theoretician but came to Socialism because he saw it as a practical solution to the poverty and misery he had personally witnessed.[10]

Blatchford wasn't allowed to write about Socialism in the *Morning Chronicle*, so audaciously set up his own newspaper, *The Clarion*. It was a gamble, but many of his readers followed him and his weekly editions became hugely popular, not as a dusty political tome, but a jovial mix of news, comment, short stories, songs and poetry.

The readers of *The Clarion* in turn set up a network of societies and clubs (including the Clarion Cycling Club which exists to this day throughout the country) which included scouts, rambling clubs, vocal groups, handicraft clubs and fellowship groups.

It was at one of these clubs, a Clarion Music Club in Bolton (which George Hilton almost certainly had a hand in setting up) where Jack Hylton took his first musical steps, with a dozen piano lessons, what was known in Lancashire as "one quarter". He was taught by Thomas Cheetham, who would later be the conductor of the Blackpool Tower Circus band:

> [He] was the first man to introduce me to five finger exercises, and the infinite subtleties of *Won't You Buy My Pretty Flowers*. Nobody, incidentally, ever bought them. Nor, at that stage of my musical scholarship, could you honestly blame them.[11]

Music was not the only thing that a young Hylton took from his father, and the Clarion movement:

> Like Blatchford, he wanted to help other people to stand on their own feet without climbing on someone else's back. For him, as for Blatchford, his political faith was not one of joyless doctrine. It was warmed by the fun of living. My Dad took after Blatchford; and I take after my Dad.[12]

It was uncommon for a tradesman to be so blatant with his politics as Hilton was but he felt a strong affiliation with Blatchford and clearly led by example in the way in which he moved positively from a menial job in the mills to working for himself doing something he enjoyed and was passionate about.

From Division Street, the family moved first to the Moses Gate area of Bolton, then to Deane Church Lane, all three homes within a few miles of each other. By the time Jack was seven years old, in 1899, George Hilton had given up working in the cotton mill and was running his own grocer's shop.[13] This did not give him the fulfilment he was looking for either and after a few years running the shop, he took up work as a 'licensed victualler', or a publican as we now know it. The pub he was licensee of was the small Roundcroft Tavern in James Street, Little Lever – just a short distance from their previous home in Great Lever; they moved there in 1902. This building has since been demolished, but it was here that George found his vocation, entertaining, whilst serving the customers.

Whilst here Jack attended St. Michael's School (which still stands on Green Lane in Great Lever) but began his musical career at his Dad's pub:

> I can remember...when my Dad was licensee of this pub...he used to lock me into the room here, which was partitioned off, and tell me to play the piano. He used to sit in the billiard room next door, and every time I stopped he wanted to know why.[14]

Although he only had those few lessons, he learned to read music and in due course began to accompany his father on those Saturday evenings in the pub – his first public appearances:

> I remember the days when he used to come in and sing his old song – *There's Nothing Like This In America, There's Nothing So Pretty In France, There's Nothing That's In It With This Little Linnet, I'll Learn It To Sing And To Dance...* And he used to play and sing one of his favourite songs *When I'm Following In Fathers Footsteps, I'm Following Me Dear Old Dad.* And he did do too. Those were rough days, when beer was a penny a gill and Woodbine were five a penny. Them were the days when Jack had to please everybody and he did, he did it well, too.[15]

These early performances began before Jack was in his teens and clearly his passion was music and not school:

> I hated school. For two whole weeks I played truant and spent the time in a farmyard. If my father had found out he would have laughed. He didn't think much of school. But it was my mother who found out. Next morning she carried me kicking and screaming under her arm to the school gates.[16]

This reluctance towards his schooling is the direct opposite of his approach to his music – he practiced hard at the piano, both when his father watched over him and when he was by himself. He wanted to be an entertainer from an early age, learning songs and stagecraft from his father and developing through his own live experience. A particular favourite at that time was a song the young Jack sang to the pub customers called *Don't Ask Me To Play 'Home Sweet Home'*, which was a 'weepy' about a street musician willing, for a few coppers, to sing anything but the tune that reminded him of the family he had disgraced. Hylton later said "the customers were so moved by this tale of a man reduced to the gutter by drink that they would order extra pints to restore their spirits!"[17]

George Hilton subsequently made a move to running a pub back in his old stomping ground of Stalybridge. The family moved there from Little Lever in 1903, to the Commercial Hotel, in Melbourne Street. Melbourne Street remains one of the central streets in Stalybridge and the Commercial Hotel subsequently became the Commercial Inn (famed for live rock music!) and then The Riverside before its demise at the turn of the 21st century.

Jack attended St. Paul's School, in Huddersfield Road, Stalybridge, a school that, at the time of writing, has been open for one hundred and seventy five years. George and Mary added to the family, giving Jack a younger brother and sister. George Whalley Hilton was born in 1898 and would grow up to look remarkably like his father, whilst sister Dorothy Elsie Hilton (born in 1906) would grow up to become a singer with her big brother's band, as Dolly Elsie.

It was in Stalybridge that the now complete family settled for some years, with George entertaining the customers in the music room of the pub on a Saturday night and managing to mix elements of music and politics, as Hylton himself describes:

> Still, he had fun. I remember the beginnings of the Variety Artists' Federation, when top-liners like Marie Lloyd came out on strike against the managements. They held committee meetings in my father's pub at Stalybridge, and, when the proceedings were over, took a little of what they fancied and sang songs. My father, by nature an entertainer, sang songs too.[18]

George Hilton spread his creative wings a little whilst running the pub in Stalybridge. He started his own Pierrot troupe, alongside Bert Maden (performing as the Maden & Hilton Pierrots), which would

8

take the two and a half mile journey from Stalybridge to Mottram, to play outside the tram terminus. They played there for two summer seasons, in a field near the Dog & Partridge Inn, attracting crowds at weekends. (Or as Hylton put it later in life; "it played regularly – usually to two deaf men and about a score of children"[19]).

However, these were Jack's first professional engagements away from the Commercial Hotel and they led to some other work in local halls, where he began an act which he would continue with until his voice broke – The Singing Mill Boy, complete with clogs, a dinner pail and red-handkerchiefed basin. Of course he never was a mill boy and it was by now many years since his father had worked in a mill, but it was the perfect approach for a young boy singer and would lead very soon to greater, if not great, things for Jack Hilton.

Chapter 2: 1905-1913

The Merrie Men Of Rhyl. Jack Hylton appears bottom middle in the picture.
(Malcolm Drew, private collection)

By the summer of 1905, at the age of just thirteen Jack Hilton (Jack being a common colloquial version of John) was enjoying an established, though modest career in local music halls as The Singing Mill Boy. He was spotted in and around Stalybridge by E.H. Williams, who owned and managed a Pierrot troupe called *The Merrie Men* who worked during the summer season out of the North Wales seaside resort of Rhyl.

A Pierrot is a pantomime clown character that originated in 17th century Italian Commedia dell'Arte. The English 19th century version was developed by singer and banjoist Clifford Essex who, on returning from a trip to France, resolved to create an English version of the French Pierrots he had seen there. The conical hatted, black and white costumed entertainers subsequently became a fixture in the seaside Pierrot troupes (or concert parties) for around fifty years, mostly on the South, South-Eastern and North-Western coasts of Britain.

At the turn of the century Rhyl had seen significant changes from the small fishing village it had been as late as the 1830s. Its place on the Chester and Holyhead railway line (Rhyl station was opened in 1848) led to it being adopted as a popular resort for Victorian holidaymakers, especially from the northwest of England. It was popular both for its beaches and its stunning views to the Clwydian hills and Snowdon. By 1867, a 2,355 feet long, £17,000 pier had been built to compliment the new hotel which had begun to appear. It was from the pier pavilion that many of the concert parties would begin to work from, despite serious damage having been done to the pier from both severe weather and boating accidents.

The *Merrie Men*, under the auspices of interlocutor[1] E.H. Williams, worked out of Rhyl between 1899 and 1906, though Williams appears to have been in charge of this evolving group for thousands of shows before this time. The size of the concert party show varied, but consisted of comedians, singers, musicians, dancers, jugglers, acrobats, and sketch artists, even female impersonators:

> The Pierrot show comprised various 'turns' which varied from company to company, depending on the talents of troupe's groups members. Usually audiences could expect to enjoy songs, instrumental turns, comic backchat and sketches, dancing and displays of particular skills, such as juggling. Companies for the most part were based in particular resorts, returning summer after summer to perform on the sands or promenade. In the early decades of the century, touring from resort to resort became more usual. Touring inland, especially in the winter, began about 1910.[2]

It would be into this environment that young Jack was thrown, and his time working in the local halls in Bolton or in Stalybridge would have given him exactly the right grounding and experience to succeed within this troupe of generally much older performers. Certainly he was never likely to be worried about leaving home for a lengthy summer season when he had been given an opportunity to embark on the career that he dreamed of. During the summer of 1905 Hilton was performing his boy soprano act from the halls for which he had initially been spotted, as well as playing the piano and clearing up the pitch after each performance – a tough life for a thirteen year old, but considerably more desirable than staying at home and working in a cotton mill.

The seaside concert party would require five or sometimes six shows a day – serenading the terraces at 9.00am, giving a show on the sands at 10.45am, serenading again at 2.00pm, back to the sands at 3.00pm, away to the terraces again at 6.00pm, and on the sands yet again at 7.00pm – this was described by veteran entertainers as 'in and out with the tides'.

Performers would have to constantly update material, and would supplement their income by walking round among the holidaymakers hoping for voluntary contributions for their collection. This six show a day summer season earned Jack the handsome sum of thirty shillings per week. He spent the money on donkey rides on the sands and landed home at the end of the season with 1s 6d.

Once autumn came and the tourists returned home, so did Hilton, with no money to show for the six months work, but a wealth of experience and his resolve to enjoy a career in entertainment undiminished.

Back in Stalybridge there was of course no chance of Jack going back to school but the bookings for the local halls continued to come in. The act continued to be honed there, and in the Commercial Hotel, adding comedy to the singing, without ever setting the entertainment world alight.

The summer of 1906 was spent at Craig-y-don, in Llandudno, North Wales with a concert party. It is worth mentioning here a matter that many sources have been confused with:

> Jack would sweep the stage at Rhyl and help his father dress as 'Happy Jack Hylton - The Diminutive Comedian' for £5 a week and a share of the 'bottle' (collection).[3]

It would appear that the Jack Hylton in question is a comedian from Liverpool, not related at all to our Hiltons or Hyltons, as explained by George in a 1941 newspaper article:

> That Jack…was a Liverpool comedian who was a big favourite at Rhyl. He spelt his name with a 'y'. We spelt ours with an 'i'. About ten years later, 'our Jack' made his first appearance at Rhyl, and, by accident or design, he

found himself billed not as Jack Hilton, but as Jack Hylton. He liked the change so much that he adopted the new spelling and the rest of the family followed suit.[4]

It seems a strange situation, but this serves better than any other situation for the family changing their name. It transpires that Jack never officially changed his name. In 1913, he would sign contracts 'Jackson Hilton', the only in print use of 'Jackson' that is known. By the 1960s, official papers showed that his name remained John Greenhalgh Hilton, and deed poll records at the National Archives at Kew back this up.[5]

By the summer of 1907, Jack was working for the Adeler & Sutton Pierrot troupe, in Girvan, on the west coast of Scotland. London.

*   *   *

Edwin Adeler, the son of a Presbyterian Minister, had previously worked with a theatrical fit-up company before he began working with entertainer W.G. Sutton. They got together in 1894 and travelled to Weymouth to try their luck as seaside entertainers, along with their pianist, who would walk his piano up and down the promenade on a trolley, until they found their pitch. They would make money by 'bottling'. Soon after, they moved to Harrogate and introduced the Pierrot outfits, complete with white make-up – made from the rather unpleasant sounding recipe of zinc and lard.

In 1898, the pair tried their hand in Southport, became the Southport Pierrots, along with the pianist and comedian Frank Lynne (Clive Dunn's grandfather). They moved from there to New Brighton, where they became resident, becoming the Adeler & Sutton Pierrots, where they worked with a young Jack Hylton. They also became supremely successful, and had twenty resident pitches by the early 1900s. By 1909, Adeler felt he had achieved everything he could in this country – he had become a very powerful influence in the summer entertainment business, given a number of artists their first break in show business and had a ball whilst he was about it. His was the first Pierrot troupe to employ a female member, Ethel Stanhope (the Pierrots had an enormous female following, and the managers of the show would keep any information on the performers being married very quiet) and he was the first to pay a performer £100 per week, in 1908! Adeler

14

moved to South Africa in 1909 and set up the first Pierrot company there. Dolly Summers was his female member there, who would go on to star in *ITMA (It's That Man Again)*, with Tommy Handley, another Pierrot troupe artist, linking us back to Jack Hylton.

*   *   *

> It was just as bad the next summer when, after working for a concert party in Girvan, I spent all my money on presents for my young brother and sister, so that Mum had to send me my fare home.[6]

After another winter back in the Stalybridge pub, the summer of 1908 was also spent with Adeler & Sutton, this time in New Brighton, a seaside resort in Wallasey, on the coast of what is now Merseyside. Much like Rhyl, the resort came to prominence in the mid-nineteenth century, having previously been a dropping off point for smugglers. Much of the land was purchased by a rich Liverpool merchant who wanted to create a resort for the gentry, similar to Brighton (hence the name). Substantial development followed, including a pier built in 1867 with an adjoining 2,000-seater pavilion theatre, where the Pierrot shows often played.

By this time Jack was being paid two pounds per week and was now a seasoned performer and accompanist.[7] After another winter making ends meet in his father's pub and in the halls, the summer of 1909 was spent with the Pierrots on the coast of Devon. Whilst there, Jack befriended the organist at Exeter Cathedral, Dr Pym, whose impact on Jack's future was significant:

> ...as a kid accompanist for a concert party in Exeter, I had become friendly with the organist of Exeter Cathedral. He said I had talent. He practically forced me to read theory. I did so. I don't remember his name but I bless his memory.[8]

By 1909, Adeler had moved to South Africa, so Jack was looking for new employment and the first of many lucky breaks fell into his lap in the autumn of that year. He replied to an advertisement in long-running trade paper *The Stage* for the job of musical director with a touring pantomime company, run by Joseph Garibaldi Kiddie (1864-

1943), a comedian who had formed a sketch company in 1907 before forming the J. Gar Kiddie & Co. pantomime production company shortly afterwards. The salary was an unimpressive forty-five shillings per week. Despite his age, Jack was able to offer the company considerable musical experience and vast energy and eagerness. He was offered the job, and gained his first experience with a baton, with this job being his first as a bandleader.

The touring company would have employed the in house musicians in whichever venue they arrived at (up to eight players) so Hylton was working with small ensembles of varying sizes and of sometimes questionable quality. This would have been challenging work for such a young man, directing jaded musicians much more senior than himself, but the sheer fact that he stayed for three seasons suggests that he was a success in his new role of pianist/bandleader:

> I went to the auditions. I must have looked young. Perhaps I looked innocent. Gar Kiddie, at any rate, conceived the opinion that there was some sort of joke being played – and that he was not in it. At rehearsals he asked me to play the music which had been composed for the fight of the wicked uncles – it was *Babes In The Wood*. It was music more descriptive than melodious. 'That', said Mr. Gar Kiddie, and there was almost a wink in his voice, 'is the principal boy's big song.' But I did not fall for that. I laughed at precisely the right moment, and in the end I was given the baton.[9]

He spent three seasons with the company, conducting pantomimes in the winter, with the summers spent with operatic companies or ballet for Phyllis Bedells and Laurent Novikoff. In the summer of 1912 Jack was back in Rhyl in a show that was significantly less successful than some of his previous contracts:[10]

> For example, in 1912 but also in Rhyl, I was an accompanist when the management went bust. The artists clubbed together and appointed me their secretary. We saw the season through and after that even managed to tour 'on the baggage', i.e., the station master impounded our trunks as security for our fares until the owner of the hall

where we were next to appear came along to bail out our belongings.[11]

This is an audacious move, typically Hyltonian, to take a show which had flopped and not only take over and finish the season but carry it on touring the provinces. It would be far fetched to call this particular example a success, given there was never enough profit even to buy the train tickets, but keeping the full company in employment beyond the summer season and into a winter tour is an impressive piece of entrepreneurial decision making. Inevitably the tour had to end and that found Jack back at the pub in Stalybridge:

I spent the rest of the winter leaning against the wall at my mother's expense.[12]

Just as it would through the rest of his career, this modest set back simply spurred Jack on to work harder and make the next step forward. 1913 would take Jack back to Rhyl for a life changing summer season that would deliver his first great loss and his first great love. This time in Rhyl, Jack was in charge. He called the act *The Comedy Cameos*, and they gave three shows a day in a tent on the sea front. For rent, he paid the owner of the ground a percentage of the takings.

Jack Hylton (far-right), as part of *The Comedy Cameos*. (Personal Collection)

At the morning performance they wear straw hats, blue coats, the highest of collars in the latest fashion, and white flannel trousers, that are whiter on Monday than on Saturday. They sing the latest smash hits: *I Do Like To Be Be-side The Sea, Who Were You With Last Night?* and *Joshua! Joshua! How Like Lemon-Squash-You-Are!*[13]

The summer of 1913 was a particularly wet one and this was a significant factor in the failure of the show. Perhaps a more significant factor was a woman called Florence Ennis Parkinson. She eventually became better known as Ennis Parkes, and found fame as Mrs Jack Hylton.

Ennis was born at 64 Hutchinson Square, Douglas on the Isle Of Man, on the 13th of November 1893, but raised in Bootle, in Merseyside. She received piano lessons as a child, and was well regarded as a singer whilst still a child. She began her professional career at the age of seven, singing, dancing and playing the piano, and worked for many years at the seaside parties in Rhyl. Her first stage appearance was at the Muncaster Theatre in 1911. She also starred in *Here & There* at Liverpool Empire and *Joy Bells* at Liverpool Hippodrome:

> A beautiful orphan girl, just seventeen, with Mary Pickford curls and the sweetest manner. A young girl, yet she sings and plays with the dash of an experienced artiste, for she too, has been singing and dancing for a living through her childhood days as a juvenile performer.[14]

The couple had met briefly the previous year, but now Hylton was employing Ennis on an eighteen week contract, paying her £3 10s per week for twelve performances:

> Jack is not romantic. There were no moonlit nights or poems in our courtship...We had no time for falling in love, but one night Jack said to me 'We are going to be married'. That's just like him. He makes up his mind suddenly but his impulses are usually right. You cannot say 'no' to Jack. I didn't. Two days later we were married.[15]

They married just a few miles away from where they were working, in St. Asaph, in Denbighshire, North Wales, in July 1913 and just two days later another week of *The Comedy Cameos* began in earnest. They would venture further than Rhyl; a week in Teignmouth in June, a week in Paignton in July, a week in Redcar in September, and presumably others. We have very few details of the outcome of this summer season other than a startling revelation in a newspaper article and no more detail:

> A few years later I was back in Rhyl with my own little show. It was a wet season. Worse, I fell in love and neglected business. I lost money – far more money than my mother could find in the best teapot or under the mattress. To get me out of that mess my parents had to sell the pub. I was ashamed. From then on I stopped being lazy and really went to work.[16]

The brevity of this quotation means that we are missing out on the whole story, but we can safely assume that whatever the details, the 1913 season in Rhyl, Jack's first production, was a disaster which left his parents in deep financial trouble and left their eldest son effectively bankrupt, a matter of weeks after marrying Ennis Parkes. We know nothing of the repercussions for George and Mary. In due course George began to work more frequently as an entertainer and in 1917 the couple moved to Cliff Place, in Bispham, a mile and a half north of Blackpool, and George would perform regularly, even broadcasting on the radio once his son had become a household name.

George and Mary would enjoy a life supported by their wealthy son, and both were leading lights in the social life of Blackpool through the 1920s and 1930s and were in a position to support local causes and charities, using the name of their son, who often returned to the north for charity events. George was described as a "well known Lancashire character"[17]; he was chairman of the Speedwell Association and Mary was the Lady President. On Boxing Day 1940, Mary was taken ill whilst watching one of her son's shows in Oxford. Despite a recovery, by March 1941 she fell ill again and died on March 13th. George carried on entertaining the troops as World War II continued, but died on July 28th 1943 at the age of 72. Jack immediately travelled up to Blackpool to arrange the memorial service to this popular local man.

Meanwhile, back in the 1910s, Jack was ready to take the next step in his career and was thinking about the bright lights of London.

Chapter 3: 1913-1921

The Queen's Dance Orchestra, c.1921. (Personal Collection)

Late in 1913 Jack's career was stalling. He was working another season as pantomime conductor, but was soon given the break he wanted and the opportunity to finally move to London, where he knew he needed to be to make the next step upwards. An un-named friend offered him the post of organist for the Alexandra Theatre in Stoke Newington, to accompany the silent films being shown at the time. The Alexandra Theatre (designed by Frank Matcham) was opened in 1897, adding to the new trend of building suburban theatres outside of London's West End theatre district:

> The Alexandra is the finest building in Stoke Newington, and the red brick and stone front is much admired. Inside it is in every respect equal to any West End house.[1]

Another new skill to develop, but after eight years in the business Jack's repertoire of songs would already have been quite large.

As soon as the pantomime season had finished in January of 1914, Jack and Ennis made their move:

> I'll never forget the journey there. After buying our tickets, my wife and I had threepence left – and two large appetites. At Crewe the man opposite produced a packet of sandwiches, and ate every crumb while we watched. At Euston we took a cab to my friend's digs, hoping against fear that he would be in. He was. We borrowed 5s from him, and on what was left of it after paying the cab-fare we prepared to conquer London.[2]

An inauspicious start to a career but nevertheless Jack was making money now and within a few months had begun a second, parallel career as what was known as a 'relief pianist'. The 400 Club, 6-8 Old Bond Street in the West End of London, was built as a theatre club in the late 19th century, and was established as a venue for cabaret and dancing in 1913. It was renamed the Embassy Club in 1919 (where reputedly there was a couch reserved at all times for the Prince of Wales). In 1914, violinist Stroud Haxton led the orchestra, and the band would play for dancing every night.[3] Haxton gave Jack the job. When Haxton's band took a break, Hylton would play the piano, providing continuous entertainment. He continued to work at the cinema whilst playing at the 400 Club:

> I used to leave the cinema at 10pm, play in the 400 till 2am, catch the tram at Holborn, invariably sleep through to Stamford Hill, travel back to our lodgings at Stoke Newington, get to bed at 4.30am and be back in the theatre at 2.30pm. I wasn't bone idle any longer...[4]

Meanwhile, Ennis was also forging a career of her own. She auditioned and was booked for a West End revue at the Oxford Music Hall (which was later demolished and replaced with a Lyons Corner House) called *Full Inside*, and subsequently performed in many shows at the London Hippodrome, for Albert de Courville (who became a film director in the 1930s).

Jack Hylton was now making three pounds a week on top of his cinema fee so finally had some money, but 1914 saw the outbreak of the Great War and of course there were implications for Jack and Ennis. The 400 Club was patronised by young Guards officers who were immediately called up to serve in the war and so, despite the best efforts of those involved, the club closed and Jack was out of a job. Around the same time Jack lost his cinema organist job too, and he had no choice but to work outside of London, taking a show on a tour of the provinces:

> With borrowed money I put on a touring show of my own. As the star, I picked an artist also hard up at the time. He was Gillie Potter.[5] I paid him £3. The show struggled on till we reached Banbury. There I found I had just enough money left to pay all debts, including wages. I paid them, and then found I'd no money for the fares back to London for myself and my young brother (who had joined me against Mum's wishes). We asked Gillie Potter to lend us the fares. He was rightly cautious. So we found out the train he was catching and, as he stood at the booking office, we rushed past him shouting something incoherent about getting the baggage aboard and would he get the tickets – we'd pay him on the train. He did get the tickets. We did see him on the train. He wasn't pleased. However, we borrowed some money at the other end and paid him. Didn't we, Gillie?[6]

This is interestingly the only mention of the young George Hilton being an entertainer and unsurprising news that Mum was unhappy about it, given the debacle of the 1913 Rhyl summer season! Sadly this would be George's only experience of show business. He was called up to the army, where he died, in France, on March 30th 1918.

Jack also served in the Great War, but not on the front line like his brother. Jack was certified as C3 – one of the lowest fitness grades, meaning "fit for Sedentary Service at Home Camps". It is unclear why Hylton was graded so low, unless this was a deliberate ploy to keep him at home and to utilise the skills he had for entertainment. His father described him as a "live wire", but given his long, hardworking life to come, it's hard to see why Hylton was certified so low.

In 1915 he was called up and joined either the Royal Naval Air Service (the air arm of the Royal Navy, which after World War I would merge with the Army's Royal Flying Corps, to form the Royal Air Force), or the 20th Hussars (a cavalry regiment of the Army, which amalgamated with the 14th Hussars in 1922 and eventually became the 14th/20th King's Hussars), depending on which source one believes. Either way, he was soon switched to the Navy and Army Canteen (NACB). His war records appear no longer to exist (along with around sixty per cent of World War I records), so it is hard to confirm any of these details and Hylton's own words are rather contradictory. He certainly became an active part of the NACB and avoided front line duty.

The NACB would later become the Navy, Army and Air Force Institutes (NAAFI), an organisation run to provide recreational establishments for the forces. They would supply shops, clubs, facilities and entertainments on British military bases. By 1917, the entertainment branch of the NACB was being directed by Basil Dean (1888-1978), an actor and playwright who would later become a film director and theatrical producer. Hylton would become the Musical Adviser to the entertainment branch, under Basil Dean:

> [I] made my little contribution to a service which here, there and everywhere, persuaded the troops for an hour or two to forget that a war was on.[7]

> But before long he was…dashing round the country from one camp to another, seeing that the men had plenty of cheery music to keep up their spirits.[8]

The work of the NACB entertainment division was distinct from that delivered by Lena Ashwell's concert parties, which launched *Concerts At The Front* in 1915 to provide entertainment on mainland Europe. The NACB were based at home and provided the entertainment as part of their services.

In 1918 Jack was duly relieved of his duties and de-mobbed. After first working as pianist for MacDonald and Young's concert party in the seaside resort of Bognor, he moved back into theatrical production, taking a concert party of his own to Bognor in the summer of 1919. This first foray into post-war entertainment included northern comedian Charlie Harvey, regarded as "the best Pierrot of all time".[9] Also on the bill was a young baritone who Jack had shared digs with at one time, Tommy Handley, who would have a lifelong association with Hylton.

Thomas Reginald Handley was born on January 17th in Liverpool and became famous as a regular comedy broadcaster for the fledgling BBC radio service in the 1920s. After writing and performing numerous scripts for the BBC alongside writers and performers such as Arthur Askey and Bob Monkhouse, Handley became a household name for his show *ITMA*. It began in 1939 and ran for ten years, and spawned a stage show (of which more later) and a feature film. The last performance was on January 6th 1949 and Tommy died suddenly just three days later, of a brain haemorrhage.

During the run of the Bognor show, Jack and Tommy formulated a double act, Hylton & Handley, with Tommy fronting and Jack at the piano. By all accounts this was another failure to add to Jack's growing collection:

> Tommy and I became Hylton and Handley, a double act which shamelessly copied the Two Bobs, then great stars. I mean 'shameless' because I'm still not ashamed at the plagiarism. Everybody copies success in the theatre. Hylton and Handley were booked to appear at the [Lyons] Popular Café, Piccadilly, on Armistice night 1919, but when we arrived we found that the audience had taken over the entertainment. We sat quietly while a number of amateurs volunteered their pieces. Then we 'volunteered' ours. Afterwards a guest said: 'With practice, you could get into a concert party.' He was about right, because together, Tommy Handley and I were a flop. We realised that when, having got a week's booking at the old Bedford Music Hall, Camden Town, we invited a well known agent to see our act, and, since we were now experienced in the business, spent all our cash on a bottle of whisky. The agent drank all the whisky, and booked another act.[10]

The setback with the Hylton & Handley act at the Bedford Music Hall in Camden deterred neither partner and they both continued to seek future projects. Towards the end of 1919 Jack wrote the music for a burlesque show called *Seasoned To Taste,* a vehicle for Tommy Handley and Bobby Howes,[11] which opened at the end of 1919 and ran until early 1920, at the Metropolitan Theatre, 267 Edgware Road, in Paddington.[12] (The Metropolitan was a music hall theatre on the site of the White Lion Inn, dating from 1524. It was rebuilt in 1836 and subsequently redesigned by Frank Matcham in 1896. It later became a TV studio, before being demolished in 1964).

So impressed was Hylton with Howes, that he foolishly gave him a five year contract (starting at £4 per week and rising to £7 in the fifth year). The show, yet another flop, lasted just ten weeks. Conveniently, Hylton found himself in a position of being able to trade Bobby Howes' contract to Herbert Clayton (later of production company Clayton and (Joe) Waller), in exchange for conducting one of Clayton's touring productions. This show also folded!

By 1920, despite having a string of successive failures behind him, Hylton carried on undaunted, picking up work where he could. He spent the first part of 1920 playing piano in a nightclub, but by the start of the summer of that year, a music publishing company in Charing Cross Road in London had employed him as a song plugger. As part of this job, Jack travelled to Blackpool to sing, play the piano and try to sell sheet music, on a commission basis.

Around this time, Hylton got together with an old friend from the Pierrot days in Rhyl, Con West. Together the pair put together a volume of 'musical numbers, cross talk, stories, monologues, burlesques, sketches, etc.' which was designed as a one-stop book of solutions for concerts and entertainment, either professional, semi-professional or amateur, and sold for four shillings. Entitled *Words & Music* (published by Reynolds & Co. in 1922), the book contains songs written by Hylton, with lyrics and sketches written by Con West. These items are somewhat dated by today's standards, but they were very specifically written for the market at the time and written with the experience of two decades in the business. The books were successful enough to spawn a second and third volume (1923 and 1924):

A few years ago the author-composers…were touring Lancashire in a Pierrot concert party, and when the party broke up the two friends went up to London. Existing on the little money they had saved, the pair set themselves to write songs – West the words, Hylton the music.

This was four years ago, and for a year they met with no success. But today their names and their songs are to be found on thousands of gramophone records and on scores of popular songs.[13]

The pair would also receive press for their co-written number *Singing*. An article from 1922 suggests it was "written on an old envelope in the trenches, and discovered in an old kit-bag".[14] That brief article suggests the pair worked together during the war, perhaps as part of an NACB revue, though it seems this is artistic license on the part of the newspaper; the pair are much more likely to have worked together with the Pierrots, as mentioned in the previous quotation, and travelled together at roughly the same time, linking up and trying to make some money together. Certainly, Hylton liked *Singing* well enough to record it with the Queen's Dance Orchestra, for the HMV label (HMV B-1364), on June 7th, 1922 at Hayes.[15]

One report suggests that Jack was working more for himself during the Blackpool trip. He would write songs in the popular style of the day, print a batch of one thousand, and sell copies on the promenade at sixpence each. Five pounds could be made on every thousand copies sold, which appears to be one of Hylton's less shrewd business ventures.

Whether working for himself, for the song plugger, or with Con West, we know Jack was back in London at the end of the season working for a music publishing firm in Wardour Street for £2 a week. The company was owned and run by Claude Ivy, a well respected and technically gifted pianist. Claude was also working for the Queen's Dance Orchestra, the band that played on the Roof Garden at the Queen's Hall, in Langham Place. This would prove to be a vital link in Hylton's career, but first Jack had another failure to endure! Perhaps Jack's own words tell this story best:

> I got a job playing the piano for a firm of music publishers in Charing Cross Road. I was sick at heart at this introduction to Tin Pan Alley, but the Alley did me proud later. A man who heard me song plugging asked me to go to France next day to work as accompanist with a concert party. I said yes, and on the boat made friends with a man, who, like me, came from the North. The name was Stan-

ley Holloway. After I had accompanied him at rehearsal, he went around singing my praises. 'He's better than Melville Gideon!' he said, with north-country loyalty. For this party was the beginning of the famous Co-optimists, with Gideon, Davy Burnaby, Laddie Cliff, Phyllis Monkman. Months later I heard how that party had turned itself into the Co-optimists and taken a West End theatre, and how they had sent me wires offering me a job at £15 a week, and how the wires had gone astray. I could have cried. But as things turned out, it was a lucky break. For only two years later, with the Co-optimists still at the height of their fame, I too, had become sufficiently famous for them to do a skit on me called Jack Stylton and His Band. My luck changed at the beginning of the Jazz Age when I got a job as assistant pianist at the Queen's Hall Roof.[16]

Chapter 4: 1921-1926

Jack Hylton and His Orchestra, c.1924. (Jack Hylton Archive)

He looked like such an insignificant man, with no special attributes, but beneath his beguiling simplicity was a forceful character and a formidable brain with prolific ideas which paved the way for dance bands in Britain. He was in every sense an original with the human touch.[1]

The Queen's Hall Roof would indeed be exactly the change of luck Jack Hylton was looking for and in no small part, Claude Ivy was instrumental in that luck. The Queen's Hall, in Langham Place in central London (next to where BBC Broadcasting House stands today) was opened in 1893, and became London's principal concert venue. It could seat around three thousand people and was famed not only for its excellent acoustics but also for being the home of the Henry Wood Promenade Concerts (The Proms) before they moved to the Royal Albert Hall.[2] Above the main auditorium was the Small Queen's Hall, which could seat five hundred people and was initially planned as a chamber music venue. In July 1894 Bernard Shaw described it as:

...cigar-shaped, with windows in the ceiling, and reminiscent of a ship's saloon ... now much the most comfortable of our small concert rooms.[3]

It was considered by some to be London's equivalent of Ziegfeld's Roof Garden in New York.[4] As early as 1899, the orchestral manager of the Queen's Hall, Robert Newman, had been persuaded by comedian, actor and musical hall star Albert Chevalier,[5] to instigate variety performances in the small hall. By 1919, the small hall was being managed by Herbert Henri (who would later found the Chez Henri Club, on the first floor of 8 and 9 Long Acre), and alterations were made to the room to make it more suitable for dancing and cabaret.

Clarinettist Edmund 'Al' Jenkins and pianist Claude Ivy were tasked with forming a band, which they would call the Queen's Dance Orchestra. Jenkins, son of the founder of the illustrious Jenkins Orphanage had arrived in England in 1914 and had enrolled at the Royal Academy of Music to study clarinet, for which instrument he subsequently held a tutorial professorship. Claude Ivy was pianist with the Savoy Quartet from 1917 to 1920 and, in October 1919, lost the audition for the Original Dixieland Jazz Band to Billy Jones. Later he became resident pianist in the Decca studios.[6] The pair recruited Dick de Pauw on violin, Bert Bassett on banjo and Harry Robbins Jr. on drums. Ivy managed to persuade Henri that the band needed to split their evening's performance into sets, with breaks in between. He then suggested his music-publishing employee Hylton as a possible relief pianist for the breaks; of course Hylton had considerable experience already as relief pianist, having worked in a similar role at the 400 Club before the outbreak of war.

Whilst the main band were trying their hand at the new ragtime and jazz styles filtering through from the States, Hylton was filling the gaps playing mostly waltz duets with violinist de Pauw:

The band itself was a real ragtime affair, busking choruses in woeful harmony to a background of kitchen furniture noises manipulated by young Harry Robbins; well, he was young then, all right, hardly out of knickerbockers.[7]

By May 1921 Jenkins was leading the band, which now consisted of Bert Heath (trumpet), Jesse Stamp (trombone), Edmund Jenkins (clarinet and alto saxophone), Bert Worth (alto and tenor saxophone), Hylton (and/or Claude Ivy) on piano, Dick de Pauw or Johnny Rosen (violin), Bert Bassett (banjo) and Harry Robbins, Jr. (drums), though this set up varied in size and in personnel greatly over the next couple of years:

> Jenkins was in charge until an Englishman named Hylton came on the scene. Hylton was jealous of Jenkins and wanted to control everything. He caused some problems, which caused Jenkins to relinquish the position in disgust.[8]

Of course Hylton himself doesn't tell it like this but certainly his personality and his managerial ability will have impacted on the former leader.

It was 1921 and Henri's wife had been holidaying in America where she'd seen Paul Whiteman and His Orchestra playing a high profile show at the Palais Royale in New York.

Paul Whiteman (1890-1967) was a classically trained violist from Denver, Colorado, who first worked with the Denver Symphony Orchestra, before moving to the San Francisco Symphony Orchestra. After conducting the US Navy Band during the war, he formed a dance band, which moved from San Francisco to New York in 1920. He began recording for the Victor record label in 1920 and received almost instant fame and acclaim. The parallels with Hylton's career should not be underestimated. Whiteman's band, at some thirty-five players, was considerably larger than the standard six to nine piece dance band line up which was popular at the time in England. Mirroring Hylton's future career, within two years of the move to New York, Whiteman would control some twenty-eight bands along the East Coast of the United States. The media referred to Whiteman as *The King Of Jazz* but many felt his style, which blended symphonic music with jazz, was far removed from the true roots of the genre. Again there are acute parallels with Hylton's style, his critical reception and his tendency to hire the finest jazz musicians whilst not playing the style of music for which they were best known.[9] He became best known for commissioning George Gershwin's *Rhapsody In*

Blue, which the band premiered in a concert *An Experiment In Modern Music*, on February 12th, 1924 in Aeolian Hall, New York, with the composer at the piano.

Upon Madame Henri's return to London from a holiday in New York, she brought with her a copy of an early Whiteman gramophone record,[10] which she and her husband felt was stylistically the direction in which the band should develop.

It was clear to Jack Hylton that Whiteman's orchestra was playing from sheet music. Most of the jazz music being attempted at that time (including that of the Queen's Dance Orchestra) was improvised and extemporised by the band, though based on existing songs:

> Thereupon, greatly venturesome, I said to Henri, "If I only had a gramophone at home I could write down that music", and so enthusiastic was he about the record... that they actually hired a machine for me and sent me home to carry out my threat. I did the job, but, of course, had to adapt the parts for our instrumentation, and when I told Henri that I should have to have a trumpet added to the band to get anything like the real effect, he readily acquiesced. Well, after a lot of rehearsal, we actually did succeed in making sense of the parts and getting them to sound more or less, mostly less, like Whiteman's Orchestra.[11]

We have a little more detail, also in Hylton's own words:

> I had to analyse the secret of this new and heady music by the next morning. Through that night I kept the maid at my diggings winding the gramophone while I listened raptly and wrote...By the morning, very punch drunk, I had one complete dance tune, as scored by Whiteman. By late afternoon, that Queen's Hall Roof band was playing it reasonably near to the Whiteman way. That evening the Roof guests were ecstatic...Well, the owner of the Roof wanted to get more Whiteman records. I told him it wasn't necessary. I knew how to score thanks to the Exeter organist. You might almost say, in fact, that British jazz was born in Exeter Cathedral.[12]

These new arrangements were hugely popular with the dancers of London, eager to hear the latest sounds from America live in their own dance halls, and this didn't go unnoticed by the bosses at the HMV record label and very soon, the Queen's Dance Orchestra recorded four songs in the *His Master's Voice* studios at Hayes, Middlesex, on May 28th, 1921:

> Meeting with Mr Coolidge of HMV one day, I told him that we could make records like Paul Whiteman, and he agreed to give us a test session. We did four titles from my arrangements and they were promptly put out.[13]

Emile Berliner had founded the Gramophone Company in 1892, whilst William Barry Owen founded the partner UK Gramophone Company in 1897. Owen bought the famous Francis Barraud painting *His Master's Voice*, of Nipper the dog listening to the gramophone (which had *His Master's Voice* painted over the original *Edison* phonograph label by Barraud himself). The Gramophone Company in the States became the Victor Talking Machine Company in 1900 and the image of Nipper was first used on record labels at this time. By 1908, The Gramophone Company in the UK had begun using *His Master's Voice* on labels to distinguish newer labels from older ones. By 1908, these now familiar trademarks had been registered and a bespoke recording studio and record-producing factory had been opened in Hayes, in Middlesex, in the outskirts of London (with the foundation stone having been laid by Dame Nelly Melba). By the 1930s HMV had merged with EMI (Electric and Musical Industries Ltd.) and opened Abbey Road Studios in London, which superseded the Hayes studio.[14]

Each song recorded would be regarded as a 'side', as it would appear on one side of a 78rpm disc. It was common to record in groups of two 'sides', one for each side of the record. The tunes on this occasion were, *Turque*[15], and *I'm Wondering If It's Love* (catalogue number HMV B-1236) followed by *Idol Of Mine* and *The Wind In The* Trees (catalogue number HMV B-1237). These early recordings are scarce and don't bear repeated listening. Not only is the playing rather staid, by comparison to the bands' later work, but the recording quality is very poor.

Jack Hylton

Sound reproduction had begun with Thomas Edison's invention of the phonograph, but things began to take shape by 1893, by which time Emile Berliner had perfected his gramophone, and the process of recording and reproducing discs that could be played repeatedly. From the turn of the century, The Gramophone Company began recording a variety of artists, mostly operatic stars of the day and later ragtime. The first jazz on record was in 1918, with a famous series of recordings of The Original Dixieland Jazz Band. Pictures of these early acoustic recordings show the ensemble huddled round a large conical horn, which transmitted the sound into the recording mechanism and directly onto disc. The results were passable, but coloured by the horn and the resonances that it created. In 1924, two engineers from the Bell Telephone Laboratories created a workable public address system, with its necessity for large power outputs with a wide frequency range and low distortion. They then turned their attention to recording and developed a similarly high fidelity system on which to record:

> The results blew acoustic recording away virtually overnight. For the first time something like a full orchestra could be successfully recorded. Transients and sibilants were there, studio ambience and atmosphere, and all these things made for far greater fidelity. Now the gramophone could compete with the radio.[16]

The Hylton band would make acoustic recordings for their first four years, but within a few weeks of the invention of the electrical versions, HMV and Victor had converted all their equipment and never returned to the acoustic versions. Recordings from this later period are considerably more enjoyable and sonically sophisticated.

The band was paid thirty-five pounds for their first HMV session, giving each of the seven band members five pounds. Of course Hylton was leader of this band, pianist and arranger, but was being paid the same five pounds session fee. He felt rightly uncomfortable about this, and asked that the fee be split differently to compensate Jack for the time spent arranging. He asked for an extra ten shillings per session. The band refused:

34

"All right", I said. "What about putting *directed by Jack Hylton* on the labels of the records?" They said yes. That was it. I was 29 years old. I had had more downs than ups. But that moment I knew I was there.[17]

It is easy for Hylton to state, some thirty years later, that this moment was significant but it really proves to be the pivotal moment in this story. To say he had 'more downs than ups' is something of an understatement, with almost every job for the previous fifteen years ending up either with the sack, or with near-bankruptcy. This one piece of greed from those six musicians literally turned Hylton's life around and set him on the road to staggering levels of success.

The early recording sessions and their subsequent record release (amongst the first dance bands to be released on record) were a roaring success. On the 7th of August the same year the band went back to Hayes and recorded four more titles – *Love Nest* and *Mon Homme (My Man)*[18] (Zonophone 2155) coupled with *Billy* and *Wang Wang Blues* (Zonophone 2167), released on their cheaper Zonophone label, as Jack Hylton's Jazz Band. These were 3 shillings, as opposed to 5 shillings for the HMV discs, but the differences in the recordings were minute, if noticeable at all.

The first recordings of the Queen's Dance Orchestra to contain the words 'directed by Jack Hylton' were made on November 15th, 1921, after some nineteen sides had been recorded for HMV and a further ten sides had been recorded as Jack Hylton's Jazz Band for Zonophone, so the beginning of Hylton's recording career isn't quite as clear cut as it would first appear. Altogether, Hylton made some thirty-three recordings in the first eight months and a further sixty-one the following year, under various guises, first using *Jack Hylton and his Orchestra* in 1922 after leaving the Queen's Hall.

After Edmund Jenkins left the band in November 1921, a saxophonist named Rudolph Dixon replaced him. Hylton hired Dixon, but the pair disagreed to the point where Hylton offered an ultimatum to Henri of 'either he goes or I go'. Henri took the rather cowardly approach of letting the band make the decision. Bizarrely, given the success he'd help create for the band, Hylton was out. He would be away for just three months:

The owner called the band together and told them to vote on which of us should quit. I waited smugly while each dropped a folded paper into a hat but when the votes were counted I saw that every member of the band had voted to fire me. I was out. But it didn't matter. I was there.[19]

During a brief holiday to France,[20] Jack had just the stroke of luck he needed, meeting the owner of the Grafton Galleries, 7 Grafton Street in London, which was about to open for dancing. The Grafton Galleries was a Mayfair art gallery, originally opened in 1893, which moved to a site in Bond Street. The original venue kept the name and opened as a dance club in 1922:[21]

"This place has been the Valhalla of dancing for more years than one cares to remember", Dolly tells me as I have only just joined the club "and I have been here countless times…you will love it here…It is rather marvellous", I say, "and certainly not like those postage sized dance floors that are seemingly popular in the more intimate smaller night clubs or restaurants."[22]

Of course with the directing credit on the records (and more importantly, having retained the HMV recording contract for himself), Hylton's name would have been well known to the kinds of people in London who had the money to open such venues, and he was offered £120 per week to lead an eight-piece band. Four members of the Queen's Hall Roof band came to him asking for jobs with the new band, perhaps realizing the error of their ways in letting their boss be sacked:

I *ran* my orchestra, arranging, conducting, sometimes playing. Mum's lazy boy had properly got the itch to work now that work meant money. We played far into the night; we made records in the mornings and afternoons… All the time I was working on new stunts for winning popularity for my band. I was remembering what great old George Robey once told me: "You can't, in show business, stay still and still stay."[23]

Within eight weeks of the Grafton engagement, Monsieur Henri was asking Hylton to take his new band back to the Queen's, which he did for an inflated £135 per week and immeasurable increase in status. He was now leader of Jack Hylton and His Orchestra and on December 22nd 1922, the first HMV sessions were recorded under the new banner. With subsequent sessions on the 29th and the 9th January 1923, the first records were released on HMV as Jack Hylton and His Orchestra – *Oh, Star Of Eve/Dancing Honeymoon* (HMV B-1523), *Who Tied The Can On The Old Dog's Tail?/I Ain't Nobody's Darling* (HMV B-1524) and *Where The Bamboo Babies Grow/Sheba* (HMV B-1525. These tunes have hardly become standards in the intervening years, but I suspect their huge sales would have made up for that; in 1923 Hylton sold 190,818 records.[24]

A new show at the Queen's Hall Roof, called *The Cabaret Follies* was presented by Hylton (in fact the programme displays *Jack Hylton's Cabaret Follies*) and produced by actor Jack Buchanan and opened on September 7th, 1922, where it would stay, constantly evolving, until 1925.

Walter John "Jack" Buchanan (1891-1957) was a Scottish theatre and film actor, singer, producer and director. He came to London as a music hall comedian, later working in the West End, in silent films, and eventually musicals and movies in the inter-war years. He was famed for "the seemingly lazy but most accomplished grace with which he sang, danced, flirted and joked his way through musical shows.... The tall figure, the elegant gestures, the friendly drawling voice, the general air of having a good time."[25] He made twenty-nine films, the last being in 1955.

The initial contract for *The Cabaret Follies* was for eight weeks, and was extended with no formal agreement, a tactic that Jack would employ throughout his career. He was also booking the acts that performed in the show, writing and arranging the music, and playing the piano. Of course during this time records were continuing to be made at a startling rate, for HMV, Zonophone and the Ariel label.[26]

As was stated in the press at the time, this was "not a series of turns in the concert platform manner; this is a fully fledged revue in miniature." This type of show was new for Britain and indeed the word *cabaret* was new.

Jack Hylton

Cabaret was supper entertainment in a venue other than a theatre. It provided food, drink, jazz music and other entertainment, but it also gave the public the opportunity to dance. Of course each of these elements was available elsewhere but the idea of offering all of this in one place was new. So new, in fact that venues did not exist to house this new art form, hence the use of venues like upstairs at the Grafton Art Gallery, or in the small hall above the otherwise classically orientated Queen's Hall. Many others followed and many bespoke venues sprung up in the 1920s and 1930s. Hylton would become a major player in this new world:

> If it is crowded and difficult to dance it is fashionable. Expensive couture gowns rustle, glasses are chinked and conversation and laughter abound. Above the noise we order our drinks and supper from the excellent menu and become part of the unfolding revelry. The room is packed with an eclectic mix of people of all ages but they have one thing in common: they are all immaculately dressed and the men have large wallets. On the stroke of midnight the music suddenly stops and the lights are dimmed. The drums roll, trumpets blow a fanfare and in the distance at the end of the room the curtains open to reveal a small stage lit by several spotlights. The orchestra takes up a new tune as a bevy of show girls appear in their rather brief, yet colourful feathery costumes. The chorus sing and dance and then disappear to hysterical cheers, wolf whistles and clapping. In their place emerge the principals of the show in their first number, a dancing duo of international renown, beautifully dressed and full of grace and skill, whirling across the dance floor causing gasps of delight. The stars of the time included such famous names as Moss and Fontana, Sielle and Mills and Divina and Charles (British); Fowler and Tamara, Maurice and Walton and Cortez and Peggy (American); and Mitty and Tillio, Roseray and Capella and Guy and Van Duren (French).[27]

Of course, this was happening in London. It could have been Paris or New York, but nothing like this was happening for the majority of towns in Britain and indeed for the majority of the working class people of London itself. It is important to understand that whilst those indulging in the *jazz age* are a vital part of our story, it was going on un-noticed by most of the population. Fortunately Jack Hylton was not one to forget his roots and soon he would take this jazz tinged cabaret to the provinces.

By February 4th 1923, *The Cabaret Follies* was already celebrating its 150th performance and by mid March was celebrating its 250th performance. Ennis Parkes (who kept her maiden name as a stage name) had been a part of the show since late 1922 and was performing a hit song that she had composed, *Evergreen Eve*:

> I'm singing and playing my own songs here…I like cabaret work tremendously. For my sort of stuff it's really the only way. You don't have those bothering footlights and miles of space to get over.[28]

Personality Photo Press

A glimpse at the "Cabaret Follies" at the Queen's Hall Roof. The Company includes the Trix Sisters, Henry de Bray, Tim O'Connor, Flora Lea and sixteen Folly Girls

Publicity shot for *The Cabaret Follies* (Jack Hylton Archive)

Dinner would be served at 10.15pm, with 'a series of turns in evening dress.' The full cabaret show would begin at 11.00pm, with six or so principal performers and a 'beauty chorus' of sixteen. Stars at this time included the Trix Sisters (an American duo who were fined eight shillings for having incorrect papers), Violet Doreen, Tim O'Connor, Henri De Bray, Flora Lea and Beatrice Lillie. These performers could come and go depending on circumstances and it was Hylton's job to arrange the performers for each show. Even at this early stage Hylton had a central London office, moving from his initial office at 59 Conduit Street, just off Regent Street, to 'a comfy little office' at 40 Albermarle Street, just off Piccadilly.

Prince George visited the show twice in three days, along with Lady Louis Mountbatten, the Marquess of Milford Haven and the Earl of Westmorland. Hylton recounted in later years:

> Those late hours! I remember how the Prince of Wales came to a supper club where I was playing, and went on dancing long after we were supposed to close. At last we played *God Save The King* as a hint. The prince came over to me and said, "Now you've put the old man to bed, Jack, what about some more dance music?" We grinned and played.[29]

The Queen's Hall Roof closed for refurbishment in the summer of 1923, so Hylton took a company comprising various members of his current show and the Grafton Galleries, to the Westover Dance Hall in Bournemouth. They performed their *Midnight Follies* to record crowds. Hylton took *The Cabaret Follies* back to the Roof in September but by the end of the year, that show would be over and Hylton had moved to the Piccadilly Hotel, alternating with their in-house 'London Band'. The Queen's Hall Roof would replace Hylton with an orchestra led by Frenchman Paul Gason.

This show was known as *Piccadilly Revels*, subtitled, *Playtime at the Piccadilly*. Meanwhile the impresario Hylton was already in full flow, putting together an orchestra for the Shaftsbury Theatre, on Shaftsbury Avenue. Already simply having Jack Hylton's name attached to a band gave credibility, but more importantly, sold tickets.

The band worked solidly through the end of 1923 and into 1924 but Hylton never rested and felt the weight of his previous failed enterprises:

> In this atmosphere of insecurity I planned as much as I could for other worlds to conquer, and one of the ideas I got was to go on the stage.[30]

So he continued to move. The band was offered an engagement at The Karsino from May 17th 1924 for the summer, so he kept the band running for the Piccadilly Revels and simultaneously they worked at The Karsino, rushing from one venue to the next, organising set times to make this work.

Programme for the *Piccadilly Revels* show. (Personal Collection)

The Karsino was the brainchild of Fred Karno (stage name of Fred Westcott) a music hall impresario who had made a considerable amount of money, which he invested in rebuilding the hotel on Tagg's Island (an island in the mid-Thames near Hampton, up river from Molesey Lock). It was luxurious and it was an instant success. In 1914 he added a six hundred seat Palm Court Concert Pavilion.

From here Hylton made an audacious and fundamental decision, which would impact upon the subsequent two decades. Jack approached producer Harry Day to book his band as top of the bill in a variety show – a variety show which Hylton himself would book, from amongst the artists he was already working with. It was unheard of to put a dance band in a variety show and unheard of to have a syncopated band performing in such a venue. Of course, the audience for the exclusive clubs like *The Karsino* was very different to the music hall audience of the day. Hylton felt confident; Harry Day booked them into the Bedford Theatre in Camden Town (scene of his previous failure with Tommy Handley). Also known as the Bedford Palace of Varieties and the Bedford Music Hall, this was a spacious variety theatre opened in 1899 on the site of an old music hall, built with an elaborate Renaissance frontage and incorporating its own public house. It was an immensely popular theatre, built exclusively for variety and as such was a good venue for Hylton to choose. The fee he accepted was £50 for a week. This was not enough to cover the expenses of the eleven-piece band, but Hylton knew this was a good decision:

> Up till then dance bands had never been on music halls. After that they all went on the boards, for (let's not be modest about it) we were a riot.[31]

It was a decision that showed staggering vision. The following week, the band played at the Holborn Empire for £120, still not vast amounts of money, giving Hylton a net profit of £11. A month later the band was paid £200 for a week at the Alhambra Theatre, Leicester Square, a venue which was to become almost like a second home for them.

The Alhambra was built in 1854, as the Royal Panopticon of Science and Arts, closing two years later to have a circus ring installed. It opened as the Alhambra Circus in 1858. Many name changes and rebuilds occurred until theatre architect Frank Matcham redesigned the building in 1912 and it opened as the Alhambra Theatre. The building was demolished in 1936 and the current Leicester Square Odeon was built.

By 1924, the Hylton band was recording prolifically for HMV (as Jack Hylton and His Orchestra) and for the cheaper Zonophone (as the Grosvenor Dance Orchestra). Over seventy titles were recorded in 1923 and another eighty in 1924. In 1924 Hylton sold 332,436 78rpm records, earning him £1,385. This was on top of all the money from shows, money taken from bands he was merely putting his name to. He was doing very well, but very far from taking things easy. Recording techniques were far removed from what they are today, as future vocalist Sam Browne recalls in a radio interview:

> *Sam Browne*: Oh, the pre-war – entirely different to what it is today – you didn't get that fifty microphones round the studio. All you had was one microphone, set in the middle. The instruments were placed round. I would be on the floor, more or less, waiting for my cue. Four bars before, I would bob up, sing the vocal chorus, bob down again and have to wait there till the record was finished.

> *Interviewer*: In those days of record outputs where they were issuing many different records per week, how long did you actually get to learn a song?

> *Sam Browne*: Learn a song? No man – I read music! Er, I learnt to play the violin when I was a boy and I knew what music was. It shocked a lot of people, but none of this, er, six weeks to learn a song. No, six minutes just to look through it.[32]

By now the idea of a dance band 'on the boards' as Jack put it, was firmly established, and the dates flooded in. Through record sales and word of mouth, the news of this new and exciting band had spread beyond London, into the provinces, and Jack was keen to exploit this new market. The band played at London Coliseum, Islington Empire, Manchester Palace Theatre, Finsbury Park Empire, a return trip to the Alhambra, Shepherds Bush Empire and Chiswick Empire. Each of these visits would be twice nightly for a run of a week. Meanwhile, his newly formed band Jack Hylton's Metro-Gnomes, led by his wife Ennis Parkes (or Mrs Jack Hylton as she was now being called) was starting to tour the provinces as well, beginning in Bognor Regis at the Pavilion Gardens.

And so it went on: return trips to the Alhambra (three weeks) and Finsbury Park Empire, new shows at Hackney Empire, an election night special variety performance at the Royal Albert Hall, another four weeks at the Alhambra, the annual Variety Ball at Covent Garden Opera House, Wood Green Empire, Victoria Palace and a performing visit to the children's ward of Guy's Hospital. A proposed seven-week trip to America was cancelled due to the sheer volume of work available in England. Meanwhile the Metro-Gnomes were at Bedford Palace, Ilford Hippodrome, Willesden Hippodrome, the Coliseum and back at Bognor.

Each of these shows was a full variety bill, put together by Hylton, and with the band as the star attraction at the 'top of the bill'. Jack Hylton and his Orchestra would often perform before the interval and such was the hysteria surrounding the band, that the in house orchestra would strike up the interval music, to curb the constant calls for encores from the band! The bill changed often on these shows, but as an example, one week at the Alhambra consisted of Jack and the band, Masu (a Japanese equilibrist), Rupert Hazell (a comedian instrumentalist), Eva Parke and Pauline Crothers (violin and piano), Mme. Lillebil (dancer), Alba Tiberio (singer), Lee Sisters (singers), Jay Whidden (violinist) and The Brocks (clown/tumblers). Jack's band would typically perform for around thirty minutes, making these shows often three hours long or more. This, along with the eighty recordings, made for an astonishing workload.

August 29th 1924 saw Jack Hylton broadcast for the first time on BBC radio. The British Broadcasting Company (BBC) was formed on October 18th 1922, by British and American electrical companies doing business in the UK, with the aim of creating a product for which to sell their radios. The first broadcasts from London came in November of 1922, with further broadcasts in Birmingham, Newcastle and Manchester happening by the end of the year. Also by the end of that year, John Reith (1889-1971) was employed as General Manager. Reith (who felt he could manage a company but had no knowledge or experience of broadcasting) saw the BBC as way of educating the masses, an idea which was retained by the BBC for many years.

Chapter 4: 1921-1926

The first dance band music programme had been broadcast on February 27th 1923, when Marius B. Winter and his band played for more than an hour, with a news bulletin as an interlude. From October, the Savoy Orpheans and the Savoy Havana Band broadcast from the Savoy Hotel several times a week.[33] (The Savoy Havana Band was set up by American saxophonist Bert Ralton in 1921 and was resident in the Savoy Hotel from 1921 to 1927. The Savoy Orpheans were a British band, formed in 1923, led by Debroy Somers, an ex-army bandmaster. They were resident at the Savoy Hotel from 1923 to 1927. Both bands were under the management of Wilfred de Mornys).

Other bands also broadcast in these early days – the Piccadilly Orchestra first broadcast on 27th April 1924 and Albert Sandler and the Orchestra from the Grand Hotel, Eastbourne first broadcast on 28th July 1925.

In 1923, there were 595,496 wireless sets in Britain; by 1926, this had increased to 2,178, 259:[34]

One day I thought, "Now, this new-fangled wireless – there's something to go for." I went to Savoy Hill, where a sombre-looking man named Mr Reith told me the Broadcasting Company was tied to the dance band at the Savoy Hotel. I bought myself a copy of the charter given to the BBC. It contained some interesting restrictions on monopoly. Primed with these, I obtained an interview with the Prime Minister, Mr Lloyd George. That wonderful little Welshman, after talking to me knowledgeably about music, and singing a few bars to prove his points, gave me a letter to Mr Reith. In a few weeks my orchestra was broadcasting and the BBC dance band monopoly was bust. I hate monopolies unless they're mine.[35]

This reference seems rather muddled, though it is a fascinating anecdote and must surely be based on facts. Of course the Savoy band was not the only band being broadcast on the BBC, and whilst they broadcast frequently, certainly did not have a monopoly. That Hylton approached the Prime Minister says a great deal about not only Hylton's status in London at the time, but also the way life has changed since the early 1920s. However, we know that Hylton's first

BBC broadcast was in 1924, but the BBC Royal Charter was not created until January 1st 1927, when the British Broadcasting Company became the British Broadcasting Corporation. John Reith (later Lord Reith) would move from being Managing Director of the company, to being Director General of the corporation.

This first Hylton broadcast, from the BBC's 2LO studio, at 10.30pm on August 29th lasted forty-five minutes (with a break in the middle, presumably for a news report or some kind of discussion) and featured *Shanghai Lullaby*, *Who Did You Fool After All?*, *Honolulu Blues*, *It Ain't Gonna Rain No Mo'*, *Pasadena* and *It Had To Be You*. After the break, the band played *My Time Is Your Time*, *Blues* (this title may be wrong), *And That's Not All*, *When You And I Were Dancing*, *What'll I Do?*, *Raggedy Ann*, *Oo Baby* (probably *Oh Baby (Don't Say "No" Say "Maybe")*), *The One I Love* and *Why Did I Kiss That Girl?*

The band would not feature again on the radio until November 1925, from the Piccadilly Hotel, and in March, April and July in 1926.[36] The band would, in time, be famed for their radio broadcasts, but for their scarcity rather than their ubiquity. The band would be too busy playing lucrative theatre shows around Europe to be in a hotel for dancing and simultaneously broadcasting on the BBC. This was a situation Hylton was more than comfortable with; whilst the radio was high profile, the headlining theatre shows, along with his voracious appetite for recording, was seen by him to be more important for the development of his band.

1925 started much as 1924 ended and the constant workload would continue in a similar vein for a decade. The band was now back at the Alhambra Theatre for £175 per week, constantly renewing the contract as the massive audiences continued to be entertained. The key for Jack was to keep the programme changing regularly, and constantly be trying to add spectacle to the show – if the audience was not being distracted by dancing (as they were in most dance venues) then he felt they needed to be distracted with scenery, props and gimmicks. This was the development of the 'show band' as opposed to the 'dance band':

> It was now becoming clear to bandleaders, and to those
> who aspired to that exalted status, that there were in fact

two distinctly different kinds of band, the dance band and the show band; that the two were mutually exclusive and that you had better make up your mind which of the two you wanted to lead. If you chose to lead a show band, then you and your musicians were going to need skills and talents that were only remotely connected with the making of music. It was Jack Hylton who was setting the pace and laying down the ground rules for success upon the stage. What you needed was what he had: singers, dancers, comedians, elaborate concert arrangements and grandiose finales.[37]

The Alhambra contract would eventually amount to thirty-eight weeks in a one-year period, a record that still stands today. Meanwhile, the band was still performing at the Piccadilly Hotel, and they managed to find time to perform a week at Finsbury Park Empire, for dancing at Covent Garden Opera House, a first visit to Bristol (Victoria Rooms), as well as weeks at New Cross Empire, Victoria Palace, charity balls for the Faculty of Arts Ball at Grosvenor House Hotel, the Orange Grove Ball at Claridges, the Jewish Board of Guardians at the Alhambra, and the Samaritans Social and Literary Club at the Westminster Palace Rooms. This is merely a snapshot of the workload. The Metro-Gnomes we're also touring extensively throughout this period (Watford, Shepherds Bush, Leicester, Sheffield, Bognor, Liverpool, etc.). 1925 also saw somewhere in the region of one hundred and twelve titles recorded for HMV, including the first electrical recording for HMV on June 24th 1925, *Feelin' Kind O' Blue* (HMV B-2072). 485,803 records were sold during the year with overall profits of £2,024.

During late 1925 and early 1926, the Alhambra was taking up most of the band's performance time, but they still managed a number of other contracts that would often run concurrently. Contracts show weeks at Brixton, the Metropolitan, Walthamstow, Chelsea and East Ham, with a percentage deal giving Jack 50% of takings over £130, as well as a week at Kensington Kinema at £300, with an extra couple of Christmas shows at £75 per show. Hylton very soon became inundated with offers. Early in 1926 Jack was asked to form a band to act as resident orchestra in the new Kit-Cat Club in London's Haymarket.

Jack Hylton

The Kit-Cat had opened the previous year; it was sumptuously decorated and a famously decadent nocturnal haunt. At the time, it was the only venue purpose-built as a club. It was in the heart of London's West End, in the basement of the Capitol Theatre, with its entrance on Haymarket. It had a large glass fronted entrance, a spacious lobby and a ballroom twice the size of the Piccadilly Hotel. It was a troubled venue, being closed due to licencing issues in late 1926, then closing for good in 1931 due to financial problems. It would later re-open as a restaurant and of course, Jack Hylton would be involved with the music there:

> It was an ultra-chic members only club described as "luxurious, but wonderfully comfy…a vastly patronised and fashionable resort" and such was its popularity that within a short space of time membership exceeded 6,000 including princes, cabinet ministers, dukes and peers.[38]

Jack put together a ten-piece orchestra – Jack Hylton's Kit-Cat Band, under the direction of Al Starita, the American clarinettist and saxophonist (formerly of the Savoy Orpheans band). The band also featured a young Ted Heath (who would famously go on to lead his own highly successful band) on trombone, Len Fillis on banjo, and Sidney Bright on piano. They would go on to record over a hundred and eighty titles for HMV (as Jack Hylton's Kit Cat Band and Jack Hylton's Hyltonians in late 1926 and into 1927). Al's brothers, Ray and Rudi Starita would also later be on the Hylton payroll. Ray, also a saxophonist and clarinettist, would front the Piccadilly Revels Band back at the Piccadilly Hotel, while Rudi was drummer and xylophonist for the same band.

Paul Whiteman came to the UK on tour in April of 1926, his first visit since 1923 and was booked to appear at the Tivoli Cinema in The Strand after his theatre tour. The Musicians Union rules stated that there needed to be an English band of equal size to Whiteman's if he was to be allowed to play at the club. Hylton increased the size of the Kit-Cat band from ten to fifteen with the addition of the Paignet String Quartette, which consisted of Eric Siday and Jean Paignet on violins, Harry Berly on viola and David Cameron on 'cello, as well as second pianist J. Clark. Whilst the Whiteman orchestra was rightly lauded during their trip (where 10,000 people attended the Royal Albert Hall show, with many thousands turned away) the Kit-Cat Band more than held its own and was very well regarded:

> The simple fact, however, is that the Kit-Cat band put up a show which, although somewhat of a different character, was in its way as good as Whiteman's, and was just as well received. This is 'saying some', but it is the opinion voiced by all who heard both bands.[39]

Whilst Hylton's Kit-Cat band was playing against Paul Whiteman's Orchestra, Hylton's own band was embarking on its first UK tour. The schedule was exhaustive, as reported in Melody Maker in May of 1926, the first year of its publication:

> By the time these words appear in print Jack Hylton's big provincial tour will have been fairly launched, and, if one can judge by advance bookings, is likely to exceed, both in popularity and as a money-drawer, any similar effort yet undertaken in this country by a syncopated band. So many performances have to be undertaken in the short period of the tour, sometimes only allowing just a few hours to go to and from places many miles apart, that a rest-cure may be necessary afterwards.[40]

The tour consisted of six weeks of twice nightly variety, six nights a week, with as many late night dances and Sunday concerts as could feasibly be fitted in, from London to Edinburgh. The fourteen piece band line up was now Johnny Rosen (violin), Hugo Rignold (violin), George Shannon (string bass and tuba), Claude Ivy (piano and celeste), Arthur Young (piano[41]), Emile Grimshaw (banjo and guitar), Lew Davis (trombone), Jack Raine (trumpet and violin), Charles Pemmel (trumpet), Noel 'Chappie' d'Amato (soprano, alto and baritone saxophone and guitar), Edward Pogson (soprano, alto and baritone saxophone, clarinet, oboe, cor anglais and violin), Gerald Hoey (soprano and alto saxophone, bass clarinet and 'cello), Johnny Raitz (soprano and tenor saxophone and clarinet) and Arthur Wiltshire (drums and timpani).

It was during this period that Jack employed arranger Leighton Lucas for the first time. Leighton Lucas (1903-1982) was a composer and conductor who would later be famous for his orchestral compositions and film scores. After learning the piano as a child, he studied as a classical dancer, appearing with Diaghilev's Russian Ballet, before becoming a conductor of opera. Jack Hylton put an advert into Melody Maker for a new arranger and Lucas replied – he scored two numbers as a test and Hylton gave him the job, at £1,000 per year:

> Now Mr Lucas arranges exclusively for Jack Hylton. He averages about three symphonic arrangements a week, in addition to all sorts of other duties for the Hylton concern...Mr Lucas says the real secrets of arranging for dance bands lie in being able to score a perfectly balanced dance rhythm with a variety of truly musical harmonies and tone colours.[42]

In May Jack was invited to appear at his first Royal Variety Performance, to be held at the Alhambra Theatre on May 27th. For this he used a fifteen-piece band, playing new Leighton Lucas arrangements. The band travelled from Glasgow for the show, then back to Glasgow to carry on their tour. Through the summer, the band would spend eight weeks back at the Alhambra (including the 850th show at the end of July), plus dates in Bournemouth, Brighton and Margate. In Bournemouth, box office records would be smashed as Jack's manager grabbed every available seat in the Winter Gardens to increase the capacity from 1,800 to 2,139, leaving the theatre manager scratching his head as to how so many tickets could be sold. Jack would also be fined £15 plus expenses for dangerous driving (with the court citing six previous driving convictions) and there would be reports that Jack had been offered £34,000 for a fourteen-week tour of Australia and New Zealand (which would never materialise).

It was also reported that Jack was raising the stakes with the on stage antics and using two live racehorses on-stage for a number (which was never recorded in the studio) called *Horses*. August of 1926 saw the first reported use of the phrase "Jack's Back" (at the Victoria Palace in London) which accompanied an enduring image of the maestro, hands aloft, conducting the band. The image and the phrase would be used throughout his career.

By September of 1926, with barely a moment to catch their breath, the band were off on another tour of the provinces, taking in two weeks in Blackpool, and weeks in Leeds, Cardiff, Birmingham,

Brighton and Manchester as well as dates in Eastbourne, Tunbridge Wells, Scarborough and Harrogate, other London engagements and two charity shows in his home town of Stalybridge. An American tour is announced then cancelled, due to American Federation of Musicians wranglings.

On December 19th the band gave a rare Sunday afternoon concert at the Royal Albert Hall and featured some new Leighton Lucas arrangements, including the Eric Coates composition *The Three Bears Fantasy*, Gershwin's *Valse Moderne* (which featured a piano duet of Arthur Young and former Queen's Hall Roof pianist Claude Ivy), Lucas' own *The Dance Suite* and the Hylton composition *Hyltonisms*, which was a feature for soloists Hugo Rignold, Johnny Rosen and Harry Berly (on strings), Lew Davis (on trombone) and Johnny Raitz (on saxophone and clarinet):

> All the compositions were excellently rendered; in fact, good as Hylton's band is known to be in the interpretation of 'legitimate' works, Jack Hylton surprised one and all, not only by the control he has over his combination, but by the keen appreciation he possesses of the lighter Russian school, which showed continually throughout the renderings.[43]

Before the year was out, Hylton had signed a contract to become Musical Director of both the Piccadilly Hotel and the Kit-Cat Club, after a little jostling and legal threatening earlier in the year.

On New Year's Eve 1926, Hylton and his orchestra shared the bill of a charity concert in aid of a Middlesex Hospital, and featured a BBC Radio broadcast at 2.00am, as part of their New Year celebrations. Sharing the bill with Hylton was the Kit-Kat Club band, under Al Starita, the Piccadilly Revels Band, under Ray Starita, and The Metro-Gnomes, under Mrs Jack Hylton. These were all, of course, bands on the Hylton payroll.

> The Albert Hall was full to its utmost capacity and the full dancing floor which was laid for the occasion was a wise forethought as nothing smaller would have accommodated so many revellers…The ball was a riotous success and Jack Hylton, who, though it is not generally known, has

done much in the past for charities, had the satisfaction of knowing that he had backed a winner on behalf of the crumbling portals of the Old Middlesex.[44]

It is also worth noting that this was the very first broadcast for the BBC under the new charter. The music was relayed from 2:00am. The list of songs played, as provided by the BBC, was *I Am Lonely Without You, Silver Rose, Am I Wasting My Time On You?, No Fooling, Lady Be Good, The More We Are Together, When It's Twilight On The Trail, Missouri, Follow The Rainbow, Couldn't You Care?, Me Too, When, It's June Down There, In My Gondola, Just A Rose In Old Killarney, Out In The New Mown Hay, While The Sahara Sleeps, Lavender, A New One For Two, Ukulele Dream Girl, Speak, Sunny Swanee, Good Night, I've Never Seen A Straight Banana, My Cutie's Due At Two To Two, Cross Your Heart, Charleston, Smiling Joe, Tell All The World, Let's All Go To Mary's House, That Certain Party Of Mine, Caring For You, Ukulele Dream Man, Bye Bye Blackbird, Because I Love You, Always* and *Heart Broken Rose.*

1926 had proved to be a landmark year and the progress from 1921 was staggering. In 1926 alone, just when gramophones were beginning to take hold and become popular in people's homes, Jack Hylton recorded around one hundred and twenty sides for HMV and sold 790,449 records with a profit of £3,294. It is extraordinary to realise that the band was some considerable way off its peak.

Chapter 5: Symphonic Syncopation

Hylton's band on New Year's Eve 1926, after a charity show for a
Middlesex hospital. (Jack Hylton Archive)

You know, we were never a jazz band, but Jack would
use such elements of jazz as...would improve the show,
because for him, the show was everything.[1]

Exploring the idea of 'what is jazz?' is somewhat too broad a top-
ic for this book, but the ideas of to what extent Jack Hylton was
playing jazz, what his feelings towards jazz music were, and the impact of this on his contemporaries is certainly worth considering.
Throughout this we shall explore Hylton's own words where possible.
In the 1920s he wrote often on the subject; given that as an art form it
was both new and misunderstood, and that the matter was often talked
about in the music press and the mainstream press, makes Hylton's
insistence no surprise. The word jazz, its associated music and the
kind of occasion on which it was played in the first quarter of the 20th
century, led to the mainstream press often speaking disdainfully of

jazz, and Hylton sought to disassociate himself and his band from this negative media coverage, whilst at the same time trying to suggest that elements of jazz were required for his band. He also managed to coin the phrase *symphonic syncopation*, which he used throughout the life of his band to describe the music they played.

Jazz music has a vast academic legacy in the 21st century but when Hylton transcribed his first Paul Whiteman record, things were very different and studying jazz was unheard of. The roots of jazz are muddled but it is generally thought to have originated in the late 19th century in southern states of America, an amalgamation of African drum music (which was associated with festival dances), church music (which developed gradually by slaves, taken to America, using the harmonic styles of hymns and turning them into what we would now call negro spirituals), European orchestral music (made mostly by African slaves playing European instruments discarded by the European settlers and imitating their harmony and melodic sensibility), and the added influence of the South American *habanera*, itself a development of Spanish dancing music. This paragraph is a gross simplification, but gives the new reader a sense of what was involved.

The abolition of slavery led to many African Americans being offered the opportunity of education and employment and in turn many found work as entertainers. Pianists developed *ragtime* and in turn *ragtime* began to appear in written sheet music form, especially once classically trained Scott Joplin published his first set of ragtime music *Original Rags* in 1898.

Blues was developing concurrently, especially in the 'deep south' of America, with spirituals blending with slave work songs, field chants and ballads. Meanwhile, a culture of marching bands was developing; small bands with European musical sensibility, played by African American musicians, in the bars and brothels of lively New Orleans.

From within this melting pot of varying styles, artists such as cornettist Buddy Bolden and pianist Jelly Roll Morton loosened the distinction of these genres and very quickly a new style developed. By the time trumpeter Louis Armstrong began his career in the late 1910s, a style known as *Dixieland* (a polyphonic style with a theme and collective improvisation) had developed. Armstrong is known not simply for his longevity but for the way in which he moved jazz on with his chordal, rather than melodic improvisation style:[2]

> *Jazz:* A music created mainly by black Americans in the early 20th century through an amalgamation of elements drawn from European-American and tribal African musics. A unique type, it cannot safely be categorised as folk, popular, or art music, though it shares aspects of all three. It has had a profound effect on international culture, not only through its considerable popularity, but through the important role it has played in shaping the many forms of popular music that developed around and out of it.[3]

By the 1920s, bands such as the Original Dixieland Jazz Band had begun to receive international acclaim, and were one of the first high profile recording acts early in the decade

Much of the history of jazz and its mainstream appeal comes from the 1930s onwards, by which time Jack Hylton was well established. When he took his first tentative steps as a bandleader in 1921, very little authentic jazz had been heard in the UK and although some bands in the UK were attempting the new style, the standard is thought to have been some way off what was being heard in America:

> The Savoy Hotel it was, in 1922 or thereabouts, which presented the West Enders with their first recognisable dance band. Until then, bands had been a raggle taggle of assorted instruments – cornet, trombone, soprano saxophone, piano, banjo and drums – the players slavishly imitating the sounds they had first heard when The Original Dixieland Jazz Band crossed the Atlantic in 1919 and astounded the natives assembled at the London Hippodrome and the Hammersmith Palais with their raucous, undisciplined, mostly improvised music. To ears unfamiliar with the real McCoy, it passed for jazz.[4]

It's also worth bearing in mind that most dancers would be unfamiliar with this new style and not necessarily keen on hearing it played, especially when it was played badly. Also of note is that most of these new experimental musicians would have been working in

London, and outside of the capital very little of this new music would have been heard until at least the mid 1920s.

Of course, just because Jack Hylton was at the forefront of the dance band movement, doesn't mean he was a trailblazer and jazz lover:

> Jack didn't like jazz music, didn't like it at all. Jack's scene was the songs of the period just before and after the First World War. When he went to Berlin, a short time before I joined the band, he did become aware of Continental music and this opened up a new world to him. He made records of *I Kiss Your Hand, Madame, Handsome Gigolo*, and similar things, but he still didn't like jazz. It was a battle for the youngsters in the band to try and get some jazz feeling into our music. We tried to all the time - never stopped, in fact.[5]

Contemporary opinions of jazz widely confused both the term itself (with origins considerably less savoury than a new brand of dance music) and what the word represented. Many commentators saw only what Whiteman was doing; others saw a synthesis of the music from the southern United States and the Tin Pan Alley composers such as Irving Berlin, Jerome Kern and George Gershwin. Still others felt that the music that had filtered across to the UK was not even jazz at all, but some kind of post-jazz refinement:

> Jazz, as I understand it, describes only the first stage of development of modern syncopated music, when its outstanding feature was improvisation. Improvised noises of the sliding trombones, cowbells, the train effects, shouting of negroes and all varieties of spontaneous exclamation – these embellishments, superimposed on the basic dancing tune, combined to create the early 'true jazz'.[6]

Critical analysis of jazz began in the early 1920s, especially when 'serious' composers began using the jazz vernacular, most notably Gershwin's *Rhapsody In Blue* and his *Concerto in F*. This argument was very often based on whether jazz should be deemed as serious *art music*, but perhaps a link is more relevant to jazz as dance music, or as music descended from indigenous folk music rather than orchestral (art) music. Meanwhile there were a number of commentators for whom this *art music/folk music* idea was of no relevance because jazz by its very existence was immoral:

> They blamed jazz for the supposedly rebellious behaviour of the younger generation, and argued that this music led to everything from immorality and out-of-wedlock pregnancies to criminal activities and dementia. "Moral disaster," predicted the *New York American*, "is coming to hundreds of young American girls through the pathological, nerve-irritating, sex-exciting music of jazz orchestras." Automobile tycoon Henry Ford likewise condemned jazz music...Jazz, he believed, was nothing more than "monkey talk, jungle squeals, grunts and squeaks and gasps suggestive of cave love," and his newspaper, the *Dearborn Independent,* regularly published attacks on what he called "moron music."[7]

For Hylton, the crucial element appears to have been a driving and constant rhythm, a quality which jazz possessed in no small measure. However, Jack's love of Victorian parlour songs, ballads and dance music would stay as the fundamental starting point – the 'good tune', as he often called it, was vital. That, presented in a modern English way (though clearly influenced by the developments across the Atlantic), was what he sought to offer the public. His music was more of a natural development of the 'old style', rather than an adoption of the 'new style'.

The development of printing technology in the 1820s and 1830s led to a proliferation of printed sheet music and advances in lithographic technology led to publishers making ever more desirable front covers for the sheet music which in turn increased sales. The cost of the music, despite having gradually decreased (perhaps three or four shillings per song) meant that the biggest market was the middle classes, who could afford pianos in their parlours.

Meanwhile, the saloon bars of pubs, where music would be performed, started to be replaced with music halls by the 1850s. These were distinctly different to theatres, as they were designed for eating, drinking and talking, whilst the show was being performed; essentially like large saloon bars. The popular songs of the day would be played in the smaller pub venues too, and it was these songs, performed in pubs and music halls, which were printed. These were the songs which Hylton was brought up with, performed as a child and as a young man, and which influenced his future career.

Jazz would have been a little unrefined for the ears of the British public, so Hylton used all his experience and everything he learned from the Paul Whiteman records, to develop his own unique take on this most modern of sounds, calling it *symphonic syncopation*. Here is a good example of his writings at the time, this from 1926:

> Symphonic syncopation is not 'jazz', that nerve-torturing riot of sound which made its appearance during the war, when everything, music included, was topsy-turvy. 'Jazz' and syncopated music have one thing only in common – a pronounced rhythm. Once upon a time, we are told, all music was crude rhythms, but it gradually came to be embellished with harmony and melody.

> Harmony and melody are, of course, essential, but there is rhythm as well in modern symphonic syncopation, which I believe is the first really successful combination of these three elements ever evolved. The rhythm of all syncopated melodies, however, is not identical, as many critics assert. *Castles In Spain* and *Ida I Do*, both new dance tunes, are good examples of different rhythms.

> Why, then, is syncopated music so popular? As I see it, music, to be popular, must express what people in the mass are thinking or desiring. Modern syncopation does this. It expresses cheerfulness. We all want to be happy, to radiate cheerfulness. That is what all this work-weary world is wanting most of all today.

> By broadcasting syncopated music, the BBC is scattering throughout the land among countless listeners, cheer, hope and vitality. The full truth of this fact may not be realised at present, but here lies the reason why I believe that symphonic syncopation will find an increasing place in future radio programmes. The critics cannot stop it. Like everything else, broadcasting programmes are gov-

erned by the inexorable law of supply and demand. Undoubtedly, the public wants syncopation. Undoubtedly, they will get it.

No song succeeds nowadays unless it is also a dance tune. But, to be really popular – to be a best seller – the dance must be expressive of joy and cheerfulness. It is the happy lilt, characteristic of symphonic syncopation that counts.[8]

This refinement of the American sound, combined with the history of Victorian parlour music led to visual refinements on stage, again drawing from the European tradition:

But by 1923, bands were taking on a new look. Seven or eight dinner-jacketed gents, slick haired and well scrubbed, presenting themselves in an orderly row across the front of the bandstand...Front and centre, smiling urbanely, groomed and polished, dressed as for a royal banquet, stood the bandleader...And before each of these musicians there stood a music stand, its metal struts tastefully hidden from view by a velvet banner proclaiming the name of the band. Music stands, for goodness sake! These guys could actually read music!...That wild and woolly Yankee music had been tamed and domesticated; it had been disciplined and deodorized and forced into respectability, rendered suitable for the ears of kings and princes, for the dancing feet of duchesses and debutantes.[9]

A great deal of the 'refinement', which Sid Colin speaks of in the above quotation, is to do with rhythmic drive and tempo. The incoming bands, such as The Original Dixieland Jazz Band, would present shows in music halls and also for dancing, where they were hugely popular, and their sound was faster, louder and more potent that the British bands. It is this visceral sound and approach to playing which was so foreign, whilst the stage-show itself and often the song choices and instrumentation were not so far removed from what the public were already comfortable with hearing:

However, the music of the ODJB was generally regarded as being different in style from most extant dance music in London. In particular, the band's rhythmic drive and tempi were different to anything that dancers would have experienced before, and this seems to have thrown the conventionalists of the dancing world into panic. The ODJB's fast one-steps were probably responsible for introducing a freer style of dancing in Britain. Therefore, it was at dance clubs that their actual musical performance was appreciated, through the response of those dancing, and in this context it is hardly surprising that the music of the band became synonymous with jazz in Britain for many years to come.[10]

Perhaps of more interest to Hylton was another band that visited Britain from America in 1919, the Southern Syncopated Orchestra (SSO). Their band was larger (twenty four instrumentalists and twelve singers) and their repertoire was much broader than the ODJB, including spirituals, ragtime, the work of contemporary black composers and classical pieces (Brahms, Grieg, Dvořák and others.) We don't know whether Hylton heard either the SSO or the ODJB, though he would have been in London at the time and would have known of their engagements:

> Interestingly, the performances of the SSO provoked an increased appreciation of the evolution and developments that had taken place in black American music since the minstrel shows and performances of spirituals in the nineteenth century. The juxtaposition of plantation songs and spirituals with instrumental ragtime and blues thus provided in effect an illustrated lineage of the evolution of black American music. It is significant that the SSO linked the new styles of syncopated music with black American musical forms with which the British public would already be familiar.[11]

The idea of mixing a programme of classical pieces with what was ostensibly dance music was something that Hylton would later adopt, though whether there was any direct influence from the SSO or from Whiteman is unclear. There is an abundance of classical repertoire in both Hylton's recorded and performed output. One of his best selling records consisted of two Rachmaninoff Preludes, the *Prelude in G Minor op.23 no.5* and the *Prelude in C# Minor op.3 no.2*, both arranged by Peter Yorke. These were recorded in Kingsway Hall in London on February 19th 1930 on HMV (catalogue number C-1864). These were 'played straight' and sound simply like re-orchestrations of the original.

It is of note that without exception, Hylton was never guilty of 'jazzing the classics'. A number such as *The Light Cavalry Overture* as arranged by Harry Roy for his own orchestra (recorded in February 1942 in London) features marching drums with a swing feel, a trumpet fanfare introduction and a swinging dance band arrangement. We see the difference when compared to a typical Hylton arrangement, such as his version of Sieczynski's *Vienna, City Of My Dreams*. This is a waltz, prominently featuring strings, with unison wind figures and flute and clarinet arpeggio figures above the melody. There is a great deal of rubato tempo work in the short number and the overall feel is rather melodramatic. This Billy Ternent arrangement would certainly not be classed as jazz, but is perhaps trying to reach the same audience as the *Light Cavalry Overture* already mentioned – something for those looking for a little more than the average dance band numbers.

The idea of adding classical pieces fitted well with Hylton's all encompassing idea of being a 'show band' rather than just a 'dance band'. His work was extensive and in a world of supply and demand, its clear Hylton's record buying audience was as ready to purchase his classical pieces as his foxtrots or his comedy numbers. Hylton knew Eric Coates (1886-1957) well and On February 19th 1926, Hylton recorded a twelve-minute version of Coates' *The Selfish Giant*. The length of the number was such that it had to be spread over two twelve inch 78rpm records (the standard size was ten inches), which were simply called *Part One* and *Part Two* (cat. no. C-1253).[12] This is a more adventurous work, pre-empting some of the band's future concert arrangements, with many tempo changes, dramatic use of orchestral timbres and use of instruments not normally associated with a dance band, such as an oboe, a flute and a harp. This work was followed in December 1926 with Coates' *The Three Bears*, again spread over two sides of a twelve inch record (cat. no. C-1309) and named *Part One* and *Part Two*.

As well as these, Hylton recorded Ravel's *Bolero*, Liszt's *Nocturnes*, Stravinsky's *Mavra* (discussed in Chapter 7), a Schubert *Serenade*, Tchaikovsky's *Violin Concerto*, and works by Paganini, Chopin and Mendelssohn. Many of these classical traits were also expressed in the concert arrangements the band were famed for, which were rarely recorded due to their length, and which were very different in tempo and arrangement to the regular version 'with vocal refrain' and once in the environment of the concert hall rather than the dance hall, these longer more expansive versions worked well.

Alongside the concert arrangements and classical pieces, Hylton was famed for his comedy numbers. Indeed his biggest selling record was a sing-along comedy number, written by Leslie Sarony, called *Rhymes* (released, in different versions as Zonophone 5997 in October 1931 and Decca F-2679 in November 1931). It was so successful that a follow up was released just a month later, called, unsurprisingly, *More Rhymes* (Decca F-2750, December 1932):

> A number of the comedy records contained hot solos but these were not actually Jack's idea. The reason for them was that the musical content in these records was so appalling that the arrangers had terrible trouble doing anything with the material to make it last a whole eternity of three minutes. The way arrangers used to get out of this was to stick in a hot chorus, then a vocal chorus, then another hot chorus, and so on. That is the reason hot solos were used so frequently in comedy numbers and they rescued some of these from complete mediocrity. Anyway, that's my opinion.[13]

Hylton was always meticulous in his recording, despite the prodigious output. A memo from Hylton to Gramophone Company executive W.L. Streeton attests to this:

> On Thursday last Mr Anderson brought me up a master of *Moanin' Low*. On hearing it I found right in the very first eight bars the trombone player 'duffed' his passage and again later in the trumpet chorus there are many cracks, as well as some of his hot playing being in the wrong chord. Also in my opinion, the record was amplified far too

much...I should be most glad if we could make a ruling once and for all, that we must consider the artistic performance of a record more than its strength.[14]

Clearly, despite his punishing schedule, Hylton was personally involved in the process of choosing the music he wanted to record, the recording process and the finished product, from both a musical and technical viewpoint. HMV clearly agreed; they continued to release hundreds of records every year and they continued to sell in their millions.

In due course the moral arguments against jazz dissipated but Hylton was still fighting the *highbrow/lowbrow* argument for a considerable number of years. Here are his own words:

Many hard things have been said about jazz – or dance music by people who have wrapped themselves in a cloak of sham 'highbrowism'. But none of these remarks has had the power to check the triumphant progress of dance-music, which is now part and parcel of the lives of the people. That dance-music has an important place, and a rightful one, in our lives is admitted. For to say that music should consist alone of such glorious works as those of Beethoven or Schumann is as absurd as to say that classical music must take second place to the works of Noel Gay and Irving Berlin, and the like. I am a keen student and lover of all types of music, even that which many people would term 'highbrow', but I am not ashamed of having devoted my career to dance-music. I have played dance-music with genuine sincerity of purpose; for I believe that in many ways clever and melodious 'jazz-music' portrays the spirit of this age. Remember that the majority of those whose lives are devoted to such music are accomplished musicians. That is to say, they can, and do, play classical music as well as modern, while many of those who write our dance-numbers are also fully capable of writing 'highbrow' stuff, and writing it well.[15]

Matters came to a head in 1926, when Robert L. Bigg wrote an article in *The Gramophone* in June of that year, which was a review of the recent visit of the Paul Whiteman Orchestra, which derided Whiteman's contemporaries in London, Hylton included:

> We need a Whiteman band in this country to make us appreciate fully the much-abused term 'jazz'. Hylton and the Orpheans are very limited in their orchestrations, and nibble in a fresh field only very occasionally. Naturally the arrangement is the chief obstacle, for there are no Ferdie Grofes [sic][16] in England.[17]

Hylton, being the type of chap he was, and by this time a significant force in British dance music, chose to reply with his own article in *The Gramophone*, in August of 1926, entitled *The British Touch*. In it he responded to Bigg, again muddying the waters of the term 'jazz' as well as 'show band' and 'dance band':

> Mr Bigg may not be inclined to agree, but I assert without fear of contradiction that we have at least two men in this country who, so far as arrangement is concerned, can produce work equal to anything we get from America or, indeed, elsewhere in the world.
>
> In America the public have grown up with 'jazz'. Everything is 'jazzed'. Over there the world moves to 'jazz' time, for public taste has kept pace with the evolution of this type of music. But if you attempt to perform the most modern American arrangements of syncopated music in this country you are not likely to be successful. I know, because I have tried repeatedly.[18]

Whether this is strictly true is a moot point, as Whiteman received a fantastic reception in 1925 when he visited the UK and subsequently throughout Europe. If anything the Hylton/Bigg spat in the UK music press merely fudged what was a complex issue of semantics that almost do not matter at all. Hylton shouted loudly that he was not playing jazz, though clearly there were heavy jazz influences throughout his repertoire and his link with Whiteman, who clearly used elements of jazz music, is incontrovertible. Hylton clearly had a major impact on the dance band style of the 1920s in Britain and in calling his music 'symphonic syncopation' he was trying to remove himself from any suggestion that what he was playing was associated with a genre some saw as immoral. Meanwhile the addition of vaudevillian comedy songs, classical pieces 'played straight' and, subsequently, complex concert arrangements, perhaps gave validity to the fact that he did not want to be, and was not trying to be associated with jazz. The fact that Hylton's style has, for now, fallen out of favour is little to do with the fact that the population of 1920s and 1930s Britain and Europe didn't much care what the style of music was called. Hylton's dance band reigned supreme for almost two decades:

> I hope that Mr Bigg or anyone else does not think that Americans have a corner on syncopation. They have not. Symphonic syncopation, which I feel proud to have developed in this country, is pre-eminently British. In the dance hall or on the gramophone record alike, it makes subtle appeal to our British temperament. It is fast becoming a truly national music. [19]

Chapter 6: 1927-1931

Jack Hylton and His Orchestra outside the Palais de la Méditerranée, Nice, 1928. (Jack Hylton Archive)

"Everyone plays everything – and dances, and sings equally," reported one account. Hylton himself conducted with great verve, "his hands explaining his music…his body elongates and shrinks…He jumps, goes, twirls, comes back, boxes a little, then in an instant, seems to hold a sword, fakes, jabs, while the instruments appear to change themselves rising or falling and one doesn't know how."[1]

1927 started in a predictable enough fashion, with a number of weeks at the Alhambra Theatre in London's Leicester Square. On January 19th, Ennis Parkes set sail for America, along with Hylton's manager George Samson and composer Horatio Nicholls and his wife. Hylton would stay in England tending to the band's busy schedule.

Horatio Nicholls was the pseudonym of Lawrence Wright (1888-1964), the Leicester born songwriter and publisher who went on to write six hundred songs under his own name and his pseudonym. He opened a music shop in Denmark Street in London in 1906, established the Lawrence Wright Music Company in 1912, was the founder of Melody Maker in 1926 and was awarded an 'Outstanding Contribution to British Popular Music' Ivor Novello award in 1962. He had been living in Blackpool since the early 1920s, where he lived in a mock castle house, which would later be known as the Castle Casino.

This trip was meticulously planned and all went well. Whilst on board The *SS Majestic, en route* to New York, Wright would compose a new melody. Once they arrived, he would engage the lyric services of his writing partner, American songwriter Edgar Leslie, at his 40th floor Broadway office in New York. The title of the song, *Shepherd Of The Hills*, came from the name of a horse that Wright had seen in the sports section of a newspaper whilst on board ship.[2]

On the morning of February 10th, Lawrence Wright cabled to London to alert Jack and his office that the song would be ready that evening. This is when things started to move quickly to make the plan play out in the way Hylton imagined. The chairman of Melody Maker Ltd., Llew Weir and chairman of the Lawrence Wright Music Company's orchestral department were alerted and Jack agreed to be in his office at 5.00pm to answer the transatlantic call. These men being present were simply part of the publicity stunt. At exactly 5.00pm Wright called, Hylton answered, and the transatlantic phone line didn't let them down:

> "Yes, this is Hylton. I can hear you. Speak up" we heard Jack say, and then as he repeated what he heard, so that all might take it down. "Yes, I hear...*Shepherd Of The Hills*. Foxtrot tempo. Key of Eb. Verse starts. First note G, minim; second note F# crotchet; third note G crotchet; first bar ends. Next note Bb, minim; then F crotchet and F# crotchet; second bar ends," and so on, with but an occasional call for repetition until the verse and half the chorus was completed.[3]

At this point, with the telephone call costing many pounds per minute, it was felt things needed to be speeded up. Mrs Hylton came on the line and sang the remaining part of the song to her husband and he duly wrote it down on the manuscript paper. Wright's secretary Miss Hain then took down the lyrics in shorthand and the call was ended, costing the pair £150 for half an hour. Hylton's manuscript was then handed to a waiting car, which contained Leighton Lucas, and he was taken to the Alhambra Theatre where the band were playing two shows, along with another two at Finsbury Park Empire. He arranged the brand new song and had the parts ready for the band to play at the second house of both venues, with Jack himself on vocal duties. Within five hours it was show time in New York and audiences there were also treated to an arrangement of this brand new song.

Ennis Parkes telephoning *Shepherd Of The Hills* to her husband, from New York to London with Horatio Nicholls holding the new sheet music. (Jack Hylton Archive)

Jack Hylton

The publicity alone would have been sufficient to make this song a hit in sheet music sales, but Hylton naturally took the extra step and on the morning of February 11th the band met up at the HMV studios in Hayes to record it.

There was heavy fog that morning and Jack's chauffeur, Mr All-wood, was in something of a hurry; Hylton was taking care of business in the back of his luxury Spanish Hispano-Suiza sports car when a student from Oxford, travelling in the opposite direction, lost control, skidded, and collided with him on Bath Road in Hounslow (the A4), just a few miles from the studio. The front of both cars were smashed; Hylton was thrown heavily against the glass partition of the car and was found on the floor of the car bleeding profusely from severe cuts to his head and face. The chauffeur was unharmed and the student, J.W. Collins suffered only slight cuts to his legs and wrists:

> As he was lifted from the car by passers by, and laid by the roadside, he was just conscious, and said to his helpers, "I am Jack Hylton, if anything happens, everything is to go to my wife."[4]

Hylton was given first aid by an AA man, and then taken to the nearby Hounslow Hospital by a passing army ambulance, suffering from concussion and severe cuts. He lost five teeth and would receive eighty-five stitches to his face, gaining a long scar on the left hand side of his face, which he would sport for the rest of his life.

Typically, Hylton was not prepared to let this near fatal car crash get in the way of the '3,000 miles a second New York to London hit'. The band was in place waiting for Jack to arrive when the message came through, from Hounslow Hospital: "American hustle ends in disaster. Tell the boys to carry on." This they did. Chappie d'Amato was instructed to lead the band and take the vocal chorus on *Shepherd Of The Hills*. Their second take was the one that was released (as HMV B-5207). The other sides recorded that day, *Baby* and *Lantern Of Love* were rejected and no more recordings took place until Hylton's four week convalescence had taken place.

Hylton still working whilst recuperating. This show was taken at the nursing home
where Hylton was convalescing, as published in *The Daily Chronicle*, February 1927.
(Jack Hylton Archive)

The subsequent recording, on March 2nd, would be Hylton's own
vocal version of *Shepherd Of The Hills*, recorded at the Small
Queen's Hall in London. The Chappie d'Amato version on HMV B-
5207 was then replaced with Hylton's vocal. Both versions therefore
exist with the same catalogue number, though Hylton's vocal is seen
to be the superior take. Perhaps significantly, the band did not return
to Hayes for six months:

Nothing could have so markedly demonstrated the perfect
unanimity of Jack's band as this enforced absence of the
directing head. The bands carried on in perfect accord,

Jack Hylton

Chappie d'Amato assuming the leadership, and Jack's new manager, Mr Hunt, attending to all the stage detail. Everything went smoothly, everyone making it a point of honour to relieve Jack of all business worries.[5]

And so whilst Hylton recovered, the schedule continued for the band. By mid March he was back at work, with dates in Brighton, Birmingham, London, Manchester, Bolton, Newcastle, Blackpool, Dundee, Glasgow, Edinburgh, Paisley, Hamilton and Leeds. He also formed Jack Hylton's Piccadilly Band for the show *Piccadilly Follies* at the Piccadilly Club. The Kit-Cat band was on tour, and Hylton's Hyltonians had been formed. At least on paper, this was an ensemble just for recording, primarily drawing musicians from the Kit-Cat band, but essentially using any available Hylton alumni.

April saw the band back at the Alhambra with a new show (including comedy vocalist and future Hylton regular Leslie Sarony, Little Tich, the Houston Sisters, Conn Kenna and his pilot and Sandy Powell "in his spoof Russian dance and ludicrous sports medley"!) Week long variety dates followed, many doubling two venues each night, whilst the newly opened Kit-Cat Restaurant featured the Kit-Cat Band, and the Piccadilly Revels band was resident at the Piccadilly Hotel. Jack, in another little bit of publicity announced the winner of a competition to name Hylton's next band. E. Hamblin of Levenshulme in Manchester won £10 for suggesting Jack Hylton's Rhythmagicians, which he said he "hopes to make use of in the not too distant future."

Somehow the band found time for a week's holiday, before a staggering four thousand people danced to the band at the Tower Ballroom in Blackpool, before they appeared in a new revue show, composed and produced by Laddie Cliff, called *Shake Your Feet*. The show opened at Liverpool Empire, but soon moved to the West End, into the Hippodrome, to universally good reviews. Jack also found time, with his wife, to be photographed on the inaugural Imperial Airways flight to Deauville, which for the first time gave people (with sufficient funds) the opportunity to take a day trip to the Normandy town.

Shake Your Feet would run at the Hippodrome for the rest of the year, but plenty of other dates would run concurrently. Jack Hylton and His Orchestra were now by far the most popular and biggest selling show band in the country:

> Is there anything to approach the success of this outfit in this country? But it's not done without enormously hard work and clever thinking.[6]

Another publicity stunt occurred in September, again with the aid of the Lawrence Wright Music Publishing Company. On September 4th, the largest passenger aeroplane in the UK was hired and the band, Mr and Mrs Hylton, along with Mr and Mrs Nicholls, drove from London to Croydon airfield to pick up the Imperial Airways twenty four seater plane. It flew, via a stop-off at Chester, to Blackpool, along with the band parts for a new song, written by Joe Gilbert and published by Lawrence Wright, called *Me And Jane In A Plane*. Crowds swarmed the sea front at Blackpool and when the plane arrived, flying low, the cacophonous engines all but drowned out the band playing the song live from the plane. After a couple of circles round Blackpool Tower, a small parcel was dropped, attached to a parachute, and was picked up by a 'day excursionist' from Eccles. In it were the band parts for *Me And Jane In A Plane*, which were dramatically rushed to Ray Starita, who was performing with Hylton's Piccadilly Revels Band all week in Blackpool. They then took the parts to their Sunday concert at the Palace Theatre in Manchester, and performed the new number. There was also a standard sheet music version, which was dropped for the use of Walter Williams, who performed the song that evening on the North Pier, and subsequently nightly for the rest of his season. The aeroplane flew away from several thousand excitable music fans on the ground and when the sheet music was delivered by car to the Lawrence Wright music demonstration pavilions, there was almost hysteria with five thousand copies sold within an hour. Hylton, with a vocal trio of himself, trumpeter Jack Jackson and Billy Ternent, later recorded the song.

Meanwhile, after leaving Blackpool, the aeroplane flew to Harrogate, where the band was playing that evening. Of course they played the new song and after flying back to London the following morning, the song was featured in their shows at the London Hippodrome and the Camberwell Palace. Following this, the manuscript was sent to America, where Irving Berlin bought the rights, and many orchestras made recordings of this now famous song. Music publishers employed many gimmicks to increase sheet music sales but this was one of the most elaborate and most successful.

Bookings continued to rush in for the band, whilst *Shake Your Feet* continued in London. By the end of the year, Hylton was ready to embark on his first continental tour. A farewell party took place on December 20th, at the Ambassadors Club. Naturally music was provided by one of Hylton's own ensembles. Mrs Hylton (recovered from a recent spell in hospital) sported a diamond 'Jack's Back' brooch. The band would be away from December 31st until February 1st, 1928, visiting Paris for twelve days, then Hamburg, then Berlin, where they would be resident at the Scala Theatre for three weeks.

The Scala was the most famous Vaudeville stage in Germany and was hugely popular. It was built in 1920 by a wealthy consortium of Jewish business people and by 1941 was the largest in the country. The onset of World War II would have a catastrophic impact on the venue, first by Goebbels' decree that banned the role of 'Conferencier', or MC, (which reduced the cabaret to an unconnected string of song and dance numbers) and then on November 22nd, 1943, when the building was all but destroyed by a bomb. The site of this former theatre is currently a nondescript apartment block, shop and multi-storey car park.

For Jack Hylton and His Orchestra, the crowds at the Scala were huge and the reception was overwhelming. Box office records were broken at the Empire Theatre in Paris.

They arrived back in London with news that they had been added to the bill for their second Royal Variety Performance, to be held at the London Casino on March 1st. A tour of the provinces preceded it, with dates including Nottingham, Birmingham, Blackpool, Buxton and Leicester. After the Royal Variety Performance the band embarked on another Continental tour, though it was not without a hitch. Jack flew ahead to Paris, with the band following by boat. When they arrived in Calais they were told that there were problems with all but three of their passports and they were refused entry to France. They sailed back to Dover and Jack was alerted. He reacted in his usual short tempered way, contacted the manager of the Palace Theatre in Paris, where they were due to play the following evening, who contacted the relevant authorities, whilst the band took a rare night off in a hotel in Dover. The authorities fixed the issue with the passports, Jack chartered a private plane, and the band was flown to Paris just in time for the first show at the Palace.

The band opened in Paris to critical and commercial acclaim and stayed there for two weeks. They moved to Marseilles for ten days at The Capitol Theatre, before returning to the Empire Theatre in Paris until April 21st.

They returned to London, having barely played a show there in three months. A week at the Victoria Theatre was insufficient to appease the fans, but as quickly as they had arrived, the band was off on another tour of the provinces, finally landing back in London in May, with a week at Holborn Empire, a week at Finsbury Park Empire and more touring around the UK, including dates in Bradford, Bridlington, Scarborough, Burnley, Harrogate, Newcastle, Bristol, Cardiff, Liverpool, Southport, Manchester and Glasgow, amongst others. The summer months were spent touring round the seaside resorts of the south coast, before more weeks of variety in September and October, at New Cross Empire, Holborn Empire, Penge Empire and Brighton Hippodrome. During the summer of 1928 Hylton turned down a year's contract at Leicester Square Cinema, which was due to open on October 1st for a staggering £42,000. Of course Hylton was making plenty of money, and could see potential for not just more money, but more prestige if he stayed out of the Leicester Square orchestra pit:

> I have turned down the contract...I objected to the company having the power to add a minimum of 15 players to my band when it was in the orchestra pit, and I also objected to my band playing in the pit. I think it, and I, would lose prestige...It is essential for me to move about from place to place; I'm doing bigger business now than ever. By playing in various towns my gramophone records are advertised. When I leave Manchester the sale of my records will go up 500 per cent...So that's why I'm not worrying about this £42,000.[7]

Variety Programme for Glasgow Alhambra, June 1928. (Personal Collection)

This confidence manifested itself during an engagement at the Palladium in London, where Jack had a dispute over top of the bill status. Hylton simply stated that if his band was not top of the bill, there would be no band. The Palladium baulked, reprinted the posters and the show went on.

Meanwhile Jack's wife Ennis was suffering another bout of ill health and was given her third 'serious' operation of the year during the summer. Jack was on stage in Sheffield with his band, when a call was received to give authority for the operation, which he gave and skipped back on stage to finish the show, with no sign that his wife was ill. Overnight he drove from Sheffield to Glasgow to visit Ennis, driving back the following day to conduct the next show.

*   *   *

76

In late October 1928, Hylton was in France, ahead of another European tour. It was here he would famously encounter French gypsy guitarist and banjoist, Django Reinhardt (1910-1953). Hylton travelled to Paris, to where Django was playing musette music, accompanying accordionist Maurice Alexander. Hylton entered La Java nightclub, much to the excitement of the audience, who of course knew who Hylton was, being a huge star in France by this time:

> He stood just five feet, four inches tall, but bore a beautiful woman on each arm, one dressed in a sumptuous mink coat, the other in a jacket of Tuscan lamb, their Chanel *le numero cinq* overpowering the sweaty scent of the dancers. He made his way through the crowd, which parted like the fabled sea of old... The appearance of this suave entourage raised the hackles of the regulars, and they greeted them with whistles and lingering appraisals of their diamond necklaces.[8]

Hylton had heard of Django's jazz skills, especially his ability as both guitarist and banjoist, and as an improviser, and had come to France specifically to see him. Hylton offered Django a place in his orchestra on the spot, and the pair arranged to meet the following day to finalise terms, at the bar Chez Fred Payne on Pigalle's Rue Blanc.

At the end of the night, Django's partner Maurice Alexander encouraged him to accept the job, saying there would still be a job for him if things did not work out. As Reinhardt returned home to his gypsy caravan, his pregnant wife dropped a lighted candle and both were set on fire. Django saved his girlfriend, but became very badly burned.

His clothes had to be scraped off his skin, the right side of his body was scorched from knee to chest and his right leg was almost amputated to avoid gangrene. His left hand was semi-paralysed by the flames with muscles, tendons and nerves all damaged.

Django's rehabilitation would take several years, and the contract never materialised with the Hylton orchestra, Jack having to look elsewhere for a guitarist. Reinhardt would ultimately only have use of his index and middle fingers and would develop a whole new style of guitar playing, whilst going on to be regarded as one of the greatest guitarists of all time, never playing a note with the Hylton orchestra.

*   *   *

After forming yet another band, this time for the Green Park Hotel (led by violinist Jean Pougnet), the band headed off on their next European tour, beginning on October 28th in Cologne, with a visit to Frankfurt the following day, followed by a month's engagement at the Scala Theatre in Berlin. Most British theatres were tied up over the Christmas period with pantomimes, so Hylton saw this as an opportune time to visit Europe. In early December the band played six countries in seven days, with shows in Vienna, Budapest, Prague, Frankfurt, Antwerp, Brussels and Paris, finishing off the year with a private concert for the head of Citroën cars on New Years Eve. The band hired two planes to take them and their equipment the six hundred miles to their concert in Hamburg the following evening, little knowing that Mr. Citroën was going to present Jack with a brand new Citroën Six Weymann Saloon, which ultimately was delivered to the UK, complete with a miniature 'Jack's Back' figure in the place of the Citroën logo:[9]

To say the least of it, Jack Hylton and his boys... have created a furore in Paris, where the standard of good dance orchestras is fairly low. He has shown them quite a lot of things they did not know before, both in style, accuracy, and last, but not least, stagecraft... The band was kept on stage for nearly an hour, which tells its own story. The general performance of the band was definitely very creditable, particularly in accuracy, as no music was used, and also in the whole-hearted interest shown by every member of the band.[10]

The Tatler. 22.5.29.

A FAMOUS CONDUCTOR AND HIS CITROËN SIX
Mr. and Mrs. Jack Hylton with their Citroën Six Weymann saloon

Hylton with his brand new Citroën Six. (Jack Hylton Archive)

They stayed in Hamburg, at the Hansa Theatre throughout January, with dates in February in Amsterdam, The Hague, Antwerp, Brussels and Paris, followed by ten days in Switzerland, two weeks in Nice, followed by dates in Marseilles, Barcelona, Toulouse, Lyons and Paris, with a quick stop off in the middle to do a rare BBC radio broadcast on February 11th 1929, at 8.15pm. The band finally arrived home in March, having been away for more than four months and having travelled over five thousand miles. The seventeen strong band opened at the Victoria Palace in London on March 25th, now consisting of Johnny Rosen, Hugo Rignold, Harry Berly, Jack Raine, Jack Jackson, Lew Davis, Leo Vauchant, "Poggy" Pogson, Billy Ternent,

Johnny Raitz, Chappie d'Amato, Billy Herbert (who replaced Eddie Grimshaw, who had played banjo for Hylton for eight years), Peter Yorke (who came in as pianist and arranger, and had replaced Claude Ivy, who had worked with Jack since 1921), Sam Browne (the first featured vocalist the band had used on tour), Basil Wiltshire, Clem Lawton (replacing long time bass player George Shannon) and Harry Robbins (who replaced Ray Starita on xylophone).

The band was now a formidable outfit, playing to houses of over seven thousand in Europe, selling out every show they could perform in the UK and selling records at an unheard of rate. 1927 saw around one hundred and twenty sides recorded, with another hundred recorded in 1928, with sales into the millions, but 1929 would make the previous years seem like a warm up, with over one hundred and fifty sides recorded for HMV. Despite this, Hylton continued the expansion of his empire and was in control of a surprising number of musicians:

> With three bands under his direct control and several lesser ones touring under various names, he is one of the leading exponents of jazz in this country. "In addition to the bandsmen regularly employed," Mr Hunt [his manager] continued, "we have hundreds of bandsmen on our lists waiting for occasional engagements, so that we can fit out half a dozen extra bands any time they are wanted."[11]

Talking films were beginning to take hold in the UK this year. *The Jazz Singer*, the first talking film, was released in 1927 and by the 1930s they would be a global phenomenon. In 1929, Hylton was very aware that there would be a huge impact on musicians, especially the number of musicians employed in cinemas. He wrote a piece in *Encore*, entitled *The Menace Of 'The Talkies'*, though with typical Hyltonian vision, he foresaw no major issues for his own band:

> As far as stage bands are concerned, I do not think that making sound films will be any disadvantage. When broadcasting began a few years back everyone told me my band was doomed and that, in a couple of years, my gramophone sales would dwindle to nothing. The effect

has been the reverse, wireless having become the biggest advertising medium in existence for the sale of gramophone records. There is something inseparable from the actual presence of an orchestra and its leader which has not yet been captured successfully either by the gramophone, radio or the films, and in the case of my own band I feel, even though we recorded before the best "talkie" apparatus, it would not supplant our stage show, but would act like our records and broadcasting to stimulate people to hear the real thing.[12]

Put simply, he was right. The Victoria Palace shows were followed by a week doubling the London Palladium and Collins' Music Hall, then a week at the Metropolitan doubling with the Willesden Empire. Mr and Mrs Hylton had a moment to savour when the Bolton Wanderers football team engaged them as 'mascots' for their ride to Wembley stadium for the FA Cup Final on April 27th, Jack having been a diehard Bolton fan since he was a child living within a mile of their ground. Jack returned the favour by inviting the team to be guests of honour at the second house of their Holborn Empire show that night (which they did, despite losing the final 2-0 to Portsmouth).

Also in April, news reports began to filter through that Jack had accepted an invitation to travel with the band to America, to work in the Roxy and Paramount Cinema theatres in New York, for a substantial $5,500 per week. Of course they accepted, and contracts were signed, but the American Federation of Musicians had other ideas and threatened strike action if the band were allowed to perform. Despite the numbers of US bands performing in Britain, Hylton's shows were cancelled.

The summer of 1929 consisted of a formidable schedule, relentless performing, with four shows a night the norm, coupled with an equally formidable recording schedule. They spent weeks in Leeds, Brighton, Glasgow, Manchester (where they visited and played for the animals at Belle Vue Zoo!), Cardiff, London Palladium, Liverpool, Sheffield and Edinburgh, as well as countless other shows, including a record crowd of 4,500 in Bridlington. On June 22nd, they were so well paid for a private show for Baron de Rothschild in France, that they sailed there and had a little time off.

Jack Hylton

In August, Jack, Ennis and manager Kenneth Hunt travelled to America on the *Ile De France* where they stayed for three weeks, apparently to try and iron out the issue of work permits for Jack and the band. It was widely reported at the time that Jack had signed a £20,000 movie deal, though this seems to have fallen through. Hylton himself told reporters that he had witnessed how sixty thousand American musicians had been made redundant by the talking films, so he arrived back in the UK with no firm booking, circumspect, but still keen to take his band abroad. When he arrived back in the UK on September 4th on the *Berengaria* at Southampton, he suffered a puncture and a breakdown on the way to that evening's show at Plymouth Empire, arriving for the last three numbers to huge applause!

A steady stream of shows followed, and a quick trip to Europe began on October 17th, with two nights at the Champs Élysées Theatre in Paris, breaking box office records and with hundreds of people turned away at the door. The band then visited Antwerp and Ghent (where their van broke down and a 9.00pm show finally began at 10.45pm). On the 20th, they became the first act to perform at the brand new Palais des Beaux Arts in Brussels, for Crown Prince Leopold and Princess Astrid. So taken were they with the show that they called for Jack after the show, congratulated him and insisted he stay another night. Of course there were already shows booked in for London the following night, so Jack politely declined.

In November, Kenneth Hunt left Hylton after four years as his business manager, to become Ambrose's manager. Edgar Jackson, who had been editor of Melody Maker since its inception in 1926, would replace him the following month. Also in December, after a charity concert in his former hometown of Stalybridge, Jack employed pianist Billy Munn. Munn (1911-2000) was a Glaswegian pianist and occasional accordion player and joined the day on which trumpeter Jack Jackson left the band. His own reminiscences (serialised in *Memory Lane* magazine shortly after his death in April 2000), were told to Ian Horner and transcribed by Gordon Howsden:

> ...On Monday morning down Archer Street, where the musicians hang around, Jackson [Edgar, Jack's manager] came looking for me and asked if I could go up to Glasgow right away, as Jack now wanted me to audition for

the main band. Ray Broderick, who was the leader of the Cecil Band and an awfully nice old man, raised no objection and I went straight up to Glasgow, did my audition on the Tuesday and started in the band on the Wednesday night. I firstly did an audition for Jack in the Grand Central Hotel, Glasgow, and then another audition for his number one boys - Bill Ternent, Leo Vauchant, Rignold and Pogson, at the theatre. Rather amusingly, I had only left Glasgow two months before and here I was back again and joining the number one stage band in the world. I was walking on air I can assure you. The Hylton band was never permitted to use music on stage but an exception was made in my case for about three nights whilst I memorized the show. And what a magnificent show it was, a terrific experience, but difficult to describe. First of all the band was beautifully rehearsed and 'together', and so funny I could hardly play for laughing. Amazing!

At the beginning of December, the band played a week at Edinburgh Empire. To give a sense of the line up at this time, the programme included Gillie Potter (an old colleague of Jack's), "Three Girls and a Boy" – a harmony group which included Ennis Parkes, Miss Belle Avalon ("The Skating Girl"), the Hengler Bros. ("Strong, Silent Men") and Daimler & Eadie (in "International Nonsense"). Shortly before Christmas the band accepted a rare engagement for dancing, their first in around four years, beginning a ten-week residency at the Kit-Cat Restaurant on December 23rd, whilst also performing through the month at Brixton Astoria (now the Brixton Academy). Hylton was paid £1,000 per week for the Kit-Cat job alone and the band would broadcast for the BBC regularly from here during the run.

This exhausting schedule meant that during 1929 the band gave 736 performances, to over 1,500,000 people, and travelled 15,745 miles. In December alone they played to 63,000 people at Brixton Astoria. Their total record sales for 1929 of 3,180,000 mean six records were sold every minute.[13]

1930 continued this trend. On January 12th, there was a concert at the Dominion Theatre in aid of Middlesex Hospital and the Musicians

Union; an audience of 3,000 attended. Five hundred musicians were said to be out of work due to the introduction of sound films ("talkies") and this concert was partly to help them.

Long-term vocalist Sam Browne left the band at this time. Sam had been chief vocalist with the band since 1928 when he recorded *That's My Weakness Now* (HMV B-5520), making over a hundred records with Jack Hylton. He left to work with Ambrose and recorded hundreds of records with Ambrose before eventually returning to the Hylton fold in the late 1930s. Sam Browne was replaced by Pat O'Malley who recorded many hundreds of sides with the band and is regarded by many as *the* vocal sound of the Hylton band. Pat O'Malley would stay with Hylton until the end of 1935, when he settled in America. He remembered a specific occasion when the band made some enjoyment of their own:

> We had several funny ones... with, Freddie Bamburger [pianist] and Clem Lawton on the bass. I was telling you, this number, I think it was *Pagan Love Song*. We had a beautiful passage, where Clem is playing the sousaphone and when he was playing sousaphone he used to lay the bass down so that the neck was right next to him and he could catch up on it and swing it up and start playing right away. Freddie unscrewed the peg [of the double bass]... and pulled it out so that it was at least three feet protruding from the end of the bass, and screwed it up ready, which Clem didn't see... Clem had to pick up the thing and go 'dum dum dum dum dum'... and the bass fiddle reared up about twelve feet in the air and he can't reach the strings...everyone's in complete hysterics![14]

Meanwhile, the band performed weeks at Stratford Empire, Holborn Empire and Brighton, whilst still performing (and broadcasting for the BBC) from the Kit Cat Club. That engagement finally ended on March 2nd, and after a week at the London Palladium, the band embarked on yet another continental tour. On March 16th the Ambassadors Club held a huge farewell party for the band, attended by Jack's parents, friends and family of the band. They then embarked on their most gruelling tour to date, taking in twenty three cities in twenty four nights, in total taking in forty-two cities in sixty-nine days, travelling a total of 9,763 miles. It's worth recounting in full the article entitled *The Travels Of Jack Hylton* from *Encore* on June 7th 1930 as it beautifully encapsulates the essence of this most engrossing of trips:

> Well, Jack Hylton is back after covering 9,000 miles in sixty-two days and playing in capital after capital! In Brussels Princess Maria Jose and an Italian prince sent for Jack after the performance. At Antwerp the hall, which held 3,000 people, was packed, and the crowd nearly rushed the doors. At Luxembourg there was a concert run by the students for their own pleasure. They organised it all themselves and there were no free seats. The hall only held about 400, and everyone was there by invitation. "After the show," says Jack, "they asked us to go and have wine. We were taken to a smart restaurant, where a carefully thought out supper had been ordered, and during it a gramophone played all the latest Hylton records. I suppose they thought we should enjoy these. Of course, we were tired of them."
>
> In Paris, at the Salle Pleyel, the hall was sold out eight days before the concert, although there had ben no newspaper advertisements. "We were worried to death all the afternoon by people ringing us up and imploring us to help them to get seats for the concert," says Jack, "but, of course, it was impossible. All the smart people of Paris seemed to be at our concerts, and the jewels and dresses worn were wonderful. The Rothschilds came round and said the band was better than ever. You may remember that Baron Rothschild recently paid the band a full week's salary and took them all over to Paris by aeroplane, just so that they could play at the private opening of his wonderful new theatre – the Pigalle." After the concert the people bought their records in the foyer of the Salle Pleyel, and this went on until well after midnight.
>
> Jack still wonders why none of the band got lost in Paris. Some of them had only two hours' sleep, but when they

started for Lausanne, a nine hours' journey, all the band seemed to have caught the train.

Jack has got quite lyrical over his journey from Paris to Lausanne. After talking about the meals they had he adds, "The scenery on this route was beautiful. High, snow-covered mountains and deep gorges, with crystal clear water flowing at the bottom, and wonderful forests of pine trees. When eventually we reached Lausanne we all stepped off the train looking like two-year-olds. It was very gratifying to find the people abroad love and appreciate every little thing that my boys and I do. Lots of things, which go unnoticed in England, are never missed on the Continent..."

At Geneva, where the band played for a private dance for the Automobile Association, the people got so excited at the band, they all crowded round it instead of dancing. Zurich also inspired the muse in Jack Hylton's soul.

"What a hotel!" he said. "So up-to-date and the last word in comfort, and with a very efficient staff! The cleanliness in Germany, Sweden and Scandinavia is worth noticing," he adds. "We have a lot to learn in England about running hotels."

The scenery of Europe and the hotels seem to have impressed Jack Hylton very much – and the way the people liked his records! That almost inspired him.

"At Basle all the latest Jack Hylton records are being sold, and in one candy stall," he says, "they were selling records made of chocolate and with the HMV Hylton labels. We were told that the Basle public were very stiff and we must not expect them to applaud very much, as they never do, no matter how much they like anything. Judge our surprise when they went just as wild as they do in every town."

There is none of my mock-modesty stuff about Jack Hylton. "We went everywhere," he says. "At Milan, after a beautiful journey through the Alps, we arrived only to be told at the Italian border that everything had to be taken out of the luggage can in order to pass the Customs. As we travelled three tons of baggage, this was some job and a waste of time, as not one thing was open. The price of seats in Milan was 300 lire, or about £3 10s, and the public paid it willingly. There was not one vacant seat. At what should have been the end of the show the people refused to leave, and then, after many encores, it was difficult to make them understand that the concert must finish"...After the concert Jack Hylton met the other great European nobility – Siegfried Wagner. Mrs Wagner said she loved jazz, but her husband said he hated it. "He was a very nice man," says Jack, "and had a great sense of humour, and was very amused because all the people in the place were so obviously talking about Jack and Wagner being next to each other." I am glad they noticed Wagner.

At Turin Jack really began to feel that he was somebody. "Everybody in Italy calls Jack the Maestro," is the official note I have received... It was at Turin that they allowed in HRH the Duke of Pistoja and HRH the Duke of Bergamot. "Prince Umberto should have been there," says Jack, "but he had to stay home because he had measles. However, on the second night he had the concert relayed to him by radio." What he suffered then is not recorded. "Nice looked so lovely," says Jack, "it was too bad we could not stay longer than one night. After the concert, which was said to be the success of the season, we went to the Salle Baccarat... We slept five hours and got the excellent Pullman train to Marseilles. On the train we were able to dance."

Montpelier seems to have disappointed the band. "It was a smallish town," says the official record, "but there were 2,000 people in the hall. It was so packed that about 100 people had to stand on the stage"...

Still, at Bordeaux, on the next night, they found the seats sold out a week before, with the band having to play a special matinee before a very smart audience. "Cup Final Scenes" are reported at Marseilles. "Jazz band jams the traffic, which is such an attraction, and the street in which the hall was situated became a seething mass of humanity fighting for admission." At Marseilles, by a strange mistake, the instruments got put on a boat going to America, and were only discovered just before it sailed.

In Germany Jack Hylton had a shock. "At Mannheim," he says, "I went into a restaurant and felt as thought I was looking in a mirror. I saw my own act performed by another band identically. At Cologne, when one of the boys played a German solo, the people went wild. At Dusseldorf, when we were guests of the British Club, I was mentioned during the speeches that I was the finest British Ambassador of Music ever sent out."

At Copenhagen everybody was flying Union Jacks when the Hylton Band arrived. "On our first evening the stage was covered with flowers. It was like Covent Garden itself. There were more flowers at the hotel. Went to manufacturers' works", is reported. "Went to Tuborg Brewery... At Gothenburg we were met by a brass band at the station," he says. "Bands across the sea. The conductor was so excited he went on beating after the band had finished."

Towards the end the notes of this triumphant tour began to get a bit short. In fact, at Berlin, the only note is "Concert at ___ Palace." You see, they had all forgotten the name of it; while at Magdenbourg they merely give the name of the hall. Of The Hague they merely say, "Holland is the most enthusiastic country of the lot."

I am not surprised that, after leaving Holland, the aeroplane on which the band travelled tried to lose them. It went up in the air and refused to come down until two and

a half hours after it was due. It chose a nice fog, and
stayed in it as long as it possibly could..."

This unprecedented reception had become the norm for the
Hylton band. Whilst on this tour, Hylton also met Russian composer
Igor Stravinsky, who was at the time becoming intrigued with modern
syncopated music. The next chapter covers their encounter in full.

Also unreported in the above article is that Hylton turned down
the opportunity of £2,500 per week in Germany, whilst also turning
down a week at the London Palladium for £475. It is a measure of the
European success that these figures are so disparate. Whilst the band
could take on more than one weekly engagement in London, the opportunities open to them on the continent, and the size of the venues
meant the rewards were huge. Hylton was insisting on £600 per week
at the Palladium and whilst Jack Payne took his place, Hylton would
bide his time and ultimately be rewarded for being the premier show
band in Europe.

Another incident from this tour harked back to a performance at
the London Palladium in September the previous year. One of the
Hylton band's comedy numbers contemplated, musically, how bands
from different parts of the world would render the popular song *Bye
Bye Blackbird*. One such verse of the number required the band to
jokingly announce, "Now Mussolini and his Fascists will play *Bye
Bye Schneider Cup*". The Schneider Cup was a race for seaplanes that
ran between 1913 and 1931, with a prize of around £1,000. Initially to
advance aviation techniques, the race became a simple speed trial
over a triangular 280km course. The winning country would host the
following year's race. Frequent winners Italy had been beaten in the
previous two meetings, one in England, and one in Italy. Both Hylton
and the British public, but not the Italian authorities soon forgot this
trivial skit. When the band arrived in Milan, the fascist authorities
were waiting to receive them. Jack was taken to the police station and
questioned about his reference to Mussolini:

I had no idea what was the matter. I called in the British
Consul, who explained that I was being questioned about
a piece I played in London last September...This apparently, had given offence, and I was cautioned not to repeat

my indiscretion. I was kept at the police station for two and a half hours.[15]

On their return to England, the band, along with songwriter Horatio Nicholls embarked on another cross-country song writing stunt. Amy Johnson was an aviator (or, in the common parlance of the day, an *aviatrix*) who broke many records in her short career. In 1930 she flew from Croydon on May 5th and arrived in Darwin, Australia on May 24th, making her the first female pilot to fly solo from England to Australia. On May 30th, whilst Amy was resting on medical advice, a song dedicated to her, (written by Nicholls with words by Joseph George Gilbert) was played simultaneously by Jack Hylton's band at the London Palladium and in Sydney, Australia by a local band when Miss Johnson arrived there. Ten per cent of the royalties would be sent to the *Daily Sketch* fund to buy Amy a new plane. The song (*Amy, Wonderful Amy*) was recorded by the Hylton band on June 2nd and released on HMV B-5836.[16]

The summer of 1930 was spent in familiar circumstances, with weeks at Holborn Empire, Finsbury Park Empire, Bournemouth Pavilion, Piccadilly Theatre, Glasgow Alhambra and Victoria Palace, along with shows in Southampton, Eastbourne, Manchester, Blackpool, Liverpool and Bolton. Significantly, in August Hylton was given the Officier de l'Instruction Publique – this is a French title, an Order of Chivalry, awarded by the French government in Deauville and usually given to distinguished academics (originated by Emperor Napoleon to honour eminent members of the University of Paris). It was later broadened to include notable figures in the worlds of education and culture and it was for Hylton's services to jazz music for which he was honoured – something which goes some way to convey quite how popular the band was on their continental tours.

After an autumn tour of the provinces (which took in New Cross Empire, Nottingham, Hastings, a first time visit to Hanley in Stoke-On-Trent, Bradford, Burnley, Halifax, Bridlington, Brixton Astoria and Fulham, amongst others) the band embarked on a two part continental tour, carrying on the now familiar pattern of winter in Europe. This time the tour was split up with a rare Christmas back in the UK, starting in Holland and moving into Germany with concerts in Berlin, Leipzig, and Dresden, before returning to Holland to play at the Carlton Hotel in Amsterdam. Here they took the rare step of playing for dancing, for a four-day residency. They continued the tour through France, Belgium and Switzerland, before returning to Holland, where a radio broadcast was made of their dancing set. Their success in Europe was unmatched and they faced receptions quite unlike anything they had experienced in Britain:

> So tremendous was the band's reception at all its dates, that the applause was positively embarrassing at times. On one particular occasion, the boys had just played a number, when, quite unexpectedly, a great and thunderous crash of applause broke out.
>
> Leslie Sarony, the singer...had, up to this time, been accustomed only to the moderate receptions which even the best British shows receive at home, and this continental outburst of approval left him gasping.[17]

The band performed thirty-six shows in thirty-six days, and then flew back to Edinburgh for a two week run over Christmas and New Year. Even then Christmas Day wasn't a holiday – there was a one-night trip to Paris! They then fulfilled dates in Southampton, Portsmouth, Stratford Empire, Holborn Empire, Southsea, Stratford, Birmingham, Chelsea Palace Theatre and Kilburn Metropolitan Theatre and a week at the Palladium in London. They then headed out on tour again, beginning in Paris with a historic performance at Paris Opera House, which is described in more detail in the following chapter.

During the tour, a series of radio broadcasts took place, from each major venue the band visited on their travels. They broadcast four times from Nice, six times from Prague and five times from Vienna. On these dates, the wide-ranging repertoire of the band was increasing. One programme listed no less than sixty-four items ranging from Franz Lehar's *The Merry Widow* and Rachmaninoff's *Prelude in C# minor* and *Prelude in G# minor* through the current hits of the day, to tunes which were already deemed to be jazz classics, such as *St. Louis Blues*, *Tiger Rag*, and *Limehouse Blues*.

By now the band was famed not only for their props and stunts, but also for the way they would utilise any party trick or extra ability a band member could display. Indeed this would impact on the possible employment of musicians into the band. Pianist Billy Munn recalls this aspect of the band's work:

Advert for the London Palladium, February 1931. (Personal Collection)

Jack had an uncanny ability to get the best out of any of his band. If they could do anything at all, if they had any little facet, or any party trick, sooner or later he brought it out and it had to go into the show. For example, if you played yo-yo very well, you could bet your boots that yo-yo would be in a subsequent number in the show; that actually did happen. We had a violinist who could turn somersaults while he was playing. That was one of our biggest numbers, *Crazy People*.[18]

Pianist Billy Munn himself could do a passable impersonation of Louis Armstrong, both vocally and on the trumpet and during the band's version of Armstrong's *St. Louis Blues* (Decca F-3239, recorded October 1932), he would stand on his piano stool and shout "New St. Louis Blues!" to introduce his act, before going on to sing, play piano and play trumpet; it would go on to become a live favourite.

Chapter 6: 1927-1931

1931 would also signify the official end of a long-since dead relationship, that of Jack and wife Ennis. She would continue to run a band under the name Mrs Hylton & Her Boys for several years, but they had been apart for many years. 1931 saw them both sign a deed of separation, though Ennis refused to grant Jack a divorce and remained that way until her death in 1957, despite a long-term relationship with alto saxophonist Jock Scott (estranged father of Ronnie Scott, the famous jazz club owner) who would become part of her band.

On the band's European tour in early 1928, whilst in Berlin, Jack had met Frederika Kogler (known to all as Fifi) who was a model and seamstress (two occupations which worked hand in hand then). Fifi (born in 1906) was a well-known figure in the social scene in Berlin at this time. They met and fell in love and Fifi moved to London with Jack shortly afterwards. She was, by all accounts a beautiful, stylish and intelligent woman. Together they had two daughters, Jacqueline Frederika (known as Jackie, born in 1932) and Jillian Georgia (known as Georgie, born in 1938). Jackie went on to marry Irish champion jockey Liam Ward in 1962, with whom she had William (born 1953) and Nicola (born 1956); they were divorced in 1977. Georgia chose to remain unmarried and lives in Arundel in West Sussex.

Jackie began her life-long interest in horses, through her father's keen interest:

> After an early rebellion against anything to do with the theatre, her main preoccupation was with horses. Right from the start her interest was professional and she soon outgrew the local riding stables, where in 1940 we would spend many a happy day. Becoming a racehorse owner at an early age, she graduated to a racing stables at Ferring where she worked as one of the lads. By the age of about eleven she had made a complete life for herself in the racing world...[19]

Jack and Fifi, personal photo shoot, c.1935. (Jack Hylton Archive)

Partly because of this shared interest, Jackie managed to spend a great deal of time with her father, when she was younger. By around 1946, when Jack was buying a number of horses from France, Jackie was appointed to look after them, running all aspects of her father's horses' needs. During breaks in rehearsals for shows, members of the band would attend the local racecourse, for betting and Jackie was always on hand to advise them on the likely winners, at the same time as placing the bets on behalf of 'father'. By 1958, she had bought her own stud farm.

During her first eight years, Jackie witnessed the prime of Jack Hylton and His Orchestra and has memories of tours and meeting such luminaries of the entertainment world as Duke Ellington and his son Mercer, with whom she stayed in touch for many years. Jackie now lives in Kentucky, USA, where she runs a stud farm with her second husband, Frank Ramos, whom she married in 1982.

The relationship between Jack and Fifi was a stormy one, as Jack made no secret of his many other affairs. Despite this, Fifi was fiercely loyal, very strong willed and quietly continued her family life out of the spotlight; she refused to speak to the press about her relationship and remained part of Jack's life until he died:

> She was a wonderful person; she didn't have an enemy in the world. She worked through it – all the others were just 'fly by night'…there were dramas, but nothing that bad – that's just the way it was.[20]

When their romance began, Fifi moved to London and took the Hylton name. She moved into 36 Cumberland Mansions (off Edgware Road in London), in the late 1920s. She would accompany Jack on all his subsequent continental tours, and would be on hand as translator throughout most of the countries they travelled to. Both she and Jackie went with Jack to America during his time there and Jackie remembers pictures being taken on her fourth birthday, in the Drake Hotel in Chicago where they stayed. When they returned, the family moved into Villa Daheim, Kingston Gorse, in the village of Angmering on the south coast of England and also lived in a bungalow at 28 Gilbert Street, Mayfair, more of which shall be discussed later.

Author Maureen Owen was a close childhood friend of Jackie Hylton:

> One day I arrived as the phone was ringing. She answered, saying, "Mrs Hylton here", and then went white to the lips. Unaware of the complex Hylton relationships at the time, I was surprised when Jackie abruptly removed

us both from the room. I later learned that the caller at the other end had said, "There's only one Mrs Jack Hylton, and that's who's speaking."[21]

Chapter 7: Hylton and Stravinsky

AN EXCLUSIVE PHOTO of the Russian composer, Strawinski, and Jack Hylton on the stage of the Opera during a rehearsal.

Hylton and Stravinsky on stage, February 1931. (Jack Hylton Archive)

The mixing of different genres always turns out badly. The jazz version of *Mavra* has just confirmed this truth in striking fashion. Let jazz stay as it is, played by specialist musicians who know the technique; and let other musicians keep to their own genres where they are sufficiently distinguished.[1]

One of Jack Hylton's particular strengths as a bandleader and one that made him ultimately so successful was that he knew exactly what his audience wanted to hear and gave them exactly that. He also appeared to know how to develop his band when they moved from the dance halls onto the concert platform and one tactic he and his team of arrangers used was to borrow from the 'classical' world, producing what became known as 'light classics'. This appears to have been more of a shrewd show business move than a deliberate attempt to bridge the gap between popular and classical music.[2]

One example of borrowing from the 'classical' world is worthy of particular note. Hylton and Igor Stravinsky collaborated on one of Stravinsky's works and the result was, at the very least, disappointing. This unprecedented story begins around 1930, a time when the band was as big an attraction on the continent as they were in their home country and France in particular made the band feel very welcome on their numerous visits:

> Hylton empathised with Paris completely; and there can be little doubt that Paris reciprocated in the same way. He seemed happy to spend more time there than anywhere else; and of course we had to be there with him.[3]

One of these tours began on February 17th 1931 with a concert at the Paris Opera House. This was no ordinary event, as this was the first non-classical concert ever to be given at the venue. It was widely reported in the French press at the time as being a landmark occasion for the Opera House and a landmark also for jazz music – a suggestion that this music was gaining a respectability which had been lacking during the first part of the century. At least as important as the venue, was the choice of music:

> Jack Hylton will perform a completely new programme, the main attraction of which will be the first rendition of a symphonic fragment of the comic opera, *Mavra*, by Stravinsky.[4]

With the Hylton band approaching the height of their popularity as a stage band, the Paris Opera House was an ideal venue to perform in – a well loved and well respected concert platform. It was never Hylton's intention to play a classical concert but it was to prove a good opportunity to display one of the band's most serious arrangements to date, the idea for which began the previous year:

> During one of these periods [in France] a chap hung around quite a bit. He and Hylton did quite a degree of chatting; mostly with the hands and gestures and sidelong

looks at the band. Jack introduced him as Stravinsky, the famous composer.[5]

The amount that Stravinsky 'hung around' with Hylton varies from report to report. Chappie D'Amato contradicts the above quotation from Les Carew by suggesting that Stravinsky attended one of Hylton's concerts in Berlin in 1930.[6] Whatever the case, it appears that Stravinsky liked the band enough to ask them to play an arrangement of one of his works. It is perhaps strange that Stravinsky would be so keen to associate himself with dance music, but sections of his output suggest a man who not only wanted to push the boundaries of his art, but also embrace elements from other genres. For example, *Ragtime* from 1918 speaks for itself and the *Ebony Concerto* from 1945 was written for clarinet and jazz band. These pieces certainly captured a flavour of jazz and may have satisfied Stravinsky's desire to be 'modern', but would not be considered as 'jazz music'. These works borrowed from the jazz idiom in the same way that works such as *Le Sacre De Printemps* borrowed from indigenous Russian folk culture.

It is perhaps an indication of Stravinsky's knowledge of the genre that he took to Hylton's band, rather than a more pure form of the music by one of the American bands from the same period. Although Duke Ellington, for example, did not appear in Europe until the summer of 1933 (coincidentally brought over by arrangement with Hylton himself), Stravinsky did not appear to have heard any Black-American jazz, or sought it out. Rather, he favoured the music that he had stumbled across or had been prompted to listen to by mutual contacts. It is unlikely that Stravinsky was a fan of jazz music, or a fan of Jack Hylton's music in particular. What he saw was a proficient orchestra playing modern, popular music and he saw a way to further his knowledge of the genre and become better known amongst the public. Whatever his true reasons, Stravinsky did approach Hylton regarding the project. Richard Taruskin cites an account in *The Voice* from August 1930:

His meeting with Igor Stravinsky was one of the most memorable events of Jack Hylton's recent continental tour. It was at a concert in Holland that the creator of *Petroushka* first heard Jack and his boys and he was so interested that he followed the band to the next city on their tour and attended the concert there. After the performance he went into the artists' room and spent over an hour with the wind and percussion players of the orchestra asking each man to demonstrate the capabilities and limitations of his instrument...[7]

There appears to have been some kind of discussion between Hylton and Stravinsky at this time and this is confirmed in Hylton's letter to Stravinsky on September 10th 1930:

I am coming to Paris next week for a few days and I am writing to ask you if it is possible for us to meet and discuss the music which you honoured me by asking me to play.[8]

Billy Munn[9] suggests that Hylton's French agent had the idea originally and introduced them. However, it has been suggested that Hylton himself presented the idea to Vera Sudeikina, Stravinsky's mistress and later wife, on March 20th 1930, over lunch.[10] Stravinsky himself has in print contradicted all of these sources, saying that Hylton himself, who then sought permission to arrange a particular section, perceived the 'jazz' element of Mavra.[11]

This appears to be a good example of Stravinsky contradicting himself; something that he appears to do in his extensive published writings and something that has hampered progress on the confirmation of details for this matter. Both Les Carew and Billy Munn suggest that Stravinsky chose both the piece and the section of the piece and it would seem unlikely that Hylton would have had enough knowledge of Stravinsky's work to pick a specific section from one of his lesser known operas. It may be that retrospectively Stravinsky wanted to disassociate himself from the whole episode and so is suggesting that the idea came from Hylton; this is hard to accept. Indeed, Stravinsky has mentioned in his writings that the piece had a jazz element, a clear contradiction of the last point:

I used wind instruments principally [in *Mavra*], both because the music seemed to whistle as wind instruments whistle, and also because there was a certain 'jazz' element in it – the quartet especially – that seemed to require a 'band' sound rather than an 'orchestral' sound.[12]

The Times, from January 29th 1931, concurs with the most likely scenario of Stravinsky seeing the band in concert in Paris on a previous trip and admiring the performance so much that he suggested they might like to play something of his. This agrees with the article cited in Taruskin's book. It is also worth considering what appears to be misinformation from *Melody Maker* of February 1931. It suggests that Stravinsky heard the band in Paris and was "enthralled by the performance of the combination". The article goes on to quote Stravinsky:

> I was told I should hear a jazz band, and instead there is a combination with all the qualities of the symphony orchestra. I felt a great desire to hear Mr. Hylton play one of my works, and I have chosen my composition, *Mavra*...I have rescored a great deal of the work to make it suitable for a modern combination...[13]

Evidence shows that the work was arranged by the band's staff arrangers and that at no time did Stravinsky aid them by giving them a version to work from. Perhaps Stravinsky was misquoted and was merely pointing out that he had chosen the section of the work that he wanted Hylton to use, suggesting a way in which voice parts could be translated into instrumental parts successfully.

The phrase "I was told to hear a jazz band" lends weight to the argument that Stravinsky was encouraged to seek out this music, rather than discovering it himself. It is interesting to note that he had a great desire to hear this band play one of his own works and not simply to hear more of the band playing their own music. This may suggest that Stravinsky heard an unfamiliarly orchestrated band showing a high level of technical skill and musicianship and saw that as an opportunity to have his music played to a new audience, or that he felt he could explore new avenues with his music in what was to him, a new idiom. His mention of a 'modern combination' suggests again a need for something new. There was (and still is) a great deal of scope for different combinations within the accepted orchestral set-up, but he may have felt that something seen by popular culture to be modern was a better canvas to work with than a combination which was merely seen to be radical. Either way, the piece played by the band was an arrangement of an existing work and it may have benefited both parties if Stravinsky had composed a new work specifically for the band. The whole occasion would be seen now as having historical importance for both 'classical' and 'jazz' music if this had been the case.

Certainly, by the end of 1930, preparations were underway for the arrangement and it became clear that the band would need a little more rehearsal for this piece than for a stock concert arrangement. The band were not averse to complex arrangements – when they were free from the strict tempos required by dancers, the arrangers were allowed to explore more elaborate changes of tempo and meter, but the band simply were not used to time signatures changing every few bars or even every bar, as in the chosen section of *Mavra*. They realised it was a challenge, but these were some of the very best dance band musicians in Europe and expected perfection of themselves.

There is very little information on the arrangement and rehearsals of this piece and all the evidence put forward here has come from the reminiscences of Billy Munn (who could remember the details clearly, some sixty-five years after the event) and from the Les Carew article already quoted. It is known that Stravinsky had nothing to do with the actual arrangement of his work. He certainly chose the sections that were to be arranged (although the final version may be shorter than was originally intended), but he did none of the arranging. The score was sent by G.G. Paichadze, Stravinsky's publisher, to Hylton at the end of 1930[14] and Hylton asked his foremost arranger, Billy Ternent, to begin work on the new piece. However, Ternent was a man of modest ego and suggested that Leighton Lucas would be more suited to the style that was needed.

Indeed, theoretically Lucas was better equipped for the job. The career paths of both men following the break-up of the Hylton Orchestra corroborate this idea. Lucas was one of the drafted men from the band in 1940, where he served in the RAF. Following that, he became known as an orchestral composer, noted for his film work. He wrote a number of ballets and works for varying groups; chamber orchestras, string orchestras, solo voices, piano trios, etc. Ternent stayed with the band for some fifteen years, both as arranger, violinist, baritone saxophonist, friend and confidant of Hylton and leader of the band in Hylton's absence during rehearsals. He had more to do with the running of the band than any other individual after Hylton. When the band split up, he went on to a career with his own band, which enjoyed considerable success, in a time when dance bands were fading.

Leighton Lucas' arrangements for Hylton were, unsurprisingly, lightly textured, orchestral in colour and perhaps more suited to a Stravinsky transcription. Ternent wrote in a more sectional way, much as a modern big band is written for, with the saxophones and brass playing as blocks, being supported by the rhythm and string sections. This created a fuller sound, one that Hylton perceived as being the 'Hylton sound'.

Lucas took on the task, with only a couple of months to the concert at the Paris Opera House. He took the duet and quartet from *Mavra* (from section 44 to section 92) and arranged it for flute (doubling on clarinet), oboe (doubling on clarinet and alto saxophone), alto saxophone, tenor saxophone, baritone saxophone, two trumpets, two trombones, piano, three violins, 'cello, bass and percussion (kit, timpani, xylophone). Lucas had apparently listened carefully to Stravinsky's orchestral version and tried to make a true re-working of the piece. The Lucas version consists of two parts simply titled *Part I* and *Part II*. *Part II* remains unfinished and it is unclear where this part might have concluded. It picks up the score just a few bars after *Part I* and finishes eighty-six bars later. The next logical place in the score where it could finish is after a further twenty-four bars, but this would only make *Part II* around two-and-a-half minutes long, against the six minutes of *Part I*. It could well be that Hylton and Stravinsky's original idea was for an extended work that would have gone on to the end of the original score and would have made more musical sense. This is more likely when considering the scale of the pre-concert press:

> In due course, Leighton arrived with the parts and wished us luck. Well! It was a case of 'What the hell's all this? What's it all about? How are you supposed to read this'...it was nightmarish![15]

Indeed, to a band that was more used to regular time signatures and regular numbers of bars, this arrangement must have come as a shock, despite their ability. Due to the nature of Lucas' sparse writing there could be no reliance on other members of the section, as there was no sectional work. As an example, in one section (three bars before section 47) the alto and tenor saxophones are playing one melody by themselves. Two trumpets are playing a counter melody, while baritone saxophone and bass play a simple crotchet pattern. The dynamic on the score is *forte*, but the score does not display the sheer volume of instruments associated with *forte* in the usual Hylton sense. At section 67, the woodwind double the strings, but the orchestration of the woodwind section is not thick with saxophones, but features flute, oboe and clarinet. The brass at this point is playing dissonant offbeat quavers, across the changing 3/4 and 3/8 time signatures. It is certainly well arranged and compares favourably with the Stravinsky original score at section 67, which features just oboe, violins and one voice on the main melodic line, with the trombones and low strings taking the offbeat quavers. It is unclear whether this was an approach to arranging that Stravinsky would have been happy with or whether he required a closer approximation to the 'Hylton sound'. Certainly, there would be no impact on the audience of the famous Hylton brass or saxophone sections:

> The rehearsal was a shambles. Leighton struggled valiantly, but it was only towards the end that it began to show any effect. Luckily, Stravinsky wasn't there. Even as it improved it made little or no sense. Odd squeaks, grunts, groans, snorts at completely unrelated moments seemed to happen at the whim of the instrument concerned. Hylton looked bewildered. Disbelief was in his eyes as he surveyed the ruins of his lovely band. What could he do? He was obviously committed – no backing out now. Maybe it needed more thorough rehearsing – more and more, until the idiots could think of nothing else.[16]

Nevertheless, despite the efforts of the musicians, it was not a suitable vehicle for the band. Jack realised this and decided Ternent would have to re-arrange the whole piece.[17] It was not uncommon with a band such as this to rework an arrangement with a different arranger, but this was an exceptional work and many hours had already been spent on rehearsal; the band (and Leighton Lucas) were not pleased. Jack had stated that it did not sound like his band and that Ternent's job was to make it exactly that. Ternent took the orchestral score and Lucas' arrangement, but time was short (the concert had only been around two months away when Lucas began working on his arrangement). He made no reference to an original recording and simply blocked out the notes he saw, for the instruments that he had at his disposal.

This version was therefore scored differently and more heavily than Lucas'. Three alto saxophones (doubling on either clarinet or flute), tenor saxophone, baritone saxophone (Ternent himself, doubling on violin), two trumpets, two trombones, three violins, 'cello, bass and percussion as before. On the end of Ternent's score are the words "Thank God!" which, one assumes, sum up his feelings on arranging this particular piece in these particular circumstances.[18] However, the changes seemed to work, despite the whole band having to learn new parts and the arrangement was certainly a lot 'fuller' than the previous one. Alto and tenor saxophones and two trumpets carry the melodic line, while two other alto saxophones, trombones, bass, strings and drums all carry a much heavier offbeat quaver pattern. This process applies throughout the arrangement. The essence of the piece is the same and the orchestration is similar, but there are simply more people playing more of the time in the Ternent arrangement:

> Whether it would suit Stravinsky was another matter, but Jack began to relax a little. The music became smoother and notes began to seem to have a reason for existence.[19]

It was during the period of rehearsals that Hylton informed the band that this piece was to be the centre of attention at the Paris Opera House and the band recognised this as the reason for his anxiety. As the date drew closer however, the ensemble improved to the point where *Mavra* was being played as competently as anything else in their repertoire.

When the arrangement was polished, Hylton took over the conducting, as he often had before, after Ternent had rehearsed the band. Unfortunately, Hylton was more of a showman than he was a conductor, and the arrangement was simply too hard. As Billy Munn put it, "the *Mavra* arrangement was not too hard for the band...but it was too hard for Jack to conduct."[20]

Ternent attempted to guide Hylton through the score, which he did successfully – Hylton was a competent musician and had arranging credits of his own, so will have developed some level of understanding of the piece.

This is how the situation stayed. The piece had been chosen, the arrangement had been worked out, the piece was well rehearsed and Hylton was to front his band as he always did. *Mavra* was to be the special feature throughout this European tour, which was to run for exactly two months.[21]

On January 29th 1931, *The Times* gave a review of a concert from the previous evening. Stravinsky was a guest soloist for the BBC Orchestra, conducted by Ernest Ansermet, at the Queens Hall in London.[22] On the morning of the concert, Hylton's band was rehearsing in the small hall next door and it is from this meeting that the famous photograph of Stravinsky, Hylton, Ansermet and some of Hylton's musicians is taken.[23] Billy Munn was lucky enough to have assistance from Stravinsky himself who sat next to him at the piano and explained the score that he was using and some of the more tricky fingerings. Some of these can be seen on the piano reduction score that Munn used (as there was no piano part scored by Ternent).[24] From the report in *The Times*, we can judge that the piece was sufficiently rehearsed for performance, as indicated in the descriptions given by Carew and Munn. Indeed, the press, or at least the reporter from *The Times*, was witness to this rehearsal with Stravinsky and favourably commented on the bands' arrangement and performance:

> The general effect, however, when played with the subtlety of which Mr Hylton's band is capable, is satisfactory, and as a piece of music it stands securely on its own feet without the dramatic context from which it is taken... Mr Stravinsky... ought therefore to be gratified by the result of this experiment in rescoring.[25]

This is glowing praise and the only example of such positive predilection towards the piece. It also confirms that the band was capable of playing the piece, that Stravinsky heard it played well, and that there were more than the Paris concertgoers of February 17th who heard it. These are important points to consider, as will become clear when looking at Stravinsky's reaction to the concert performance.

What is missing is any record of Stravinsky's reaction at this rehearsal. If the unnamed reporter from *The Times* is correct, then the performance was a good one, the arrangement worked well and Stravinsky's idea of having his work performed by a 'jazz band' was realised.

During Hylton's career, press agencies were hired to keep records of any mention he or his band were given in newspapers and magazines both in Britain and in Europe. These, as part of Lancaster University's Jack Hylton Archive have proved a valuable source of information for the *Mavra* episode and show how much attention was given to the Hylton/Stravinsky collaboration. Hylton's office was keen to point out the inclusion of *Mavra* as part of the programme, but also the inclusion of an arrangement of *The Merry Widow*, and of a Rachmaninoff *Prelude*, which were also planned. It is known that the band recorded Rachmaninoff's *Prelude In G Minor, Op.23, No.5* and the *Prelude in C# Minor, Op.3, No.2* in London on February 25, 1930.[26] What is not known is which of the Preludes (or perhaps both) they intended to play on this occasion. These and other 'light classics' are discussed elsewhere:

> We learn that this Tuesday evening [February 17th], for the first time, the Paris Opera will play host to a jazz concert and that the orchestra chosen for this sensational first is Jack Hylton and his Boys...For the occasion, Stravinsky has presented Hylton with a special arrangement of a symphonic fragment of his comic opera *Mavra*.[27]

This article also mentions the plans to play *Mavra* the following evening at the Salle Rameau in Lyon:

> To have a composer of the standing of Stravinsky writing for the band must be put down as yet another of Jack's great triumphs, and there must be dozens of enthusiastic English musicians who bitterly regret that the recital is not going to take place in London.[28]

The culmination of all the preparation, rehearsal and press coverage came on the day of the concert, in Paris on February 17th 1931. This was during a period when the band was generally regarded as being the most successful band in Europe, if not the world. Consequently, the French audience had no problem in accepting the band in the hallowed Paris Opera House, as they would have done at any other French venue.

We do not have a list of the numbers that made up the first half, but we know it was a regular mix of the band's most popular tunes, such as *Body And Soul* and *Dancing Tambourine*[29] and their latest arrangements (no doubt soon to become favourites). We also know it was a huge success. The audience (numbering somewhere in the region of four thousand) roared their applause and the band performed in awe of what was must have been a glorious place to play. "The concert itself was a regal affair," said Les Carew.[30]

The second half began with another popular number and then French trumpeter Phillipe Brun walked forward and explained to the audience the circumstances regarding the meeting of Stravinsky and Jack Hylton. At this point, he introduced Stravinsky who, eight or so rows back, rose to acknowledge the tremendous applause.

Saxophonist Chappie D'Amato recalls the day's events:

> We performed this almost unknown work of Stravinsky to a packed audience at the Paris Opera House with the composer present with his family, also the President of France and all the diplomatic corps – what is known, I believe, as a glittering assembly.[31]

There is understandably a difference in the reaction to the performance of those members of the band whose recollections have been mentioned (saxophonist Chappie D'Amato, trombonist Les Carew and pianist Billy Munn) and the French and English press. Firstly, the band themselves: Billy Munn described the occasion as "a horrifying nightmare". At first, Hylton got lost, as was expected. Consequently, the whole band got lost, despite how well they knew the piece – "it was a nightmare". Trumpeter Jack Raine decided to play out a particular section towards the end, where the trumpet had the lead and as the band knew the piece so well, they all picked up on it and the piece ended together. Hylton knew he had done a bad job and was very annoyed that the performance had not been a success; consequently, he dropped the rest of the planned set and carried on with his normal stage show. This concurs with one of the French newspaper reports, which says, "...he forgot to play the Rachmaninoff

Prelude which we had been promised."[32]

Of course, it was not forgotten, but rather cancelled. Chappie D'Amato described it a little more casually, saying it was "a little nerve-wracking", but that the band "got through it", which for many people listening was how it seemed. Les Carew described those few minutes in more detail and it is best to quote him in full:

> We started off alright, maybe a little tentatively, and confidence grew slightly. Then, funny things began to happen, Jack's arms began to flail meaninglessly, aggravating a situation that was already dicey. His face went pasty-coloured and shiny with sweat...The flailing of his arms became more pronounced and more off-putting. Between the odd burps and coughs from the instruments we heard him muttering, only just audibly, 'Take no notice of me, I'm bloody lost!' We sailed on without a captain to the bitter end – eyes screwed on parts and trying to ignore Jack. Every now and again Jack Raine, our lead trumpet, would poke in his few notes with all the confidence in the world and set us back on course. Nothing barring an earthquake could have shifted Jack Raine. Through him I suppose, we all finished together.[33]

At that moment, Jack Hylton turned to the audience with outstretched arms to take the applause, which had been freely his during the rest of the evening. This time, the audience may have been a little perplexed and the applause may have been a little muted from some, but it was huge applause nevertheless. Billy Munn described their reaction as "uproar":

> ...we got through it, with no one knowing whether we'd played any wrong notes, except, perhaps, Igor Stravinsky.[34]

> Only we, Jack and Stravinsky knew the facts. Perhaps Jack also knew that Stravinsky's music was so unfamiliar in those days, that none of the audience was aware that anything had been other than was intended by the composer; you know, fashionable, debatable...[35]

Following this change of direction for the programme, the concert went smoothly and was as successful as one would expect. Reports suggested that while the concert should have finished around 11.00pm it went on, due to demand, until nearly midnight, by which time the band was resurrecting old numbers to please the crowd. The receipts for this one concert totalled around £1,400.[36]

The press reaction to the concert seems to have concentrated mostly on the six minutes of *Mavra*, rather than the other three hours. It is very interesting to compare the opinions of the writers from the French press to those of the *Melody Maker* article already cited and Stravinsky's reactions on the day as well as after the event. It is clear that Stravinsky rose to his feet at the end of the piece, as he had done before the piece. *Melody Maker* suggests that Stravinsky did not attempt to disguise his pleasure at the performance and that he was most open with his praise. However, *Le Carnet de la Semaine* suggested that Stravinsky left the Opera House immediately after *Mavra* "cursing both jazz and Jack Hylton".[37] They go on to suggest that Stravinsky's departure led to Hylton's change of programme.

Before the concert, on February 12th 1931, Stravinsky wrote to Hylton, regarding the publication of this arrangement of *Mavra*,[38] saying that it "must not use my name otherwise than as the composer of the original"[39]. This was not a very positive attitude to take into the Opera House, but he seemed happy with the arrangement when he helped on January 28th, at the Queens Hall and was not sufficiently put off by the performance on that day, to suggest any major changes. This is perhaps another example of Stravinsky's persistent contradictions. On another occasion, Stravinsky views the experience very harshly, seemingly forgetting that it was his idea originally:

> Mr. Hylton actually conducted this *Mavra* potpourri in the Paris Opera (!) in 1932 (I believe). It was an awful flop, for the musicians tried to play the music 'strictly'. Mr. Hylton had merely transcribed the music for his combination of instruments – and *Mavra* has no place on a 'jazz' programme. Mr. Hylton was a sympathetic man, but I think this was the most bizarre concert I have ever attended.[40]

This suggests that perhaps he was not happy on January 28th, but realised that it was too late to protest about the performance, given the interest taken by the newspapers, and the number of people attending the concert on February 17th. If Stravinsky felt that the Queen's Hall rehearsal had gone badly, this may have prompted his letter of February 12th to Hylton regarding the recording.

This is the only written opinion we have from Stravinsky. Writer E.W. White adds severely, "It seems strange that the composer should have consented to such a travesty of his music."[41]

This is a particularly harsh description from someone not at the concert and who has no real cause to describe the work in this way. The French press however, was present and in a stronger position to comment:

> ...on the evening of the concert, Hylton just didn't have the Stravinsky soul...He conducted all the same, but with such evident boredom that the success of the piece was compromised...[42]

Le Monde Musical was more critical still: "The performance was and deserved to be a complete failure."[43] The article suggests that Hylton 'felt obliged' to put into the programme something of the nature of *Mavra*, to fit more into the surroundings and mood of the Paris Opera. It would be fairer to say that the arrangement would have been played at some time, but such an auspicious occasion suited Hylton's sense of theatre and hence it was chosen as the venue for *Mavra's* premiere:

> In this arena, *Mavra* seemed a poor thing, gauche, deformed, one of nature's rejects.[44]

When the whole article is considered, it is perhaps referring as much to Stravinsky's original version, as to the Ternent arrangement, but it still stands as a harsh criticism. It begs the question of why Stravinsky chose *Mavra* rather than one of his better-known works. The only information we have to suggest the reasoning behind *Mavra* is from *Expositions And Developments*, where there is reference made to the 'jazz element' in parts of *Mavra*. It is perhaps more to do with the 'band' part than the 'jazz' part, given Stravinsky's comments after seeing the band in France in 1930.

The same *Le Monde Musical* article concluded by suggesting that the audience could not hide its disappointment with *Mavra* and that it paled into insignificance alongside the usual Hylton set.

The quotations from the press get yet more critical:

It has to be said that their fears were not only justified, but far surpassed. It was in fact one of the most lamentable failures which it has been our misfortune to witness for a very long time.[45]

This article suggests that the first problem was the bringing on of music stands (something which the band very rarely used) and the calming down of the usual band antics. It goes on to suggest that the arrangement did nothing for and may even have had a derogatory effect on Stravinsky's work. It says this was the wrong work to be chosen for the occasion and that it was really one of Stravinsky's less important and less appealing efforts.

The *Paris Excelsior* gives a slightly more favourable review and almost glosses over *Mavra* as an unfortunate but forgivable few minutes:

Jack Hylton played jazz at the Opera...and it didn't bring down the roof of this august building...but nor did the applause! Indeed the audience...seemed quite cool to begin with; Stravinsky's *Mavra* ...provoked only a fairly visible boredom. In the second half, enthusiasm was revived by the clowning and somersaults in *The Merry Widow*.[46]

These were the 'clowning and somersaults' of the band's regular stage show to which they had reverted. The one point that all reports seemed to agree on was that the bulk of the audience (at the very least) was keener on the regular numbers than on *Mavra*, but surely this is to be expected.[47] *Melody Maker* points out that it was the audience's insatiable appetite for ordinary dance tunes, which led to the concert running so late.

What does become clear, is that, despite 'getting through it', despite the band finishing together, despite Stravinsky taking the applause and despite the audiences reaction, the performance of Ternent's arrangement of *Mavra* at the Paris Opera was a failure. This must be the case, as Hylton dropped it from the set for the rest of the tour. It is clear from a perusal of the European press cuttings for the rest of the tour, no mention is made of this most heralded of arrangements and Billy Munn confirmed that he had never seen his part again after that night. The fact that so much time was spent rehearsing and arranging the piece, for it only to be played once and never recorded was one of the few true indications we have of Hylton's feelings after that date. Of course, it did not put a stop to Hylton's interest with classical music:

> Unfortunately, or perhaps I should say fortunately, we never made a record of this, but from then on we ventured into popular classics more and more.[48]

When looking at Jack Hylton's career as a whole, the *Mavra* episode is almost irrelevant, but it makes for a fascinating story. It is also an excellent example of the genre mixing, which has gone on to such an extent in 20th century music. Hylton never wrote his autobiography, so of course his true opinions on the matter will never be known and through Stravinsky's conflicting writings his opinion will remain similarly elusive, but it stands as a wonderful piece of musical history:

> Anyway, in retrospect it was great fun – and after all – we're all human. A fascinating episode – one such in a lifetime and how many of us are here to remember it? I suppose every conductor has his own particular *Mavra* hiding somewhere in his career?[49]

Chapter 8: 1931-1935

Jack Hylton & His Orchestra on stage c.1933. (Jack Hylton Archive)

The European tour of early 1931 would be the biggest to date, with dates in Paris, Lyons, Marseilles, Rome, Naples, Milan, Turin, Venice, Bologna, Vienna, Prague, Berlin, Dresden, Magdeburg, Frankfurt, Leipzig, back to Italy, Monte Carlo, Nice, Cannes, Madrid, Barcelona, Pau, Biarritz and back to Paris (this time at the Empire Theatre), travelling some 25,000 miles and performing seventy-eight shows in seventy-eight days. They returned on April 20th, but of course were straight in to more work, beginning with a week at Brighton Hippodrome and continuing in the usual vein with weeks in Leeds, Manchester, Blackpool, Bristol, Bath and Holborn Empire. The press at the time noted that the band was playing an entirely new programme:

> Of particular note was a Billy Ternent vehicle, entitled *One Man Band*, which featured him playing all the saxophones, the violin, all the brass instruments and other 'sundry instruments' such as the ocarina.[1]

Again there were reports of taking the band to America but again they were denied after threats of strike action from the American Fed-

115

eration of Musicians. In due course Jack would find a way to finally resolve this ongoing issue.

Meanwhile a string of summer dates would ultimately take its toll on Jack's health and almost a decade of non-stop work finally caught up with him. In August of 1931 he took two weeks off, suffering from nervous exhaustion:

> Jack Hylton has broken down in health and is now taking, under doctor's orders, his first holiday for years. He has had to cancel all his engagements, and has gone into the country for complete rest.[2]

After his enforced recuperation, Hylton continued the previously planned schedule, with a string of dates in London and the south coast.

There had been a few changes in personnel in the previous few months. Violinist Hugo Rignold left after five years, to begin an illustrious career as a conductor (with the Liverpool Philharmonic and later the City Of Birmingham Symphony Orchestra). Stanley Andrews replaced him, whilst trombonist Lew Davis was replaced by Les Carew and saxophonist Joe Crossman was replaced by Phil Cardew. Drummer Basil Wiltshire was replaced first by Gilbert Webster, then by Neville Bishop and long serving saxophonist 'Poggy' Pogson was replaced by Australian Abe Romaine:

> 'Poggy', now retired, is one of those instantly likeable characters, and everything seemed to happen to him. On arrival in the band-coach in Hamburg, 'Poggy' stepped out of the door nearest to his seat, straight into the canal, and played the engagement that night in borrowed clothes.[3]

Abe Romaine recalls his first engagements with the band:

> To catch up on the programme I was allowed to use music for my first appearance, but after one or two shows I had memorised the current programme, and from then on, no music was allowed on stage. This I have always felt was a great 'selling point' for the band, and I'm sure that much

of the success on the continent had stemmed from the great 'ease' which was apparent on all the programmes.[4]

October saw Jack cause a sensation in the dance band world by choosing not to renew his long standing recording contract with HMV and take up a new deal with fledgling label Decca, with whom he had become a major shareholder. Decca (named after the portable gramaphone the Decca Dulcephone) had only formed in the UK in 1929 and Hylton signed despite a general feeling that the sound quality of the Decca records was inferior to the more established companies. At that time HMV had both the Hylton band and Ambrose's band on their roster and Jack began to feel that Ambrose had first call on the hit songs of the day, despite Jack's huge sales. When the Decca deal appeared, he jumped, the promised £58,000 in royalties helping somewhat! In 1931 Decca badly needed an artist of international repute and Hylton was just the kind of artist they wanted. The event was met with a predictable flurry of publicity and the Hylton band immediately became the number one attraction on the Decca label. In 1932 Jack would also sit on the board of directors, which gave him 40,000 shares and an undisclosed sum of money.

Throughout this punishing schedule, the recording output grew. In 1930 the band recorded 174 sides for HMV. In 1931 they would record a staggering 266 sides, of which seventy-seven were recorded for the new Decca deal, in just two months at the end of the year. One of the tunes recorded for the new label was *Rhymes*, the Leslie Sarony comedy number. A version had been recorded in October and released on the HMV subsidiary Zonophone (Zonophone 5997) but was re-recorded in November (with a slightly different arrangement) for Decca at their studio at Chenil Galleries in Chelsea (Decca F-2679). This nonsense song, which included the first three lines of rather gauche limericks, followed by a "la da da" finale, rather than the presumably rather rude (for the time) punchline, became a huge hit for the band:

There was a young man of St Paul's,
Who once did a turn on the halls;
His favourite trick, was to stand on a stick,
La-da-da-da-da-da-da-da-da.

Jack Hylton

Perhaps in 1931 it was funnier than it seems to this author in the twenty first century.[5] It went on to sell over a million copies and spawned a sequel, *More Rhymes*, (Decca F-2750), which was recorded in December 1931.

It was during these early Decca sessions that Jack first met Patrick 'Spike' Hughes. Spike Hughes would subsequently play double bass for Hylton and was widely regarded as an excellent jazz player, although he is perhaps better known for his writing in *Melody Maker* (under the pseudonym 'Mike') and his later critical writings:

> The company was fun and I found myself being taken off to tour Amsterdam, Brussels or Paris for a week at a time with the band...I don't think Jack will mind my saying that I was bored to hell playing at his sessions, but there I think he was too and anyway, I could do with the money.[6]

*   *   *

Each Jack Hylton and His Orchestra tour show would offer the audience a souvenir programme and, much as today, programmes would be full of adverts, pictures of Jack and the band, information on the band personnel, but also a list of repertoire. Due to the ever-changing programme and Hylton's insistence on fiddling with the running order on an almost daily basis, the programme would list possible repertoire, but not a definite set list. Whilst individual running orders are hard to come by, it is worth sharing the list of numbers. On this occasion, a concert in Strasbourg on March 15th 1931:

Mavra (which we have seen wouldn't have been performed), *Rachmaninoff Preludes, St. Louis Blues, Limehouse Blues, Dinah, Whispering, Bye Bye Blues, Piano Duet, Cheer Up And Smile, Telling It To The Daisies, Sing You Sinners, Merry Widow, The King's Horses, Absence Makes The Heart Grow Fonder, Nobody's Sweetheart, You Brought A New Kind Of Love, Silly Little Tune, Adeline, Dance Of The Raindrops, Oh Donna Clara, We All Go Hoo Ha Together, Here Comes The Sun, Sing, Somewhere In Old Wyoming, Singing A Song To The Stars, I'm Yours, Sweet Jenny Lee, Betty Co-Ed, Choo Choo, Moanin' Low, Kiss Waltz, Reaching For The Moon, If You Can't Sing Whistle, Sittin' On A Five Barred Gate, Song In My Heart, Swinging In A Hammock, Punch And Judy Show, One Night Alone*

118

Chapter 8: 1931-1935

With You, Rhineland, Memories Of Paris, Fine Alpine Milkman, Bitter Sweet, Harmonica Harry, A Cottage For Sale, It Happened In Monterey, The Stein Song, When It's Springtime In The Rockies, Tiger Rag, Piccolo Pete, Singing In The Rain, He Kissed Her, Handsome Gigolo, Body And Soul, Happy Days, Ain't Misbehavin', Pagan Love Song and Go Home And Tell Your Mother.

Interestingly, whilst obviously there are a large number of Hylton hits and recorded numbers, there are quite a number of songs never recorded by the band. Given the band's prodigious recorded output, the sheer number of numbers performed but *not* recorded means the band had a staggering number of arrangements written. Whilst the Jack Hylton Archive at Lancaster University has thousands of sets of parts, it is only a fraction of what Hylton will have used at some point or other in the years he was running a band.

*   *   *

In November of 1931 the band was expanded, for just one night, to sixty members, to play for a film, *Splinters In The Navy*, at the New Victoria Cinema. This was part of a policy to employ live musicians at cinemas in the West End that were also showing 'talkies'. It would appear the use of such a famous band was to bring this scheme to the attention of the media and the public. The fee was, naturally, a record for the time of over £1,000. Another record fee of over £1,000 was given to the band the following month when they finally made contact with America, albeit only via radio. The band made history as they became the first British band to broadcast live to America, which they did at 3.00am British time, on December 16th. The programme (which consisted of two fifteen-minute slots, with a similar sized break in between) was relayed live from Savoy Hill to the American NBC network, in a show sponsored by Lucky Strike cigarettes. The deal was struck with the American Federation of Musicians whereby there would be a twenty-four-piece band standing by in a studio in New York, doing nothing, but being employed for the duration of the recording:

> The price paid to Mr Hylton for this broadcast is claimed by him to be a record one. He also states that the sum he

119

receives will be duplicated to the band on the other side. An American official of the National Broadcasting Company informs me that five million listeners will tune in to hear London's broadcast of jazz, and pointed out that Mr Hylton has created broadcasting history by being leader of the first English jazz band to broadcast to America. "I think the explanation of the withdrawal of their opposition is due to the fact that recently gramophone records recorded by my band have had an enormous sale in America," said Mr Hylton.[7]

The numbers played were *My Sunshine Is You* (HMV C-2283), *Running Round The Trees* (Decca F-2700), *When The Guards Are On Parade*, (HMV B-6015), *You Are My Heart's Delight*, (HMV B-6071), *Tom Thumb's Drum*, (Decca F-2672), *Oh What A Night*, (the other side of Decca F-2672) and *Goodnight Sweetheart* (HMV C-2283). It was a huge success, as reported in Melody Maker in January:

> The complete success with which the Atlantic was bridged, for the first time by a British dance band, the unqualified approval with which the broadcast was received by the American people, the programmatic and propaganda value of the material chosen, and the brilliance of the band's playing, have contributed enormously to British prestige throughout the States.[8]

The same article brings to light the issue of the broadcast output of the Hylton band, which mysteriously had been restricted to just five broadcasts in six years, a figure which *The Melody Maker* was appalled with. It was especially unhappy that the band had been able to broadcast to America and many times in other European countries whilst abroad, but despite offers of relaying these concerts for no fee, or working in London for a fraction of the costs involved, the Hylton band was very often refused. The paper asked rhetorically why this situation was persisting:

> There is, apparently, no other reason at all why the BBC ignores Hylton's band in this unnatural manner. There has been no domestic trouble at any time, no difficulty of fi-

nance, no real obstacle of convenience. It just happens that Hylton is never approached by the BBC and that he has grown tired of making offers which are inevitably turned down. What is all the mystery about?[9]

On Christmas Day 1931, the band were working on another continental radio broadcast, this time in a Decca sponsored hour-long show on Radio Paris. It was normal for this to be a show playing records, but Decca were keen to make exceptions for the Hylton band. This fitted in well with a three-week engagement in Paris at the Empire Theatre.

The New Year began with a series of weeks including the London Palladium, Finsbury Park Empire and the Victoria Palace, before heading off, in early February of 1932, to the Carlton Hotel in Amsterdam. By February 14th, they had moved to Brussels and were again graced with the presence of the royal family, including King Albert himself at the Palais Des Beaux Arts. This short tour finished in Nice on March 21st, having also travelled through Italy and Monaco.

By now Jack had begun indulging one of his great passions – racehorses. He bought his second horse, Bonanza, to add to his previous purchase Kakine, which he bought after seeing it win in Deauville. He would continue through his life to buy and sell racehorses and after encouraging his daughter Jackie's love of horses he would buy a stud farm that she ran on his behalf. Horses, greyhounds, football and cricket were all passions of Jack's in which he indulged throughout his life. No Saturday would be complete without either a visit to the football (if his beloved Manchester United or Bolton Wanderers were playing in London) or to the races or the dogs.

He was also beginning to show signs of his future career as an impresario, when in February he brought Ray Ventura's Collegians over from France to take part in one of the shows at the London Palladium. Ray Ventura was seen by many as the 'French Jack Hylton', one of his most famous recordings being the very Hylton-like arrangement of *St Louis Blues* where Ventura imagined how Mozart, Chopin, Wagner and Ravel might have conceived it!

They became probably the most popular of the European dance bands in Britain, who all struggled due to the intransigence of the

Jack Hylton

British Musicians' Union, and his ranks would later include Hylton trumpet ace Phillipe Brun.

After the band's return from Europe, they again hit the variety stage, with a series of shows which took in Penge Empire, Holborn Empire, Brighton, Hull, Bolton, Glasgow, Aberdeen and the London Palladium. Perhaps due to the cajoling of *The Melody Maker* or perhaps related to Jack Payne leaving the BBC and Henry Hall setting up a new BBC band, Hylton was given an hour-long broadcast on March 1st. It was, of course, a huge success. On May 30th the band performed at their third Royal Variety Performance, at the London Palladium. They played *Today I Feel So Happy*, (HMV B-6070), *Rhythm Like This*, (Decca F-2958), *By The Fireside*, (Decca F-2802) and a medley. Further dates around the country and performances at a number of Empires and Astorias around London followed, as well as another US broadcast (this time at 5.00am on June 9th, at the BBC studios, as guests on Paul Whiteman's NBC show) and an hour long BBC broadcast from Daventry on June 24th. A trip to Ireland, more dates in UK theatres and seaside resorts followed, but the summer included enough time for Jack to buy the aforementioned bungalow at 28 Gilbert Street in Mayfair, around the corner from Grosvenor Square, where he would later live. Press reports showed Mr and Mrs Hylton moving in and refurnishing Gilbert Street, though we know that in 1931 they had split up and Jack and Fifi had just had their first child together and were living less than a mile away in Cumberland Mansions. The 'happy family' picture was being maintained for a press who were happy to fall for it, or at least go along for the ride. Jack would later live in this house and one assumes that at this time Ennis lived here by herself. Their housewarming party was well attended by both friends and press alike; band members played, George Formby sang and the sound-proofed rehearsal room which Jack had had built was put to good use!

*　　　　　　*　　　　　　*

There were parallels in the careers of Jack Hylton and George Formby. Both of course were born and brought up in the North West of England and both went on to major national and international success, without ever losing sight of their roots. George Formby (1904-

1961) was a little younger than Jack, hailed from Wigan and found fame as a banjolele playing singer-songwriter. When Hylton moved from HMV to Decca in 1931 he found he was a label mate of Formby's and it was only a matter of time before they worked together. Their first recording session was on July 1st 1932, though Hylton and his band were not credited, with Decca F-3079 being credited to 'George Formby with orchestral accompaniment'. They recorded two sides that day at the large studio in Chenil Galleries in London, *Do De O Do*, and *Chinese Blues*, which is now better known as *Chinese Laundry Blues*, and would become Formby's theme song and the first in a series of songs referencing 'Mr Wu'. *Chinese Blues* was a song about a lovesick Chinese laundry worker in the Limehouse dockland area of London, which housed a large immigrant Chinese population. The song is still used on occasion, some eighty years later, in the *Aladdin* pantomime.

They may have recorded again on the 4th October, on a song entitled *How Are You?* (Decca F-3204). The song is officially credited as featuring a vocal trio of Jack Hylton, Pat O'Malley and Philippe Brun, but it sounds very much like Formby. Possibly Hylton is channeling his inner Formby, but towards the end of the song it sounds like Hylton and Formby overlapping. No firm answer has been given from experts of either Formby or Hylton.

The next time their paths definitely crossed was on October 13th 1932, at a particularly busy recording session for Hylton, when thirteen tunes were recorded, of which eleven were released. Three of the tunes featured Formby, two without any banjolele. They were *The Old Kitchen Kettle* (Decca F-3222, on which Formby was uncredited, despite there being no doubt who is singing), *I Told My Baby With The Ukulele* (Decca F-3219, on which Formby plays and sings) and *If You Don't Want The Goods, Don't Maul 'Em* (the flipside of Decca F-3219, again with no banjolele).

A story accompanies this session, but given the expansive solo on *I Told My Baby With The Ukulele*, and the sheer number of songs recorded by the band that day, this seems unlikely, but it is worth sharing: Formby stumbles across a rather anxious Hylton at the Decca studio on Vauxhall Bridge Road, having a rather heated discussion with a Decca executive. Formby's wife overhears that Hylton's vocalist has failed to turn up for the session and if they do not record soon, they willlose their slot and the band will have to squeeze the session in another day. 'Excuse me Mr Hylton, what number were you hoping to record?' Jack replied, 'Just a little novelty called *The Old Kitchen Kettle*.' 'Why, my Georgie can do that, give him a go Mr Hylton.'

Of course Hylton had already 'given him a go' earlier in the year, so perhaps the story is muddled (or simply apocryphal).

The final time they recorded was January 29th, 1933, when they cut fours sides, all credited to 'George Formby'. They were *Why Don't Women Like Me?*, *Running Around The Fountains In Trafalgar Square* (Decca F-3524), *Sitting On The Ice At The Ice Rink*, and *Levi's Monkey Mike* (Decca F-3458).

Hylton and Formby remained friends for the rest of their lives, though Formby found Hylton's high living too much to take – Formby's idea of a good night was dripping on toast, a mug of cocoa and twenty Churchman No.1s!

*   *   *

During 1932, the French Government again honoured Hylton, when he was appointed a Chevalier in the Ordre National de la Légion D'Honneur, again for his services to France and to jazz music. This is the highest decoration possible to award a foreigner in France. He wore both this and his Officer De L'Instruction Publique with pride when travelling in Europe.

The rest of the summer and autumn was spent recording (there would be 156 recordings made in 1932) and working at the London Palladium again, at Torquay, Exeter, Eastbourne, Hastings, Margate and Brighton, whilst planning for the biggest European tour yet, which would cover some 20,000 incident filled miles. The twenty-five-piece band left England on November 14th and planned to visit Germany, Austria, Belgium, Hungary, the Balkan States, Switzerland, France and Holland before returning home. Although a problematic tour in some respects, it also was the first time Hylton employed German saxophonist and 'clown', Freddy Schweitzer. At the time Schweitzer was playing with a German band led by Efrim Schachmeister, alongside British musician Tom Dallimore. When the Hylton band were in Berlin, Dallimore would socialise with the boys of the band, and introduced Hylton to Schweitzer, acting as translator.

Chapter 8: 1931-1935

Freddy joined the Hylton band for the 1932 European tour and was an instant hit:

German newspaper photo – Freddy Schweitzer. (Personal Collection)

Schweitzer was a clown, and a great one. Dave Shand, the lead alto player with the band from 1931-1935, remembers him well: 'As I sat next to him on the bandstand, I became the straight man to his clowning; he used to call me 'mein partner'. One of his acts was to balance a violin on his forehead while playing a jazz chorus on the clarinet. (It was good jazz, too). I remember one concert in France when someone in the audience shouted something... 'Why don't you do it with a bass fiddle?'... Sure enough, after a few days practice, Freddy was balancing the huge bass fiddle on his forehead while playing the same jazz chorus on his clarinet.[10]

The band finally arrived in Königsberg, duly performed their concert there and were due to be escorted through to Leningrad, to perform twice there and subsequently twice in Moscow. They had a contract that had been signed by the Director of Gomez (the Soviet government department responsible for the engagement of foreign artists). The Soviet minister in London had accepted the application for permission to enter and had forwarded it to Moscow.

The arrival of the band in Königsberg coincided with the termination of the Anglo-Russian trade agreement, and permission to cross the border was refused. There was also a suggestion that authorities felt that Hylton's orchestra was only suitable for the wealthy classes and because of that it would not be suitable for the comrades and workers:

> How absurd the latter idea is, I leave to the British public, whom, I am sure, are satisfied that my appeal is to the people of all classes...I pointed out to him that I had complied with Russian law in every way, and that I was really interested in entering the country for the purpose of giving the people the opportunity of hearing my band.[11]

A series of calls were made between Königsberg, Moscow and London. Forty-eight hours passed and another concert was hastily arranged in Königsberg, which of course was another sell-out. Very soon though, the contract for their stay in Königsberg meant that they had to move on, cancel the Russian engagements and go to Vienna. Extra concerts were arranged for the two weeks in Vienna, after which the band spent two weeks in Munich before continuing the tour through Germany as planned.

Problems continued though. Whilst in Vienna, Hylton's insatiable love of sport manifest itself as it often did on the continental tours, with a hastily arranged football match between the band and a local team. This time they lost 1-0 in a match refereed by Austrian international Martin Hiden and watched by around 3,000 spectators. Bass player Clem Lawton, going for one tackle too many, broke his leg and was taken to hospital, where he stayed until November 28th, missing the rest of the Viennese dates and picking up the band in Munich, with his leg in plaster of Paris.

Towards the end of the tour, in Hungary, Jack was presented with yet another problem – the huge sums of money earned were not allowed to leave the country. As Hylton himself said, "international finance is a deep subject". Never one to miss a trick, Hylton spent £3,000 on a block of buildings in Budapest:

> Always a believer in good real estate, there is only one thing to do. Good bricks and mortar are as safe as anything, and in a surprisingly short time I am the tentative owner of a block of smart modern flats.[12]

Not all of the money was spent – some found its way into the air gap in the band's accordion, whilst more still found its way into Clem Lawton's plaster cast!

Whilst still in Hungary, Hylton was summoned to see Admiral Miklós Horthy, Prince Regent to the kingdom of Hungary between the wars. Hylton was expecting another hiccup, but found Horthy presenting him with the score for a new song that he had composed and wanted him to perform with the band. Hylton watched whilst the Admiral performed the waltz at the piano, with his son accompanying on the drums. It was, he said, "as corny as can be" and the band never performed the song.

So the eventful European tour came to a close at the end of the year and the band returned to the packed houses of London, following the packed houses of Europe; a week at Victoria Palace, a week at Stratford Empire, a week at Brighton Hippodrome. Jack also formed Mrs Hylton And Her Boys, a vehicle for estranged wife Ennis. They were a moderately successful band, which would tour the variety halls extensively and record for the Crown label. They never had the standard of musicianship or arrangements that the main band had, but would continue to record and perform until 1937, when Ennis bowed out of band leading for good, due to ill health.

Jack Hylton

At the end of January 1933, the band were back in France, for a fortnight at the Rex Cinema in Paris. The previous week, Johann Strauss, the 'Viennese Waltz King', had entertained the Paris audience. Asked about Jack Hylton he spoke in glowing terms:

> Jazz music is a drug, the product of war frayed people's craving for the deadening of their troubles in rhythmic noise. But your Jack Hylton and his music belong to a different category. He has come to stay. There is room both for his music, clever, symphonic syncopation, and for mine, the graceful melody of the classic tradition.[13]

After a number of engagements in Belgium, they returned to the UK with dates at Holborn Empire, London Palladium, and Glasgow Empire. Newspapers reported the extraordinary story that Jack had been elected as Honorary Musical Advisor to His Majesty Bao Dai, in the Court of Annam, a French protectorate in central Vietnam. Presumably his links to France had something to do with this most bizarre appointment:

> His Majesty is planning to install a jazz band at the Imperial Annamese Court, for the enlivenment of his courtiers, and has instructed me to guide him in his new adventure as to the choice and combination of instruments, as well as on suitable modern music that should appeal to his court.[14]

Whilst fulfilling their regular schedule of UK shows through the spring of 1933, Hylton was planning his most audacious entrepreneurial move to date. On June 9th Duke Ellington and His Band sailed into Southampton on the *Olympic*, and were welcomed ahead of a UK tour 'by kind permission of Jack Hylton, by arrangement with Irving Mills'. This was a major venture both for Ellington and for Hylton and a big financial risk for Hylton. Of course it was just a stepping-stone for the kind of work he would ultimately move into. They appeared as part of a variety bill at the London Palladium for two weeks, before embarking on a six-week tour of the UK, including theatre shows, Sunday concerts, radio broadcasts and dances. Hylton spoke of the process in his tour programme notes:

Because I knew I could count on the discernment of British music lovers, I decided that Duke Ellington and his Band, with their provocative style and methods, their peculiarly individual compositions, their undoubted genius as instrumentalists and the spontaneous joy and feeling of their playing would not be wasted on British audiences.[15]

After the UK tour the band would head out to France and Holland, with the Hylton band appearing in a package show. Ellington was a star in America and much loved by the jazz-loving record buying public in the UK, many of whom would have expected never to see their idol in the flesh. Some of Ellington's biggest hits had been released by this point in his career; *Black & Tan Fantasy*, *Mood Indigo*, *It Don't Mean A Thing*, *Creole Rhapsody*, *Sophisticated Lady*, etc.

Whilst Ellington's audience in the States was mainly African-American, the audience in the UK and Europe was predominantly white, and huge concert halls were filled in every town they visited; concerts were very well received, by press and audience alike. However, some American commentators were not so taken with Hylton himself, or his attitude towards discipline, which was somewhat different to Ellington's approach:

But I learned that Jack Hylton had specifically forbidden Duke's men to play outside the concerts or they would be fined fifty dollars...In fact, Jack Hylton was there [at 'Bricktops', a cabaret venue in Paris] too. Flabby and pot-bellied like an English pork butcher, he was rocking grotesquely in his chair. Overwhelmed by heat and liquor, he had a red, congested face and was splattering food on his neighbours and wiping it off mechanically when it fell on his jacket. Alongside him, Duke gave the impression of a prince of the blood, on whom had been imposed the company of a stupid upstart.[16]

There appears to have been a mutual respect amongst the two sets of musicians though. In November of 1933, Hylton's band recorded *Ellingtonia* (Decca F-3764), a medley of Duke Ellington tunes and would later play in concert a separate *Ellington Medley* (the score of which remains, though it was never recorded). In Brian Rust's *The*

Dance Bands, he suggests that when listening to the Hylton recording, the Ellington band recognised the playing of the others, though not their own, suggesting that Hylton's musicians had done a fine job in approximating the Ellington style.[17]

The summer of 1933 consisted of the usual array of summer dates around the country, stretching into the autumn. In July, Billy Ternent had been admitted to hospital for a duodenal ulcer and in October Hylton himself was admitted to hospital for an undisclosed but 'serious' operation. He stayed at Park Lane nursing home and the band took three weeks off, with a number of shows cancelled. Upon his return to work in November, fighting fit, the band performed a charity show for Charing Cross Hospital before working on a new show with songwriter, radio presenter and producer, Eddie Pola. They named the show after Pola's radio show *America Calling* and the show would include the stars of the radio show, as well as Hylton's band. They opened at Finsbury Park Empire on December 11th, shortly before the band embarked on their inevitable Christmas and New Year in Europe. *America Calling* would return to the UK when the band returned in 1934. Whilst at Finsbury Park, just before setting off on tour, the band was part of a Post Office experiment with short wave radio. They transmitted from on board a Heracles air liner 4,000 feet above London, at 100mph, where they played dance tunes for two hours, whilst engineers on the ground picked up the music at Baldock in Hertfordshire, and relayed it for broadcast at the Post Office exhibition in The Strand. It was the first time a broadcast of this nature had been attempted and also represented one of the first engagements for the band by trumpeter George Swift, previously of Baldon Colliery Brass Band.

The end of 1933 saw the end of Hylton's two-year contract with the Decca record label. After recording over four hundred titles for the label, the band simply stopped recording after suffering what Jack felt was a similar problem to what had befallen them at the start of the Decca deal. By now Decca had Roy Fox and Lew Stone on their books and Hylton felt that he was not being offered to top songs to record. His solution, as before, was to leave. They wouldn't record again until March 1935, when Hylton signed again with HMV.

The Continental tour, more modest than the previous year, would take in Antwerp, Brussels and Paris, including a long season at the Rex Cinema in Paris, as well as a record breaking week at the Gaumont Theatre in Paris, from December 22nd to 28th, which earned 1.2 million francs.

1934 would represent the tenth anniversary of the band, and they celebrated with, of course, a big concert at Holborn Empire in March along with a double page tribute in *The Melody Maker* paper. Before that, *America Calling* had been running at London Palladium to great acclaim, many saying the band were sounding better than at any time in the previous ten years, whilst another band had been formed to play for the show *Here's How*, both shows opening within a week of each other. Other dates followed, of course, round the UK and in April Hylton brought jazz tenor saxophonist Coleman Hawkins over from America to tour with the band. Hawkins had contacted Hylton after a planned UK tour had fallen through, sending a wire that simply stated, "I want to come to England". Hylton obliged, replying the following day, and soon 'Hawk' came to the UK as guest soloist both with Jack's band and with Mrs Hylton and Her Boys. He arrived on March 30th and took dates at the Palladium as well as York, Leeds, Sheffield, Bridlington, Glasgow, Southport, Blackburn, Finsbury Park Empire and New Cross Empire, amongst others. Quite what Hawk thought of the variety audience in provincial northern towns is not recorded, but he stayed touring and recording in Europe until 1939, linking up again with the Hylton band in May 1939 to record *Darktown Strutter's Ball* (HMV BD-5550) to great acclaim.

Cab Calloway was on tour in the UK at this time, to the consternation (and legal wrangling) of Hylton who was apparently the sole representative of Irving Mills artists in the UK, of which Calloway was one. Hylton therefore was happy to change his plans, cancel concerts and take over from Calloway at the Palladium when ticket sales for Calloway's shows dropped too low. One suspects that if Hylton had been in charge of the tour, things may have gone more smoothly. Cab Calloway simply had not sold enough tickets during his four-week residency:

It was intended that Calloway should carry out such an engagement, but so disappointing has been the public response during the current week that the old cry went up, "Where's Jack? Get him!" If any Managerial Mogul gets into a jam nowadays, the sovereign remedy seems to be to put Hylton into the bill![18]

Soon after this, Louis Armstrong was the next US jazz artist for Hylton to represent. He embarked on a successful tour with Coleman Hawkins and a dance band put together by Hylton. Meanwhile Jack was also in charge of the Mrs Jack Hylton and Her Boys European tour, the first time an Englishwoman had presented an English band on the continent. Another Royal Variety Performance (the fourth for Jack and the band) took place on May 8th at the London Palladium, which was broadcast live. There was another radio broadcast on July 7th, this time featuring George Formby, there were UK dates, seaside resort dates – a staggering volume of work to be involved with.

Louis Armstrong with Jack Hylton and His Orchestra. (Jack Hylton Archive)

August saw the band's first venture into film, with an appearance in *Two Hearts In Waltztime*, a British musical romance film, starring Carl Brisson, Frances Day, Bert Coote and Roland Culver, with music by Robert Stolz. The film tells the story of a composer who falls in love with the star of an opera company. It's not clear what role the Hylton band played, but it seems to have been a brief appearance.

The band were long overdue a holiday and in September Hylton and Billy Ternent went to America and the band were given three weeks off. Only a couple of months after *The Melody Maker* reported news of a ten week American tour, Hylton's office was forced to assert that this trip was merely a holiday and not a planning mission for the upcoming tour. Despite apparently not working, Hylton brought over vocal group The Ink Spots to appear in their autumn variety programme, where they appeared for weeks in Manchester, Glasgow, Newcastle, Chiswick and the Palladium, as well as numerous other dates.

By this stage, Billy Ternent was a fundamental cog in the Hylton band wheel. He was regarded as Hylton's 'second in command', but he became much more than that, often taking care of every stage of rehearsals, with Jack appearing in time to count the band in and lead from the front. It was an arrangement that suited everyone and Ternent used this experience to hold down a celebrated career as a bandleader long after Hylton died:

> What Billy said went and as far as rehearsals went, he was always there. In fact, for the Palladium show for that year *Swing Is In The Air*, the big show of all, er, Billy was behind the scenes all the time and you seldom saw Jack around anyhow. He'd pop in in the evenings to see how things were going in general and sort of went down to the dressing room with Ternent and discussed the matters and would look in and take over the baton when time came to say go, you see, but Billy was always there, the whole workout, completely was governed by Ternent; I would say, anyhow. Billy I feel was the one who brought all the discipline in and he was 'Right, lads, this is it' with a snap of the finger, everything quiet and rehearsals went on.[19]

Jack Hylton

After their three-week holiday, the band played on in Jack's absence, firstly in Rhyl, then for three weeks in Ireland. This time, Pat O'Malley was the musical director. Around this time, long serving saxophonist Johnny Raitz and violinist Johnny Rosen left the band, and blind pianist Alec Templeton joined the band. The current line up was Maurice Loban, Eddie Hooper, Jack Farrell and Richard Willows (violins), George Swift, Phillippe Brun and Jack Raffle (trumpets), Les Carew and Eric Breeze (trombones), Billy Ternent, Harry Carr, Freddy Schweitzer and Benny Daniels (saxophones), Billy Munn and Alec Templeton (pianos), Sonny Farrar (banjo and guitar), Gilbert Webster (drums and percussion), Andre de Vekey (bass) and Brian Lee on vocals. Jack hired Lee after stumbling across a crooning competition on Plymouth pier whilst the band were performing in the town. He performed with the band that night and featured on a radio broadcast on December 7th. He had to then give up his job as assistant in the grocery department of the Plymouth Co-op.

The band embarked on their winter European trip, beginning with a run at the Gaumont Cinema in Paris, performing up to five shows per day. The band moved on through The Hague and into Germany, where the Nazi authorities denied access to Coleman Hawkins due to the colour of his skin. The band carried on without him and performed for eight days at the Berlin Philharmonic Hall. They then travelled back to Britain, via Amsterdam, arriving on February 11th to start rehearsal for their next project.

1935 would see a brand new show, with the band integral to the whole show, rather than simply being a featured headlining act. The band would be onstage throughout, accompanying, introducing and leading into the acts. They called it *Life Begins At Oxford Circus*, with a host of new Billy Ternent arrangements and an augmented band (featuring Dutch pianist and arranger Melle Weersma for the first time), and aided by variety acts Flanagan & Allen and the Western Brothers. The show was a huge success and would run into June, whilst the band restarted their recording career with HMV.

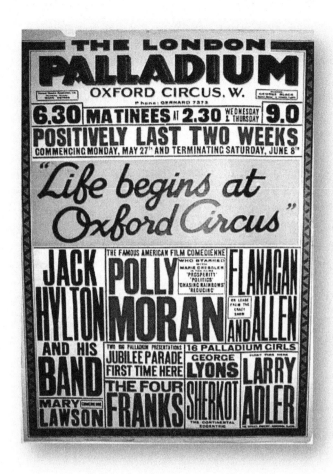

Life Begins At Oxford Circus bill poster. (Personal Collection)

Also on the bill was Stanley Holloway (1890-1982), who Hylton had met when he had a near miss with the Co-Optimists in 1922. According to Holloway's autobiography, *Wiv A Little Bit O' Luck*, the pair had previously met at Victoria station on their way to a World War I show in Wimereux, in Northern France, entertaining the troops.[20] Holloway sang on a number of Hylton recordings, from as early as 1926 (*Mama's Gone Young, Papa's Gone Old*, on HMV B-5170) up until 1935 (*Gentlemen! The King*, on HMV BD-157 and *Jack Hylton's Jubilee Cavalcade*, along with Flanagan & Allen, on HMV C-2744). Holloway was already a very well known comedian,

135

singer and poet, especially as part of the aforementioned Co-Optimists, whose show at His Majesty's Theatre would run for eight years and 1,568 performances. This would ultimately be overshadowed by his film career and subsequently his portrayal in 1956 of Alfred P. Doolittle in *My Fair Lady*, in its original Broadway run, its transfer to the Theatre Royal, Drury Lane, and the 1964 film version. He continued to have a successful film and television career and was awarded an OBE in 1960.

Another 'first' for the band occurred in the summer of 1935, when they were working at Twickenham Film Studios, on their own vehicle, *She Shall Have Music*, a similar production to their recent revue at the Palladium. The film featured the band playing on a broadcasting ship touring the world and showed the band's varied talents of comedy, singing and dancing, with the grand finale vocal taken by Jack himself. The cast included Claude Dampier, June Clyde, Gwen Farrar, Brian Lawrance, The Delmona Can Can Dancers, Leon Wazikovsky ballet, Terry's Juveniles and Diana Ward. The film also featured an uncredited newcomer, Magda Neeld, who would feature in Hylton's next project.

Chapter 9: The Rival Bands

Lambert & Butler cigarette cards – "Dance Band Leaders" from 1936. (Personal Collection)

This is not the place to offer an exhaustive history of British dance bands, but there is room to give an essence of the maestri with whom Jack Hylton shared a rivalry during the 1920s and 1930s. It is not meant to be exhaustive, or to offer anything new, but more to add a little context to our story. The reader is pointed towards a book for which the chapter holds a great debt – *This England's Book Of British Dance Bands.*[1]

Ambrose (1897-1971)

Benjamin Baruch Ambrose (Bert, or 'Ammie' to his friends) was born into poverty in London's East End, the son of a wool merchant. He took up the violin at an early stage but never became an accomplished musician. He was taken to America by an aunt and he became a proficient if unremarkable musician. By the late 1910s, however he found his strength was in band leading and when he returned to London in 1920 he formed a band at the Embassy Club in New Bond Street. He returned to run a band in New York in 1922, but was persuaded back in 1925, partly by a cable from his fan Prince Edward,

Prince of Wales. He moved to the Mayfair Hotel in 1927, where he stayed for eight years.

He would hire a high calibre of musicians, including future bandleaders Ted Heath, Sid Phillips, Sydney Lipton, Lew Stone and George Black and became renowned for setting a minimum price for the band, from which he would never drop. The band would visit Monte Carlo, Biarritz or Cannes for lucrative summer seasons.

Ambrose provided music for dances and would play subtle, quiet 'sweet' music, always maintaining that if he could hear the dancer's shuffling feet, all was well. He would broadcast regularly on a Saturday night from the Mayfair Hotel and recorded prodigiously for the Decca label. His records, dances and broadcasts were immensely successful, his strength being in the band's sheer quality of musicianship and its sense of rhythm. Whilst they explored the comedy song, their forte was quicksteps, foxtrots and waltzes. By the end of the 1930s he was widely regarded as the finest exponent of dance music on either side of the Atlantic.

Much like Hylton, his band was decimated by the call up for World War II, with many of his alumni becoming the core of the Squadronaires Dance Orchestra. He limped on through the war, still recording for Decca, but by the 1950s the new era of swing music left him somewhat out in the cold. His career continued in show business in various forms. He died a bachelor in 1971 with a formidable reputation as perhaps the greatest dance band leader of the era.

Jack Payne (1899-1969)

John Wesley Vivian Payne was brought up in Birmingham where his musical parents' encouragement helped him become a proficient pianist at an early age. He was also a very keen cadet in the Officers' Training Corps. Towards the end of World War I he became Lieutenant Payne in the Royal Flying Corp and could well have started a career in the fledgling airline business after the war.

However, music became his love, especially after setting up a dance band of sorts that included some American saxophone players with whom he was serving. After leaving the RAF he worked with his own bands in the Birmingham area before moving to London in 1924 where he persuaded the Hotel Cecil in The Strand to employ his band. His initial four-week contract ran for four years.

The key to Payne's future success came when the BBC decided to form its own dance band and employed Payne as its leader. The band broadcast every weekday between 5.15pm and 6.00pm and consequently he became hugely popular and famous with the listening public. He eventually left the BBC in 1932 and took the band on tour, in the provinces and onto the Continent. His line up included such Hylton luminaries as Jack Jackson, Eric Siday and 'Poggy' Pogson. His BBC band featured on the first ever BBC television broadcast in 1929.

Payne, with chief arranger and future bandleader Ray Noble went on to record extensively with Imperial Records, and starred in the film *Say It With Music*, which was his signature tune. After a brief stint on HMV during World War II, he gave up band leading to concentrate on work as a television presenter and disc jockey, as well as a five-year stint as Director of Dance Music at the BBC, starting in 1941.

Geraldo (1904-1974)

Gerald Walcan Bright, Geraldo to his fans and Gerry to his friends, was born in the East End of London into a working class Jewish immigrant family. Like many Jewish families at that time, music was important and he became a child prodigy on the piano, attending the Royal Academy of Music. He began his professional life as a theatre organist, then as a pianist in Liverpool and Blackpool.

He formed his own band in Blackpool before setting up Geraldo's Gaucho Tango Orchestra, which performed at the Savoy Hotel from 1930. As well as performing in a Charlie Chaplin film, they recorded, as Geraldo and His Rumba Band, and were chosen for the Royal Command Performance in 1933, complete with comic Latin American moustaches.

The following year, Geraldo began moving towards a sweeter style, incorporating everything from the current dance band trends to his trademark tangos and classics. They re-launched as Geraldo and His Sweet Music. (Gerry's twin brother Sidney joined as deputy leader following a period with Jack Hylton's Kit-Cat Band.)

The band began broadcasting frequently on a number of different shows, performing in revue shows, appearing in films and even performing to the modern taste of jazz fans with their *Jazz Jamboree* and *Sunday Night Swing Club* shows. He wrote most of his own arrangements, so his workload was huge and his working days of Hyltonian length! During World War II the band toured extensively and Gerry was supervisor of the ENSA Bands Division, under Hylton's chairmanship.

His was the first band to appear on TV after the war and later he became the musical supervisor for the Cunard/White Star Line. His band limped through until the early 1960s, after which he ran a successful theatrical agency.

Henry Hall (1898-1989)

Henry Robert Hall was born to Salvation Army parents in Peckham in South-East London. His father was a blacksmith turned greengrocer. He began his musical life playing cornet and concertina in his local Salvation Army band and would go on to a scholarship at Trinity College of Music, where he studied piano and trumpet.

His first job was at Salvation Army headquarters, where he worked as general office boy and music copyist. When war broke out Henry became a member of the army military band, stationed in the UK, and when war was over he hit the variety stage both as a soloist and as part of *The Variety Three*.

He also worked, like Jack Hylton, as a cinema organist but found himself deputising in a dance band in Manchester in 1922. A stroke of luck on that job led to him not only running the Midland Hotel band in Manchester, but soon afterwards was in charge of five bands under the London, Midland and Scottish Group (LMS), including a time spent at the Gleneagles Hotel. All this before he was 25. The following year he began broadcasting for the BBC from Gleneagles, which he would do for eight years. By now this unassuming young man was in charge of all thirty-two of the LMS bands.

Due to his links with the BBC, when Jack Payne resigned from the BBC Dance Orchestra, Hall was offered the job. The public took rather a shine to his apologetic, typically English style, which was so different to the swaggering American styling of most of the dance band leaders.

After five very successful years at the BBC, by which time Henry Hall had become a national institution, he left to pursue the touring variety circuit which so many of his peers had enjoyed (which Jack Hylton had instigated back in 1925). However, the wartime closure of theatres led him back to the BBC (this time in Bristol, where much wartime broadcasting took place) where he developed his famous *Henry Hall's Guest Night* programmes, thought to be an early form of our modern day chat shows, which appeared on both radio and TV.

By the 1950s, the band had become less popular and Hall's time was spent more and more as a radio and TV personality. He wrote his autobiography in 1955, was awarded an OBE in 1970 and enjoyed a long and happy retirement.

Lew Stone (1898-1969)

Louis Steinberg, yet another Jewish East Ender, whose family changed their name by deed poll to Stone was an exception to most of his peers in that he was an exceptional arranger, musical director and composer for films and West End shows, and that side of his career was of equal importance to his band leading.

His early love of football gradually gave way to his love of music and after a few professional engagements he became pianist for Bert Ralton's Savoy Havana Band. The band had been afforded a recording opportunity for Columbia and without an arranger, Lew stepped up and took on the work. He soon found himself with an office on 'Tin Pan Alley' (Denmark Street, in London) supplying scores to Carroll Gibbons, The Savoy Orpheans and Ambrose, for whom he became resident arranger, producing some eighty scores between 1927 and 1931. Those recordings are as well known for the standard of the arrangements as for the standard of the playing.

When Roy Fox's first visit to England flopped, Lew Stone put together a crack band of top musicians for him and took on arranging duties. The band performed and broadcast every Tuesday night from the Monseigneur Restaurant and when Fox was ill, Stone took over. Six months later, when Roy Fox returned, Stone had transformed the band, recording for Decca and becoming a household name in his own right. Fox never returned to the band.

When the Monseigneur closed down, Stone toured, then took up residency at the Hollywood Restaurant in London. He also began conducting orchestras for stage shows and writing film scores, whilst still leading the band of an evening. During the war, he spread his creative wings still further, recording jazz tunes with his band Lew Stone and His Stonecrackers, recording Russian folk songs and light classics with his Concert orchestra, and touring the music halls and service camps.

On the cusp of retirement he accepted the post of musical director on the 1947 production of *Annie Get Your Gun* (into which Hylton is said to have had financial input), where he led a twenty-eight-piece orchestra for two very happy years. After *Annie Get Your Gun* he took a residency at the Pigalle Restaurant, broadcast with his big band for the BBC and subsequently with his sextet for *Music While You Work*, and toured the Mecca Ballroom circuit, before retiring in the early 1960s. Whilst never gaining much fame as a composer he left a legacy as one of the finest arrangers of his generation.

Nat Gonella (1908-1998)

Nathaniel Charles Gonella began life in poverty in East London and was taken into care and schooled at St Mary's Guardians School in Islington. He turned to music at an early age but would make a very slow and steady rise to fame.

He began on the cornet and after a stint in the St Pancras British Legion Brass Band, got his first professional engagement with *Archie Pitt's Busby Boys*. This led to the cornet being replaced by the trumpet and along with his brother he would tour in various Archie Pitt shows for four years. His first dance band experience was with Bob Dryden's band, where he would stay for a further four years.

After a brief spell with Archie Alexander's band, Nat found himself working with Billy Cotton's band and earning sums he could previously only dream of.

Gonella became known as an exponent of Louis Armstrong's style and indeed the two became good friends, though vocal comparisons to Armstrong were unfair and there could hardly have been a jazz trumpeter at that time that wasn't influenced by him.

Much of Cotton's material was 'hotter' than the competition, which suited Gonella, as did a move to play for Roy Fox when he went to the Monseigneur Restaurant as part of Roy Fox's band, with whom Nat stayed for three years after Lew Stone took over the reins.

Nat finally set up his own band to work as a relief band for Stone's. By 1935, Nat's six-piece band The Georgians (named after his favourite track and theme tune, *Georgia On My Mind*) had become a name in their own right and began touring and recording for Parlophone. They recorded a mixture of jazz, dance music, novelty jive numbers and outright corn. They rapidly became very popular both in the UK and abroad, especially in Holland.

During the war, he set up a modern big band and toured the variety hall and worked under Hylton for ENSA, under the name *The New Georgians*. He was conscripted, but managed to avoid frontline duties due to his musical abilities and also served as batman to Major Alexander Karet, who subsequently offered Nat a butler job post-war.

He turned this down and returned to touring, but the musical climate had changed since his heyday in the late 1930s and he began to struggle to recreate his previous fame either at home or abroad. He had an ill-advised venture into bebop, but returned to the variety stage, with ever diminishing returns.

He continued to receive plaudits through his life from his peers and had occasional success, especially during the trad-jazz revival of the late 1950s, but declined steadily, finding himself in pubs and working men's clubs in Blackpool. His final flourish came in 1997 when a sample of a 1932 recording became part of a number one hit for White Town, called *Your Woman*.

Ray Noble (1903-1978)

Raymond Stanley Noble was not born into poverty in the East End. The opposite was true; he was the son of a wealthy London surgeon and was destined to follow in his father's footsteps, studying at Dulwich College and Cambridge University, before switching to the Royal Academy of Music to satisfy his love of classical music.

Jack Hylton

This love switched to a love of dance music when he first heard
Kitten On The Keys at a dance in Wimbledon. He began to write and
arrange in this style and by 1927 came to the attention of Lawrence
Wright, who employed Ray at his music publishing company in
Denmark Street, in London.

When Jack Payne began the BBC Dance Orchestra, Ray was employed as one of the staff arrangers. His original songs did not set the
dance world alight but they soon would. Ray became leader of
HMV's house band the New Mayfair Dance Orchestra in 1929, a re-
cording-only outfit, which borrowed players from various other
bands. Noble raised the standard from that of the previous incumbent
Carroll Gibbons, using high-class musicians and his own arrangements. He also used top vocalists, including many that at one time or
another would work for Jack Hylton – Pat O'Malley, Elsie Carlisle,
Sam Browne and Gracie Fields.

In 1930 the band was renamed Ray Noble and His Orchestra and
they employed the services of upcoming South African singer Al
Bowlly. This would prove to be a turning point, especially when Noble wrote a song for Al, *Goodnight Sweetheart*, which would go on to
be one of the biggest selling dance band records of all time. Even
more famous songs, *Love Is The Sweetest Thing*, followed this and
The Very Thought Of You, which were huge hits on both sides of the
Atlantic. The latter made him world famous and the band eventually
went to America, a year before Hylton. They suffered the same issues
as Hylton, and Ray, Al Bowlly and Ray's manager/drummer Bill
Harty hired an all American band (which included a young trombone
player called Glenn Miller).

Ray chose to stay on in America, after Bowlly returned to England in 1938, and forged a successful career as composer for radio
shows and movies and would often make guest appearances in films.
He neither played an instrument nor sang with his band and the nature
of his early fame meant that his face was less recognisable than many
of his peers, but his song writing made him wealthy and famous
around the world. He retired to Santa Barbara, and then to Jersey in
his later years.

Jack Jackson (1907-1978)

A name that has cropped up a number of times already in this chapter is Jack Jackson, son of a Kent brass band player and conductor, who was playing the cornet by the age of six.

After a brief spell with Bert Ralton's Havana Band, he played trumpet prominently with Jack Hylton. His 'hot' style was slightly at odds with the Hylton oeuvre but he featured on a number of very popular records. He left in 1929 and played with a number of bands, including two years with Jack Payne, before taking up residency at the Dorchester Hotel in 1933 and recording for HMV (initially as John Jackson and His Orchestra). He would stay at the Dorchester for five years and would also broadcast extensively on radio, including a regular show on Radio Luxembourg in 1939.

His final residency was at the Mayfair Hotel, but the inevitable wartime issues that faced bandleaders also affected Jackson. Being apparently a somewhat carefree, happy-go-lucky chap, he neither soldiered on with the band nor worried about what would come next. His personality inevitably led him to presenting on radio and he began a new, equally successful career as a disc jockey, beginning with *Record Roundup* that gained popularity and moved from its initial afternoon slot to a peak time 11.00pm spot. Much of what he introduced was decades ahead of his time, using sound effects, fast-moving chat and the use of fictitious characters, to add to the popularity of his shows. This was a clear influence on later DJ's such as Kenny Everett and Noel Edmonds.

After a brief chat show on TV, he retired in the 1960s, more famous for his radio work than for his influential and heavily featured 'hot' trumpet playing of the 1920s and 1930s.

Harry Roy (1900-1971)

Harold Lipman, the son of a cardboard factory owner, was born in Stamford Hill in London and began playing the piano at an early age, moving to the clarinet and saxophone in his teens. His musical outlook was heavily influenced by a visit in 1919 to see the Original Dixieland Jazz Band in their ground breaking visit to London, at the Hammersmith Palais.

He formed a band with his brother Syd, The Darnswells, which later became The Lyricals, accompanied by a modest recording contract. By 1930, Harry had formed his own band (his brother would later be his manager) and after success at the Bat Club in London, he was hired for the new Leicester Square Cinema, to play in between the RKO films. Harry Roy and His RKOleans later moved to the Café Anglais in 1933 and the following year to the Mayfair Hotel, recently vacated by Ambrose.

Harry soon established himself as one of the premier bandleaders in the country, with regular broadcasts and bill-topping variety theatre tours. He was an energetic livewire on stage, with an unusual Al Jolson-like vocal style and a penchant for tricks and ad-libs throughout his set, much to the delight of the audience. This onstage demeanour was matched by a lively, jazz-tinged style, epitomised by his signature tune *Bugle Call Rag*. His fans referred to him as 'The Little Hotcha-Ma-Cha-Cha".

During the war, Harry led a smaller band Harry Roy and His Tiger Ragamuffins both in a residency at the Embassy night club, but also touring Europe and North Africa for ENSA (with an enormous drop in revenue). With the decline in post-war dance band music, so the decline in fortunes for Harry Roy. He staggered on into the early 1960s, though never really retired. He died in 1971.

Billy Cotton (1899-1969)

William Edward Cotton was rare amongst these names as being a bandleader who defied the dance band post-war downturn and successfully managed to run his band for decades after the war. He was born in Smith Square in London and began his musical training as a choirboy, before becoming a drummer. He falsified his age to enlist into World War I, serving in Malta, Egypt and Gallipoli. He became a drummer-bugler in the London Regiment (Royal Fusiliers). He learned to fly and flew solo before his nineteenth birthday.

He flirted with a number of jobs, from boxer to bus driver, from circus acrobat to footballer for Brentford, before setting up his own band The London Savannah Band, in 1924. They had contracts in Brighton, Southport and Liverpool before opening at the Astoria Ballroom in Charing Cross Road in 1928 and then Ciro's nightclub in

1929. By now Clem Bernard was Cotton's pianist and would go on to work with him as arranger and deputy conductor for thirty-three years.

By now Billy Cotton was recording for Decca and broadcasting regularly, featuring vocalist Alan Breeze, who would sing with the band for four decades. Other Cotton vocalists would include Hylton alumni Sam Browne and Jack's sister Dolly Elsie. During the war the band worked extensively for ENSA, and Cotton performed in a number of Hylton's touring shows. By the time the war ended the band were broadcasting regularly on what became *The Billy Cotton Band Show*, which ran until 1957 and continued on television until 1968, always beginning with his idiosyncratic call of 'Wakey, wakey' and signature tune *Somebody Stole My Gal*.

The band continued through five Royal Variety Performances and Cotton never retired, despite a stroke in 1962. His band through the 1930s had been unremarkable, though successful, and his sheer spirit, amiable nature, and continued use of popular entertainers seems to have seen him through the post-war years.

Debroy Somers (1890-1952)

William Debroy Somers (known as Bill to his friends) was the son of an Irish Army bandmaster, and born in Dublin. He was a multi-instrumentalist who trained at the Royal Irish Academy Of Music. He became the very epitome of the charming debonair superstar bandleader; a tall, dark haired, white toothed, moustached figure, but he was a serious musician, composer and musical director, not just a baton waver.

He was engaged by the Savoy Hotel and formed the Savoy Orpheans in 1922 and the band made the very first broadcast from the 2LO studios at Savoy Hill for the BBC (next door to the Savoy Hotel where they were working). They also recorded for Columbia and for HMV under the names The Albany Dance Orchestra and The Romaine Orchestra. They moved to the concert stage in 1925 at the London Hippodrome, and this led to Somers leaving the Savoy and setting up a band in his own name, Debroy Somers and His Orchestra. The Savoy was left to Carroll Gibbons, who made his name there. Somers' early bands included Hylton band members Jean Pougnet (on violin) and Harry Robbins (on percussion) and had previously worked with Al and Ray Starita who would work for Hylton for many years.

By 1927, Debroy stopped working in nightclubs and, whilst still recording prolifically, began working as a conductor in West End musicals, which he would continue to do throughout the 1930s. He also took his loyal band of musicians into the world of film, appearing in *Aunt Sally*, *Music Hall*, and *Stars On Parade* between 1934 and 1936.

Before war broke out, Somers was broadcasting on well-remembered programmes such as *Shipmates Ashore* and the well-loved *Ovaltineys* on Radio Luxembourg.

Other theatre shows followed, but ill-health rather took its toll on Debroy, collapsing during the run of George Formby's *Zip Goes A Million* in 1952. He died shortly afterwards.

Joe Loss (1909-1990)

Joshua Alexander Loss was one of only two bandleaders, along with Billy Cotton, who truly made a success from running a band long after the end of World War II. Joe was born in Spitalfields in London to immigrant Russian Jews. He began playing violin aged seven and would go on to study at both the London School of Music and Trinity College of Music. Initially he had no interest in dance music, playing violin for silent films at Ilford, but in due course he learnt studiously about strict tempo music for dancing and was rewarded when he was made musical director at the Kit-Cat Club in 1930.

His eight-piece band made broadcasts from the Kit-Cat Club and they recorded for the Edison Bell Winner label. By the late 1930s the band had established a reputation for being amongst the finest bands for dancing, whilst also scoring a smash hit with *Begin The Beguine* (featuring a Chick Henderson vocal) in 1939.

By now Joe had given up playing the violin and conducted his band, ever increasing in size, for the forces overseas, then in peace-time in the music halls and ballrooms around the country. The band became hugely popular, despite the fact that Joe neither wrote nor arranged for the band; most of their repertoire coming from whatever was popular with the current crop of American bands. It was this approach which gave him longevity – not sticking with the formula which had made his name in the 1930s, but moving abruptly with the times and playing whatever tunes were biggest. Indeed his signature tune, *In The Mood* was a hit for Glenn Miller and really had no particular relevance for Joe Loss.

This astute attitude to supplying the public with whatever they pleased saw him through to the late 1980s, many more decades than any other band leader and he died in 1990. The band continued under the leadership of vocalist Todd Miller and the band still tours to this day.

*   *   *

Honourable mentions are also due for other famous band leaders at the time, Carroll Gibbons, Charlie Kunz, Fred Elizalde, Victor Silvester, Sydney Lipton, among others. Of course several whole books could be filled with detail on these bands, but a serving of those working in and around the scene that Jack Hylton found himself in helps our story.

Back to our story then, with Jack about to finally perform in America.

Chapter 10: 1935-1936

Queuing for *Jack Hylton and His Continental Revue.* (Jack Hylton Archive)

This very strange affair opens up all sorts of prospects, because it has been known for years that the American populace would be only too delighted at an opportunity of hearing and seeing Jack Hylton and his band, which is now accepted all over the world as the greatest stage band entertainment on earth...Having played virtually every capital of Europe, his eyes have for a long time been turned to the West, where he is anxious to prove that he has an act of international merit, and that he is in a position to challenge the big guns of American stage bands at their own game.[1]

Jack Hylton

Late 1935 would finally see Hylton perform in America, though not as he had originally planned. After several failed attempts, Jack would take a band to America, let them holiday (without playing a note) then return home and he would stay on with a band of American musicians. Yet again the American Federation of Musicians was responsible for this situation but so was American bandleader Paul Specht. He exploited the disparity in the respective musicians' union approaches of America and Britain and subsequently manipulated and exaggerated the situation to the chagrin of Hylton and most other major bandleaders of the time.

Paul Specht began his career in the 1910s, running the American Collegians, followed by his own dance band appearing in an Atlantic City hotel, to great acclaim. He soon started running a number of different bands from his office on Broadway. His first visit to the UK was in 1922, when he brought over two bands, the Frisco Syncopators and The Criterions, to perform at the Empress Rooms in Kensington and the Trocadero, the Popular Café, the Empress Rooms and the Grafton Galleries. They were replaced at the Trocadero by another Specht band. In 1923, Paul Specht and His Orchestra opened the new Lyons Corner House, to great fanfare, and returned to America, already complaining that he may have problems with a return visit.

In 1924 his band were refused labour permits, despite them being halfway across the Atlantic. Conveniently, they were travelling with a large legal delegation and some of those were cajoled into helping Specht when they landed and he was refused entry into the country. Eventually permits were granted and his band performed but he remained angry about the situation, and threatened to set up a rival organisation to the Musicians' Union (despite them having little say in the matter of labour permits) and offered Jack Hylton a contract whereby Hylton would manage American bands in the UK and Specht would manage UK bands in America. This system could never work due to the power yielded by the American Federation of Musicians, but he seemed not to mind. Hylton did mind, especially when the small print of the contract stated that Jack's organisation would have to pay Specht 50% of all earnings, however they were derived, as well as 10% booking fee in America. Hylton, even in the mid 1920s was in no need of such a restrictive contract.

From this point, Specht became somewhat vitriolic towards Hylton and towards all the British bands, being a major voice in getting all attempts to take bands to America thwarted, no matter how popular they were and how many people wanted them to visit. Meanwhile Hylton remained happy for American bands to visit the UK, despite Specht continually reporting otherwise. Hylton was offered dates in America on a number of occasions but each time the AFM (with the help of Paul Specht) flatly refused to allow it, threatening strike action from their members.

Specht's strange approach continued – he persisted in trying to get American bands to the UK, yet persisted in refusing the reciprocal venture. He circumvented the system by employing a Canadian band to appear in the UK (Canadians, being part of the British Empire, did not require work permits).

In 1926 his band was refused a permit to appear at the Kit-Cat Club, and again he lobbied the government, this time to no avail. Ironically, it was Hylton who would ultimately take that contract at the Kit-Cat. It would appear that Specht stopped trying to get into the UK from this point on, though his lobbying to stop movement in the other direction carried on for many years.

In 1929, Hylton was again approached and again the AFM objected. Specht chose this time to attack Hylton in print, with a lengthy article in *Rhythm* magazine, suggesting Hylton was to blame for all the refused work permits. By 1934, when yet again there was talk of Hylton going to America, Specht wrote another lengthy article in *Rhythm* about this, complaining this time that the Musicians' Union (MU) were to blame for all the problems. The MU simply did not carry that much weight, had little to do with governmental input into granting or otherwise of work permits and indeed had very few members who were dance band musicians at the time of Specht's attempts. In fact it was well into the 1930s until the MU opened a Dance Band Section. Still he refused to leave it alone, and in late 1934 Specht was threatening to sue Hylton for $100,000 as recompense for all of his difficulties obtaining work in England.

By late 1935 of course no such claim had been made and Specht was more and more becoming a lone voice. He wrote an article in American magazine *Down Beat*, to which Hylton wrote at length in response. By now, *Rhythm* magazine in the UK was reporting,

"Specht spoke for no-one but himself." Hylton's response seems to have shut Specht up once and for all, with its close attention to detail and point-by-point rebuttal of everything that he had been ignoring for the previous decade:

> There can be no doubt that Mr Specht's action and the views he expressed at this time have been the source of any trouble since. He has only himself to blame.[2]

Specht left Hylton and the Musicians' Union alone after this, perhaps admitting defeat. He continued to be a successful band leader in America through to the late 1940s.[3]

Meanwhile, despite having finally silenced Paul Specht, Jack Hylton struggled to find a solution to taking his band to America. The AFM carried sufficient weight politically to stop this from happening, but what became clear was that Hylton himself could not be stopped, neither could singers, entertainers or arrangers, none of whom were covered by a union for musicians. With that in mind he arranged his trip to America. On August 31st 1935, *Melody Maker* reported on a deal that had been signed by Hylton, with the radio sponsors Standard Oil, for a series of thirteen hour-long broadcasts known as *The Standard Hour*. So keen was the company to engage the services of Hylton that they agreed to pay not only him and his American musicians, but also the members of the English band, who would be paid not to play, in a similar way to how the American band had been paid not to play during the Hylton radio broadcasts.

Later plans emerged as to how Hylton would be received on his arrival in America; 'Aeroplane Escort Of Honour Arranged To Receive Hylton On Arrival At New York – Triumphal Ride Down Broadway Also Planned' was the *Melody Maker* headline on October 5th:

> America is agog with expectation. Julius Stein has put the whole weight of his wonderful organisation, the Music Corporation of America, through which Hylton is booked, behind the plans for Jack's reception and exploitation. Standard Oil are all out to get the maximum publicity from the engagement, for which money, with the utmost

indifference, is being paid out on a scale suggestive of the wealth of the founder of the firm, John D. Rockerfeller.[4]

There was to be an escort of honour from six or more aeroplanes, followed by an open-topped car journey down the length of Broadway, then a cocktail reception in his honour and finally on to a charity ball. The article also detailed plans to record the first show for broadcast in London a few days before departure, with his British band, with another broadcast from the boat, the French liner *SS Normandie*, three miles outside New York – neutral territory. The broadcasts would then continue on American soil, with the new group of American musicians.

The first broadcast to America was duly completed on October 13th 1935 from St. Georges Hall in London and the *Melody Maker* reported it as 'a raging success':

So said hundreds of telegrams from America arriving at Jack Hylton's office last Monday morning following his 'regardless of cost' Standard Oil broadcast... Both reception and performance were adjudged by the sponsors in New York as supremely successful, and it seems that the American public started straight away to concur.[5]

This success was despite a crippling schedule – the band had spent the day at Twickenham Film Studios filming *She Shall Have Music* (as previously mentioned) and this was followed at 10.00pm with a few hours rehearsal before the 3.30am radio broadcast.

On October 16th, the band made a very public departure from Waterloo Station and onward to the *SS Normandie*.[6] The British band would holiday in New York for over a week before returning to Britain to work under the baton of either Sonny Farrar, or guest conductor Buddy Rogers (an American film actor). Between March 30th and April 4th 1936, Charles Manning conducted the orchestra and it was then disbanded.

Along with partner Fifi and daughter Jackie, Hylton had taken to America his manager Arthur Wilcox and arrangers Billy Ternent and Melle Weersma. He also managed to take two members of the band, saxophonist Freddy Schweitzer and pianist Alec Templeton, under the guise of them being 'speciality acts'. Vocalists Peggy Dell, Eve

Jack Hylton

Becke, Magda Neeld and Pat O'Malley also sailed, giving a solid core from which Hylton could easily add the cream of American dance band musicians:

> The orchestra included such great names as David Rose, Arthur Layfield, who was Isham Jones' drummer and one of the greatest swing drummers in America in those days, George Wettling; we even had Miff Mole playing trombone on occasion.[7]

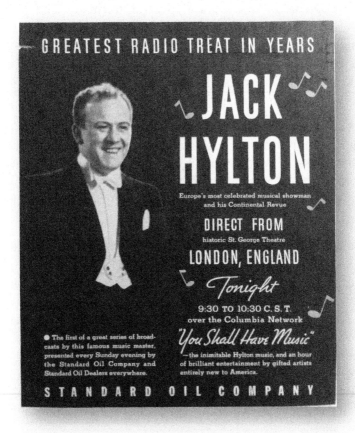

Magazine advert for the Standard Oil radio show. (Jack Hylton Archive)

Jack Hylton And His Continental Revue was a smash hit. Radio stations claimed that after the October 27th broadcast, Jack received more than 10,000 letters from American fans. Since his arrival, Jack had been courted by almost every big theatre, but was unable to take up any offer, as his contract had restricted him just to radio broadcasts. After much negotiation from Hylton himself, the ban was lifted and within hours, on November 20th, he had signed a deal with the Palace Theatre in Chicago. The engagement would last for six days, after which the show moved on for a Thanksgiving Day performance in Cleveland. These theatre shows would run for just one hour, (as the American bands tended to share the bill with a feature film) and displayed the home grown talents of Pat O'Malley (who would marry a few days later and subsequently settle in America), Magda Neeld, Peggy Dell, Freddy Schweitzer and Alec Templeton (already a successful radio personality in America).

By the beginning of 1936, the Standard Oil contract had expired, but the company re-signed Hylton for a radio series of *The Standard Hour*, which began on January 5th, 1936. Manager Arthur Wilcox takes up the story:

> We were standing at rehearsal, quite quietly and with no thought of harming anybody, when up sailed Mr Hylton with a piece of manuscript under his arm and sat down at the piano. 'All right, let's try *Cup Of Cold Poison*' says he with Wilcox taking his part. Our embarrassment was immense and increased rather than abated when genial Jack, having heard our rendition of the part, opined that we were OK. Have any of you ever walked to a microphone before a large audience feeling that you have forgotten your abdomen? We did, on that Sunday, the 12th January 1936, a red-letter day in the history of American broadcasting. This was the first performance in America by the Jack Hylton Orchestra of the Box and Cox tune *With A Cup Of Cold Poison Beside Me*. The butler and heroine of the piece were personified by Pat O'Malley and the fruity Lord Ebenezer by myself. But the audience was kind and Pat O'Malley very amusing, so that the performance was applauded with vigour. We bowed and retired gracefully, myself wondering just how mad Bing Crosby and Eddie Cantor would be, and hoping that Jack wasn't mad at us![8]

Jack Hylton

By now, Jack was also free to play almost anywhere he pleased and on January 24th, the band were at the Gold Coast Room at the Drake Hotel in Chicago, where they played for dancing:

> Jack Hylton might well be called the little Corporal of the dance band world. Having pretty well conquered all of Europe with his rhythms, he set out from his native England some months ago to conquer America...Now, having let the radio and theatre taste the power of his guns, he has moved his regiment into the Gold Coast Room at the Drake and for his first dime and dance engagement in this country, he is quickly conquering a new field...On the large orchestra stage at the Drake...it is easy to see that Hylton's men respect him. Their eyes are riveted on his baton and on his left hand, which shades their music.[9]

They were also free to record and on January 2nd 1936, Jack's American band embarked on their only recording session, in Chicago. Four titles were cut, three of which were released by HMV in the UK – *Lights Out* and *The Music Goes 'Round And Around* (HMV BD-5030) and *Eeny Meeny Miney Mo* (HMV BD-5035). The tunes retain the classic Hylton sound, though they swing a little harder than most tunes Hylton recorded.

On April 4th, the Standard Oil contract again came to an end, but only a day later Jack signed for the rival NBC network, to appear on the Real Silk sponsored programme, *Life Is A Song*. On April 11th, the previous resident band at the Drake Hotel, Horace Heidt's Brigadeers [sic] were due to return, but Hylton was so successful that he was retained instead. When the run at the Drake finally ended, Hylton took the band on a short tour of Canada, eventually returning to conclude the Real Silk shows on June 28th. This orchestra was then disbanded, but Hylton made one last broadcast from America, with an all-star session band, in New York.

Things were not straightforward during the time in America. Singer Magda Neeld (known on this trip as "Australia's Star Of Song") sent her unpublished memoirs to Lancaster University, where they remain in the Jack Hylton Archive. With them are details of two incidents involving Jack. If they are to be believed (and we only have this one source) they reveal a shocking undercurrent of mafia led treatment of musicians and entertainers and go some way to explain the power of the AFM. I offer them here in full:

The first was in Chicago in the beautiful Gold Coast Room, after many months of enormous success there with the *Continental Revue*, and after finishing a grand show we were horrified to see Petrillo [James Petrillo, leader of the AFM] standing in the wings chewing his big cigar. He went immediately over to one of Jack's outstanding American trumpet players and said, "You, pack up and get out now!" The boy was shaking. "You spoke nastily about me in the bar room and you were overheard. So go now or I'll see that you will never get any other job, coast to coast in this country, even again!"

The trumpet player said quickly, "OK, I'll go now" and Petrillo left. Then this fine musician said to me and some others nearby, "I have to leave you, but please tell Jack to be very careful from now on, every step he takes. He's on their hit list. I've been very solidly told. I know!"

I felt my skin creep, but said nothing... So on we went, in spite of everything, with tremendous acclaim everywhere. But the second very close danger for Jack's life came in Detroit during our last show there...Jack was under protection from Standard Oil, and near the end of the last show there his bodyguard said "Come quickly Jack. We've got the word. Out the back of the theatre, now please! For the final number and spotlight, you dare not stay! Bill Ternent and Pat O'Malley both agree that they must take the bow and stand in for you. They both look very different from yourself and so say 'don't worry', it will be quite OK." In a flash, Jack was taken quickly out the back way, to safety. The next time I saw him was for our final appearances and farewell broadcasts in the great NBC studios, before returning to London.

This story may be somewhat apocryphal and some other parts of Magda Neeld's memoirs don't seem to tie up with other sources, but it may be a fascinating and otherwise unreported insight to Hylton's time in America.

The party sailed back from New York on the *Ile De France*, arriving on July 7th 1936 after ten hugely successful months in America, matching if not exceeding his level of success in Europe. He took a month long holiday in the South of France, where he would begin to spend more and more time, eventually purchasing a pair of villas in Antibes, Les Arbrets and L'Hermitage, at La Garoupe.

When he returned to England after his well-deserved holiday, Jack Hylton would have no band, so a fresh start, some new faces and a modern sound would dominate the next few years.

Chapter 11: 1936-1940

Jack Hylton and His Orchestra, performing at the Scala Theatre, Berlin, 1937.
(Personal Collection)

Whilst Hylton was in America, the band still had recording commitments for HMV, so as well as Hylton's recordings with his American band, the British based band continued to record. Banjoist Sonny Farrar directed the band on January 3rd and February 14th 1936, whilst Billy Ternent took the baton on January 19th. A number of very popular Hylton numbers were recorded at those sessions, including *She Shall Have Music* and *Do The Runaround* (HMV BD-5017), *My First Thrill* (HMV BD-5018), *Why Did She Fall For The Leader Of The Band?* (HMV BD-5023), and *This'll Make You Whistle* (HMV BD-5037). In total, twenty sides were recorded whilst Hylton was still across the Atlantic.

Barely a month after arriving back from America, Jack Hylton was back working and recording for the BBC. The broadcast on October 7th would be done with a 'scratch band'. There had been no performance work for the band in any form for over four months, so some old hands were hired, some new faces and a new vocal group that Hylton had been working with in America and had brought over – The Swingtette. This accomplished vocal group were second choice after The Merry Macs, whose schedule did not fit in with Hylton's. The Swingtette were such a success that not only did they follow Hylton back to Europe, but they recorded solo and with the band for several years. They consisted of sisters Jewel, Dorothy, and Frances McCarthy, Ben Late and Gene Lanham, originally from Kansas City.

The British stage debut for The Swingtette came on August 12th 1936 with Mrs Jack Hylton and Her Orchestra at the Paramount Theatre in London. At the same time, Jack was recording his ensemble of old and new members, using arrangements by Melle Weersma. The session was notable as being the last to feature vocalist Pat O'Malley who, following his success in the USA with Hylton, was to pursue a career there.

The musical influence on Hylton's musical output from his time in America was clear, but whilst he saw 'swing' as the natural successor of what he was now calling 'jazz', this wasn't necessarily to the taste of all his fans in Britain. The October 7th broadcast had received criticism, as reported in the Radio Times, ahead of their December 2nd broadcast for the BBC.

On October 7th, in Jack Hylton's first broadcast since his return from America and his first in this country since September, 1935, a goodly part of his programme was swing music. He did it, as he said, to illustrate a further advance in the progress of that which we once knew as Jazz. He got hundreds of telegrams and messages of congratulation, but also hundreds of letters from his fans. "Give us what we know you by. Give us the sweet music you played before you went away." So tonight and again on Saturday Jack Hylton, though he will play a little swing music (which he still believes is the music of the future) will make the greater part of his programme "sweet". It is good news that he intends to start his band again as a permanent concern in the New Year. Many of the fine musicians to be heard tonight and on Saturday will be in his new orchestra.[1]

Chapter 11: 1936-1940

The band made many more recordings during 1936, with Jack and his arrangers refining his sound and making changes. On January 11th 1937, the band embarked on another European tour, travelling through Berlin, Prague and Vienna before settling into the Scala Theatre in Berlin for a month long run. There they were to break box office records, regularly playing to over five thousand people per performance, taking £8,000 per week. Nazi leaders such as Herman Goering and Dr. Goebbels saw concerts on the tour. The same Nazi authorities were responsible for making sure there were no Jews visible in the band. They spoke directly to Hylton about this and were assured that no performers of Semitic appearance were to be clearly on display at the front of the stage during the performance. Questions were asked about specific performers and Hylton deflected the questions and the band remained intact. Whilst travelling in Nazi Germany, people, greeting them with a raised right hand and the inevitable "Heil Hitler", would approach the band. The band soon learned to respond by raising their right hand and replying "Heil Hylton"!

So called 'hot jazz' had been banned in Germany, but *The Melody Maker* reported that Goering and Goebbels liked the hot music and Hylton's band played 'hotter and hotter in each city.'

Jack and 'the boys' returned to England, via Holland, on March 22nd 1937 and just a week later was opening in a London Palladium show, *Swing Is In The Air*. By now the band consisted of twenty-four musicians and thirteen entertainers, including Joe Rossi (French boy accordion champion), Wilbur Hall (ex-Paul Whiteman trombone comedian), Dick Murphy (American guitarist and entertainer), Alice Mann (vocalist), The Swingtette, Peggy Dell and Canadian contortionist Babs Laval, as well as the first appearance on the variety stage of a Hammond Organ, played by Robin Richmond. The band themselves had five costume changes, and were on stage throughout the show, in a set designed to replicate the Rainbow Room of Radio City. All the music had been specifically written and arranged by Billy Ternent. After two years away from the Palladium, advance ticket sales were unprecedented for a performance as lavish as anything seen at the Palladium:

Swing Is In The Air bill poster. (Personal Collection)

Hylton has returned to London a greater showman than ever before...His band...is exceptionally brilliant and, when the music gives it the scope, is well able to justify the title of the show.[2]

The Melody Maker also notes around this time that Hylton is becoming less of a bandleader and more of a 'variety impresario', which is tellingly astute. Certainly it is becoming clear where Hylton is pitching himself for the future.

Whilst the show was running, Hylton and the band performed for the first time on the fledgling BBC Television network. The show, simply entitled *Jack Hylton And His Band*, aired at 3.00pm on May 14th 1937, running for thirty-five minutes. It featured Joe Rossi, Dick Murphy, Alice Mann, George Lyons and Freddie Schweitzer. Televisions were still extremely rare at this time, and the broadcast was not deemed important enough to warrant a mention in *The Melody Maker*. (There would be further television broadcasts on January 20th, August 29th and September 3rd 1938, and March 15th and June 27th 1939.)

Swing Is In The Air ran successfully until June 26th, after which the band made another of their rare BBC broadcasts and would spend the rest of the year touring the provinces – where the band had not been for over two years. There were just fifty sides recorded in 1936, and only twenty-six sides recorded in 1937. When the eighteen-month HMV contract expired in May 1937, Hylton chose not to renew it, for reasons that aren't entirely clear.

Their provincial tour continued quietly through the rest of the year, a strangely quiet one for Jack.

An article published in *Rhythm Magazine* in December 1938 spoke of Hylton's working techniques during a performance. The article is worth reproducing in its entirety here:

> What impression do you form when you see Hylton on the job? He's a very different fellow back-stage, say when he's just finished a show. Then, first thing he invariably does back in the dressing room is to chat with his second-in-command, Bill Ternent, about the way the public has just reacted. "Think we'll put the waltz back, next house – and we'll take out so-and-so and put in so-and-so in its place. It'll go better there." Always scheming, that's Hylton. Never blaming the audience for lack of response. Seeks a reason for anything wrong and puts it right. Talks so quietly that you have a hard job to follow him. Darts off at conversational tangents. Suddenly breaks into a song in a most disconcerting manner, or absent-mindedly puts on the gramophone in the middle of what you're saying. Seems never to be listening, but damn it, has the most embarrassing habit of remembering every word, and confounding you with something you may have said in the past and which is not consistent with what you're saying

now. Capable of great burst of generosity, but does not readily forgive a bad turn. Always has a motive for everything he does, works like a horse and is faintly surprised if anybody else can't keep up with his tempo. Knows everything that's going on in the profession of popular music. You'd think he maintained a highly paid espionage service. Fiery temper. Once saw him kick the outboard motor of his rowing boat with such force that he hurt his foot, but immediately recovered, laughing as he realised how funny it was. Can keep his temper, though, when he's most provoked, and when he goes a bit pale under the strain of it, then he is at his most menacing. A little sleepy and offhand, outwardly, but a volcano of latent energy within, frequently erupting with seismic effect. Above all, entirely free from snobbery and affectation.[3]

In early 1938 Hylton embarked on his first theatrical collaboration with the BBC, an untested idea but one that Jack would successfully run with for several years. He bought the rights to a radio show, in this case *Secrets Of The BBC* and made a theatre version of the show, complete with the performers from the BBC version and put it on a variety tour of the UK. Along with Bryan Michie, this show also featured Dorothy Duval, Jean Bamforth, Arthur Tolcher, Eric Bartholomew, Archie Glen, Rosie and Alice Lloyd, Donna Sisters, Al and Hilda Heath, Iizuka Brothers, George and Jack D'Ormonde, Martin Lukens and Mary Naylor. Jack didn't involve himself or his band directly in this show, another feature of his future work. This would be the first show to feature the strap line of 'Jack Hylton Presents...'; the first of several hundred.

In January 1938, Jack and the band embarked on what would prove to be their sixteenth and final European tour. The band set sail for Holland on January 26th, with a twenty-piece band and seven featured vocalists, including newcomer June Malo:

I was singing in a club in London and [Hylton] brought in Val Parnell one night and heard me singing and...asked me if I would like to join the band. Of course, I was very delighted and excited, but I said, "well of course I'm under contract here and I don't know whether I can". But

being Jack...he was able, within twenty four hours, he'd
got another girl to take over my contract and in my hand
was an airline ticket to Berlin and I was due to fly two
days later to open with the band at the Scala Theatre,
which I did and it was the most exciting experience because I'd never heard anything like it before...Then I
realised as the tabs opened and Jack started his signature
tune *Listen To The Band* it was the people stamping their
feet, in applause and I've never heard anything like it and
it's an experience I'll never forget.[4]

The tour took the band through Holland and into Germany for a
second month-long residency at the Scala Theatre. Again, the band
broke the box office records. On the return journey, they played briefly in Paris before returning to England in early March.

Typically, there was little time to rest. On March 14th, they set
out on another tour of Britain, beginning with a two-week stay at the
Birmingham Hippodrome. The show featured Peggy Dell, June Malo
and Dick Murphy on vocals, alongside accordionist Joe Rossi, vocal
duo The Henderson Twins, Freddy Schweitzer as a self-contained
comedy act and trombonist Wilbur Hall, who also played violin, a
foot pump and indulged in comedy dancing!

By May, the band was back in London rehearsing for a new variety show, *Happy Returns*, at the Adelphi Theatre. The show ran from
May 19th until July 2nd. Also in May, Hylton's second BBC radio
based production opened. *Palace Of Varieties* at the Paramount Cinema on Tottenham Court Road in London, was a stage version of the
BBC feature of the same name, which attempted to capture the essence of the Victorian old-time music hall. Ernest Longstaffe, the
producer of the original series, conducted the orchestra and Herman
Darewski performed the traditional role of chairman. Following another show at the Paramount, *Monday Night At Seven,* which followed
a similar pattern, Hylton already had plans for a fourth BBC radio
production, which would gain much more attention and critical acclaim. In July, Jack put together what amounted to a 'greatest hits'
show:

Called *Cavalcade*, it resurrects in sequence all those big
numbers which Jack, either by scenic or mechanical aids,

or else through brilliant orchestration, turned into national hit tunes – tunes which are now indelibly associated with his name.[5]

The sixteen piece band was smaller than the twenty-four-piece unit which was put together in late 1936, consisting now of Billy Hill and Freddy Bretherton (pianos), Bruce Trent (bass), Lew Stephenson (drums), George Swift, George Taylor and Stan Howard (trumpets), Jack Bentley and Woolf Phillips (trombones), Andre Budegary,[6] Reg Cole and Les Maddox (violins), Les Gilbert, Ben Daniels, Rudy Loeffler and Freddy Schweitzer (saxophones) with Peggy Dell leading a number of vocalists. Hylton took the *Cavalcade* show on tour, with weeks in Aberdeen, Glasgow and Manchester, before reaching the London Palladium where Hylton and the band received acclaim at a level that even they had never experienced:

> This is not a show which can be adequately described in cold print and I am certainly not attempting to do so... Success in this sphere can only be won by finding one's own formula, albeit I feel very strongly, and have done for years, that Hylton has well-nigh said the last word that can be said on stage band presentation. My hat is raised high as I pay this tribute, and I can only conclude with this pious wish that if the show proves to be the money spinner that it promises to be, then may everyone in the company gather in a fair share of the doubloons.[7]

In September, after a short holiday, Jack signed a new deal with HMV and began recording again, fitting in some thirty sides before the end of the year, and the BBC booked a series of shows, once a month, entitled *Jack's Back* which would signal a new interest in the BBC and the band, long overdue. Hylton was given free reign to present whatever he chose, perhaps an indicator of how Hylton was now being recognised within the industry. The band continued to tour, with a slightly re-jigged show, entitled *Bands May Come*.

Also in September the band took part in the annual National Radio Exhibition, at Olympia, in London, known as *RadiOlympia*. This had been running since 1926, but since 1936 the major attraction was television. This was a trade exhibition that sold radios and subsequently televisions, but also included celebrity appearances. On September 3rd 1938, Jack Hylton and His Orchestra performed in the glass-walled television studio, with Peggy Dell, The Henderson Twins, Bruce Trent, June Malo and young dancer Maureen Potter. The show was performed twice during the day for the visitors to the exhibition and was broadcast live at 2.30pm that day. Amazingly, footage of this event exists, in colour, filmed on a cine camera by Desmond Campbell, who worked for the Baird Television Company. This silent, one minute film can (at the time of writing) be viewed on YouTube. Jack can be seen conducting the band and discussing matters with musicians and the production team.[8]

Towards the end of the year, two new important projects began – neither of them featuring the famous band. *Youth Takes A Bow* would ultimately prove to be a huge theatrical success under the auspices of Bryan Michie, but initially Hylton conceived the idea as a series of fifteen-minute radio shows, featuring the cream of upcoming young entertainers. He pitched the idea to the BBC and they accepted. It would run in one form or another for many years.

Meanwhile, Jack had also bought the theatrical rights to the very popular *Band Waggon* radio series and set to put it on the stage. A number of the original artists were contracted, most importantly the star of the show Arthur Askey (whom Jack had helped to 'discover' several years previously). A young nine-piece band was put together under the baton of Billy Ternent. After weeklong try-outs at Finsbury Park Empire, Hammersmith Empire, Ilford Hippodrome and Croydon Empire, Hylton leased the Princes Theatre (now the Shaftesbury Theatre on Shaftesbury Avenue in London) and opened the four-week run of *Band Waggon* on Boxing Day 1938. This was a full-scale variety show, with Ternent in charge of proceedings, but featuring a thirty-minute spot from the full Hylton band, conducted by Jack himself. A young Ernest Wiseman was part of both of these shows, firstly alongside Arthur Askey in *Band Waggon*, and subsequently alongside Eric Bartholomew in *Youth Takes A Bow* where, with Hylton's assistance, they would become Morecambe and Wise.

Band Waggon bill poster. (Personal Collection)

Ernie was auditioned in Manchester and Hylton immediately gave him a job. He was subsequently given a five-year contract at six pounds per week (double what his father was earning at the time). He was thirteen years old and about to become a major West End star. Hylton personally developed Wise's stage persona, swapping his brown clogs for smart black tap shoes, his battered bowler hat for a new straw boater and his haphazard coat and jacket for a white dinner suit and black trousers. Jack was a major influence on Ernie Wise and allowed him to stay at the family home, Villa Daheim, in Kingston Gorse in Sussex. He wrote to Ernie's father in Pontefract in September 1939:

> Ernest is staying with me at my house at the seaside. He is very welcome to stay down there with me and I shall be glad if you will let me know if this is OK or if you would prefer that he is back home with you. We have six other children there, and his being with us does not inconvenience us at all.[9]

Given how much work Hylton was juggling at this time, this is an extraordinarily generous, though far from exceptional gesture. Wise remembered Hylton fondly:

> I got my first taste of luxury the moment I joined Jack Hylton. He gave me a flat in Albany Street and a sort of governess, and sent his Buick every day to take me to the theatre from a school nearby. When we went on tour, Jack and his Austrian wife, Fifi, decked me out with some fine clothes. I took my new life in my stride, spending time at the Hylton's grand home and mingling with the stars who came to visit.[10]

Jack became a surrogate father to Ernie, buying him meals, sharing in the Bolton-imported pork pies that Hylton would have delivered to London, buying Ernie clothes and suitcases when he needed them, and extra cash when the earnings had run dry. Of course there are parallels between the two and Hylton saw something of himself in little Ernie – the northerner with the working class parents, moving to London to make his name in show business. In turn, Ernie looked up to Jack as a role model – to someone who could come from such a background and make it to the very top of his profession.

Hylton would have a significant impact not only on Ernie's career, but the setting up and developing of the Morecambe & Wise duo, which would dominate the light entertainment schedules for decades. The pair had become friends whilst working separately on Hylton's *Youth Takes A Bow* show, but were struggling to find work as a duo. Having worked previously with Hylton, Ernie approached Bryan Michie and asked him to speak to Jack about hiring them. Hylton was at first reticent, but agreed to watch their act whilst he was in Liverpool checking up on the show. He liked it, tweaked it, added a song, and then removed another act in the show to make way for Eric & Ernie. Hylton stood with Sadie Wise as they watched from the wings at Liverpool Empire on August 28th 1941, when Bartholomew & Wise made their professional debut. Whilst featuring nothing particularly ground-breaking, the act received a warm welcome and Hylton kept their act, along with both their solo acts, on the bill as the show moved to Edinburgh.

At the end of the run at the Princes Theatre, Hylton sent *Band Waggon* off on tour, to huge success, but without Jack and his band. Theatres had queues just for the advance booking of tickets and every town sold out. Meanwhile the regular Hylton band continued their touring schedule and hooked up again with Coleman Hawkins, who was back on tour in the UK, before returning, after several years, to the USA. It was at this time that the band finally recorded with Hawk.

In April, Jack put an eleven-piece orchestra together under the baton of violinist and ex-Hylton employee Maurice Loban. This band was to perform with singer Diana Clare (a pseudonym of Esther Coleman, who had appeared in the third series of *Band Waggon* on the radio) in a Sunday afternoon broadcast, *Sunday Afternoon at Clare's*, for both Radio Luxembourg and Radio Normandy, in a spot known as *The Lux Programme*. The band featured Jack Raine on trumpet, Johnny Raitz on tenor saxophone and Freddie Bretherton on piano, all of whom were ex-members of various Hylton bands. By the summer, both *Band Waggon* and Jack Hylton and His Orchestra were enjoying huge success and recording continued apace – over a hundred sides would be recorded in 1939, and in August they had embarked on the filming for their second feature film, *Band Waggon*.

The film starred Arthur Askey, Richard 'Stinker' Murdoch and Hylton singer and bass player Bruce Trent, with songs composed by Noel Gay and Harry Parr Davies. The songs included *Heaven Will Be Heavenly* (HMV BD-5557), *After Dark*, *The Melody Maker* (HMV BD-5558) and its flipside *The Only One Who's Difficult Is You*. The big hit of the film was written by Annette Mills (sister of actor John

Mills), entitled *Boomps-A-Daisy* (HMV BD-5499), which would become a hit later in the year. Jack and the band played themselves in the film, which was released in March 1940.

Also in August, yet another band was put together under Hylton's name, this time at the London Casino and under the baton of Hylton band violinist Cyril Stapleton.

In September, Prime Minister Neville Chamberlain declared war with Germany and this would ultimately signal the end of Jack Hylton and His Orchestra. It was clear that Hylton was looking to new avenues and perhaps beginning to lose interest in the running of the band and this would continue for the next few months. There would be no great fanfare and no great send off – such things were understandably inappropriate in the circumstances.

Basil Dean and Leslie Henson set up the Entertainments National Service Association, known as ENSA, to provide entertainment for the troops during World War II. Hylton was appointed chairman of the dance band section, which also included Billy Cotton, Geraldo and Eddie Jones, and a great deal of his time over the next few years would be spent organising bands, many of them his own bands, to provide shows all over Europe.

With the outbreak of war, a wave of patriotism had swept the country, and many of Jack's old marching style songs from the early 1930s were re-issued by Decca. Jack also began to broadcast more regularly on the BBC. In September, the band was featured in *Band of the Week* on the BBC, appearing twice daily for five days. In October, Billy Ternent conducted for two radio broadcasts of dance music, while Jack took over for the concert music later during the same week. Meanwhile, on November 27th, Freddie Bretherton replaced Billy Ternent for the continuing tour of *Band Waggon*. On December 20th, Jack conducted for another BBC broadcast, while Ternent took his place for the last week of the year for another set of *Band Of The Week* performances.

By December, the band had performed eight shows for the troops, and after a Christmas Eve broadcast called *Hylton Harmony*, the band flew to France for a very different series of concerts than they were used to at that time of year. Many bandleaders were beginning to feel the strain, with essential members being called up for service. Ambrose suggested publicly that a few musicians from each band should be exempt, to form a morale boosting National Dance Orchestra to entertain the troops. Hylton openly retorted in an article published in *The Melody Maker*:

> The entertainment and dance band business is very important and essential, but winning the war comes first. Four of my boys have already been called up and I need hardly add that I made no effort to get them exempted. As all of us can and will do, I am carrying on with the boys I have left and not doing too badly either I hope.[11]

In February 1940, Hylton and his band broadcast yet another series of *Band Of The Week* for the BBC, starting on February 11th, while Hylton announced that he had bought the rights to another BBC radio feature, *ITMA (It's That Man Again)*. In fact he had bought the rights six months previously, even before the show had become a big hit. By now it was huge and Hylton employed the services of the show's stars, old friend and colleague Tommy Handley, Jack Train and Maurice Denham. It would prove to be another 'Jack Hylton Presents...' smash hit. Billy Ternent wrote the music and Hylton hired Billy Cotton and his band to provide the musicians. They opened at Birmingham Hippodrome on February 26th.

Also in February, Hylton and his band recorded two songs with vocalist Celia Lipton (who had made her name singing with her father, Sidney Lipton's band) – *Let The People* Sing, (HMV BD-5562) and *There'll Never Be Another You* (HMV BD-5563). Hylton would within a year manage Celia Lipton, and he would continue in this role for over a decade. Lipton toured the country in vaudeville for £100 per week and famously played the lead in *Peter Pan* on tour, in Manchester and at the Scala Theatre in London. In the early 1950s, she moved to America and became a famous movie actress, before marrying the inventor of the cardboard milk carton, Victor Farris. When he died, Celia Lipton-Farris inherited $100 million.

On March 6th 1940, the band went into the recording studio for what would prove to be the last time, cutting four sides all of which featured vocalist Sam Browne, the last of twelve sides recorded in 1940, after the eight produced on February 1st. The last songs, released on HMV BD-5570, *Give A Little Whistle*, and *Little Wooden Head* were unremarkable. On April 12th it was decided that due to the on going 'phoney war', a previously postponed Paris show could be honoured. The band flew to Paris and performed at the Paris Opera House, featuring Jack Warner, Josephine Baker, Jack's sister Dolly Elsie, and Frenchman Maurice Chevalier. A forty-minute broadcast was made by the BBC, which featured the first broadcast of a popular song from the Opera House, Dolly Elsie's rendition of *Over The Rainbow*. A Week later, they flew back to Paris for their final foreign performance, again at the Opera House and again with a broadcast in Britain.

The final concert by Jack Hylton and His Orchestra took place at the Drury Lane Theatre, in London, on April 30th and the BBC broadcast the entire show. It wasn't billed as the last show and in *The Melody Maker* the show did not even warrant a mention. In December, the paper mentioned in passing that Hylton was "momentarily discarding his baton" whilst busy with other projects. With seven members of his band called up in quick succession and all the other projects he was involved with, Jack Hylton quietly chose that time to hang up his baton and not compromise the quality of his product any more. He had been working both as bandleader and entrepreneur for some years and now had given himself a chance to focus on just one of those things. Despite many theatres closing down in London during the war, Hylton would progress steadily with more and more projects coming under the 'Jack Hylton Presents...' banner. Many of his former colleagues, both musicians and entertainers, would continue to work for many years as part of Jack's ever increasing empire.

Meanwhile, the remnants of the band reformed in Bristol under the direction of Billy Ternent for the BBC, as The Dance Orchestra. For a time, this band was controlled by the Hylton office, and would later become The Billy Ternent Orchestra, which began recording for Decca in 1941.

Perhaps this is a good moment to share a few personal reminiscences of Jack as bandleader. First, from bass player, Andre De Vekey, via journalist Chris Hayes:

> As a journalist, I found Jack Hylton brusque and testy, but this was not characteristic according to Andre de Vekey, who played bass for him from 1933 to 1938. Andre...told me: "He was a strict disciplinarian, a hard taskmaster, a

straight talker and a tough businessman, who liked to have his own way, but he had a kind streak and often helped his musicians when they were in trouble. He was a good bandleader, who generated a lot of charisma and loyalty. Musicians liked him and enjoyed being with the band, although some resented his all-in contracts, which meant one salary for everything we did. He worked hard himself and expected everyone else to do likewise. He was a grim perfectionist and our rehearsals could be interminable."[12]

And from Spike Hughes, journalist and double bass player with Hylton from 1931-1932:

I took to Jack Hylton personally very quickly, once I had overcome my initial embarrassment on finding myself in his company at all. I liked his peculiar unostentatious generosity, his sly sense of humour, and his willingness to try anything once. I admired too, the contempt he showed for most of his own activities as a musician, his alarming perception of any second rate or lazy playing by his band, and his prodigious vitality, which enabled him to talk business sense long after the rest of us were under the table and long before we were conscious the next morning.[13]

And finally from vocalist Pat O'Malley, interviewed for BBC radio in 1971:

It was a great education. All I can say is that the years I was with Jack Hylton, who was my boss and a very good friend, I never had a contract with him from the day I joined him and everything we agreed upon was a handshake and to me it was a marvellous education. It would cost me a million dollars to do what I did with him, if I wanted to go out and do it on my own, you know. So for my way of thinking, this was a marvellous training and a marvellous education.[14]

Chapter 12: The Boys In The Band

The band relaxing at the beach, c.1932. (Personal Collection)

Jack Hylton's orchestra was exceptional for the number of members who would go on to be either bandleaders or important soloists in their own right. In this chapter, I do not intend to break new ground but to give an overview of just some of the talent that worked through the ranks of the Hylton band and where they progressed to after their departure. It is not meant to be exhaustive, merely an interesting diversion.

Billy Ternent (1899-1977)

Frederick William Ternent was born in Newcastle, where he took up the violin at the age of seven. He had his first trio aged twelve and was conducting his first orchestra on a cinema circuit run by George Black. He joined the Hylton band in 1927, after a spell playing in Hylton's Kit-Cat Band at the Piccadilly Hotel, and would remain a fundamental part of Hylton's musical output for the rest of his career.

He became Jack's second in command and chief arranger. In the latter years of the band he would run most of the rehearsals.

It was no wonder that when Hylton's orchestra disbanded, Ternent took charge of the remainder of the band, which became the BBC Dance Orchestra. Later, Ternent formed his own orchestra, featuring top class musicians playing his own elaborate and sophisticated arrangements. He continued to work as an arranger and musical supervisor for Hylton and arranged and conducted for many West End shows and visiting American stars (including Frank Sinatra, who referred to him as 'the little giant') as well as several Royal Variety Performances as part of his role as musical director of the London Palladium. Despite the gradual demise of light-music on the radio, the quality of Ternent's work allowed him to continue broadcasting well into the 1970s.

'Poggy' Pogson (1904-1980)

Edward O. Pogson began his multi-instrumental career at Wimbledon Palais, before joining Herman Darewski's Stage Band, the Bert Firman Orchestra then the Hylton-owned Kit-Cat Band, run by Al Starita. He finally joined Hylton in the mid 1920s, as all-round reeds player (though his skills extended beyond the saxes, to the bassoon, the violin and he was a competent vocalist).

In 1931 he left Hylton to join Jack Payne's band, before moving to Jack Jackson's Orchestra until 1939. During this time he freelanced with a number of other orchestras, which of course his Hylton contract wouldn't have allowed. The 1940s were fecund for Pogson, he played with Billy Ternent, Geraldo, Jack Jackson (again), Chappie d'Amato and Jack Payne (again).

His freelance career continued through the fifties, notably working with Victor Sylvester, Kenny Baker and on BBC radio's *Goon Show*. Illness in the 1960s saw him move away from London and into teaching.

'Chappie' d'Amato (1897-1976)

Noel Albert Gennaro d'Amato began his career playing banjo in Louis Mitchell's Syncopating Sextette, before working with Hylton throughout the 1920s. He began his Hylton career on banjo and guitar, before moving to alto sax and occasionally piano. He would also take on the role of leader on occasions when Hylton was otherwise engaged. He sang often with the band, as part of a three part male vocal chorus, consisting of a combination of Jack Jackson, Billy Ternent, Hugo Rignold and Hylton. He also sang a number of solo vocals throughout the 1920s, from *I Ain't Nobody's Darling* (HMV B-1524) in 1922 to *Digga, Digga, Do* (HMV B-5638) in 1929.

Chappie left Hylton in early 1933, to play guitar for Jack Jackson, before working again with Hyltonian Billy Ternent, then forming his own band at the Piccadilly Hotel in London. Further engagements included a time with Arthur Young's band, Denis Moonan's Band and an eight-year residency at the Hatchett's Club, from 1942 to 1950. He later became a radio disc jockey and occasional musical director.

Ted Heath (1902-1969)

London born George Edward Heath began playing tenor horn aged 6, before switching to trombone. He was discovered busking in a quintet that included his brother, outside London Bridge Station, by none other than Jack Hylton, who invited him to play in the band at the Queen's Hall Roof. His tenure didn't last long but he would go on to have a long relationship with Hylton in various outfits.

He worked with Bert Firman, the Ennis Parkes fronted Metro-Gnomes, Al Starita's Kit-Kat Club Band, and Sydney Lipton, as well as long spells with Ambrose and Geraldo. During this time he became regarded as the finest trombone player in the country, and his time with these great bandleaders taught him everything he needed to know to form his own band, which he did in 1944.

Ted Heath's orchestra moved away from the model of the bands he had previously worked with, and took its reference from Glenn Miller, sporting a modern, American big band sound. Ted Heath and His Music became very popular both in the UK and in America, where they toured in the 1950s, along with extensive radio work and further touring commitments in Europe and Australia. After his death, the orchestra continued for over thirty years, giving their final concert in December 2000.

Billy Munn (1911-2000)

William Munn was born in Glasgow, and began taking piano lessons aged seven. By the age of eleven he was accompanying children's matinees in a local cinema and by fourteen had joined his first dance band – he was a professional musician before leaving school.

He moved to London in 1928, and after playing in West End clubs and hotels made his first recordings with Jack Roseberry's band. He soon joined Hylton, where he stayed until 1936, playing piano, occasionally accordion and sometimes singing, most notably on *St. Louis Blues*. After five years with Sydney Lipton, he was conscripted, and made aircraft instruments during the war. He later formed his own band, which played at the Orchid Room, Mayfair, at Ciro's Club and at the Casino in Deauville.

In 1949 Munn took a job as bandleader at the Imperial Hotel, Torquay. Intending to stay for a season, he remained there for thirty years, until his retirement. Chapter 6 features a little more on Munn joining the band.

Freddy Schweitzer (1907-1950)

Born in the Saar region of Germany, Freddy began playing the piano from a young age, moving to the saxophone, clarinet (and subsequently almost any instrument for comedy effect) in his teens.

Jack was introduced to Freddy in Berlin, whilst the band was on a continental tour. He had previously built up quite a reputation in Berlin not only as one of the finest saxophonists in the city, but also as a comedy multi-instrumentalist, and these two sides to him would be valuable for his lengthy time with the band. He had led his own band in Germany, and had appeared in the film *Five From The Jazz Band*. His comedy antics were shown to full effect in Hylton's films *She Shall Have Music* and *Band Waggon*.

Freddy joined the band in 1932, and replaced long-standing Hylton associate 'Chappie' d'Amato in 1933. He would remain a main feature of the orchestra, both on tour and on record until it disbanded in 1940. He continued to play and formed his own comedy band, Freddy Schweitzer and His Fun Makers in the 1940s, which toured in the UK. The reformed Royal Variety Performance of Jack

Hylton and his Orchestra would prove to be one of Freddy's last engagements, as he died just a month later, aged forty-three.

Hugo Rignold (1905-1976)

Violinist Hugo Henry Rignold was a vital part of the Hylton Orchestra but would ultimately be remembered as a conductor. He worked not only with Hylton but also with Ambrose, Jack Harris, Lew Stone, Jay Wilbur and Mantovani. After taking charge of a number of recording sessions and rehearsals for the Hylton band, he eventually ran his own band, with Hylton as his mentor. He also sang on many songs that Hylton recorded as part of a three part male vocal chorus, consisting of a combination of Jack Jackson, Billy Ternent, 'Chappie' d'Amato and Hylton.

Whilst serving in the Royal Air Force in 1944, Hugo formed the Cairo Symphony Orchestra and conducted the Palestine Orchestra (which became the Israel Philharmonic Orchestra) and from that point, dance band music was never a part of his professional career. He went on to conduct at the Royal Opera House in Covent Garden, succeeded Malcolm Sargent at the Liverpool Philharmonic Orchestra, became Musical Director of the Royal Ballet, and conducted the City of Birmingham Symphony Orchestra.

Phil Cardew (1903-1960)

Phillip Cardew was a graduate of the Royal Academy of Music, before working as saxophonist and clarinettist with Al Starita's Kit-Cat Club Band in 1926. He worked with another Hylton owned band, the Piccadilly Revels (under Ray Starita) before joining the number one Hylton band until 1931.

He went on to work as an arranger for many top bands, so kept his association with Jack. He also wrote for Jack Payne, Henry Hall, Lew Stone and Roy Fox, whilst later writing for film, television and radio.

Lew Carew (1908-1994)

Leslie Priestley Carew was a trombonist and vocalist, from Shipley, in Yorkshire. His musical career only began when he was seventeen, having previously worked as an apprentice in a local mill.

Moving to London, he worked first with Billy Cotton, then Ray Starita, before becoming Hylton's main trombone man in 1930, where he stayed until 1937.

He then moved to Jack Harris' band and Ambrose's band until he was conscripted into World War II. After the war he joined Ambrose's smaller band, the Octet, as well as working with previous Hylton band mate Chappie d'Amato and Geraldo, with his association with Ambrose lasting well into the 1950s. He continued to freelance for many years, with Mantovani, amongst others. He married John Dankworth's sister Avril.

Paul Fenoulhet (1906-1979)

Trombonist and trumpeter Paul Fenoulhet began his musical life in his early teens when he led a band called the Metro Five, but later worked for bandleaders Arthur Rosebery, Percival Mackey and Carroll Gibbons, as well as Jack Hylton, for whom he also arranged a number of songs.

During the war, he led the famous RAF band, the Skyrockets, and after the war took the band into the London Palladium, where they stayed for many years. In 1947, he formed his own orchestra, which he toured until 1950, before embarking on a twenty-year association as leader of the BBC Variety Orchestra.

Woolf Phillips (1919-2003)

Woolf Phillips was one of the last surviving members of Hylton's orchestra. He was born in London to a musical family, working as a young man for Lawrence Wright's music publishing house. His first arrangement was recorded by Ambrose's band when he was just fourteen; two years later he was playing trombone in the band. After a spell with Joe Loss, he became Hylton's featured trombone soloist, where he struck up a life-long friendship with guest tenor soloist Coleman Hawkins.

He was by now rated as the premier jazz trombonist in Britain. After a time in the RAMC band during the war, he worked as arranger for Geraldo, and then was founder member and arranger for the Ted Heath band. Woolf later led his own band before taking over the Skyrockets from Paul Fenhoulet, and then becoming musical director at the London Palladium. He worked with a staggering array of artists whilst at the Palladium, and subsequently toured the UK with Frank Sinatra, who described him as the finest conductor he had ever worked with.

He would later work extensively on film and television, writing the theme tune to *What's My Line?* and hosting *Goon Shows* for his friend Peter Sellers.

Monia Liter (1906-1988)

Pianist Monia Liter was born in Odessa, where he studied piano and composition at the Imperial School of Music. During the Russian Revolution of 1917, he left for China where he performed with an Italian opera company, and subsequently his own dance band.

Whilst later working in India, he met young singer Al Bowlly, and the pair travelled to England, where Liter eventually settled in 1933. Liter would eventually play for almost all the big name bandleaders, Lew Stone, Nat Gonella, Hylton in 1936 and 1937, Harry Roy, Stanley Black and Victor Silvester.

During the 1940s he toured and recorded with artists such as Larry Adler, Mantovani and Sophie Tucker, recorded Gershwin's *Rhapsody In Blue*, and began writing for film and television.

His composition work began to take precedence over his piano playing, until his death in 1988.

Philippe Brun (1908-1994)

Paris born Philippe Brun studied violin and taught himself to play the trumpet, the instrument for which he would be most closely associated. At the age of sixteen, he led his own small café orchestra, before falling in love with jazz when working with an American band in Biarritz. He would become one of the best-regarded jazz musicians in Paris, working with *Grégor et ses Grégorians*, before moving to London to work first with Ray Starita in 1928, before promotion to the number one Hylton band from 1930 to 1937.

He would later work with Django Reinhardt, Stephane Grappelli and Bert Ambrose. During World War II he fled to Switzerland and went on to have a lengthy career as bandleader and freelance musician.

Melle Weersma (1908-1988)

Arranger, pianist and accordionist Melle Weersma was born in Harlingen in Holland to musical parents, with an organist father and a cellist mother. From 1927 he studied pharmacy, but also worked as an amateur pianist.

He turned professional and toured Germany and Switzerland as arranger and pianist with Eugen Wolff and Gricha Nakchounian, whilst beginning to arrange for a vast number of German films. Hylton employed him in 1935 as pianist and arranger, travelling with Jack to America as chief arranger.

After leaving Hylton, Melle wrote for Benny Goodman, Duke Ellington and Henry Hall before moving to Argentina for a number of years, writing for orchestras and radio programmes. After serving in the American Navy, he returned to South and Central America, before finally returning to his native Holland in 1954, where he continued to write and arrange extensively on record, and for radio.

Chapter 13: 1940-1950

Hylton in his office at Hylton House, with trademark cigar. (Jack Hylton Archive)

There was no transition period for Jack Hylton between his career as a bandleader and his career as a theatrical entrepreneur; indeed the two had crossed for some years. Even as far back as the band's first foray into the variety theatre, Hylton had been in charge of booking the other acts which would play alongside his band, and this simply developed and focuses changed. It is easy to see 1940 as a transition year, but it was simply another year of hard work in the entertainment business. Hylton had, for several years, been producing shows, predominantly ones he had bought from BBC radio and successfully transferred to the stage. By the summer, Jack was hitting the headlines for another financial risk, and one that this time, despite huge success, he would lose out on financially.

Hylton was reading the *News Chronicle* on the train to watch his *Band Waggon* show in Blackpool in early July 1940, when he read a piece by J.B.Priestley stating that the London Philharmonic Orchestra was on the cusp of disbanding due to financial collapse.[1] The orchestra had recently suffered a disastrous opera season in Cardiff (in October 1939) followed by heavy losses with a Bach festival and an Anglo-French festival. Grants and donations were heavily depleted due to the war and the orchestra would shortly be disbanded. Despite having no previous experience with orchestral music, Hylton sensed an opportunity, and knew that his vast variety experience could help.

He watched *Band Waggon*'s successful performance and got on the next train back to London. A mere forty-eight hours later, Jack had secured the services of the orchestra, taken on full financial responsibility and arranged a concert tour of music halls and variety theatres round the country, with Sir Malcolm Sargent and Basil Cameron as conductors, and fellow impresario George Black supplying the venues. The tour would musically be run along the lines of the Queen's Hall Promenade Concerts, playing a constantly varying programme of popular works, with the standard (for variety) twice nightly shows, and a maximum ticket price of 3s 6.d The idea was that their music would be opened up to a much broader audience, who eschewed the opera houses for the music halls. Hylton agreed to pay all seventy members of the orchestra Musicians' Union rates, and after expenses the profits would be shared out amongst the members in the form of bonuses.

Hylton was in such a position financially that he felt he could run the tour and pay himself nothing, whilst also taking the financial hit if things went wrong; an extraordinary gesture. Malcolm Sargent was widely quoted at the time:

Chapter 13: 1940-1950

I think it is one of the most amazing gestures which has
ever been made – and from such an unexpected quarter
too. While various ministries were wondering what to do,
Jack Hylton acted.[2]

The tour began in Harrogate on August 11th, before moving to
Glasgow the following day and beginning a regular pattern of weekly
runs in provincial theatres across the country. Unsurprisingly, they
were a huge success. There was a suggestion that classical music in
music halls would flop, but there was a peculiar defiance in the air
and people felt an urge to retain their culture – despite much of the
music not being British – despite burned out, bombed theatres, lack of
accommodation, the blackout and irregular railway timetables, the
tour was an enormous success.

Simultaneously, Hylton was beginning a long period of producing plays, musicals, pantomimes and variety shows in theatres in
London and putting them on tour, whilst continuing to put together
bands and variety shows for the troops. The sheer number of shows
that Hylton had a hand in literally becomes too many to mention.
Whilst planning the London Philharmonic series, straight play *Dear
Octopus* went into the Adelphi Theatre and *French For Love* (a comedy play that had run for eight months at the Criterion Theatre
starring Alice Delysia and Cecil Parkes) began a UK tour at Brighton
Hippodrome. *Let The Band Play*, a variety show featuring Billy Cot-
ton and his band was also out on tour. As with all these shows, the
'Jack Hylton Presents…' banner took pride of place. *Let The Band
Play* featured Jack's sister Dolly Elsie and snooker world champion
Joe Davies, who toured with a large mirror, which allowed the theatre
audience to see him play. Hot on the heels of *Band Waggon*, Arthur
Askey, Richard 'Stinker' Murdoch and Pat Kirkwood toured with a
new show, *Hello, Playmates*. Joe Davies would also feature in another
BBC radio adaptation, *Garrison Theatre*, which ran for 225 perfor-
mances in 1940. The show also featured former Hylton vocalist June
Marlow:

It was through Jack that actually I married Joe Davis. Of
course, in 1940 I think it was, Jack put on a show *Garrison Theatre* at the London Palladium and Joe was one of
the acts with his billiard table and the mirrors and of

187

course before the show, I was saying to Jack "Who's going to be in it?", and he said, "a speciality act", and he said, "Joe Davis", and I said, "What does he do – wire walk or something?", and Jack was absolutely furious that I hadn't heard of the world snooker champion. Of course, eventually he introduces me to Joe and quite a few years after that, I married him! I can really thank Jack for my marriage![3]

In September, *Swing Is In The Air* was a title that would guarantee success; this was a new variety show with Nat Gonella and his band topping the bill. Another variety show, *Dorchester Follies* was also sent out on tour, under the baton of Maurice Winnick and his Broadcasting Orchestra, along with Georgie Wood (with Dolly Harmer) and Renee Houston (with Donald Stewart). The show would eventually rack up over a thousand performances. Meanwhile *Youth Takes A Bow* had moved from the wireless to the theatres and was doing immense business under the auspices of Bryan Michie. All of this happened in the same year that started with Hylton as a bandleader, with his last concerts and last recordings. In fact, there was so much of 1940 left that Hylton found time to return to America, return to his band leading role, and conduct an American band for twelve broadcasts on the NBC network for the American Forces.

Of course he was developing a strong and talented production team and a slick office set up, but Hylton was a focussed, extremely hard working, astute producer and businessman and would continue to be so for many years. Arthur Askey joked, "that's where Jack lives", while pointing to four phone booths in a hotel lobby:

Talking to him this week for half an hour, Jack was called to the phone five times, and by the time we were through he had given important business decisions to Edinburgh, Birmingham, Liverpool, Leeds and Manchester. Only a few hours earlier he had arrived back from London, having spent some eighteen hours travelling to attend to a couple of hours' business...[4]

He was also thoroughly enjoying his life and made the most of every opportunity afforded to him by his staggering success:

He could manage with the minimum of sleep and expected everyone to work 18 hours a day seven days a week, as he did! His vision as an impresario was as sharp and productive as it had been as a bandleader and he went on working actively until the end of his life. Dapper, silver-haired and cherubic, he spoke so softly that you could hardly hear what he was saying. He revelled in his hectic existence with fast cars and private planes.[5]

He was very short tempered...but he was strangely patient, he was outstandingly generous, he had a wild sense of humour, he was quick to rise to temper and quick to fall away. If there was ridiculousness in his argument, he would see it. He basically wanted to enjoy himself, I think. I've never seen anybody who wanted to enjoy themselves as much and I've certainly never seen anybody who succeeded to quite such a degree.[6]

1941 would begin much as the previous year had ended, with a gradual takeover of London's West End. London by now was being heavily bombed, theatres were closing, often at a moment's notice, yet Hylton seemed to flourish. Shows would be moved to different venues if air raids occurred, problems arose with resources for set building and painting, and costumes, so solutions had to be found to these problems – shows would be based around whichever costumes were available and sets would be painted over previous paintwork, depending on what was required.

More radio shows were bought and put on tour: *How's About It* was a variety vehicle for singer Adelaide Hall, which opened in Oxford before going on tour, *Carlisle Express*, a radio show starring Elsie Carlisle was toured with Eddie Gray, and *Piccadixie*, again starring Adelaide Hall also toured, also featuring former Hylton band singer Primrose and radio personality George Elrick.

Lady Behave, which opened at His Majesty's Theatre, would become a long running success for Hylton. It opened on July 24th and starred *Band Waggon* regular Pat Kirkwood, alongside Stanley Lupino (who was replaced by long time Hylton associate Bobby Howes) and Sally Grey. It eventually closed on April 25th 1942, after 401 performances, after which it was taken on a very successful UK tour. The original conductor for the show was Anglo-Italian conductor and entertainer Mantovani, who would go on to sell millions of records in his string-laden idiosyncratic style. During the war, 'Monty' was struggling to find sufficient touring opportunities, so jumped at the chance of regular work and a job close to his family. Freddie Bretherton (who scored the show, along with Billy Ternent and Phil Cardew) took most of the rehearsals and some were surprised that Monty had been given the baton.

An initial try-out at Manchester's Palace Theatre was well received and reviews for Monty and the band were favourable. In spite of this, there seemed to be a conflict with Hylton, who appeared to prefer Bretherton in the role. In his Mantovani biography, author Colin MacKenzie suggests that 'people power' defeated Hylton and his plans were quashed. This seems most un-Hylton-like – there are few if any other examples of a band standing up to Hylton and him not having his way.

In due course Hylton got his way of course. Sackings ensued over the subsequent months and Mantovani finally left the show in early November, to be replaced by George Windeatt. Bretherton by now had moved on to other projects. The official reason for him leaving was never made public and Mantovani subsequently commented, "it came off extremely well." (Mantovani would have another brush with Hylton in 1951, when he briefly conducted the Crazy Gang show *Knights Of Madness*. He left three weeks later by mutual consent, the consensus being that the Crazy Gang was perhaps a little *too* crazy!)

Peter Pan appeared again in the West End – Hylton's first revival of this popular pantomime was as early as 1936, which was repeated for two years. This production would be repeated for another five seasons. In Christmas of 1941 'Jack Hylton Presents...' appeared at the top of the bill of five shows in the West End and countless others on tour.

*   *   *

In 1941, the Hylton's seaside home in Kingston Gorse, outside Angmering in Sussex, was requisitioned by the government due to its south coastal aspect and its sheer size. Of course Hylton, Fifi, Jackie and Georgie still lived in their flat at 36 Cumberland Mansions in central London, and Jack also owned the bungalow at 28 Gilbert Street where Ennis may have lived at some point. The building next-door in Gilbert Street was bombed and Hylton's house was badly damaged.

The family moved from Angmering to Milton Common, a small village eight miles outside Oxford into the grand seven bedroom Langsmeade House, with its ten acres of gardens. The house, built in the late 1920s was bought from motorcycle salesman and self-made millionaire Stan Hailswood, who was notable for being the father of world champion motorcycle ace Mike Hailwood, who was born in Langsmeade house in 1940, a couple of years before the Hyltons moved in.

Jack had begun to use the New Theatre in Oxford as the try out venue for almost all of his shows, so a home near there made sense, especially when he used some of the land close to the house to build a large rectangular barn, which was used as a props store, which doubled up as a music rehearsal room. Very nearby, next to the newly built props store on the estate was Langsmeade Cottage, a two bedroom building much less grand than the house, which for several years Arthur Askey lived in. Soon after his arrival at Langsmeade, Jack put on an all-star concert at the New Theatre to raise funds for redevelopment. Jack also engaged in local life by joining the Oxfordshire Farmers Union!

Jack would eventually have the Gilbert Street bungalow refitted and the family used the London home as a base, with Langsmeade House as a weekend residence. Petrol rationing was in place during the war, and the house became a useful halfway house between London and Bristol, where the bands were still regularly recording. Cars would travel to Oxford, and a different set of cars would carry people on to Bristol.

Inevitably, the house also became something of a party hotspot for those working on Hylton's shows in Oxford or London, and those making passage between London and Bristol. Rose Ilbury was a young maid in the house during the Hailswood years and the Hylton years. She remembered vividly the scene at the time:

Life was merry in Langsmeade House in those years. No upper crust atmosphere, but more the looseness of the jet set. Many famous people from the London theatrical scene came to stay. I frequently had to recover from shock when I found people in bed together who were meant to sleep in separate rooms. I clearly remember how amazed I was when I brought tea in the morning to a sleeping can-can dancer, who had pegs on her fingers to keep her red lacquered nails in the right shape. I left Hylton's employment before the end of the war because I became enlisted to work in the airplane factory in Cowley as part of the war effort scheme for women. I know that Jack Hylton sold the house to Brigadier Brett [a local councilor].[7]

Jackie, Jack, Georgie and Fifi at home in Angmering. (Jack Hylton Archive)

The house became surplus to requirements in 1946 and the properties were sold on to Rupert and Olive Brett in March of '46. The house and the cottage deeds were split in the 1970s and Langsmeade House became a Bed & Breakfast in 1988, and in 2014 the props stores were being demolished in order to facilitate extensions and repairs to the nearby Langsmeade Cottage. The original oak panelling is retained, as are many period features from Hylton's time.

Chapter 13: 1940-1950

Jack retained ownership of the Villa Daheim in Kingston Gorse (of which much less is known, as the property has since changed name) and after Jack's death, and after Gilbert Street was sold, Fifi moved back there. After the requisition order had been removed, various people, including Fifi's parents, had lived there.

*   *   *

In 1942, more shows went out on tour. The plays *Grand Manner*, starring Dame Irene Vanburgh and Alfred Drayton, *The House Of Jeffreys*, starring Dame Sybil Thorndike, *Flare Path*, and political war play *It Happened In September*, starring Eva Moore, Anne Frith, Joan Kemp-Welch, Gordon McLeod, Harry Hilliard and Lyonel Watts.

Variety shows appeared also; Flanagan & Allen opened in Oxford before heading out on tour, as did *Glamourflage*, starring impressionist Florence Desmond and Claude Hulbert.

Piccadilly Playtime, featured Jack Warner, Jerry Hoey's band, Clifford & Marion and Bryan Michie presenting the best of *Youth Takes A Bow*; *Mesdames et Monsewers* featured Eddie Gray, Elsie Carlisle, comedian Hal Monty, comedians George & Jack d'Ormonde and burlesque artists The Three Renowns; Ivy Benson was put on tour. By now, 'Jack Hylton Presents...' was a mark of quality and was almost a guarantee of success.

On March 5th 1942, Jack Hylton appeared on fledgling radio show *Desert Island Discs*. He was just the sixth person to appear on the show, with the previous weeks including singer Pat Kirkwood and theatrical impresario C.B. Cochran. Hylton chose a varied programme, including a number of his own songs:

1. *Tchaikovsky Symphony No. 5 in E minor* (performed by the London Philharmonic Orchestra, conducted by Thomas Beecham)
2. Jack Hylton and His Orchestra – *Rhymes* (Zonophone 5997)
3. Jack Hylton and His Orchestra – *I Kiss Your Hand Madam* (HMV B-5602)
4. Reginald Gardiner – *Trains*
5. The Royal Air Force Squadronaires – *Sand In My*

Shoes
6. Jack Hylton and His Orchestra – *Grinzing* (HMV C-2856)
7. Jack Hylton and His Orchestra – *Cavalcade Of Popular Songs* (Decca K-619)
8. *Rachmaninov Piano Concerto No.2 in C Minor* - performed by Rachmaninov

Sadly, these early shows went out live and were never recorded, so we don't know Jack's motivation for choosing these particular numbers, but certainly his own band choices represent his biggest sellers and some that we know to be his favourites.

At the end of 1942, Hylton scored another big hit, with his revival of Franz Lehar's *The Merry Widow*. This operetta, based on a play from 1861 about a rich widow and the attempts of her countrymen to keep her money in the country by finding her a new husband, enjoyed extraordinary international success from its 1905 premiere in Vienna, through to its English language version which opened in London in 1907 and ran for 778 performances. (There were subsequent successful runs in 1923, 1924 and 1935).

Hylton's lavish production opened in Manchester in December, and starred Madge Elliott (as the merry widow herself), Cyril Richard (as Prince Danilo) and George Graves (as Baron Popoff), who not only played the role in the Hippodrome revival in 1932, but played the part in the original London production in 1907. He was by now in his late sixties. After its run in Manchester, the show toured, culminating in a two week run at the New Theatre in Oxford, after which it transferred to His Majesty's Theatre on 4th March 1943, where it would run for 322 performances. The show closed on October 23rd, and after another three weeks in Oxford it went on a three-work tour for ENSA, to Egypt and Italy.

Also in 1943, Hylton was spreading his cultural wings and producing many kinds of theatre. In January and February he brought over the German Carl Rosa Opera Company for a season of La Traviata. Although the company had toured often in the UK during the 1920s and 1930s it had been some years since they had visited and this was the first wartime visit. Hylton also put Jan Cobel's Anglo-Polish Ballet Company on tour during April.

Noel Gay's *The Love Racket*, a musical play starring Arthur Askey, opened on October 26th at the Victoria Palace and ran for 324 performances before a UK tour, with an orchestra under the baton of Hylton alumnus Freddie Bretherton. It would eventually find its way to Australia, still with Askey in the lead role. Revue show *Hi-De-Hi*, featuring Flanagan & Allen opened at the Palace Theatre after an opening in Oxford; it would run for 340 performances. The show was such a big hit that Flanagan & Allen would split £1,200 per week.

In August, Jack Hylton was in court, being sentenced to fourteen days in prison for fuel misuse. It was reported that a van had been used to convey actors and actresses and occasionally Hylton from London theatres to various addresses, including the Savoy Hotel, the Ambassadors Club and restaurants. The fuel in question had been allowed for the use of the van only in connection with Langsmeade House in Milton Common, and its grounds. The defence lawyer argued that the van was only being used whilst Hylton's two cars were under repair. (Permission to use the van in the way alleged would probably have been granted if application had been made.) In due course, despite pleading guilty, Hylton won the appeal against the prison sentence and he paid costs and fines totalling £175.

This was not the first or last time driving had cost Jack and he clearly enjoyed driving his beloved Mercedes cars at speed. In 1937, he was fined £10 for dangerous driving. In April 1941, he was fined £2 for speeding. In June 1942, he was fined twice in two days for speeding, £3 each time and just a month later was banned from driving for three months and fined £10, for his fourth conviction in just over twelve months. In January 1944 he was banned for six months for yet another speeding conviction and fined another £10, and incurred yet another fine in March 1947. In 1951 he crashed his car on Marylebone Road, causing head injuries to the other driver and narrowly avoiding more court action (though he was uninjured) and in June 1955 received yet another fine for driving between 40mph and 50mph in a 30mph zone in Barnes.

Each year he would buy a new Mercedes car from the Motor Show in London (spending £12,000 on two brand new models in 1962), and he risked the wrath of many during the war years for consistently buying a German car. Often one of his cars would be in the garage having damage repaired following a misguided attempt to dissuade him from using such a vehicle.

On the subject of cars, a story often told of a Rolls Royce surely happened in one of Jack's Mercedes. Both Jack and fellow theatrical impresario Val Parnell loved gadgets and always wanted to have the latest thing, so Parnell was furious to find out that Hylton had one of the first in-car telephones installed in his car. Parnell straight away had his car fitted with the same new toy, and called Jack's carphone. Nicky, Jack's chauffeur answered and advised Jack that Val was on the phone. "Tell him I'm on the other line", was Jack's speedy and sharp reply!

By 1944, Jack's twelve-year-old daughter Jackie had caught the horseracing bug from her father. Jack appeared to own three horses at this point, though he would buy and sell often – Wings Of Song, Gold Enamel and Fieldfare were running for him and he added to that when he bought Smoky for his daughter, making her the youngest racehorse owner in the country. From then to the present day, Jackie would dedicate her life to racehorses.

In 1944, Jack would bring *The Merry Widow* back to London, where it opened at the Stoll Theatre on June 26th, followed by a summer tour of the provinces, before landing back in London at the Coliseum in September. Theatre audiences were rather variable by now, as the regular bombings in central London made theatre trips somewhat risky, but Hylton continued to present shows and continued to make money.

Slightly different in tone to *The Merry Widow* were *Merrily Yours*, a variety show starring Eddie Gray and *By And Large*, another variety show, both of which toured through the autumn, as well as a variety show put together for twice nightly performances at the Pavilion in Leamington Spa.

A major revival of *The Lilac Domino* began life with a six week run in Manchester, where it took £34,000. The show first appeared in London in 1918 (adapted from it's German original version *Der Lila Domino*) where it ran for 747 performances. Hylton's version starred former Jack Harris singer Pat Taylor, with whom he would later have an affair.

Chapter 13: 1940-1950

At the end of 1944 Jack played a small part in a rather tragic event, the death of American bandleader Glenn Miller; but two months previously, Miller had persuaded Jack to pick up the baton once more. On October 12th, the American Band Of The AEF, which Glenn Miller had conducted since he disbanded his regular orchestra to join the war effort, were performing a radio broadcast from the Queensbury All Services Club in London, for the American Forces. It was a rare foray back into radio and a much rarer appearance as bandleader. Glenn introduced Jack live:

> **Miller**: "Tonight our British guest star is a man who is as famous back home in the big forty-eight as he is over here. He used to be the leader of an orchestra, a mighty swell one too. A few years ago he decided to sort of go straight. At that time he embarked on a career that made him what he is today: London and I dare say Britain's greatest theatrical producer and impresario. Ladies and gentlemen, Hylton's back. Here's Jack Hylton."

> **Hylton**: "Thank you, Glenn, for those kind words and even more for the invitation to join you on this programme."

> **Miller**: "Well, there's no thanks necessary, Jack. As a matter of fact, we invited you here to sort of put you to work."

> **Hylton**: "Sounds bad."

> **Miller**: "Sounds good! There's not a guy in the band or a Yank in the audience who doesn't remember and admire the records you've made and sent to our nation."

> **Hylton**: "Well, what's that got to do with putting me to work?"

> **Miller**: "Well, just this, Jack. We dug up an arrangement that sold a heap of records over on our side of the Atlantic and tonight we want you to conduct the American Band of the AEF playing that same arrangement."

Hylton: "You might find me rusty or a bit dusty, you know."

Miller: "Well, we'll take that chance. The band's all yours, the pleasure's all ours, and the tune, *She Shall Have Music*."

The band then played Hylton's concert arrangement of the song, which had never been recorded. During the rehearsal the musicians of the AEF Band spotted the fact that Jack conducted the band with a drumstick and as a spontaneous gesture Glenn Miller and the band purchased a baton previously used by many famous conductors at the Covent Garden Opera House. The baton was presented to Jack by Glenn, which attracted wild applause from the audience.

During Miller's time in the UK, he often would spend time with Jack and many of the musicians employed in Hylton shows would relax together with Miller's musicians post-show. On the evening of December 14th, Jack was with Glenn. Jack recalled the event on the twentieth anniversary of Miller's disappearance:

It was a quiet night for London. Piccadilly was almost deserted. The Germans had oddly laid off for a while with their V-1's. I'd been having a little late party at my flat, and Glenn was one of the boys – mostly musicians – who'd dropped by." Miller…was the last man to leave the party. Hylton continued: "I walked outside the flat with him. He looked up in the cold night sky, and said "Well, Jack, it'll soon be over now." I'm sure he was referring to the war.[8]

Glenn Miller flew to Paris the following day, and was never seen again, his plane's engine icing up in the terrible weather and plunging into the English Channel. The plane was never recovered.

In 1945 theatrical matters continued at their usual pace for Jack Hylton. The first suggestions of future work with the Crazy Gang began to appear – Jack had hired ex-Crazy Gang members Nervo & Knox to appear in *Babes In The Wood* for the Christmas season, whilst concurrently employing Flanagan & Allen in a variety show at the Victoria Palace and working on a number of shows over the previous few years with 'Monsewer' Eddie Gray. The whole team would soon be working together, but their paths had unsurprisingly crossed many times before; two such occasions spring to mind from when Hylton was still leading a band. Before the war, the band was working with Flanagan & Allen, and they were all to attend a special supper party after the show, for which Jack would be wearing a brand new, tailored suit. He changed after the show and was horrified to find that his trousers were six inches shorter than they should have been.

"I can't understand it", he said. "I had three fittings too!"

Bud Flanagan replied, "you shouldn't have hung it on the wall. It's damp, and now your suit's shrunk."

Jack attended the party feeling very self-conscious and it wasn't until after he arrived home that he found out that the pair had taken his suit to one of the wardrobe mistresses and forced her to shorten the trousers by six inches! Hylton got his own back by padlocking the buttons of Bud Flanagan's new suit together and throwing away the key! Hylton's own words describe the other, rather elaborate practical joke:

> Some years before the war I was conducting my band on the stage at the Palace Theatre in Manchester, when the show was suddenly invaded by Eddie Gray and Nervo and Knox. They crashed the stage door, scrambled on to the stage and started doing their crazy stuff all around me! "What the dickens are you chaps doing here?" I asked. The three comedians looked at one another with an air of feigned perplexity. "Isn't this the Hippodrome?" they asked, trying to look simple.

> The next night I retaliated. I marched the entire band across the street playing *Colonel Bogey*. We charged through the stage door of the Hippodrome and filed round the stage, making as much noise as we could, while Eddie Gray, Jimmy Nervo and Teddy Knox tried in vain to make themselves heard."[9]

Amidst the variety shows, Hylton was again staging *The Merry Widow*, on a bigger tour than ever, which began in February 1945 and would run well into the summer of 1946. Meanwhile, he also brought the operetta *Can Can* to the Manchester Opera House over Christmas in '45, before sending it to the Adelphi Theatre in London, where it starred Margaret Davison, Charles Dorning, Elizabeth French and Clifford Mollison. The Manchester leg starred Pat Taylor. This curious piece had a book written by novelist Max Catto, with the numbers using music by Jacques Offenbach. Whilst the run in Manchester and subsequent short tour went well, the show flopped at the Adelphi, running for just thirty-two performances.

Another show that opened successfully in Manchester was *Follow The Girls*, another Arthur Askey vehicle, which opened on August 22nd, also starring Evelyn Dall, David Dale, Wendy Toye and Bruce Carfax. It would transfer to His Majesty's and eventually clock up 572 performances in a two-year run. Notably, Hylton's old writing partner Con West was one of the major contributors. This show had been one of Broadway's most popular attractions, opening on April 8th 1944 and running for 882 performances. Jackie Gleason played Goofy, and the show made a star out of Gertrude Niesen in the role of Bubbles. The plot was merely an excuse to string together a series of dance routines and comic specialities. In London there was great praise for Arthur Askey's non-stop energetic clowning, for Evelyn Dall, and for a show-stopping dance speciality by Wendy Toye.

Meanwhile at His Majesty's, Jack was reviving the Harry Tierney and Joseph McCarthy musical *Irene*. It had run successfully both in London and on Broadway in 1920, and this production, starring Pat Taylor and Frank Leighton would notch up 158 performances. It is notable for including the standard *Alice Blue Gown*.

World War II was finally over and with it the rebuilding programme began in London. Many of the theatres had somehow avoided bombing, and Hylton would simply continue in the same fashion as he had throughout the war, though travel through Europe would become easier and audiences would become more reliable. Rationing was still in place and Hylton's wardrobe department would continue to struggle for several more years, being as inventive as possible with the restricted resources available to them. Clothing coupons were issued but numbers were not generous:

> My wardrobe mistress recently found herself rummaging among a pile of odds and ends in a little draper's shop in the East End for an article which, before the war, she

could have got simply by ringing up any big store or deal-
er...Nowadays we achieve an equally good effect with
much more limited means. We concentrate, for example,
on coupon-free materials like lace and net.[10]

In 1946 *The Merry Widow* would again be sent out on tour. This
perennial classic, from its first Hylton revival in 1942, would clock up
over 2,000 performances, two West End runs, three provincial tours
(1942, 1945 and 1946) and two ENSA trips (to the continent and the
Middle East). Before the end of the year, Hylton also had, amongst
many others, *Romany Love* running in Manchester, before a short run
at His Majesty's the following year, *Duet For Two Hands*, starring
Mary Morris at the Lyric Theatre, and the usual collection of pantomimes, including *Peter Pan* (starring Alastair Sim as Captain Hook)
and *Little Red Riding Hood* at the Adelphi, starring Nervo & Knox,
Noele Gordon and Janet Brown. With pantomimes at that time opening on Boxing Day, Hylton's Christmas Day meal would often consist
of a sandwich and a cup of coffee whilst sitting in the wings fixing the
latest issue on stage before opening the following night.

Gypsy Lady, written by Robert Wright and his collaborator
George "Chet" Forrest, was based on songs by Victor Herbert (com-
bining elements from *The Fortune Teller* and *The Serenade*). The
show closed after just seventy-nine performances on Broadway.
Hylton bought it, brought it to London, changed the name to *Romany
Love*, but despite favourable reviews and having Maurice Chevalier as
the leading man, a perplexed Hylton lost £21,000.

*   *   *

1946 was also notable for beginning a seven-year working relationship with Italian opera singer, Beniamino Gigli. Gigli (1890-
1957) was the most famous tenor of his generation and widely regarded as one of the finest opera singers in the history of recorded music.
He rose to fame in his mid-20s, after the death of another fine Italian
tenor, Enrico Caruso. He was famed for his roles in Boito's
Mefistofele, Donizetti's *Lucia di Lammermoor* and Puccini's *La
Bohème*. He shared Hylton's love of life and of women and they
would spend evenings together when Gigli was on tour. Jack was also

a great admirer of his voice and when Gigli began to move from the opera house to the concert stage, Hylton saw an opportunity to involve himself. Gigli had previously been to London in 1939 in *La Bohème* at Covent Garden, but his first UK concert tour was under the 'Jack Hylton Presents...' banner, in conjunction with Gigli's personal manager, impresario Harold Fielding, and ran for six weeks, beginning on November 13th 1946, in Glasgow.

The tour was a runaway success, with queues for advance bookings, sell-out shows and rave reviews. Gigli was earning between £1,100 and £1,300 per show.

The following year, Hylton and Fielding inevitably had Gigli back, this time with a tour starting on November 16th in Newcastle, taking in twenty towns and netting Beniamino up to £1,500 per show. Despite a bout of flu and a late start to the tour, it remained a huge draw.

A planned return in 1950 was severely affected by a throat infection, with nineteen of twenty dates cancelled, but in 1952 a 62-year-old Gigli toured the UK from February 25th until May 2nd, earning £1,000 per show. A ten date return a year later would include a £1,500 show at the Royal Albert Hall and a rescheduled date in Manchester which moved the show from the Free Trade Hall to a 5,000 capacity (sell-out) Belle Vue outdoor stadium.

During these visits, Hylton and Gigli would often be seen together at the Albany Club, late into the night but their friendship had turned sour by 1954 when Gigli announced that he was being represented by Hungarian agent Sandor Gorlinsky. Both sets of agents had announced shows and were selling tickets, and legal action ensued. Gigli would complete his 1954 tour without Hylton and he retired in 1955 after an exhaustive farewell world tour.

*   *   *

As well as the usual string of new shows in 1947,[11] including *High Tide* (a revue starring Arthur Askey, Florence Desmond and Eddie Gray which began life in Manchester before a move to London) and *Anna Lucasta* at His Majesty's (a Philip Yordan play based on Eugene O'Neil's *Anna Christie*) there would be two landmark productions.

The first would be another philanthropic excursion into classical music for the masses. Hylton inaugurated the Haringey Festival, which ran from June 7th to July 6th. Haringey Arena, in North London, was built in 1936 primarily as an ice hockey venue but soon also became a famous boxing venue. It seated 10,000 and nothing remotely approaching classical music had ever been staged there. In his wisdom, Jack decided that something along the lines of his 1939 tour of the London Philharmonic should take place – regular popular concerts with cheap tickets – tickets for the festival ranged from 1s 6d to 10s. He put together a wide-ranging programme featuring the Royal Philharmonic Orchestra, the Liverpool Philharmonic Orchestra, the London Symphony Orchestra and the French National Orchestra, using the services of conductors Sir Thomas Beecham, Dr Malcolm Sargent, Stanford Robinson, Otto Klemperer, Andre Kostelanetz and Manuel Rosenthal.

The whole event was audacious. At the early shows, 80% of the arena was empty and people complained of noise coming from the nearby railway sidings. Unperturbed, Hylton put up sound baffling curtains and arranged with LNER to not shunt trains during the performances. Word of mouth improved matters; by the second week audiences were regularly 5,000 and by the last show well over 9,000 people attended. Hylton said he had "very nearly broken even" and planned a repeat of the festival for the following year.

The second landmark production of 1947 would be Hylton's reformation of the Crazy Gang, which he did in April with a show simply titled *Together Again*. Former Crazy Gang member Bud Flanagan had the initial idea:

> I thought we ought to come out of retirement. So I went to Jack. All he said was: "Come and have lunch". And that was the start of seventeen years at the Victoria Palace. We never had a contract. Jack's word was always good enough.[12]

That first show would run at the Victoria Palace for a staggering 1,566 performances and the Crazy Gang would inhabit the Palace almost non-stop for almost two decades. (Incidentally, the show would feature a Bud Flanagan song that went on to become a classic. Hubert Gregg's *Maybe It's Because I'm a Londoner* was written as a morale booster in World War II, but did not see the light of day until February 1947. Jack Hylton asked Gregg if he had any songs suitable for Flanagan. At first Gregg failed to find anything suitable, but then he remembered the simple little tune he had composed a few years earlier. The song was accepted and used by Bud, who went on to make the song his own during the show's four-year run. The song later earned Hubert Gregg the Freedom of the City of London.)

Producer George Black had put together a show called *Crazy Week* in 1931 at the London Palladium and hired three double acts – Jimmy Nervo and Teddy Knox, Charlie Naughton and Jimmy Gold, and Billy Caryll and Hilda Mundy. Other *Crazy Week*'s followed, with the addition of Bud Flanagan and Chesney Allen. Each of these double acts were already established, but enjoyed greater success together than they had apart. The first show was booked for two weeks and ran for eight months. By 1932 the *Crazy Week* had become *Crazy Month*, which ran for fourteen months, and the group were a regular feature at the Palladium until the outbreak of war.

By 1937, the group was established and the Crazy Gang name was being used, with Caryll & Mundy having been dropped and Nervo & Knox's old comedy sidekick 'Monsewer' Eddie Gray being added to make a seven-piece line up. After making several films (and starring with Hylton and his band in *Life Begins At Oxford Circus*) the members split back into their constituent double acts working extensively for ENSA during the war.

Their run of shows under the 'Jack Hylton Presents…' banner at the Victoria Palace was an unprecedented success and made all involved wealthy. Indeed the money generated by the show gave Hylton scope to explore almost any show he wished, whether it was likely to make money or not. The gang were into their fifties when *Together Again* began but full of life they would perform twice nightly for many years, always to packed houses and all would remain very close friends with Hylton and all sides of his family, long after Jack died.

*   *   *

Pat Taylor (born Emily Maud Pope) had been involved with Jack for some years by now. She initially was suggested as a singer for *Band Waggon*, but her then boss, Jack Harris would not allow her to leave. She became a West End star in 1938 in the revue *Happy Returns*, following that with roles in *Let's Pretend, Shephard's Pie* and *Fine And Dandy*, as well as playing Julie in *Show Boat*. Hylton hired her first for *Lilac Domino*, then *Can Can*, and they began an affair.

Magazine cover star Pat Taylor, June 1944. (Jack Hylton Archive)

At the age of twelve Pat Taylor (or Pat Pope, as she was then) was performing with Beam's Breezy Babes, in pantomime and touring revue and by fourteen was performing with The Eight Step Sisters. She performed as a singer with John Watt's BBC series *Songs From The Shows*, before working in a double act with Hylton vocalist Sam Browne; all this by the age of seventeen. Whilst returning from a concert with Browne she was involved in a serious car crash, which killed one girl and left Pat with a double fracture of the pelvis. This major set back left her in plaster for several months. She eventually returned to work and despite suffering from synovitis in both knees, accepted an offer from bandleader Jack Harris to sing with his band at the London Casino. This led to a number of recordings and broadcasts during her four-year stint with Harris, followed by the shows mentioned above.

But Pat Taylor would not end up as just another Hylton girl-friend, as she bore him his only son, John (known as Johnnie and more recently as Jack Junior) on June 10th 1947. Their relationship floundered in the years following John's birth and understandably there was animosity between the two camps, with the loyalties of the children staying with their respective mothers. John is now married to his second wife Joyce and has two children, Catrina Lee (born 1968, from his first marriage) and Ianthe (born 1985). John lived and went to school in London and saw his father a great deal in the school holidays. In his final years they spent a great deal of time together, with Jack nurturing his son into the business that they both loved. John would eventually work as Assistant Stage Manager for his father:

> For a pittance! Lousy wages – I was the lowest paid person in the company and life was made as difficult as it possibly could be for me, because that way if I stayed in it, it was because I wanted to, not because it was the easy option. I didn't find that out until after he'd died – just as well because I'd have killed him if I'd known![13]

He would go on to work in theatrical production for many years. Pat Taylor had no more children and her career floundered somewhat in the years she was bringing up her son. They lived together in The Cottage in St. John's Wood, behind North Gate and Hylton made sure his son was looked after financially. Her relationship with Jack was sporadic for a few years, but Pat struggled to get over it and never married. When John was in his early teens she decided to try and get back into performing. She auditioned for Noël Coward's *Sail Away*, and despite having been friends with Noël, by now Pat was drinking heavily and she failed to get a part. That marked the end of her career and a slow descent into alcoholism.

Chapter 13: 1940-1950

Her son moved out of their home in the mid 1960s when their relationship began to break down. She died whilst he was working in Australia in the 1980s.

*   *   *

As the 1,000[th] performance of *Together Again* was taking place in 1948, Jack Hylton was again investing in classical music, with the second Haringey Festival, which ran from June 6th to July 4th, in just the same fashion as the previous year. Attendances were up. The first concert saw 9,000 people attend and by the final concert in July, 155,980 people had attended and the festival took £9,175 per show. Performers included American soprano Lily Pons, Australian pianist Eileen Joyce, Norwegian opera singer Kirsten Flagstad and to great acclaim the ten year old Italian conductor Piero Gamba. The boy from Rome not only received the acclaim of his peers, but 10,000 people attended his concert – a sell out at the arena. He would go on to have a career conducting the Winnipeg Symphony Orchestra, and the Adelaide Symphony Orchestra, before pursuing a teaching career in New York. (The following year, Hylton would pursue the idea of making a film about Gamba, though the idea eventually proved fruitless).

Also in 1948, Hylton took the musical *High Button Shoes* from Broadway to the West End. This comic story about the Longstreet family and their dealings with a pair of con men featured songs from musical heavyweights Julie Styne and Sammy Cahn in their first Broadway hit. The London production, which ran at the Hippodrome for 291 performances, was notable for two of the chorus girls, Alma Cogan and Audrey Hepburn, who Hylton himself chose from 4,000 hopefuls:

> Next Audrey became a chorus girl in *High Button Shoes*, a musical comedy by Julie Styne. She knew absolutely nothing about musical comedy; she had never learned modern jazz and her audition seemed to her so disastrous that she went home in tears, certain she had made a fool of herself. It's true Audrey was not hired for her talents. "She's no good as a dancer but she's got lots of verve", noted the co-producer Jack Hylton about her audition. It

was her personality and her grace that charmed the selectors – she was hired.[14]

Whilst setting up *High Button Shoes*, Hylton was also setting up the operetta *Chocolate Soldier* (a revival of a show originally staged in London in 1910, written by Oscar Straus and based on a George Bernard Shaw play, *Arms And The Man*). Jack had also set up an autumn season for French singer and actor Maurice Chevalier, with whom he had first worked in 1930, when Hylton had recorded a lengthy Chevalier medley, spread over four sides (HMV B-3686 and HMV K-3065). Whilst Chevalier had visited the UK before, this was his first solo West End run – *An Evening Of Songs And Impressions*, with Fred Freed at the piano (who was the composer of many of Chevalier's songs), which ran for six weeks at the Hippodrome. They would return the following autumn for a UK tour.

Another musical, *Burlesque* would open in 1948. This began life as a straight play, originally staged in London at the Queen's in 1928 with Nelson Keys and Claire Luce. Because of its back-stage settings it seemed an ideal subject for a musical. After five weeks at the Prince's Theatre it transferred to the Garrick – playing twice-nightly – and with Annabella Ross replacing Zoe Gail as Maizie. It ran another three and a half weeks and then went on tour.

Less successful would be *Calypso*, a musical by Ronnie Hill and Hedley Briggs, which was an odd mixture of comedy, revue, ballet, negro spirituals and West Indian music, with very little dialogue and a lot of song and dance, performed by a cast that was half West Indian and half British. The run at the Playhouse Theatre in May lasted just thirty-two performances.

No matter; the following year, *High Button Shoes* would begin an extensive and lucrative UK tour, beginning of course, at Oxford's New Theatre, starring Sid James. Along with the Gigli tour and the Chevalier tour, and a tour for the Stanley Black Orchestra, business continued to boom for Jack Hylton Ltd. and his other company Musical Plays Ltd. In fact Hylton's business dealings were becoming rather complex, as each new show would have its own company formed, leaving the Hylton office running hundreds of companies. This he managed with a punishing schedule, choosing to be in his office from 9.00am until 9.00pm, after which the current crop of shows would be visited, sleeping at most five hours per night "but very solid". The post-show hours would be spent wining and dining stars of the shows, visiting entertainers and whichever theatre beauty was his current girlfriend, although 'wining and dining' was often with a nod to his roots – "get me some potato pie and a bit of red cabbage", he was said to have demanded on entry to an exclusive London club. He worked hard not because empires would fall otherwise, but because he enjoyed keeping on with the business.

Of course the shows mentioned in these pages are a mere snapshot of the workload taken on by Hylton and his team. Up to 1950 there was also *Dear Octopus* at the Adelphi (which he now owned), *Bless The Bride* at the Adelphi, *Follow The Girls* on tour, *The Gorbals Story* (a dour play about working class Glaswegians which he brought from Glasgow with the original cast), *Starched Aprons*, *Rocket To The Moon*, *This Walking Shadow*, *Take It From Here* (a variety show at the Victoria Palace), *Ann Veronica* (which lost Hylton £22,000), *Parade Sur Grace* (music hall from Paris) and *Take It From Us* (a revue at the Adelphi); the list goes on and all of this before 1950 was over.

*   *   *

Hylton acquired the lease for the Adelphi Theatre in 1943, which he kept until his death, and his estate would retain it until 1984. The archive currently stored at Lancaster University was stored in the leaking roof space at the Adelphi for many years until its move to Lancaster in the same year.

The theatre was built in 1806, as the Sans Pareil ('without equal'), founded by John Scott. It was renamed the Adelphi in 1819, and rebuilt in 1858, built by J. Wilson to the designs of T.H. Wyatt. More renovations happened in 1879 and 1887, before another rebuild, with the third Adelphi opening in 1901, after a complete demolition of the previous building, this one built by Frank Kirk to the designs of Ernest Runtz. Yet another rebuild came just thirty years later, with the fourth and current Adelphi Theatre opening in December 1930, built by Pitcher Construction Company to the designs of Ernest Schaufelberg. Just twenty years later, having produced a number of shows there, Hylton took over. In 1955, Woolworths bought the block on The Strand where the Adelphi stands and for a time it looked as though the theatre may close, but London County Council fortunately refused the planning application. Another plan was submitted and approved in 1961, this time with a new theatre, but this never material-materialised. In 1984 the lease of the theatre was taken over by the famous American Nederlander Organisation, one of the largest theatre owning companies in the USA. In 1992 the Nederlander Organisation shared the ownership with Andrew Lloyd Webber's Really Useful Group and a year later an extensive refurbishment programme began to bring back the art deco glory of this 1930 theatre (prior to Lloyd Webber's *Sunset Boulevard*).

*   *   *

By now Hylton was well known both publicly and privately for his love of work, money and women, coupled with his quiet, fastidious, ruthless approach to business and his unerring but very private generosity:

> Of all the great ones on this earth Hylton, perhaps is the most unchanged. He is short, thick set, his hair whitening noticeably now. He talks with the same Bolton accent, which he has never tried to disguise. His voice is the same, soft, husky drawl. None of the attributes permissible to great showmen are noticeable in the Hylton make-up. No pompous strutting or braggadocio. He is quiet, dignified, serene and at all times imperturbable. Never, at any time, is he too busy or too important to spare a few moments conversation.[15]

His financial success meant he could be carefree with his generosity. There are many instances of him giving money to employees for holidays, for private medical care, or to alleviate some financial problems, once writing a cheque for a thousand pounds to pay for medical care for the disabled child of one of his stage managers. These huge acts of generosity were never mentioned in his many interviews. On one particular occasion, in 1959, Hylton bought the house of a friend, Louis Khronberg, who was facing bankruptcy and allowed him to live in it rent free, for an indefinite period. When the man finally went to court regarding the bankruptcy, Hylton was called to the stand, on the grounds that the £21,000 paid by Hylton was an inadequate price and therefore he was looking to make money on the venture. Hylton told the judge that he sought no financial reward for the purchase:

> "Are you suggesting that you expended £4,000 in order to gratify the wishes of an old friend, and for no other reason at all?"

> "Yes."

> "What sort of person are you Mr Hylton?"

> "I can tell you, Mr Finer, we are human beings, but you wouldn't know much about us."[16]

That simple answer led to the entire case being dropped. On another occasion *Dixon Of Dock Green* writer Ted Willis was given a brand new car, after asking whether Jack might be able to get a discount from any local dealers:

> I can do better than that. Go and see Nicky, my chauffeur. There's a brand new Ford Prefect in the garage. If you like it, you can have it.[17]

Jack refused payment, and when Willis insisted that he pay something, Hylton shrugged and told him to pay whatever he could whenever he could.

Fewer stories have leaked out about Jack's notorious womanising. Whilst keeping some kind of solid family life and always staying close to Fifi and the children, Jack led almost a double life. He had a passionate desire to enjoy himself and a determined realisation that the full degree of enjoyment could only be obtained by a full degree of self-indulgence:

> Jack's generosity spilled over when it came to his girlfriends on whom he lavished cars, clothes, jewellery and even apartments. He put some of them on the pay-roll of his shows, listing them ironically as wardrobe mistresses. What they had to do in return was pretty obvious, for Jack had a voracious sexual appetite. He was, as I learned from one of his ladies, a sexual performer *par excellence*; another girlfriend described him, with evident satisfaction,

as the male equivalent of a nymphomaniac. In addition to whichever regular mistress was currently enjoying his favours, it was said that he kept a girl in a separate flat with instructions that she be there between two o'clock and five each afternoon just in case, after lunch, he felt in need of further refreshment![18]

Relationships would come and go but as Jack Hylton headed into the 1950s (and into his sixties) his appetite for work and exploring new avenues would be bigger than ever, with excursions into television and even the circus.

Chapter 14: The Impresarios

Composite photo courtesy of Jack Hylton Archive

It is understandably rare for the name of the producer or the financial backer of a theatrical show to remain in the memory nearly as long as either the writers or the stars. It goes without saying that it is those people who are taking the risks, much more so than any of the better-known names. Jack Hylton was abundantly aware of this, both to his credit and to his cost, though he was already a star before his production career began.

However, the most successful of the impresarios became stars in their own right – the names of Andrew Lloyd Webber and Cameron

Mackintosh are as well known today as Jack Hylton, Val Parnell, Bernard Delfont and Prince Littler were in the middle of the twentieth century.

As in Chapter 9, this information on Hylton's contemporaries is not meant to be exhaustive, but is included to add some background to the second part of Hylton's career.

Moss Empires

The history of Sir Edward Moss and Sir Oswald Stoll is vital to our story. In the late nineteenth century, Moss and Australian born Irishman Stoll began working with architects such as Frank Matcham and C.J. Phipps to build theatres throughout Britain, including the Grand Theatre in Blackpool, the Hackney Empire, the Coliseum (which included the first revolving stage in Britain), His Majesty's, the Lyric and the London Palladium. In fact most of London's great theatres that still exist were built or owned by Moss or Stoll at some point. The original Moss Empire was built by Frank Matcham in Nicolson Street in Edinburgh in 1891.

Moss Empires was formed in Edinburgh in 1899 from a merger of ten individual theatre companies owned by Moss, Stoll and Richard Thornton, creating a huge chain of variety and music hall theatres across Britain, probably the largest of its kind in the world at that time. The group owned the major theatres in London (Palladium, Hackney Empire, Coliseum, Theatre Royal Drury Lane, Leicester Square Empire, Bradford Alhambra, Liverpool Empire, Newcastle Empire, Glasgow Empire, etc.)

As the years passed, many theatres would come and go, falling out of fashion, being rebuilt, or sold on, but the empire remained solid and affluent. Moss died in 1912 and Stoll resigned from the board in 1910, but the company remained, under the guidance of William Houlding and later J.J. Gillespie.

Val Parnell took control as Managing Director in 1945, with Prince Littler as Chairman in 1947, and in 1964 Lew Grade took over. The company was eventually bought out by Andrew Lloyd Webber's Really Useful Group, who, at the time of writing, manage the London Palladium, Theatre Royal Drury Lane, New London Theatre, the

Chapter 14: The Impresarios

Adelphi Theatre, Her Majesty's Theatre and the Cambridge Theatre, keeping the Stoll-Moss Empire alive.

Val Parnell (1892-1972)

Valentine Charles Parnell was born in London, on Valentine's Day 1892, a few months before Hylton. Val was the son of Fred Russell, the famous ventriloquist (otherwise known as Thos. Frederick Parnell OBE). He began his love of theatre in 1907 when he worked as an office boy for Sir Walter de Frece, and then as booking manager to the Variety Theatre Controlling Company. By 1928 he had become booking manager for the General Theatre Corporation.

In 1931 he was appointed General Manager of all the shows and artists at the London Palladium and in 1945 he had become Managing Director of Moss Empires and was in charge of a number of London theatres.

Much like Hylton, he began working in independent television in its infancy, becoming Managing Director of ATV in 1956. Again, like Hylton, he was very hands on with the programming, especially the entertainment programming, and struck gold with the weekly *Val Parnell's Sunday Night At The London Palladium*, which ran until 1965 to great acclaim.

Sadly, Parnell became associated with a property development company, which schemed to sell a large number of the less successful Stoll-Moss theatres in the late 1950s and early 1960s – many of which had very attractive city centre locations. Many were sold, despite running at a profit, to be turned into shopping centres, supermarkets or offices, and there were suggestions that the London Palladium, the Victoria Palace and the Theatre Royal Drury Lane were to meet a similar fate.

A boardroom battle ensued, and Prince Littler took over the company, with Parnell's resignation not far behind. Of course in many ways Parnell was a visionary – many of the theatres could not maintain a variety programme through the 1960s and many would subsequently close, reopening as bingo halls or cinemas.

Prince Littler (1901-1985)

Prince Frank Littler CBE was born Prince Frank Richeux in Ramsgate, Kent, the eldest of five children of Jules and Agnes Richeux. The pair leased the Ramsgate Victoria Pavilion in 1906 and the Artillery Theatre, Woolwich, in 1909. After Jules died, Agnes married theatre manager Frank Rolison Littler, so beginning a long legacy of theatrical management amongst not just Prince, but younger brother Emile and sister Blanche.

The first step for Prince was the production of small scale touring companies with sister Blanche in 1927. After managing the family's Woolwich theatre, Prince bought the Opera House and the Theatre Royal in Leicester (1931), the Prince's Theatre Manchester (1937) and the New Theatre Royal, Norwich (1939), amongst others, whilst also producing pantomimes in London at the Coliseum, the Prince's Theatre and the Theatre Royal Drury Lane.

He went on to produce a number of flagship shows in London, many of which have stood the test of time; *Brigadoon* (1950), *Carousel* (1951), *Guys And Dolls* (1953), *The Pajama Game* (1955) and *Fiddler On The Roof* (1966). In due course he would become Chairman and Managing Director of several theatre companies, and Chairman of Moss Empires. He was also a major shareholder in the fledgling ATV in the mid 1950s, as well as an active member of many charities and a vice-president of the Society of West End Theatre Managers.

He was appointed CBE in 1957 and finally retired after an illustrious career, in 1966.

Bernard Delfont (1909-1994)

Baron Delfont was born Boris Winogradsky, in Tokmak in the Russian Empire in 1909, was the brother of Lew Grade and uncle to Michael Grade (now Lord Grade).

His family moved to England where Bernard became a dancer, then a theatrical agent. This second career led to Delfont becoming a major force as a theatrical impresario, presenting hundreds of shows both in London and New York, including *City Of Angels* and *Sweet Charity*, as well as countless variety shows across Britain's seaside resorts, including Laurel & Hardy in 1947.

Delfont perhaps lacked the theatrical passion of some of his contemporaries, notably when he converted the London Hippodrome into
the *Talk Of The Town* nightclub where he staged the Folies Bergere
for the first time outside Paris, as well as bringing in such entertainment heavyweights as Frank Sinatra, Eartha Kitt, Judy Garland and
Hylton discovery, Shirley Bassey.

He was knighted in 1974, became Baron Delfont in 1976, and
served as president of the Entertainment Artistes' Benevolent Fund
for many years into his retirement.

Emile Littler (1903-1985)

Born Emile Richeux, Sir Emile Littler was the younger brother of
Prince, with the same upbringing as described above. Emile's move
into theatrical production was slightly different to his siblings. He began as an actor, before moving backstage to become an assistant
manager of the Southend-On-Sea theatre in 1922, then business manager of the Court Theatre, London, in 1923, becoming Assistant Stage
Manager of Birmingham Repertory Theatre in 1925.

In 1927 he spent four years as a theatre manager in America before returning to Birmingham Rep as manager in 1931. By 1934 he
had set up his own production company, not only producing shows
such as *Annie Get Your Gun*, *Lilac Time* and *The Student Prince*, but
also indulging his passion for pantomime, presenting well over two
hundred pantos both in London and throughout the UK, writing and
co-writing many of them.

He also leased the Palace Theatre London for almost forty years
and served on the board of the Royal Shakespeare Company. Emile
finally retired in 1973, and was knighted the following year.

Harold Fielding (1916-2003)

Harold Lewis Fielding was born in Woking, in Surrey, the son of
a stockbroker. He became a child prodigy, studying violin with Josef
Szigeti and touring the country as 'England's boy wonder violinist',
before suffering stage fright and giving up.

By 1942 he was arranging performances for other musicians, and
a few years later he began a series of Sunday concerts at Blackpool's

Opera House, and summer shows at seaside resorts, both of which he continued to do for three decades.

At the same time he was developing smash hit shows in London's West End, importing from America and doing business in the other direction, as Hylton had done. His first success was Rodgers and Hammerstein's *Cinderella*, which he produced at the Coliseum in London in 1958. He went on to produce *The Music Man* (1961), *Half A Sixpence* (1963), *Sweet Charity* (1967 – a co-production with Bernard Delfont), and *Mame* (1969).

Like Hylton, Harold Fielding had his fair share of financial and critical flops, including *Gone With The Wind* (1972), *You're A Good Man, Charlie Brown* (1968) and *Zeigfeld* (1988). *Zeigfeld*, on which he invested 2.5 million pounds, closed after just seven months.

His flair, his penchant for a memorable first night party, and his insistence in sticking with a show, despite poor reviews and poor attendances, shows considerably affinity with Jack Hylton.

George Black (1911-1970), Alfred Black (1913-2002)

The two Black brothers were sons of George Black (1890-1945), who took over management of the General Theatre Corporation (GTC), a chain of theatres, cinemas and dance halls, as well as the London Palladium.

In 1931, George Snr. organised *Crazy Week* at the Palladium, which was the forerunner of *The Crazy Gang*, with which Jack Hylton would have a close association for many years. In 1932, Black was the mastermind of the merger of the GTC and Moss Empires, of which he took charge, until his death, when Val Parnell took over.

His sons George and Alfred would both have a long history of their own in theatre production. Alfred would produce numerous revues and musicals in London and throughout the UK. After their father's death, the brothers took over the family business and in 1957 were part of the consortium that became Tyne Tees Television. The pair had a number of co-productions with Jack Hylton, including *London Laughs* (1952), *You'll Be Lucky* (1954) and *The Talk Of The Town* (1954). Along with Hylton, the Blacks dominated variety in London's West End in the 1950s.

After George's death in 1970, Alfred continued with television and theatre production.

Lew Grade (1906-1998)

Lovat Winogradsky, much like his brother Bernard Delfont, began his career as a dancer, when he was known as Louis Grad. He was crowned Charleston Champion Of The World in 1926. He became a theatrical agent in 1934, in partnership with Joe Collins (father of Jackie and Joan Collins).

After a brief spell serving in World War II, Lew and brother Leslie formed the Grade Organisation, developing their entertainment interests in American, bringing Bob Hope and Judy Garland to the UK for the first time.

In 1954, Grade formed a consortium which included Val Parnell and Prince Littler and formed the Incorporated Television Programme Company, to bid for one of the new ITV franchises. Their company later became the Independent Television Company, but their bid was rejected. They joined forces with the Associated Broadcasting Development Company, which already had the London weekend and Midlands weekday contracts, and became Associated Television (ATV).

ATV would go on to have great success and Grade would move into films, with both nsuccess and catastrophic failure. Some movie failures, coupled with some curious television decisions led to Grade resigning from ATV, when it merged and became Central Television.

Lew Grade was knighted in 1969 and became Baron Grade in 1976. He would live to be ninety-one years of age.

Chapter 15: 1950-1960

The television logo for 'Jack Hylton Presents' on ITV. (Jack Hylton Archive)

The lengthy list of shows mentioned in the previous chapter would keep Jack Hylton busy through 1950, along with trips to New York with his cheque book to check out the latest theatrical offerings on Broadway. One such show was *Kiss Me Kate*, the Cole Porter musical about a production of Shakespeare's *Taming Of The Shrew* which Jack bought in 1950 and would lavish huge sums of money on the following year.

1950 would also be noted as the year in which Hylton reformed his orchestra, for one night only. Val Parnell was given the job of producing that year's Royal Variety Performance, to be staged on Monday November 13th, at the London Palladium, and suggested, somewhat flippantly to his friend Jack that he should reform. Jack was still in America finalising the *Kiss Me Kate* deal at the time, but as soon as the deal was struck he returned home and began rounding up the band, ten years after they had last played together. However, getting them together would prove to be complex and time consuming, with so many high-class musicians having passed through the ranks over the two decades that the band was together. The list that Jack ended up with was almost a *Who's Who?* of British musicians, as the programme for the evening showed:

Violins: Billy Ternent (own orchestra), Dick Willows (own orchestra), Reg Cole (conductor for the Black Bros.), Eddie Hooper (producing shows), Leslie Maddox (BBC and recording), Jack Rayne (celebrity concerts) and Stanley Andrews (BBC).

Saxophones: Dave Shand (Ted Heath's band), Joe Crossman (BBC and recording), Freddy Schweitzer ('Freddy The Clown'), E.O. Pogson (Victor Sylvester and records), Les Gilbert (Ted Heath's band) and Johnny Raitz (furrier).

Trombones: Eric Breeze (BBC and records), Woolf Phillips (Conductor, Skyrockets), Paul Fenhoulet (conductor, Prince of Wales Theatre) and Les Carew (BBC and recording).

Trumpets: Jack Jackson (BBC disc jockey), George Swift (BBC and films), Kenny Baker (BBC and records) and Stan Roderick (Ted Heath's band).

Pianos: Peter Yorke (own orchestra), Billy Munn (own orchestra) and Freddy Bretherton (conductor, Victoria Palace).

Drums: Jock Cummings (Geraldo's orchestra) and Lew Stephenson (Colony restaurant).

Guitars: Chappie D'Amato (own orchestra), Sonny Farrar (in Vaudeville).

Vocalist: Sam Browne (Vaudeville and BBC)

Bass: Bruce Trent (musical comedy star) and Clem Lawton (Yorkshire Symphony Orchestra).

A huge thirty-piece band and a huge number of stars in their own right, who learned their trade with the Hylton orchestra. The only key member missing from the performance was violinist Hugo Rignold – he was busy conducting the Liverpool Philharmonic that night!

The performance of the Hylton band was kept a secret from all but a select few and they appeared as the climax of the show. Also on the bill were Max Bygraves, Billy Cotton, Tommy Trinder, Frankie Howerd, Jack Benny, Dinah Shore and the Crazy Gang, all of whom were outshone by Jack when the opening bars of *Oh, Listen To The Band!* began to uproarious applause from the sell-out Palladium crowd. They went on to play Hylton classics *Music, Maestro, Please* and *I Kiss Your Hand, Madame*, as well as joining with Woolf Phillips house band for a finale of *There's No Business Like Show Business*, led by Gracie Fields. The following day the reception was unilaterally positive and Hylton received a message from the King; George VI congratulated Jack, saying, "You have produced a large number of stars, they have done very well."[1]

Sadly, it would be the last public performance for clowning saxophonist and long time Hylton stalwart, Freddy Schweitzer, who died later that month.

In 1951 the Crazy Gang's *Together Again* finally closed after 1566 performances, but the gang would stay at the Victoria Palace and open a new show, *Knights Of Madness*, which would hit 1361 performances. Even bigger than that was Hylton's production of *Kiss Me Kate*, which opened at the Coliseum on March 8th, 1951 after having previewed in Oxford and following on from an eighteen-month run on Broadway. Hylton originally planned to bring the stars of the Broadway version over to London, but despite lengthy meetings, Alfred Drake's terms could not be agreed on and American stage actor Bill Johnson replaced him. Drake's co-star on Broadway, Patricia Morison, did make the swap to London; bringing her forty inch long hair with her, to great acclaim and excitement in the media. She would go on to play Anna Leonowens in *The King And I*, along with a number of film roles. Her performance in *Kiss Me Kate*, was regarded as her greatest.

The show was an immediate smash hit; demand for opening night tickets was greater than for any previous show in London, with a three hundred yard queue outside the theatre on the first night.

In December, Morison was replaced by American actress Helena Bliss, On January 30th, whilst Bliss was away from the show ill, her understudy Helen Jutsen also fell ill and was taken suddenly to hospital for an ear operation. A girl from the chorus was chosen to cover the role for that afternoon's matinee performance. She was 'Paddy' Larner, from Wigan, or as she became better known, Elizabeth Larner. She not only covered the part well, with twelve curtain calls, but she would go on to take the leading role in the forthcoming tour of *Kiss Me Kate* and take leading roles in forthcoming Hylton West End shows *Kismet* and *Camelot*. She had a very successful career on television, on record and on Broadway in the 1980s; yet another Hylton discovery.

The 1951 Royal Variety Performance did not have the exciting dénouement of the previous year, but Hylton was in charge of production and filled the show with friends and colleagues including the Crazy Gang, Gracie Fields, Florence Desmond, 'Stinker' Murdoch, Jimmy Edwards, Charlie Kunz, Carroll Gibbons, Stanley Black, Alec Shanks, Sam Browne, Harry Secombe and many others. He also booked an all star line up for a charity show in Bolton for the YMCA, which included the Crazy Gang, Pat Kirkwood, Adelaide Hall and his own singing sister, Dolly Elsie, who he accompanied on the piano. Had Jack not been in a position to employ the services of such stars, the show would have cost in the region of £3,000. Instead it raised huge sums for the YMCA in his hometown.

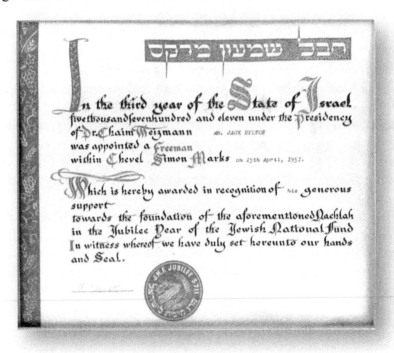

Hylton's appointment as Freeman of the State of Israel. (Jack Hylton Archive)

Inexplicably, 1951 was also the year that Hylton was honoured with the appointment as a Freeman of the State of Israel, on April

Chapter 15: 1950-1960

15th. The elaborate framed certificate still exists in the Jack Hylton Archive at Lancaster University, which states *"Mr Jack Hylton was appointed a Freeman with Chevel Simon Marks on 15th April 1951, which is hereby awarded in recognition of his generous support towards the foundation of the aforementioned Nachlah in the jubilee year of the Jewish National Fund, in witness whereof we have duly set hereunto our hands and seal."* The Chevel Simon Marks is a 20,000km^2 tract of land in the Southern Jerusalem corridor, named after British Zionist leader Simon Marks. A goal of £300,000 was set for the project. It is not known how much Hylton donated to this cause or, indeed, why he did it, given he had no apparent links to the Jewish National Fund of Britain, who launched the project.

1952 saw two major shows opening in the West End, amongst the usual flurry of plays and revues. On March 15th, *Call Me Madam* opened at the Coliseum, after *Kiss Me Kate* had vacated it to head off on a lucrative UK tour. Broadway singer and actress Billie Worth starred in this Broadway transfer, alongside Shani Wallis (an English actress in her first major role ahead of a long and illustrious theatre and film career) and Anton Walbrook (an Austrian actor who settled in the UK). This Irving Berlin penned show, a satire on American foreign policy, would play 486 times in its fifteen month run before heading off on the inevitable tour of the provinces.

At the end of the year, *Paint Your Wagon* opened in Manchester for the Christmas season, after an initial try out in Oxford. This Lerner and Loewe musical set in Gold Rush America, was another success for the Hylton organisation, moving to His Majesty's Theatre after its run in Manchester. Much like *Call Me Madam,* it stayed there for fifteen months before embarking on a tour. The show starred father and daughter pair Bobby and Sally Ann Howes. Bobby was a popular entertainer in the 1930s and 1940s, and had first worked with Hylton in 1919. He became well known for regular performances as *Mr Cinders* (based on *Cinderella*). He would go on to achieve great acclaim in the lead role in *Finian's Rainbow.* Daughter Sally Ann was predominantly a film actress, best known for her portrayal of Truly Scrumptious in *Chitty Chitty Bang Bang,* and this was one of her first stage performances since seeking singing lessons. *Paint Your Wagon* ran for 477 performances in London.

Another new musical Hylton opened was *Bet Your Life*, written by Alan Melville, Kenneth Leslie-Smith and Charles Zwar. It would again star Sally Ann Howes, along with Bill Stewart, Noele Gordon and Hylton regular Arthur Askey. It would run for 362 performances at the Hippodrome.

Meanwhile, Hylton had seen a hugely successful and popular variety show in Blackpool in the summer of 1951, which starred the Bernard Brothers, Harry Secombe and Vera Lynn (who was best known as vocalist for Ambrose & His Orchestra). Jack bought the show, changed the cast considerably and after a try out in Oxford, opened *London Laughs* at The Strand, on 12th April 1952. He was astute enough to keep Vera Lynn on board, despite her having spent the previous seven weeks starring on radio in America. In fact, her extended contract in the US was cut short as Hylton brought forward their opening for *London Laughs*. The new version of the show starred not only Lynn, but also Jimmy Edwards (a radio star for many years on *Take It From Here*) and a new young comedian, Tony Hancock (who had made a name for himself on radio's *Educating Archie*). In fact *London Laughs* was seen by many as being the last big theatre show to rely heavily for its appeal on radio names rather than those from television.

The show also featured The Jack Billings Trio, Natalie Raine, Erica York, The Happy-Go-Lovelies, Derek Rosen, Jane Shorem, The Cavendish Singers, the John Tiller Girls, Pauline Johnson, The Bedini Troupe, and Michael Dalton.

Vera Lynn scored a huge hit with *Auf Wiederseh'n, Sweetheart* during the run of the show and this was part of the reason for the extended run which they enjoyed. By February 1954 the show was still running successfully but Jimmy Edwards and Vera Lynn, having not expected such a long run, had taken other contracts and the show closed after 1,113 performances.

Also running in 1952 was a new venture for Jack – the Circus at Earl's Court, or to give it its full title, *Jack Hylton's Earls Court Circus, Fun Fair and Menagerie*. Given there were two established circuses running in London over Christmas in 1952, this was a surprising idea, but Hylton felt that with help he could add his knowledge of piecing together shows, to make a superior product, in line with a traditional variety show. Tom Arnold's circus at Haringey and Bertram Mills' at Olympia (just a short distance from Earl's Court) were initially unperturbed. In October, after Hylton announced his plans, the Chipperfield family (famous for having run a circus as far back as 1684) threatened to sue Hylton after they negotiated together to stage the show. Typically, Hylton brushed this off and stated that it was him alone who had negotiated with Earls Court, not the family. No litigation occurred. Hylton spent £350,000 on the endeavour, considerably more than the Arnold or Mills shows. Hylton suggested that in being new to the circus, his costs were considerably higher:

> Here are some of the prices he has paid: a lion, £500; a tiger, £800; a camel, £1200; an elephant, £1200; and horses up to £630. It will cost £637 a week to feed the animals at Earls Court. Star turns get £400.[2]

The same article suggested that even with very high turnouts he might lose £20,000 in the season. Of course, Hylton had the vision and the financial clout to face a loss in the first year. In the event, his circus was a huge success, helped no doubt by having 'Jack Hylton Presents…' at the top of the advertising, as well as a huge media promotion. The show ran from December 22nd 1952 to January 24th, 1953. Reviews were good, indeed better than the other circuses running at the same time. Bexley Heath Observer described the show on January 2nd 1953 as "spectacular, thrilling, colourful, gay and breathtaking." 62-year-old Billy Smart, who had been running successful touring circuses since 1946, was made General Manager of the show, and son Billy Smart Jnr. (who would later take over his father's business) was a featured performer. The show entertained 200,000 people in its first fourteen days, in the 120,000 square feet venue:

> Mr Hylton's circus has everything that the most sophisticated circus-goer could desire. It is as loud and glittering and varied as any circus should be.[3]

Earl's Court Circus, 1953. (Jack Hylton Archive)

Before the year was out, Hylton had put Maurice Chevalier on again at London Hippodrome for three weeks, paying him £10,000 for the privilege, had signed a long lease on the Prince's Theatre in London, and produced the Royal Variety Show at the Palladium on November 2nd, which featured not only Maurice Chevalier, but Gracie Fields and Beniamino Gigli singing a duet entitled *Come Back To Sorrento*. By now Jack Hylton had five theatres housing his productions in London's West End.

The circus at Earls Court would return in 1953, from December 23rd to January 23rd, as would the two competing circuses around London. Again the show was a big success and presumably more profitable for Hylton. Pianist Winifred Atwell appeared on the gala opening night in a lions cage, shortly followed by Jack himself, to present Winifred with a bouquet of flowers:

> I did it on the spur of the moment. I was due to present the bouquet after the lions left their cage. Suddenly I thought, "Why shouldn't I do it while the lions are there?" So I went in. I had butterflies in my stomach, I must admit, but once inside I didn't feel as bad as I thought I would. Still, I was glad when it was all over.[4]

The show was televised on January 18th 1954. Back in 1953, Maurice Chevalier had been sent on an extensive UK tour by Hylton from January to May and *Kiss Me Kate* was still touring the UK. *Happy As A King*, a musical revue starring Dickie Henderson and Shani Wallis was out on tour (after a dismal run of just twenty-six performances at the Prince's Theatre) and the latest Crazy Gang show, *Ring Out The Bells*, was well into its run of 987 performances, after an initial run at The New Theatre in Oxford.

Another new show would open in 1953 – *The Love Match*, which starred Arthur Askey and Thora Hird. This was a farce, rather than a variety style revue, which was new for Askey and its central plot was based around two football-mad railway engine drivers who are desperate to get home in time to see a football match. It also starred Danny Ross and Shirley Easton. The show opened at Blackpool Opera House, where it stayed for a sixteen-week summer season, before moving to Manchester, then on tour, finally heading to the Palace Theatre in London on November 10th. By June of 1954 the show was still running and moved to the Victoria Palace. Lupino Lane (an English actor turned theatre manager, who became wealthy playing Bill Snibson in *Me And My Girl*) took over from Askey in July 1954 but Askey was back in time for the 800th London performance and the subsequent second tour of the provinces.

On November 4th 1953 Hylton presented the Royal Shakespeare Company's production of Antony And Cleopatra at the Prince's Theatre, starring Michael Redgrave, Marius Goring, Donald Pleasence and Tony Britton. The show would run for 53 performances, closing on December 19th, ahead of a tour that visited France and Holland.

Jack Hylton

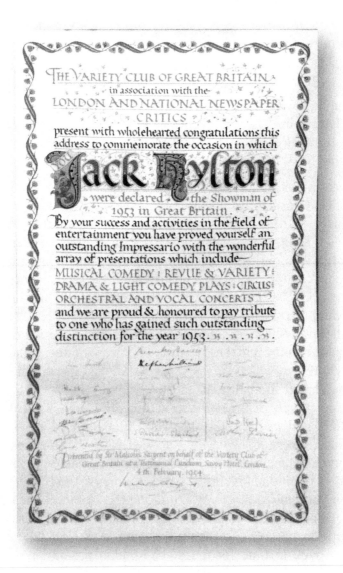

THE VARIETY CLUB OF GREAT BRITAIN
in association with the
LONDON AND NATIONAL NEWSPAPER
CRITICS
present with wholehearted congratulations this
address to commemorate the occasion in which

Jack Hylton

were declared the Showman of
1953 in Great Britain.
By your success and activities in the field of
entertainment you have proved yourself an
outstanding Impressario with the wonderful
array of presentations which include—
MUSICAL COMEDY : REVUE & VARIETY :
DRAMA & LIGHT COMEDY PLAYS : CIRCUS :
ORCHESTRAL AND VOCAL CONCERTS
and we are proud & honoured to pay tribute
to one who has gained such outstanding
distinction for the year 1953.

Presented by Sir Malcolm Sargent on behalf of the Variety Club of
Great Britain at a Testimonial Luncheon Savoy Hotel. London.
4th February 1954

Variety Club certificate. (Jack Hylton Archive)

In February 1954 Hylton was recognised by the Variety Club Of Great Britain for his services to the industry and given the title *Showman Of The Year 1953* for which he received a lunch in his honour and a large, rather elaborate certificate that currently sits in its frame in the Lancaster University archive. In his rather awkward acceptance speech he noted how he was happy to invest in shows, even if he knew they would not make lots of money:

> In fact his favourite shows are the bubbling Irish verse play *Happy As Larry* and the H.G. Wells adaptation *Ann Veronica*. He lost money on both of them. But he kept *Ann Veronica* running for weeks at a loss against all advice. "I thought it was good", he says deliberately. "I still think so."[5]

Following this acclaim, 1954 would be a huge year for Hylton shows. On March 16th, Harold Lang, Carol Bruce and newcomer Jean Brampton starred in the opening of *Pal Joey* at Oxford New Theatre ahead of an opening at the Prince's Theatre on March 31st. This Rodgers and Hart musical ran for ten months on Broadway despite mixed reviews, but closed for Hylton in October after 254 performances, losing him around £10,000. The show was sufficiently popular in the US to spawn a rather more famous Frank Sinatra movie version in 1957.

Considerably more successful was the next Crazy Gang show to open at the Victoria Palace. This one was entitled *Jokers Wild* and of course performed to packed houses, with a total of 911 performances.

In May Hylton was forced to slow down a little. He was taken ill at his office on the 14th and was taken to a Harley Street nursing home, where his appendix was removed. Hearing about this, former trumpet player Jack Jackson got in touch with his old boss:

> Jack Hylton and I shared a joke which took over thirty years to mature. You see, I joined Jack Hylton's band in the late 20's and during a week's variety at the Palace Theatre, Blackpool I went down with appendicitis. Jack was most sympathetic and arranged an operation in a private nursing home for which he paid, and he paid my full salary for the three weeks I was away from the band. Well, a few years ago, Jack, by now one of the pillars of the theatre, with shows all over London suddenly went down with appendicitis himself, so I sent him a get well telegram which read as follows: "Jack Hylton", so-and-so Nursing Home, wherever it was "I wish I could afford to

pay your salary, as you paid mine when I had the same operation thirty years ago. Get well soon, Jack Jackson". The following week, I received a letter from him: "Dear Jack, your telegram came at the right moment. I was feeling pretty low after the operation, but when I opened your telegram, the doctor thought I'd blow my stitches. Thanks again, I'm going to have the telegram framed."[6]

He recovered well and soon was in New York, fighting for the rights to bring *Kismet* to the UK, which he would do the following year. Meanwhile, *Paint Your Wagon* went out on another UK tour, *Toad Of Toad Hall* headed into the Princes Theatre, following on from the Japanese ballet company that Hylton had presented previously.

On February 16th 1954, newspapers announced the Jack Hylton was on a shortlist of four people selected by the executive committee of Bolton West Divisional Labour Party for the party's candidate at the next general election. Hylton had been a member of the Labour Party for thirty years, and in February 1952 he had become president of his local Labour Party at East Preston in Sussex. He was genuine in his wishes – if he had been concerned only with becoming an MP, he would not have bothered about the local party or the constituency. He spoke in a newspaper article in February:

> I have tried to repay a little by my work in show business; but now I would like to serve more directly by looking after the interests of individual Bolton men and women as only a Member of Parliament can. I don't want to become an M.P. for the money – which is small, nor even for the honour – which is great. I don't, in fact, want to become just an M.P. I want to become a LABOUR M.P. who sits for BOLTON.[7]

Just a few weeks later, it was announced that Hylton had pulled out of the contest. In a letter to Reg Wallis, North-West Regional Organiser of the Labour Party, he suggested that his current workload meant that he could not do justice to the job of being Bolton's M.P. and for that reason he had to withdraw. His commitment to the Labour Party would continue throughout his life and he would regularly donate thousands of pounds to the party (including generous personal cheques to Aneurin Bevan in the late 1950s and a five thousand pound donation to the party in 1964. Harold Wilson wrote personally to Jack in October 1964 thanking him for his encouragement and "everything you have done for us").

One of Hylton's most lucrative and long running shows was first presented in 1954. *Salad Days*, a musical written by Julian Slade and Dorothy Reynolds was conceived as a small scale summer show for the resident company at Bristol's Old Vic Theatre. Jack was alerted to this charming little show soon after its premiere in June 1954, bringing it to the Vaudeville Theatre in August. The cast included writer Dorothy Reynolds, Eleanor Drew, John Warner and Newton Blick. Even by Hylton's standards this show was a runaway success, going on to enjoy 2,283 performances, making it, at the time the longest running show in musical theatre history.

This success allowed Jack considerable financial leeway in his subsequent choices. Another risk and another loss occurred later in the year when Hylton presented *Joan Of Arc At The Stake*, an opera by Honegger. Ingrid Bergman was hired in the non-singing lead role, amongst a company of 120. The original opening date of July 2nd was put back and the show eventually opened at the Stoll Theatre in October. Originally Jack's old violinist Hugo Rignold was due to conduct, but the change of dates conflicted with Rignold's plans and another Hylton alumnus, Leighton Lucas took on conducting duties for the show's short run. The show closed on November 13th and Hylton was down another £17,000.

More successful was Bernstein's *Wonderful Town*, which was given a standard opening in Oxford and Christmas in Manchester, before a stint in Brighton and an eventual London run at the Princes Theatre, beginning on February 23rd 1955. The show, which had run for 559 performances on Broadway, starred Pat Kirkwood and Hylton favourite Shani Wallis, and ran for 205 performances, costing £50,000.

A typical advert, showcasing the variety of Hylton shows running in 1954.
(Jack Hylton Archive)

By now Hylton was becoming the elder statesman of show business – he had a radio programme dedicated to his work on December 21st, as part of the *Nights Of Gladness* series, presented by John Watt, and LP versions of his band recordings began to get released by EMI (who now owned all the HMV recordings). More and more articles began to be written with an overview of his career, but from his Pall Mall office, he knew he was on the brink of rather a large gear change in his career:

Apart from a piano in his office (which he rarely plays) there is no vestige of the band leader left. His room contains also a television set, a gramophone, bound volumes of his programmes and playbills, his certificate as Chevalier of the Legion of Honour, a medallion with the autograph of Franz Lehar, a photograph of George VI commemorating a royal variety performance. The heavily carved desk is tidy and everything in the room fits – the painting of a racehorse, the family photographs and the field-marshal's baton of show business – an eight-inch cigar, slightly chewed, on a huge ashtray.[8]

In March 1955, Jack opened the show he had fought so hard to buy in New York the previous year, *Kismet*. The musical was written by Robert Wright and George Forrest (who also wrote *Romany Love*, which Hylton produced in the mid 1940s) and used music 'borrowed' from Russian romantic composer Alexander Borodin. The Tony Award winning show was on Broadway when Hylton first saw it, going on to have 583 performances, starring Alfred Drake, Doretta Morrow and Joan Diener, all of whom came to London for Hylton's lavish £50,000 production. (The show also included Juliet Prowse as Princess Samaris. Prowse was a notable Anglo-Indian actress and dancer who would later star with and become engaged to Frank Sinatra. This was her first West End role after a stuttering career as a dancer in films). The show opened in Oxford on March 28th, before moving to the Stoll Theatre on April 14th. The cast would perform the show 648 times, before it closed after twenty months on December 3rd 1956.

In August of '55, Joan Diener had taken time off, then 'disappeared', to be covered by Sheila Bradley. When she eventually reappeared two weeks later, Hylton had his lawyers meet her at the stage door each time she tried to turn up for work and she was dismissed. Elizabeth Larner would take over the lead role in January 1956, whilst Bradley retained the Deiner role and Tudor Evans replaced Drake. After closing in London, the show spent Christmas of 1956 in Manchester, before a lengthy tour in 1957.

Back in 1955, Jack Hylton indulged in one final visit to his dance band days. On February 23rd *Scrapbook for 1924* was broadcast and for it, Jack put together a version of his band, as it would have been heard thirty-one years previously. Only one member of the 1924 band was still playing – E.O. 'Poggy' Pogson, who appeared with a selection of later band members and current musicians. The line up in full consisted of Lou Stevenson on drums (ex Mrs Hylton drummer), George Swift and Vic Mustard on trumpets, Hugh Akehurst on trombone, Chester Smith, Ivan Dawson, Fred Ballerini (also on violin) and Pogson on saxophones, Reg Cole on viola, Billy Bell on banjo, Cecil Norman on piano and Jack Evetts on sousaphone and bass – some unfamiliar names. Jack conducted the band on *Yes, We Have No Bananas* (Zonophone 2371), *The Charleston*, and *Horsey, Keep Your Tail Up* (neither of which the band recorded, but were representative of the period). Hylton was interviewed about the recording techniques and stylistic choices of the time.

Radio influenced another Hylton show when he produced a theatre version of long running radio soap opera, *The Archers*. The show had begun life on a provincial tour in the summer of 1953, and was a critical failure. Hylton had watched the show twice during that tour and had taken an interest in reviving it. He bought the show, a short three-act stage play, written by Edward J. Mason and Geoffrey Webb, changed the cast, edited the play into two acts and took the show to Blackpool for a summer season starring Jack Warner.

Jack Warner (1895-1981) had made a name for himself in music hall and radio, before becoming a film and television actor. He had worked both with Hylton's band and in Hylton shows in the 1940's. In 1955 he was best known for playing PC George Dixon in the film *The Blue Lamp* and would subsequently gain fame for his nineteen years playing the same character in *Dixon Of Dock Green*. He received an OBE in 1965.

Hylton's *The Archers* also starred Joyce Barber as Jack Warner's on stage wife Doris Archer, alongside Peter Byrne and Bonnie Downs as the children Phil and Christine Archer. Also starring were Anne Purkiss as Grace Fairbrother, Dandy Nichols as Mrs Perkins and

Charles Victor as Walter Gabriel. The plot revolved round someone wanting to build a holiday camp on the next-door farm, alongside the usual soap opera style love problems. The mostly positive reviews suggested that the plot was of little concern during a pleasant evening's entertainment.

After an initial opening in Wolverhampton, in May 1954 and then Bristol in June, the show opened at Blackpool Grand Theatre on June 4th 1954, playing twice nightly until *Paint Your Wagon* replaced it on October 2nd. Whilst reviews were mostly good, the box office was unremarkable, Hylton lost money, and he did not stage the show again.

After a few years away, in 1955 Jack would be involved in two Royal Variety Performances, one at the Victoria Palace on November 7th in aid of the Artistes' Benevolent Fund, and one at Blackpool Opera House on April 13th, which was highly publicised as Hylton was insisting that he would try and fill the bill with not just British, but Northern talent. This he mostly achieved. He closed the Victoria Palace for the night (at a personal cost of £1000) to bring the Crazy Gang to the show, and chartered private sleeper trains for all the acts to travel there and back from London. Gracie Fields flew in from her home in Capri. The Opera House, which lacks a royal box, had one specially built for the evening, to house the Queen and Prince Phillip. 7,500 ticket applications were made for the 3,000 seats, and given each application would grant two tickets, the show was massively over-subscribed.

As well as the Crazy Gang and Gracie Fields, the show featured Morecambe and Wise, Arthur Askey, Alma Cogan, Charlie Cairoli (Blackpool Tower Circus clown), Eddie Fisher, George Formby, Geraldo and His Orchestra, the Northern Variety Orchestra (conducted by Alan Ainsworth), Wilfred Pickles, Reginald Dixon, Al Read and many more.

In November, Hylton swiftly bought The Albany Club, a gentleman's club where he had spent many an evening over the previous twenty or so years. As he suggested to the press at the time, he would continue to run the club in its current format, but by March 1956 it was closed and in due course he would turn the building, at 3 Savile Row in the heart of London's famous tailoring district, into his palatial offices, renaming them Hylton House in the process and moving from his previous base at 125 Pall Mall. He would convert the lower floor of this five-story town house into a mock nightclub, which would be used for his next venture. In the late 1960s the Hylton estate sold the building to The Beatles when it was given a major overhaul and became Apple HQ, with a recording studio in the basement. The Daily Express of November 25th 1955 reported Hylton as saying; "We completed the deal in five minutes."

Jack's new toy, though, was television. The first of the localised independent TV contracts, the London weekday franchise was awarded to two companies – Broadcast Relay Service and Associated Newspapers, who together would be known as Associated-Rediffusion (A-R). When A-R went looking for help with their light entertainment programmes, they found that most of the big players were already signed up to other fledgling independent television companies, with Val Parnell and Prince Littler involved with the consortium which would become ATV (where Lew Grade made his name after ousting Parnell from the board). Hylton was one of the few 'big players' left and on July 15th 1955, newspapers reported the appointment of Hylton as Advisor of Light Entertainment – the signing up of Billy Ternent as Musical Director for the whole company swiftly followed:

> How a man who is chiefly remembered as a band leader and theatre impresario became involved with commercial television is a fascinating story, and one that shows how commercial television fed off the variety theatre and gave very little in return. Many big names in show business were to regret their involvement with Jack Hylton Television Productions.[9]

The association with Hylton would give A-R access to Hylton's stable of performers, as well as his inherent expertise. It was not uncommon for the new TV companies to employ a high profile figure – Sir John Barbirolli had already been appointed as Music Advisor, but Hylton took the unique move of forming a company to make programmes exclusively for the new franchise. Hylton subsequently registered Jack Hylton Television Productions Ltd., with himself as chairman, with the intention 'to engage in and produce productions of all kinds for purpose of television and broadcasting.'

His contract initially called for one hour of screen time per fortnight, with a further half hour per week. Hylton's company would pay for all artists, scripts, costumes and scenery, with all technical facilities and copyright issues to be dealt with by A-R. The assumption from Jack's point of view would be that he could save on props, scenery and costumes, with stock from previous or current shows.

The first show, on September 29th 1955, filmed sections of the current Adelphi Theatre revue, *Talk Of The Town*, pieced together with various other acts and songs filmed in a variety of theatres, featuring, amongst others, Jack Tripp and Elizabeth Larner, with Flanagan & Allen topping the bill. The newspaper reviews were poor, and suggestions that Hylton had no feel for the new medium were encouraged by his insistence on simply pointing the camera at the variety stage and hoping the quality of performer would suffice.

The next show, *Jack Hylton's Monday Show*, on October 4th fared little better. This was a mix of studio-based material and pieces from live shows. Reviews criticised his lack of live items, but once whole live shows were prepared he was then criticised for his lack of theatre based, recorded material. Hylton put his Bryan Michie live favourite, *Youth Takes A Bow* onto the television, but the rather staid interviewing technique and poor quality of performer meant that it too was criticised. Hylton then put on a performance of *Love And Kisses* (the follow-up to *The Love Match*), with Arthur Askey in a starring role. This was recorded in front of an invited audience in October 1955; four cameras were set up in the theatre and the show was performed once, recorded concurrently by all the cameras. The various angles were edited together and the show was chopped into five segments for the television shows. No concessions were made for television at all and the five segments were rather arbitrarily cut, giving a disjointed show, which made little sense in five parts and made for awkward viewing:

> Jack Hylton has very strong and personal ideas about what the television audience wants. He sees us...as a typical Monday night audience at the Theatre Royal, Shuddersford...It is, of course, a profound misjudgement...The television audience, spoiled and capricious, has nothing in common with it, except eyes and ears.[10]

Despite the almost constant criticism, viewing figures were relatively strong for these early shows, with many of the programmes regularly making the Top Ten TAM and Neilsen TV Ratings chart. The Hylton style gradually began to develop with a live one-hour variety show presented by American George Jessel, an on-going and improved *Youth Takes A Bow*, and a half-hour variety show live from Hylton House, simply called *Jack Hylton Presents*.

In 1956, one of the rare critical and commercial successes appeared in the form of *Alfred Marks Time*, a vehicle for comedian and actor Alfred Marks. His first programme was a last minute replacement for a variety show with copyright issues, but was such a success that it was commissioned for a monthly series. It was extremely well received and famous names jumped at the chance to appear – Peter Sellers, Edmundo Ros, Hughie Green, Max Wall, Max Bygraves all appeared in sketches.

However, for every big hit there were a number of flops. Hylton called on the Crazy Gang to help and even they could not manage to salvage a poor quality production. Too often the shows were badly scripted, badly edited, poorly recorded or simply too hackneyed for the modern television audience. Tony Hancock, so successful on radio with *Hancock's Half Hour* was hired (partly to release him from a Hylton theatre contract he was desperate to leave) for *The Tony Hancock Show*, which began broadcasting on April 27th 1956. This used neither the writers of the radio show, nor its format, but used various sketches, interspersed with June Whitfield doing a song or dance, which gave Hancock time to change for the next sketch. Again, the show was poorly received and Hancock would move to the BBC after his two series contract expired, to make what is regarded as some of the most classic comedy of his generation. The Hylton programmes are rarely mentioned today.

Whilst viewing figures were still very strong, the feeling was that, whilst television tastes were changing fast and the pacier feel of all aspects of ITV was moving television forward, the variety shows and Hylton's variety shows in particular were stuck in the previous decade and showed no signs of imagination of innovation. Hylton shows were also criticised for featuring too many of Hylton's acts plugging their own shows and too many shows featuring the universally derided Rosalina Neri (of which more later). Other shows appeared and disappeared, some with success (*The Robert Dhéry Show*, *The Dickie Henderson Half-Hour*), some with little or no success (*The Music Box, Hotel Riviera*).

An attempt to bring former success *Band Waggon* to the small screen came with *Living It Up*, which revived the partnership of Arthur Askey and 'Stinker' Murdoch, this time not living in a flat above Broadcasting House, but a flat above A-R's Television House. The format was much the same as the radio show from a decade previously and featured the same characters, references and storylines.

In October 1957, despite still having a year left on his contract, Hylton re-signed with A-R for a further two years, with a six-month notice period for either side. A-R were in financial difficulty and it is very likely that Hylton was forced to re-consider the costs for his programming. His output would remain, with the fortnightly hour paying £3,750 and the weekly half-hour paying £2,500. One of the first programmes under the new deal marked a new low, with the Max Wall show *That's Life*. Meanwhile the next series of *Alfred Marks Time* helped matters, but with performers apologising live on TV for either this week's or last week's poor output, things were looking rather grim for Jack Hylton Television Productions. Hylton would end the year filling his schedules with 'best of' shows from the successful parts of his output.

In 1958, Hughie Green was made presenter (and given editorial control) of *Jack Hylton's Monday Show*, but even without Hylton's input, the critics poured scorn on the material and the quality of the production. Hylton bought in scripts written by Sid Caesar from American TV and created *On With The Show* and *The Dickie Henderson Half-Hour*, which both became very popular, but even they suffered with contractual disagreements with Sid Caesar.

Another American influence was *Make Me Laugh*, where audience members would be paid for every second they could stay straight-faced whilst comedians attempted to make them laugh. The show was a disaster, paid out thousands of pounds and made a mockery of almost all the invited comedians, including the Crazy Gang, who vowed never to appear on a Hylton TV show again, despite their strong affiliation with him.

A-R were beginning to lose faith in Jack Hylton and his contract was amended in 1959 for him to create two half-hour shows per week and no more one hour shows, with a payment of £2,250 per half-hour. Things did not significantly improve. A new, restructured half-hour version of *Alfred Marks Time* bombed with both the audience and the critics, though *The Anne Shelton Show* (a comedy and music pro-gramme with special guests), and *Focus On Youth* (a new Bryan Michie show) both fared relatively well in the ratings. The shows that replaced them, *Something In The City* (a sitcom starring Eric Barker) and *Gert And Daisy* (a sitcom written by Ted Willis) were slammed by both audiences and critics.

Too often these shows were criticised for their paucity of genu-inely funny material, or their cripplingly poor production values; sometimes both. Another show, *All For Pleasure* (a themed variety show built round a different job each week) received an equally poor reaction:

> *All For Pleasure* is regularly spoiling good acts by wrap-ping them up with corny gags, tatty dancers and boy-scout-hut sets, slung on at bargain prices. ...Why, oh why, does Jack Hylton go on spoiling talent for a ha'porth of material?[11]

That Hylton could only replace this disaster with the second se-ries of *The Rosalina Neri Show* (perhaps the nadir of his entire career), says much about Hylton's television output. Throughout this continual verbal assault from the press, Jack maintained, quite rightly, that whilst the ratings continued to be high, he was happy to continue in the same vein. Even this was beginning to wear a little thin, and it was becoming clear that the relationship with A-R which gave Hylton free reign over the output was going to have to change. Not one to have his hands tied, Jack decided to jump ship.

Hylton handed in his notice in a memo to the General Manager of A-R, Captain Brownrigg, on September 23rd 1959, stating he did not want to continue in a relationship "which binds my freedom of action, or...prevents me from expressing my own individuality". Ironically, one of his better shows appeared in the last six months of the contract, in which Hylton employed the services of Sadlers Wells Opera Com-pany to produce six half-hour potted versions of popular operas, including *The Gipsy Baron, Countess Maria,* and Hylton favourite, *The Merry Widow,* and although the idea to condense so severely seems a little bizarre, the programmes were well produced and well executed. The rest of the output for the final months of the contract tended to be repeats of pre-existing programmes and the occasional strange choice of new show, including *Life Begins At Eighty,* where a cigar-toting eighty-seven year old actress, Ada Reeve, led a panel of octogenarian guests, hosted by the ubiquitous Bryan Michie, to discuss viewers' letters and reminisce about their lives. Unsurprisingly, the series was not well received by viewer or critic.

During his time in television, Jack Hylton recorded some two hundred and ninety five shows, utilising well over nine thousand entertainers. The final 'Jack Hylton Presents' logo appeared on April 13th 1960:

> Above all, there seems to have been a lack of imagination
> on the part of the Hylton organisation, an inability to
> think of new and exciting ideas for light entertainment.
> Instead of relying on Hylton's considerable theatrical con-
> tacts and expertise, the company should really have been
> thinking in purely televisual terms. On the odd occasion
> when this happened the results were encouraging... but all
> too often, attempts to re-create the atmosphere of a club
> or stage review simply didn't work.[12]

Associated-Rediffusion was not Hylton's only televisual excursion. He joined the consortium that bid for the 'South Wales and West of England' region, along with chairman Lord Derby (born Edward John Stanley in 1918) and owner of News Of The World, Sir William Carr. Television Wales and the West (TWW) were awarded the franchise in October 1956 and eventually began transmitting in January 1958. Hylton became a director and shareholder.

Hylton's role was much less hands on than that which he had at A-R, and as a consequence he retained a more stable and long lasting relationship with the company, which lasted long after he had resigned from A-R. In a surprise move, TWW lost their franchise in 1967, when HTV took over, and their last broadcast took place in May 1968, with an impetuous and very public display of their feelings towards the franchise loss. The programme was called *Come To An*

End and featured John Betjeman eulogising about the company, the franchise and the programming.

Composer Eric Coates had already completed commissions for the BBC (*BBC Television March*), for ATV (*Sound And Vision*), and for Hylton's Associated-Rediffusion (*Rediffusion March*, previously known as *Music Everywhere*), to write marches that could be used as 'theme tunes' for the stations. Given his previous links and friendship with Hylton, it is assumed that Hylton asked him to write something for TWW. Coates chose to rework a previous piece, *Seven Seas*, which he re-orchestrated for what had by now become his 'standard' march orchestration, and called the piece *South Wales And The West*. The piece is currently available to buy, wrongly labelled as being performed by Jack Hylton and His Orchestra.

*　　　　　*　　　　　*

One star of many of Hylton's TV shows was also one of his lovers. Rosalina Neri was born on November 12th 1934 in Arcisate in Lombardy, Italy. She became a cabaret singer and actress in Italy with some limited success, appearing on Italy's RIA television channel, and met Jack around the time that she appeared on *Youth Takes A Bow* on 27th January 1956. Her blond hair, Marilyn Monroe style looks (she was often referred to as the 'Italian Marilyn') and her 'pneumatic' figure clearly appealed to the 63 year old, and she was more than willing to oblige, understanding what he could offer this keen up and coming singer.

They became the most volatile of lovers and would remain so for many years. Despite her fiery temper and the frequent breakdown of their relationship they remained close and all sides of Jack's family remembered her fondly. However, Jack appears to have made a rare lapse in judgement with the amount of airtime she was given on his televisual outings:

> She was pretty dreadful, I would say...I remember thinking to myself that my father had lost his mind! But he didn't think so and to be honest, I think it was the only time he made a fool of himself.[13]

> I thought that Rosalina Neri, the blond Italian, was going to collapse last night from exhaustion in her efforts to be

sexy in ITV's *Christmas Greetings* show. She pouted, wriggled and ogled so much that she seemed like a combination of Sabrina, the young Marlene Dietrich and Mar-Marilyn Monroe – but grown to nightmare proportions. Please Miss Neri, more restraint – or you'll have us laughing.[14]

Rosalina Neri publicity shot, c.1955. (Personal Collection)

Rosa was a passable singer, but not at the standard to be exposed regularly to a television audience, and her grasp of English was such that her audience soon became alienated. Despite this, Hylton pushed her more and more into his TV shows, finally giving Rosa her own vehicle, *The Rosalina Neri Show* in 1959, which ran for nine episodes with Jack as producer and Billy Ternent as musical director. The show would have special guests who would entertain and be interviewed, whilst Rosa sang, chatted and displayed her assets. Complaints mounted up but Jack was clearly madly in love with her and persisted with her TV commitments. He also showered her with gifts, an Alfa-Romeo open top sports car, £50,000 of jewellery and accommodation for her and her many guests in the South of France.

She would think nothing of taking a dozen guests to a top restaurant and sending the bill to Jack – whether he was in the country or not.

Away from the limelight, things were just as difficult for Jack and Rosalina. Ted Willis' book *Evening All* describes in gory detail one fight to which he was a witness, which involved shouting, screaming, fast cars screeching away, finishing with the inevitable make-up back in the hotel:

> Scarcely had we ordered our meal when a stunning girl, tall and graceful as a model, came drifting across and, putting her arms around Jack from behind, kissed him on the ear and neck...Jack rose to greet this perfumed vision and I felt Rosa stir beside me. After a moment or two of conversation, the model gave Jack a kiss which hovered between friendship and passion, waved frostily to Rosa and moved on.
>
> "Who was that?...Did you fuck her?" asked Rosa, who was ever one for directness.
>
> "Rosa, Rosa!" he protested. "She worked for me, nothing more."
>
> She glared at him, her breasts heaving like twin ferrets trying to escape from a sack...Then she stood up and announced in a voice that hit the far wall of the restaurant and bounced back, "I want to make pee-pee!"[15]

Chaos inevitably ensued. The nadir of Hylton's relationship with Rosalina occurred when she persuaded him to indulge in her desire to be an opera singer. Sadly, she simply did not have the skills, but somehow she managed to persuade this most astute of producers that producing opera for her would be a good idea. He arranged a singing teacher, and then commissioned a short opera season at the Adelphi, in 1959. The results were disastrous. At her first performance, in Donizetti's *L'Elisir d'Amore,* Rosa was booed off stage and the show continued without her. She would never return to opera in Britain:

> She just about got through the rehearsals due to a large extent to Napoleone Annovazzi the conductor, but her voice could not compete with all the other singers who

were first class opera performers. I was chatting with one of the company who exclaimed "She pusha da boobs througha da television. Il Papa, he no like", and he wagged his finger as though she had committed a mortal sin...Came the opening night and Rosalina commenced her aria in the first act. She let out a strangled croak and shortly afterwards the mostly Italian audience began to hiss and boo, shouting "Annovazzi buono ma Neri cattiva". (Annovazzi good but Neri bad). The curtain was rung down and later the opera re-commenced with one of the San Carlo singers replacing her, doing a superb job. Rosalina never appeared on stage for the rest of that week.[16]

She would apparently go on to have some degree of success in her chosen field of opera. Reports in 1961 suggested that after some eighteen months out of the limelight, she had studied her craft with voice training in Rome from a cousin of Boris Chaliapin (a Russian artist whose father was opera singer Feodor Chaliapin) and returned a stronger performer. She appeared incognito at Ghent Opera House as Mimi in *La Bohème*, using her mother's maiden name, Angela Baldi.

After Hylton's television commitments ended, he and Rosa continued their sporadic dysfunctional relationship for another couple of years, until the next, less explosive young woman came into his life. When Hylton sold his two villas in the South of France in 1963, Rosalina was given the money, almost 320,000 francs (around £25,000). She attended Hylton's funeral alongside Fifi and Jack's daughters, a sign of the fondness the family had for her.

One wonders where a man in his early sixties found the energy for such escapades, and Ted Willis' book gives an anecdotal explanation:

"Not tonight, Jack," I said apologetically. "I'm too tired, I couldn't manage it."

"That's easily settled!" He pulled on a long thin gold chain and hauled a small gold pill-box from a trouser pocket. Inside were some ominous-looking off-white pills, tiny things, like grains of rice. "Put two of these on the tip of your tongue and let them dissolve. In a few minutes you'll feel like a young buck." He demonstrated by putting two pills on his own tongue and I followed suit.

...When I went to his suite the next morning, the lovely was just leaving and Jack, looking as fresh and chirpy as a newborn chick, reproached me with a shake of the head. "You must be daft, Ted. You don't know what you missed."

...Some months later I met Jack's doctor at a social gathering and out of curiosity I asked him if he knew anything about those little white aphrodisiac pills. He had taken a drop and leaning towards me he whispered, "Aspirin. Tiny aspirin. I make them up for him." He tapped his forehead. "It's all in his mind."[17]

*   *   *

Another of Hylton's 'discoveries' was given her first West End break in 1955. Shirley Bassey was working as a club singer, touring the provinces, with her agent Michael Sullivan meeting and introducing her to the great and the good of the London show business scene whenever he could. He managed to meet Jack Hylton at the Astor club, where Jack was entertaining Robert Dhéry one night after a performance of *La Plume De Ma Tante*. Bassey was performing that night and Sullivan introduced himself, fully aware of the potential in this coincidental situation. Hylton was understandably impressed with this powerfully voiced young woman and in the Hylton way, instantly offered her a job:

When she'd finished, having brought the house down one more time, he turned to Sullivan and said "She's very good, you know. Do you think she could open at the Adelphi tomorrow night?"

Sullivan looked bewildered and Hylton elaborated. "I'll tell you. This girl I've got, Pavlou, she's been taken off with peritonitis and I've got to find somebody to fill a small spot. You know lad, it's only a little time, not important to the show, but we need some girl and this one's not bad."[18]

Hylton's current show at the Adelphi was a co-production with George and Alfred Black starring Jimmy Edwards and Tony Hancock, with whom Hylton had been working on some of his TV shows. The show had a long run of 656 performances, but wouldn't be without its issues. Bassey was immediately booked, Billy Ternent was called to make full band arrangements from her piano parts and she opened to great fanfare and press interest. The Evening News the following night featured the headline 'Two years ago 19-year-old Shirley Bassey was a £3 a week factory hand in Cardiff. Last night she was a West End revue star'. Hylton, of course, took considerably more of the credit than Sullivan.

She was then added to the roster on the *Jack Hylton Presents* TV show and gained her first exposure on TV. Whilst not being an ideal vehicle for her, the exposure to the huge TV audiences the show garnered was invaluable. Her second spot ultimately rewarded her with a recording contract, and soon Hylton was putting her second on the bill for an upcoming production of comedian Al Read's revue show, *Such Is Life*, which opened at the Adelphi Theatre on December 14th 1955 and where Shirley would stay for a year.

Another new Crazy Gang show would open in 1956 and Jack and the boys had another guaranteed success. *These Foolish Kings* (a play on words of their 1938 Palladium show *These Foolish Things*) opened at the Victoria Palace and would run for a now unsurprising 882 performances. Variety would also be offered with *United Notions*, twice nightly at the Adelphi, starring Tommy Trinder and Patachou (a French singer and actress, whose real name was Henriette Ragon), *Goody Two Shoes* with Jimmy Wheeler and Tommy Fields at Streatham Hill Theatre, and *Sooty In Family Fun* running in the afternoons at the Adelphi.

Amongst the many writers for the Crazy Gang shows were Frank Muir and Denis Norden, a prolific comedy writing team for decades in British radio and television. Their paths would cross not just writing for the Gang, but writing for some of Hylton's TV shows. Frank Muir's autobiography contains an interesting anecdote:

Months later Jack Hylton asked us to call in at his office.

"I haven't paid you enough for those bits you wrote for the Gang," he said.

Not paid enough? Was this the great Jack Hylton, notably careful with money, speaking?...He gestured towards the safe on the wall and his general manager, the genial and gifted Hughie Charles...drew out a packet of banknotes. Mr Hylton took two bunches and gave them to us. "A hundred each," he said. "Unless..." he said, raising his eyebrows, "unless you'd rather have equity shares in the new Rediffusion Television Company?"

Denis and I, clutching our lovely banknotes, exchanged glances. Green we may have been in money matters, but we knew instinctively when taking a risk would almost certainly be financial suicide.

"We'll take the money!" we said, smiling quietly to show that we knew better than to be paled off with a few dodgy shares.[19]

Ted Willis later suggested to the pair that their hundred pounds could have become fifty thousand if they had taken the shares! Ted Willis would become close friends with Hylton and the pair worked together on a number of Willis' stage plays, notably *The Blue Lamp*, (which featured a young Warren Mitchell), and *Doctor In The House* which Hylton bought the rights to in 1956. It ran at the Victoria Palace for six months, ahead of a year long tour of the provinces.

Whilst visiting France, Hylton had come across a revue show devised, written and directed by French comedian and actor Robert Dhéry, *La Plume De Ma Tante*. This curious piece was a mixture of English, easy to understand French, and mime. Its success in France was easily matched in England and subsequently America. Though several English revue artistes augmented the company, the show was essentially the same as the Paris revue. Being largely visual in its appeal, no adaptation was called for, while Dhéry himself, with his air of modesty and apprehension emerged as a comedian of universal stature, like Chaplin. One of the charms of the show appeared to be that something was always going wrong but whatever disasters occurred on stage, Dhéry maintained his deadpan look, and the company stoically kept their stiff upper lip.

The show would run at the Garrick Theatre for twenty months, before transferring to the Royale Theatre (now known as the Jacobs Theatre) on Broadway, where it ran for 835 performances after taking £92,000 in advance bookings, under the 'Jack Hylton Presents...' banner.

Damn Yankees would be Hylton's next big transfer from Broadway. This retelling of *Faust* in 1950s Washington D.C. centred around Major League Baseball was surprisingly successful given the source material, running at the Coliseum for 861 performances. The show starred Bill Kerr, Ivor Emmanuel and Olympic skater Belita, who was replaced soon after by Elizabeth Seal when it became clear that Belita could not fit into the choreographical style of Bob Fosse.

Also in 1957, Hylton brought the Bristol Old Vic production of *Oh! My Papa!* to the Garrick Theatre on July 17th. The show wasn't a great success, running for just 45 performances. This little known 'comedy to music' is noteworthy mostly for the possibly apocryphal story of another Hylton discovery; film director David Lean was looking for someone for an upcoming movie and Hylton, according to the story, brought the director to see *Oh! My Papa!* He found just who he was looking for, playing the part of Uncle Gustave – it was Peter O'Toole and the film in question was *Lawrence Of Arabia.*

By now estimates suggested that Hylton shows were accounting for ten per cent of all business in London's West End. However, Hylton was now in his mid-sixties and would have to slow down. Many years of twelve hour days and incessant partying was beginning to take its toll. In June of 1957 he was admitted to University Hospital with pneumonia, and would be in the hospital for his sixty-fifth birthday. He ignored the signal and in August he was back in hospital with a recurrence of the pneumonia. He stayed for a week then flew to his preferred August retreat of Deauville. For many years he and his family would decamp to Deauville in northern France, for the month of August and Jack would fly between there and London when business required it.

On October 20th Jack's wife, Ennis Parkes died at her home in Forest Court, Edgware Road. They had remained married since 1913, despite their deed of separation in 1931. It was revealed that Hylton had given her £50,000 as well as a house and £60 per week separation allowance. Ennis left £36,000 in her will to her partner Jock Scott.[20]

Once back to full health, Hylton re-signed his deal with Associated Rediffusion for another three years of entertainment content for ITV, despite the bashing from the critics. He also put *Kismet* out on tour, before bringing it back to the Princes Theatre for a short run in June, but television was taking up more and more of his time. On June 23rd 1959 Jack was asked to organise another Royal Variety Performance, and as ever he was giving the public exactly what they wanted, by organising the first rock'n'roll performances in such an event. Along with regulars Arthur Askey, Alan Ainsworth's BBC Northern Dance Orchestra, Jimmy Clitheroe, Roy Castle, Tommy Trinder and Billy Ternent, Hylton booked Liberace, Marty Wilde and Cliff Richard. The following year (on November 6th) he would add Sammy Davis Jnr., Diana Dors and Charlie Drake to the list on a show which, due to Hylton's astute accounting, would make a record profit of £22,922 for the Variety Artistes' Benevolent Fund.

1959 would also mark the start of the sixth consecutive Crazy Gang show at the Victoria Palace. Unsurprisingly, *Clown Jewels* would run twice nightly to packed houses and would end up playing 803 performances. In 1960 they announced they were to split up, but not until after their final show had run its course. *Young At Heart* opened at the Victoria Theatre on December 21st 1960 and ran until May 19th 1962. Naughton and Gold were by then 76 years old and had been working in variety since 1908. It was estimated that there had been a total of 13,572 Crazy Gang shows, to an audience of 27,000,000 with box office receipts totalling £14,000,000. The final show was recorded and ATV broadcast a ninety-minute version the following evening, as *The Last Night Of The Crazy Gang*. Bud Flanagan would go on to make his own TV show, *Bud*, based around his comedic attempts to get a job following the breakup of the gang. Hylton would occasionally appear.

The 1960s would see a significant slowing down in both work and play for Jack, as he entered his seventies, but he still had one final shocking card to play, as well as a number of huge new shows.

Chapter 16: Jack Hylton Juke Boxes

The prototype Jack Hylton Music Maker MK-1. (Photo courtesy of Tony Holmes)

It was not just the entertainment industry in which Jack Hylton was a leading light and forward thinker, the most notable of those 'extra-curricular' adventures being his importation of juke boxes.

This is a most extraordinary diversion for Hylton, though of course with some two thousand recorded titles in circulation through the 1940s perhaps it is no wonder that he found extra ways for them to be played. It had been mentioned to this author a number of times that Hylton was the first to bring a juke box to the UK and whilst this fact is not strictly true, the story of the *Jack Hylton Music Maker* is a fascinating one.

Wurlitzer jukeboxes had been imported into the UK in the 1930s in very small numbers. Wurlitzers were popular, to the point where pre-war customers were calling any juke box a 'Wurlitzer', such as the Seeburg Wurlitzer, or the Rock-Ola Wurlitzer, to denote Seeburg or Rock-Ola juke boxes. By the 1940s, restrictions on non-essential goods into the UK had taken hold (as they had in many countries during the war) and of course jukeboxes were far from essential, despite their popularity. As a result, whilst some existed, they were not freely available, certainly not to the American GIs, based in the UK:

> "What we miss most over here are our wives and families, juke boxes, hot dogs." Families and hot-dogs were not in Hylton's line. Juke boxes were. Last week two specimens of his efforts in that direction were on show at Westminster's Royal Horticultural Hall in the first post-war Amusement Devices and Trades Exhibition.[1]

Hylton had the idea to bring jukeboxes to the UK after having a drink with a US Colonel whilst on a trip to America. He secured a deal with the US Army to supply three hundred juke boxes at £237 10s each. He then set up Music Maker Ltd with a team of investors, who sank £30,000 into the project. Soon after, another two hundred juke boxes were ordered, with thirty being supplied each week.

Each was four feet high and two feet wide, with the facility to play sixteen ten-inch records, at 1d per play. The prototype model (Music Maker MK-1) featured the words *Jack Hylton Music Maker* on the front (as the picture on the previous page shows) and was made from the American Oak used for the packing crates, which delivered the Wurlitzer Simplex mechanisms that made up the innards of the new machines. Those crates, shipped in from America in military planes, were marked as "essential war effort supplies".[2] Subsequent production models (Music Maker MK-2) would be of a different design and made of fibreglass.

Hylton enlisted the help of a Hawtins Ltd. of Preston New Road, Blackpool, to manufacture the Music Makers. They were previously known for the manufacture of amusement machines for sea front arcades, specialising in machines for travelling fairs, fitted into robust metal cabinets.

Within four months of the initial shipment, the juke boxes were on general sale at £285 each, plus 33½% purchase tax. Alternatively, the machines were rented out with a share of the cash box takings used as payment, with the juke box being moved to another site if it did not make enough money.[3] In typical Hylton fashion, he bragged that his Music Maker could play a tune within four and a half seconds after the insertion of a coin, considerably quicker than the seven seconds the equivalent American models took! At the Amusement Devices and Trades Exhibition Hylton used the stars of his current shows to garner publicity for the new machine, with stars such as Jimmy Nervo, Teddie Knox, Arthur Askey etc. all being pictured with the Music Maker:

> Almost all the stars of the various Hylton shows were on view and had their photographs taken by zealous press men – usually in clusters around the instrument, looking at it, pointing at it, or caressing it.[4]

By the late 1940s, the MK-1 machines had been transformed into fibreglass MK-2 machines by butchering the original oak versions, taking their insides and planting them inside the new fibreglass bodies. The original wood was then sold. At the time of writing, there appears to be just one original machine in existence, currently being renovated by Anthony Holmes, in Sheffield. In around 1947, Hylton's company sold the Music Maker to Norman Ditchburn Equipment Ltd., based in Dock Road, Lytham St. Annes, near Blackpool. Ditchburn manufactured the MK-2 for several years, removing the *Jack Hylton* part of the logo and renaming it *The Ditchburn Music Maker*. When Norman Ditchburn bought the Music Maker Ltd company from the Jack Hylton group, he then negotiated with Hawtin's to buy the tooling and moved it to his factory in Lytham-St-Annes. His main interest was the contract with the US Army to supply jukeboxes and also to secure his supply of mechanisms from Wurlitzer.[5]

Later, Ditchburn would butcher these models, replacing the entire front panel with a new mechanism, enabling the playing of 45rpm singles. The machines had the top of the original cabinet sawn off, and replaced with a new pre-formed glass fibre hood and screen. The whole cabinet was repainted, had some new chrome lettering added and became the MK-2R, a best seller for many years, fighting it out for popularity with Sam Norman's Bal-Ami company, who began selling British made juke boxes in 1953.

We do not know exactly why Hylton sold the company, but it can be assumed that after the initial deal with the US Army, he felt his job had been done and he could move onto other projects, which, of course, he had plenty of.

At other times in his career, Hylton is said to have invested money in a range of projects as diverse as the original UK bowling alleys (at Stamford Hill and Golders Green in North London), a car-cover factory and, in connection with northern radio comedian Al Read, the British rights to the auto-cue – "an American gadget that flashes scripts on TV studio walls for the benefit of forgetful actors and announcers."[6]

Close up of the Jack Hylton Music Maker MK-1. (Photo courtesy of Tony Holmes)

Chapter 17: 1960-1965

Jack and Beverley Hylton on honeymoon in 1963. (Personal Collection)

Early in 1960, Jack Hylton suffered a minor heart attack, along with a hernia operation, and with that he finally knew it was time to slow down. Working days became shorter, holidays became longer and parties became calmer. The television contract had now expired, with neither party wanting to continue, but there were still plenty of shows carrying the 'Jack Hylton Presents...' banner. *Salad Days* had gone on tour following its epic run in London, including two Christmases in Manchester and it would make a welcome return to the West End; there was the usual slew of pantomimes around London (in 1961 Arthur Askey was in *Cinderella*, whilst Dickie Valentine was in *Babes In The Wood* and Tommy Trinder was in *Jack And Jill*); and there were plans for new shows with associated trips to New York.

The big new show in 1961 for Jack was *King Kong*. This was billed as a 'smash hit jazz musical with an all African cast' – which opened in Johannesburg in 1959 to huge acclaim. Before Hylton brought it to London 200,000 South Africans had seen it.

Written by Todd Matshikiza and Pat Williams, with a book by Harry Bloom, it charted the story of heavyweight boxer Ezekiel Dlamini, who was known as 'King Kong'. Born in 1921, he rose to fame as a champion boxer, only for his life to degenerate into alcoholism and violence. He was imprisoned for stabbing his girlfriend and eventually committed suicide whilst in prison. Not quite the usual Hylton storyline, nor the usual musical style, but with great fanfare, a sixty-strong all-black cast shipped over from the original production, and costs of £40,000, Hylton opened the show at the Prince's Theatre on February 2nd 1961. In May ITV televised a rather brutally edited fifty minute version of the show, then, despite good reviews and solid takings, the show closed in September. It then went on tour, beginning with five weeks in Scotland, but Jack abruptly pulled the tour in December, giving the cast two weeks notice and a proposed transfer to Broadway never materialised. He lost £5,000. Many of the cast stayed on in England after the tour finished and continued to work in a variety of contexts in and outside entertainment.

In 1962, Jack celebrated his seventieth birthday. He was holidaying in the South of France and his love life was as complicated as ever. Hylton was a keen supporter and friend of the England cricket team and met the Australian team during their visit to contest the 1962-63 Ashes series. After this he became close friends with all-rounder Keith Miller, who during his career had the best statistics of any all-rounder in history. Miller, despite having a wife and children in Australia, had beauty queen and model Beverley Prowse as his girlfriend in London.

*   *   *

Beverley Prowse was born in Mackay in Queensland, before moving first to Toowoomba and then to Melbourne in 1953. A year later she won the Miss Victoria title, in an age when the Miss Australia contest and its State preliminaries were increasingly significant, but did not provide a place in the Miss World finals in London for the national winner. A year later Beverley Prowse and the reigning Miss South Australia, Pat Doran, made their way to London, and a Fleet Street paper asked its readers to decide from photographs which of them should represent Australia in Miss World. Miss Victoria was chosen – and although she came only seventh in the international competition, her career was boosted by the publicity and she was regularly engaged in London, especially to model Australian fashions, notably swimsuits, and in promotional work.

In 1973 Beverley married, at Caxton Hall in London, the News International newspaper executive Alick McKay, whose first marriage had ended in bizarre tragedy when his wife Muriel was kidnapped on December 29th 1969. She was never seen again, but two brothers were found guilty of her murder. McKay was a leading figure in London's busy Australian social and business world, and his new wife moved cheerfully into expatriate life, increasingly involved in its charitable and cultural affairs. Alick McKay, who was knighted in 1977 for his services to the media, died in January 1983.

Long based in Chelsea, Lady Beverley McKay kept up an extensive string of social, cultural and sporting activities: she was a superb skier, a fine shot, a useful golfer, tackled fencing, archery, squash and water-skiing, and played bridge keenly. A life member at Queen's Club, she continued to play tennis even as diabetes increasingly affected her eyesight. Her most notable achievement was the conception and organisation of the spectacular Bicentennial Ball at Grosvenor House in 1988, as part of celebrations marking the 200th anniversary of the founding of Australia. A dynamic organiser with a knack of enthusing colleagues, Lady McKay raised £120,000; the Australian Government matched this to help to establish the Australian Bicentennial Scholarship and Fellowship Trust. Up to six students have been chosen annually since then, in both Australia and Britain, to further studies in the other country. Lady McKay retained a keen interest in the scheme. She was made a Member of the Order of Australia for her efforts. She died on May 15th 2000 at the age of 67. She had been unconscious for almost a week, and died peacefully, survived by her mother and stepchildren from both marriages.[1]

*   *   *

Hylton was introduced to Beverley by Keith Miller at Ascot, where he would always be found in Jack's private box, and in due course the pair would holiday at Jack's villa in the South of France when Keith wasn't playing cricket. Meanwhile Jack was having a particularly tempestuous time with Rosalina Neri and finally their relationship came to an end. Miller and Prowse subsequently split up and Miller encouraged Beverley to stay on in France – Miller's love life was just as complicated as Hylton's!

Actress Pat Marlowe (with whom Jack worked sporadically over the years and with whom he had had a lengthy and passionate affair) would also visit the villa in France. Soon after one visit in 1962, she tragically committed suicide, aged 28. She had a sixteen-month-old son who for some time was suspected to be Jack's, and his financial generosity towards the child only fuelled this fire. Many years later it was revealed that Stephen was the product of an affair between Marlowe and singer Max Bygraves. (There were also rumours over Elsie Carlisle's son, Willie. Elsie and Jack had an affair and again, Jack was very supportive financially towards them, but there is apparently no substance in the rumours that Jack had fathered another child.)

Jack told Ted Willis that up until then, Pat was the only woman he had ever truly loved; certainly he kept in touch with her long after their affair had ended, helped when she fell into drug addiction and made provision for her son.

Despite the wealth of beautiful women available to him, Jack's insatiable appetite would be appeased in a number of ways, as this anecdote from a few years previously explains:

> A subdued Jack came back from the airport the next afternoon having seen Pat on to her transatlantic flight. Within a few minutes of his return there was a knock at the door of the suite and when I opened it I found myself facing two lovely girls who looked so alike that they had to be twins...There followed a few minutes of giggling and slap and tickle then the three of them disappeared into the bedroom. I went to my room to do some work and left Jack to it for a couple of hours. When I returned to the suite the trio was just emerging – the two girls looked exhausted but Jack seemed to be as fresh as ever, his spirits completely recovered. He opened the famous case and gave each girl a handful of money. When they had gone he smiled with satisfaction and said, "I needed a tonic."[2]

Chapter 17: 1960-1965

Within this atmosphere, Jack and Beverley began a relationship, after Keith Miller had split with Beverley by letter. Beverley was 28; Jack was 70. This wasn't just another of Jack's conquests. When they arrived back in London, Jack invited Beverley to the White City dog races and began to send her flowers and they began courting. Of the two, Jack was by far the most energetic, as recalled to this author:

> The first show he took me to, before we were married, he said in the interval, "Can you remember any of the numbers?" I said "Yes, yes", you know, I was very keen... I said the main one and I sang that to him without any trouble...and he sat down at the piano and played eight of the numbers. He played them all...Then he pointed out lighting things, did I notice anything about the entrances or something and he was always looking at all different things about the theatre...

> ...I was always ready to go to the theatre at the drop of a hat and to lunch, or he'd come home for lunch if he had time...We saw a lot of each other; he was very happy and so was I...We were very close. I never thought of him as being as old as he was. He was much younger than me in a lot of ways.[3]

The couple shocked the entertainment world (and their own families) when, after an eight month courtship, on April 9th 1963 Jack married Beverley in a secret ceremony in Geneva:

> I was called from Geneva and he said, "I've got married" and I said, "That's nice, is it anybody I know?" because I didn't know who he'd gone away with![4]

With a £12,000 engagement ring on Beverley's finger, the couple went on an extended holiday, trying in vain to avoid the understandably curious press. They moved almost daily through Europe into North Africa, then back through Spain, back to London and then, some five weeks later, on to their regular haunts in Cannes.

Beverley recalled trying to keep pace with the 70 year old, who by this time had slowed considerably:

Jack Hylton

If ever we were apart his friends teased him that I was probably off with a younger man, but Jack always knew where I was. If I was not with him, I was usually asleep. One day Jack took a photograph of me, dead to the world. The next time someone teased him as to where I was, he produced the photograph of me fast asleep. "I know exactly where she is," he said.[5]

A few changes followed. Jack moved out of Hylton House and back into his much less grand, old office at the Adelphi theatre. He also sold both his villas in the South of France, along with his Turbocraft and his Riva speedboat (with the money being given to Rosalina Neri). He bought a palatial new home for himself and Beverley, Flat 15, 45 Grosvenor Square in Westminster and she was given the task of transforming it to their tastes, the only direction being "you can do what you like, but God help you if you make a mistake!"

Jack still had another big show to come. Throughout his career he had never had an opportunity to put a show into the Theatre Royal, Drury Lane (which had had a theatre on the site since 1663) and he finally got the chance in 1964 when he bought the rights to the Lerner and Loewe epic *Camelot* (in later life Hylton and 'Fritzy' Loewe became close friends). Based on the legend of King Arthur, the show had its premiere on Broadway in 1960, where it ran for 873 performances. Hylton's production opened on 19th August 1964, starring Laurence Harvey as King Arthur, Elizabeth Larner as Guenevere and Barry Kent as Lancelot. (It was often reported that this was Hylton's greatest triumph, or his final dream realised, but this was simply another show, in a venue in which he had long wanted to produce a show). Hylton was typically astute, making changes from the very successful Broadway version, reinstating two songs which had previously been cut, making dialogue changes, as well as changes to the finale. The show would run for 518 performances, but unfortunately Jack himself would not make the decision to close the show.

Interestingly, a 17-year-old Cameron Mackintosh worked as a stagehand on *Camelot*, his first job in theatre given to him by Jack Hylton, which surely counts as yet another Hylton 'discovery'. Within three years Mackintosh would be producing his own shows and would go on to become the Jack Hylton of his generation!

Chapter 17: 1960-1965

On January 26th 1965, complaining of chest and stomach pains, Hylton was admitted to the London Clinic, on Devonshire Place, Marylebone. He died there three days later, on January 29th, at 3.45pm, from a severe heart attack, with Beverley by his side. Even whilst in the hospital he was plotting his next move. He was keen to be out to supervise rehearsals for Laurence Harvey's replacement and had options on two plays (Neil Simon's *Barefoot In The Park* and *Nobody Loves An Albatross*) as well as the musical *Funny Girl*, starring Barbra Streisand, which would open in 1966, produced by Bernard Delfont, who bought the rights from the Hylton estate.

Even in death, Hylton was influencing the West End. On the evening of January 29th, part of the theatre sign reading 'Jack Hylton Presents...' outside *Camelot* at the Theatre Royal failed to light up when it was put on at about 3.30pm. The rest of the sign, bearing the title and names went on in the usual way. Shortly afterwards, the theatre received the news that Hylton had died. The following day was a Saturday, and the lights came back on as normal. As a mark of respect, all West End theatres switched off their front of house lights that evening.

The funeral took place on February 2nd, at Golders Green Crematorium. The chapel where the service took place was full to bursting and there was a relay into the cloisters, which were also full. The list of mourners included fellow impresarios and producers Prince Littler, Tom Arnold, George and Alfred Black and Val Parnell; entertainers Arthur Askey, The Crazy Gang, Elizabeth Larner, Laurence Harvey and bandleaders Ambrose, Geraldo and Victor Sylvester, amongst many others. His remains would in due course find home at the graveyard in the village of Gosfield, near Braintree, where Beverley was at one time planning to live. Many years later, Beverley would be buried next to him there.

On February 22nd, a memorial service took place in the beautiful surroundings of St. Martin In The Fields church in Trafalgar Square. Here in full is the address, written and delivered by Sir Alan Herbert (otherwise known as A.P.H.), humourist, novelist, playwright, law reform activist and great friend of Jack Hylton; they would spend many a Saturday evening together in the VIP area at White City greyhound races:

Jack Hylton

A memorial is not for mourning only. It is a salute, and here, at least, a happy salute – an act of respect and affection and gratitude for a good companion who did, and deserved well in a field where many of use have worked and are working still. We fly the flag at half-mast – but we fly the flag.

Jack Hylton did not die poor or disappointed or enfeebled by the years. He died full of fun and power, on a new peak of success. He had no money, he used to say, till he was thirty, but for the last forty years he had lived with those comforting words 'house full' at the doors of more than a hundred shows. He ended as he began, giving music and pleasure to the people. As a boy he sang for pennies in his father's pub. He was known, he liked to say, as 'the singing mill boy'. He had a strong musical training. He played the piano, he played the organ. He stayed with music all his life, and in that fine garden he had green fingers. He was the father, in this land at least, of the dance band. His records made millions happy with his beat, before these famous boys were born. Always alert for the turn of the tide, always after a new thing, he was the first here to give due place to orchestration – and his orchestration he did himself. Then, in another part of the wood, did he not put the London Philharmonic Orchestra on its feet, in wartime, with Malcolm Sargent at its head? Till the last, though for so long a master, he remained a member of the Musicians' Union.

A distinguished Welshman, a poet, and a fellow director of TWW – of which Jack Hylton was the real founder – wrote to a close friend, perhaps the closest:

> *Your world will be a very empty place without him, his moods, his genius, his faults, his handshake, his generosity of spirit, at which we who loved him could always rekindle the flame of hope in the human...the great human...a man as earthy as the next, but with a rich streak of heaven running through all his smiles and tears.*

He was a generous kindly man. "Money" he said, "was made to be spent." He looked out for the young – and he looked after them. He would spot a trombone player of talent in a military band and buy him out of the army. He put many on the first step of the ladder.

Chapter 17: 1960-1965

In the bands, and in the theatres, he must have high discipline, and everything just so. But it was a rule of calm and competence, not the crack of the whip. He was not one of those generals who sit far back at the base. He was up in the front-line, attending to everything. As you may hear from Bud Flanagan and his Gang – one of Jack's prime gifts to society – he was not afraid of altering the whole order of battle on the night before. 'I'm a good plumber' he liked to say. But no panic – no blustering or shouting.

He was good company and a bundle of quiet fun. "Life", his wife told me "was never dull". He was a good loser and could laugh at himself. How he would have loved the story I heard two days ago! On the morning of his funeral a famous press agency sent a notice to the newspapers reminding them that today was 'Jack Hylton's funeral – at the Golders Green Hippodrome'. Some warm admirer, full of memories, must have made that unconscious error.

As you might expect from the beginnings, he had a high respect for the common people. He hated privilege, and pomp, and the rude. You could hardly get him to Ascot, but I met him often at 'the dogs'. He talked of going into parliament, for Labour. All this, in the theatre, made him very much an 'audience man'. He had a keen sense of what his audiences wanted – and a firm resolve to give it to them. But that, we know, in many quarters is almost a crime.

The last time I saw Jack Hylton was at the last dress rehearsal of his last show, Camelot, *such an assembly of costume and colour, and care, as has not often been seen on the London stage. My wife and I had been invited to see it by Jack and his dear Beverley. All the evening he took the usual notes, but – calm and quiet as always – nothing he said or did would have suggested to a stranger that here was the real Emperor of the evening, who of all concerned had the most at stake, for reputation or reward. At the end, I remember, I said, 'I know exactly what the critics will say. But I know too what the people will say. They will come.' I was right about both. He said, the next day, I am told, "Leave them alone. After all no critic has got a statue yet."*

'Creative joy!' That was the beginning – that was the centre – that was the end of the life of Jack Hylton. Therefore, though we must think, as we do, of all those close to him with sympathy and sorrow, let us think of him with a good, and a glowing heart. Let us go out

Jack Hylton

from this gracious gathering, in this famous church, flying more proudly still the flag of our crafts, and resolute to do the best we can with any powers that we possess to make music and laughter and – an innocent aim, I think a noble aim – to give pleasure to the people.[6]

*   *   *

Hylton in the 1960s. (Personal Collection)

Hylton's wild spending habits and generosity left his estate with £242,288, despite the countless millions that he earned during his illustrious career. With duty of £83,484, this left £151,160 to be distributed many ways, with the first £30,000 reserved for his wife Beverley, along with their flat in Grosvenor Square. As Hylton said to his son during his latter years, "I won't leave you much, but we'll have a good laugh spending it while I'm here!"[7]

In March 1965, an appeal was launched to raise £35,000 to build the Jack Hylton Music Rooms at the newly built Lancaster University. Plans were put in place for a theatrical extravaganza to celebrate his life. ITV gave £20,000 to the fund, TWW gave £5,000 and the Musicians' Union gave £500. Meanwhile Bernard Delfont's organisation took over production duties, paying a percentage to the Hylton estate. The Vice-Chancellor of Lancaster University in its formative years was C.F. Carter, who stated that the purpose of the Jack Hylton Music Rooms was:

> (a) To encourage the practice and appreciation of music, popular and classical, among the students of the new University of Lancaster; and (b) To provide a new centre for the encouragement of music in Lancashire. The university sees music as a means of self-expression and enjoyment which should be easily available to all. One of the main difficulties in making music a freely available means of enjoyment is the lack of proper facilities for practise, whether by individuals, small groups, bands or orchestras. Hylton House would provide a range of small and medium-size rooms, facilities for recording and playback, storage for instruments and a library.[8]

Unsurprisingly, the plans changed somewhat, as did an initial idea to plant a short avenue of oaks and have Hylton's remains buried under one of them. However, the rooms were built and fifty years later are still in regular use at the University despite the decline of the music course there. Some years after the building was finished (complete with large grinning portrait of Jack in his Savile Row office) a large number of documents were transferred away from a damp storeroom high up in the Adelphi Theatre to the safer confines of the Special Collections Department of Lancaster University. It then became clear that Hylton was something of a hoarder. The archive contains press cuttings from 1922 until long after his death, vast collections of band music, show music and TV music, diaries, personal photos and huge numbers of production photos from shows, scripts, records, programmes, posters, awards and various items which used to be housed in his office. The vast collection of 78s was given to the British Library and all the recorded television content was donated to the National Film and Television Archive, the source of Pamela Logan's excellent book, *Jack Hylton Presents*. At the time of writing, there is an on-going project to make a number of scores available digitally for free download with the hope that the excellently arranged scores can once again be played in public, included a large number of concert arrangements which were never recorded so have not been heard for almost eighty years.

The Stars Shine For Jack, the concert which made all of this possible, took place on May 28th 1965 at the Theatre Royal, Drury Lane. Val Parnell and Prince Littler had arranged for the building and a considerable number of artists to be available and the two and a half hour show was broadcast live on ATV. The show included the Crazy Gang, reforming for the final time, the cast of *Camelot* and other West End shows, Russ Conway, Arthur Askey, Shirley Bassey, Marlene Dietrich, and Dickie Henderson as well as video tributes from Bob Hope, Danny Kaye, Sophie Tucker and Jack Benny.

It was a suitable send off for this most successful and loved of show business personalities. He had certainly lived life to the full and is often reported to have said: "Think champagne – and you'll be champagne. Think in terms of beer and a couple of quid a week and you'll end up with nothing".[9] He said shortly before his death:

> "I'd have it all over again...the same lot with the same errors and the same successes."[10]

Chapter 18: Hylton's Legacy

Jack Hylton caught off-guard. (Jack Hylton Archive)

Jack Hylton was the last of the big spenders. He was unashamedly out to make money and just as unashamedly out to spend it. "I was born poor", he once told me. "And now I have it, I'm going to enjoy it."…He was big, obstreperous, colourful, noisy, loveable, lavish. We all miss him. We shall never see his like again.[1]

Jack Hylton

In the years following Hylton's death, various television and radio companies revisited his work, both as a bandleader and as a theatrical impresario. By now many years had passed since he last made a record and stylistically there was little interest, given the differences between Hylton's very British 'symphonic syncopation' style of the 1930s compared to the more popular big band swing style which followed it. Plans for a TV special, with film footage donated by second wife Beverley never materialised. Billy Ternent put a band together in 1967 for a documentary on TWW called, inevitably, *Oh Listen To The Band*, which gave an overview of Hylton's life.

Various radio documentaries were made but there was a tendency to give an overview of both the music and the biographical detail, with the result that they tend to suffer from considerable repetition. As the protagonists began to pass away, things became more generic both on radio and on the sleeve notes of the regular LP reissues.

Despite Hylton's consistent philanthropy, the quiet and personal manner with which he went about it, coupled with his flagrant attitude to relationships meant he never became a figure of national importance in the years following his death. He never received the recognition in Britain that he received in France but what he cared about was living for the present and enjoying himself both with his work and his private life, none of which lends itself to historical longevity. As we have seen he made a marked impact on many aspects of entertainment but neither his hometown of Bolton nor his adopted home in London have seen fit to remember him.

The music still lives on though. The age of the CD and the download have led to a considerable number of his recordings becoming easily available and there are a number of dedicated fans who have the skills and technology to repair the sound of the old records. There is still a small but determined market to buy and sell the records themselves, going back to the Queen's Dance Orchestra pre-electrical recordings of the early 1920s. All of these recordings are now long out of copyright, which gives cottage industry record companies the facility to regurgitate and release, as often as they want, versions of the recordings no matter what the quality. The result is a slightly saturated market, with limited choice (relatively), but the fact that these recordings are available at all is encouraging. Whilst there is an audience for the sound of British dance bands, it is a small and diminishing one. More and more the music is finding an audience away from mainstream broadcast radio and the niche gets gradually smaller. Occasionally, TV or radio shows spark a little interest in the period and therefore the music (including *The Singing Detective* in the 1980s and *Downton Abbey* in the 2010s), and on more than one occasion a modern dance record has been made using Hylton's original music (Baz Luhrmann's *Happy Feet (High Heels Mix)* being the best example). From 1979 until 1998, the 1929 Hylton song *Breakaway* was used as the theme tune to the Saturday morning Radio 4 travel show of the same name.

Several bands still work extensively in the UK, for dances, theatre shows and private functions. Many delve into the Hylton repertoire, though few feature the show band line-up including strings which Hylton preferred. The Pasadena Roof Orchestra have been playing since the late 1960s, releasing many albums and doing much to spread the sound of 1920s and 1930s music in the UK. Michael Law's Piccadilly Dance Orchestra formed in 1988 and the band have appeared in a number of high profile television shows, as well as mirroring the bands on which it was based, with a six year residency at the Savoy Hotel, something which few bands can manage in the current climate. The Savoy has since been home to an even younger band, Alex Mendham and His Orchestra, thereby continuing the trend and introducing the music of this period to an even wider and younger audience.

At various times over the last fifty years, people have threatened to write a definitive biography about Hylton but this has never happened. Often the curious choices he made in his personal life have put people off and that has certainly put any family members off telling the 'gory details' of the story. As the years have passed, this side becomes harder and harder to tell. Most of what I have written was already freely available in other publications and some of the 'best' stories remain unpublished simply because they need not be told – an essence of what Hylton was like and how he led his life is contained in these pages, and I have promised various members of the family that I would tell the truth but with some discretion. I hope I have done that.

Jack Hylton

I don't expect this little book to relight a fire of interest into Hylton, but since 1993 when I realised there was no biography, I have had a desire to write it and I have finally afforded myself the opportunity to do just that. Things will have been missed out and other things will create arguments (especially amongst the quite rightly protective family) as to their authenticity or factual accuracy, but I am confident it is more thorough than anything else out there and should serve as a record of the man and his work, with a little social and cultural reference thrown in.

Jack Hylton was a fascinating man with a fascinating story and his huge musical legacy remains for us to enjoy, along with the legacy of the countless performers he helped to bring to our attention.

Hylton at the piano at daughter Jackie's 21st birthday party. (Jack Hylton Archive)

Notes

Preface

[1] Writer unknown, Back Beats by The Busker, *Melody Maker*, January 1931, p.9
[2] As it turns out after considerable research, Hylton was very good friends with the editors of both the Daily Express and the News Of The World!

Chapter 1

[1] A 'mill town' is a British term referring to the 19th century textile-manufacturing towns of northern England and the Scottish Lowlands, particularly the cotton manufacturing towns of Lancashire (Manchester, Oldham, Ashton-under-Lyne, Stalybridge, Rochdale, Wigan, Stockport, etc.) and the wool manufacturing towns of Yorkshire. These are the 'dark satanic mills' that William Blake speaks of in his hymn *Jerusalem*.
[2] Peacock, Doug, *Cotton Times – Understanding The Industrial Revolution*. <http://www.cottontimes.co.uk/overviewo.htm> Retrieved June 2014
[3] Hylton, Jack. The Merry Showman, *Daily Herald*, December 22nd 1952
[4] ibid. George Hilton speaking at a party after the Hylton band's first Royal Variety Performance, in 1926.
[5] Jack's birth certificate states 75 Boundary Street, but the road was renamed early in his life to Division Street, which was then significantly redeveloped in the 1970s.
[6] Hilton, Fred, Interview. In: *Oh Listen To The Band*, TWW, October 26th 1967. Television. In the programme Fred Hilton also suggests Jack won a clock in a singing competition whilst a small child in Bolton, though further references do not exist.
[7] Hylton, Jack, Just Ask Bolton! *Manchester News Chronicle*, August 23rd 1950. In Jack's words the house "overlooked" Burnden Park; this is a slight exaggeration.
[8] ibid
[9] Hylton, Jack, My 25,000 Miles Of Jazz, July 4th 1931.
[10] Irving, Sarah, *Exploring Greater Manchester's Grassroots History – The Clarion Movement*, <http://radicalmanchester.wordpress.com/2010/08/11/the-clarion-movement/> Retrieved June 2014.
[11] Hylton, Jack, How An Inspiration Led On To Fortune, *Tit Bits*, September 9th 1933
[12] Hylton, Jack, My Attitude To Money, *Daily Express*, March 1952
[13] Hilton, Fred, op. cit. Fred suggests that Mary Hilton opened a toffee shop whilst at Deane Church Lane, though this is probably the same shop given in other sources as George's grocers.
[14] ibid
[15] Hilton, Fred, op. cit.
[16] Hylton, Jack. The Merry Showman, *Daily Herald*, December 22nd 1952
[17] ibid
[18] ibid
[19] ibid

Chapter 2

[1] *Interlocutor* was the rather grand name given to the master of ceremonies of a concert party or Pierrot troupe, often portrayed with an aristocratic demeanour. In later minstrel shows this would be a blackface character.

[2] Kershaw, Baz (et al) *The Cambridge History of British Theatre, Volume 3*, Cambridge University Press, 2004, p.101-2

[3] Mellor, Geoff J., *The Northern Music Hall*, Newcastle-upon-Tyne: Frank Graham, 1970, p.81.

[4] "Seasider", My Diary Today, West Lancashire Evening Gazette, May 3rd 1941.

[5] The government's National Archives, at Kew, states: *"Contrary to popular belief, it has always been possible to change your name without having to register the change with any official body. It is still perfectly legal for anyone over the age of 16 to start using a new name at any time, as long as they are not doing so for a fraudulent or illegal reason."*

[6] Hylton, Jack, The Merry Showman, *Daily Herald*, December 22nd 1952. This generosity and financial recklessness would continue through Jack's life.

[7] A private correspondence with Edwin Adeler's great grandson suggested that Adeler felt he had 'been robbed' paying £2 per week for Hilton's services. It feels as though this may be a retrospective humorous comment in light of Jack's subsequent success.

[8] Hylton, Jack, Fame! – And What Feverish Fun We Had, *Daily Herald*, December 24th 1952. The name of Dr Pym is reminded to us in: Graves, Charles, Jack Hylton, Bandleader, Dies At 72, *Daily Telegraph*, January 30th 1965

[9] Hylton, Jack, How An Inspiration Led On To Fortune, *Tit Bits*, September 9th 1933

[10] Hayes, Chris, Born 1921 - Still Going Strong, *Melody Maker*, March 30th 1935, p.12

[11] Hylton, Jack, Tommy Handley And I Were A Flop! *Daily Herald*, December 23rd 1952

[12] ibid.

[13] Glidoon, John, The Romance Of Jack Hylton, *The Passing Show*, May 20th 1933

[14] ibid.

[15] Hylton, Ennis, Mrs Jack Hylton – Wife Of The Band Conductor, April 1933

[16] Hylton, Jack, The Merry Showman, *Daily Herald*, December 22nd 1952

[17] Halifax Daily Courier, July 28th 1943

Chapter 3

[1] From <http://www.arthurlloyd.co.uk/AlexandraTheatreStokeNewington.htm> Retrieved June 2014.

[2] Hylton, Jack, Tommy Handley And I Were A Flop! *Daily Herald*, December 23rd 1952

[3] One source states that the 400 Club had the backing of a diamond millionaire named Dunkles. There are no other mentions of this person and I have so far found no printed reference to him. It is mentioned out of curiosity.

[4] Hylton, Jack, op. cit.

[5] Gillie Potter (born Hugh Peel in 1887) was an English comedian and broadcaster, most famous between the wars as a music hall performer, and later as a campaigner against declining moral standards and for Englishness, which was his obsession. His radio broadcasts

Notes

were introduced with his famous catchphrase "Good evening England. This is Gillie Potter speaking to you in English." He died in 1975.

[6] Hylton, Jack, op. cit.

[7] Hylton, Jack, How An Inspiration Led On To Fortune, *Tit Bits*, September 9th 1933

[8] Hilton, George, When Jack Hylton Was A Singer, *Pearson's Weekly*, July 13th 1929

[9] Hylton, Jack, op. cit.

[10] Hylton, Jack, op. cit.

[11] Charles Robert William Howes (1895-1972) began his career, much like Hylton, in revues and became famous for his performance in Mr Cinders.

[12] Bickerdyke, Percy and Arthur Jackson, Dance Band Days: Jack Hylton, *This England*, Winter 1992, p.35

[13] Unsourced article, *A Lancashire Romance – Former Pierrot's Success With "Words And Music"*

[14] *The Daily Graphic*, December 28th 1922

[15] The number was recorded again on July 5th 1922 for the Zonophone label, though it was not released.

[16] Hylton, Jack, op. cit.

Chapter 4

[1] Hayes, Chris, *Leader Of The Band*, Blackpool: Lancastrian Transport, 1994, p.119

[2] A bomb demolished the hall in 1941 and despite lobbying the government chose not to have it rebuilt.

[3] Laurence, Dan H., ed., *Shaw's Music – The Complete Music Criticism of Bernard Shaw, Volume 3*. London: The Bodley Head, 1989

[4] Chapman, Gary, The Trix Sisters, *The Jazz Age*, <http://www.jazzageclub.com /personalities/the-trix-sisters/> Retrieved June 2014

[5] Chevalier is worthy of note simply for his extraordinary full name: Albert Onesime Britannicus Gwathveoyd Louis Chevalier.

[6] Walker, Ted, The "Queen's" Dance Orchestra, *Storyville 15*, London: Storyville Publications and Co. February-March 1968, p.24-26

[7] Hylton, Jack, The High Finance Of Jazz, *Rhythm*, January 1939, p.3

[8] Walker, Ted, op. cit.

[9] Whiteman hired, amongst many others famous jazz names Bix Beiderbecke, Jack Teagarden, Eddie Lang, Joe Venuti and Frankie Trumbauer.

[10] Earlier writings by this author suggested that the tune was *Ilo (A Voice From Mummyland)*, a foxtrot, but on closer examination this initial source was wrong. The Queen's Dance Orchestra may have played this title but it was not even recorded by Whiteman. There are no further references detailing exactly what this record would have been, but the fifty or so recordings by Whiteman in 1920 and 1921 are available to view here: <http://victor.library.ucsb.edu/index.php/talent/ detail/24581/Whiteman_Paul_leader>

[11] Hylton, Jack, (1) op. cit.

[12] Hylton, Jack. Fame! – And What Feverish Fun We Had, *Daily Herald*, December 24th 1952.

[13] Hylton, Jack, (1) op. cit., p.5

[14] From <http://www.78-records.com/78s-labels-HMV.htm> Retrieved June 2014.

[15] *Turque* was written by Paul Wyer and Pierre de Caillaux, both late of the Southern Syncopated Orchestra, who are discussed in Chapter 5.

Jack Hylton

[16] Beardsley, Robert & Leech-Wilkinson, Daniel, *A Brief History of Recording to ca. 1950*, <http://www.charm.rhul.ac.uk/history/p20_4_1.html> Retrieved June 2014

[17] Hylton, Jack, (2) op. cit.

[18] *Mon Homme* ('My Man') is a foxtrot from 1920 by the operetta composer Maurice Yvain (1891–1965) and the lyricist Albert Willemetz. This sentimental 'torch song' originated in France (as a hit for Mistinguett), was popularized in America by the comedienne Fanny Brice in the Ziegfeld Follies, and was recorded by Whiteman in 1921, with Henry Busse on trumpet and Hale Byers on saxophone. See Mawer, Deborah. *'Parisomania'? Jack Hylton and the French Connection,* Journal of the Royal Musical Association, Volume 133, Part 2, 2008, pp. 270-317

[19] Hylton, Jack, (2) op. cit.

[20] A transcribed reminiscence of pianist Billy Munn (serialised in Memory Lane magazine) suggests "Jack was very disconsolate about this, which took place on a Thursday or Friday evening. As he was walking down Southampton Row he came across a pal of his, a very famous jockey whose name escapes me [Brownie Carslake]. When asked why he was looking fed up Jack confided to him that he had just lost his job. The upshot was that his jockey friend suggested that Jack should go with him to Paris as he was racing at Longchamps that weekend. So Jack went over to France and came back early the next week."

[21] Lubenow, William C., *Liberal Intellectuals and Public Culture in Modern Britain, 1815-1914: Making Words Flesh,* Boydell & Brewer, 2010, p.106

[22] *After Dark – The Nocturnal Adventures Of Fynes Harte-Harrington* <https://fynesharteharrington.wordpress.com/tag/grafton-galleries/> Retrieved June 2014. This extraordinary website offers no insight into its history or validity, but offers intriguing detail of the period.

[23] Hylton, Jack, (2) op. cit.

[24] Martland, Peter, *Recording History The British Record Industry 1888-1931. Plymouth: Scarecrow Press*, 2013, p.325.

[25] Last Of The Knuts, The Times, October 21st 1957, p. 12

[26] *The Ariel Grand Record* existed from 1910 to 1938, confusingly releasing recordings by many of the popular bands of the time under the name of the Ariel Dance Orchestra or the Ariel Symphony Orchestra. They were released by Messrs J.G.Graves of Sheffield, England, who ran a department store, which sold the records via mail order.

[27] Chapman, Gary, Welcome To The Cabaret, *The Jazz Age*, <http://www.jazzageclub.com/cabaret/welcome-to-the-cabaret/> Retrieved June 2014

[28] On The Roof, *Pall Mall Gazette*, February 17th 1923

[29] Hylton, Jack, It's Fun To Find A Star, *Daily Herald*, December 26th 1952

[30] Hylton (3), op. cit.

[31] Hylton, Jack, (2) op. cit.

[32] Fenton, Alasdair, *Jack's Back*, BBC Radio Blackburn, October 13th 1971

[33] Briggs, Asa, *The History of Broadcasting in the United Kingdom: Volume I: The Birth of Broadcasting*, Oxford: OUP, 1995, p.254

[34] ibid, p.17

[35] Hylton, Jack, (2) op. cit.

[36] The performance in July 1926 was one of Hylton's most famous. He took part in a radio debate with Sir Landon Ronald on the respective merits of jazz and classical music. Both the Hylton band and the London Philharmonic Orchestra played, with both parties 'debating' their own genre of music. See Briggs, p.255.

[37] Colin, Sid, *And The Bands Played On*, London: Elm Tree Books, 1977, p.86

Notes

[38] Chapman, Gary, *The Kit Cat Club*, <http://www.jazzageclub.com/venues/the-kit-cat-club/> Retrieved July 2014.

[39] Syncopation And Dance Band News, *The Melody Maker and British Metronome*, June 1926, p.19.

[40] ibid.

[41] Hylton was unique at this time having two pianists.

[42] England's Coming Arranger, *The Melody Maker and British Metronome*, May 1926, p.2.

[43] Syncopation and Dance Band News, *The Melody Maker and British Metronome*, January 1927, p.29.

[44] ibid.

Chapter 5

[1] Munn, Billy. Interview. In: CLARKE, Tony, *The Band That Jack Built.* BBC Light Programme, September 14th 1965

[2] Despite his later mainstream popularity, Armstrong genuinely deserves his place as a trailblazer of early jazz.

[3] Kernfeld, Barry, ed. *The New Grove Dictionary Of Jazz,* London: Macmillan, 1988, p.580

[4] Colin, Sid, *And The Bands Played On*, London: Elm Tree Books, 1977, p.15. Of course Hylton was at the Queen's Hall Roof before this, but then this book throughout has a rather anti-Hylton bias.

[5] Munn, Billy. Transcribed Reminiscences. *Memory Lane Magazine*, Private collection.

[6] Riesenfeld, Hugo, "New Forms for Old Noises", *League of Composers Review [Modern Music]* 1 (June 1924), p.25-26.

[7] Drowne, Kathleen Morgan and HUBER, Patrick, *The 1920s,* Greenwood Publishing Group, 2004, p.204

[8] Hylton, Jack, The Triumph Of Syncopation, *The Radio Times*, June 18th 1926

[9] Colin, Sid, *And The Bands Played On*, op.cit., p.16

[10] Parsonage, Catherine (2003). A critical reassessment of the reception of early jazz in Britain. *Popular Music*, 22(3), pp.315–336. This excellent article re-appraises the role of the ODJB in the popularisation of jazz in Britain and I urge the reader to read it in full.

[11] ibid.

[12] Catalogue numbers for ten-inch HMV records were prefixed with a 'B', while twelve-inch records were prefixed with a 'C'.

[13] Munn, Billy. Transcribed Reminiscences. *Memory Lane Magazine*, Private collection.

[14] Martland, Peter, *Recording History The British Record Industry 1888-1931. Plymouth: Scarecrow Press*, 2013, p.326

[15] Hylton, Jack, Jazz! The Music Of The People, *Woman's World* (supplement), week ending October 27th 1934, pii.

[16] Ferde Grofé was Whiteman's chief arranger from 1920 to 1932, his most notable work being the arrangement of Gershwin's *Rhapsody In Blue*.

[17] Bigg, Robert L., Follow The Leader, *The Gramophone*, June 1926, p.37

[18] Hylton, Jack, The British Touch, *The Gramophone*, September 1926, p.146

[19] ibid

Chapter 6

[1] Jackson, Jeffrey H., *Making Jazz French: Music and Modern Life in Interwar Paris*, Durham, North Carolina: Duke University Press, July 2003

[2] Rust, Brian, *The Dance Bands*, Shepperton: Ian Allen, 1972, p.61

[3] New Popular Song Telephoned From New York To London, *The Melody Maker and British Metronome*, March 1927, p.229

[4] Mr. Jack Hylton Hurt In Motor Collision, *The Star*, February 11th 1927

[5] New Popular Song Telephoned From New York To London, *The Melody Maker and British Metronome*, March 1927, p.229

[6] Syncopation And Dance Band News, *The Melody Maker and British Metronome*, August 1927, p.759

[7] £42,000 A Year Refused, *Manchester Evening Chronicle*, July 6th 1928

[8] Dregni, Michael, *Django: The Life and Music of a Gypsy Legend*, Oxford: OUP, 2006, p.43

[9] An Internet forum reported in 2006 that one such figure was for sale for several hundred pounds, which had come from 'Poggy' Pogson's car, suggesting that Hylton had them fitted to the cars of the band. More likely, Hylton gave Pogson the Citroen at some point after having the car delivered in 1929.

[10] Our Band Room, *Rhythm*, May 1928, p.5

[11] Jazz Means Big Business, *The Sunday People*, June 12th 1927

[12] Hylton, Jack, The Menace Of 'The Talkies', *Encore*, April 26th 1929

[13] Jack Hylton's Party – A Rousing Send Off, *Era*, March 19th 1930. These figures are from Jack's own speech on the evening of their pre-European tour party. These figures are widely misquoted (including this author's previous research), but there is no reliable source for the misquoted version. The sales are again often misquoted.

[14] O'Malley, Pat. Interview. In: Fenton, Alasdair, *Jack's Back*, BBC Radio Blackburn, October 13th 1971

[15] Offended Mussolini, *Daily Mirror*, May 29th 1930

[16] The song was also recorded by Harry Bidgood, Arthur Lally, Arthur Rosebery and Debroy Somers.

[17] Writer unknown, Back Beats by The Busker, *Melody Maker*, London, January 1931, p.9

[18] Munn, Billy. Interview. In: Clarke, op.cit.

[19] Owen, Maureen, *The Crazy Gang – A Personal Reminiscence*, London: Weidenfeld and Nicolson, 1986, p.93

[20] Ramos, Jackie. Private communication, August 1998

[21] Owen, op.cit., p.94

Chapter 7

[1] Writer unknown, Jack Hylton At The Opera, *Edition Musical*, Paris, February 1931. All French press articles at: Lancaster University, Jack Hylton Archive and translated by Marion Freyther. Unless cited, authors of these articles are unknown.

Notes

[2] 'Classical' is taken to mean non-jazz music, typified by any well-known composer from Bach through to Schoenberg, in this instance. 'Classical' is a far from adequate description, but it is a broader term than 'symphonic', 'serious' or 'high-art'.

[3] Carew, Les, How Are The Mighty..?, *Nostalgia*, Vol.10 No.40, October 1990, p.19

[4] *Le Temps*, Paris, February 17th 1931. *Mavra* is a one-act comic opera, by Stravinsky (with libretto in Russian by Koshno), based on Pushkin's *The Little House at Kolomna*, written in 1922 for four voices and wind-heavy small orchestra. It was first performed, ironically, at the Paris Opera on June 3rd 1922 and was dedicated to the memory of Tchaikovsky and Glinka. It is one of Stravinsky's lesser known works and is rarely performed in concert.

[5] Carew, op.cit., p.19

[6] Clarke, Tony, *The Band That Jack Built*. BBC Light Programme, September 14th 1965

[7] Taruskin, Richard, *Stravinsky And The Russian Traditions Volume II*, Oxford: OUP, 1996, p.1569, note 104

[8] Stravinsky, Igor and Robert Craft (1), *Selected Correspondence Vol.II*, London: Faber, 1984, p.123

[9] Munn, Billy. Private communication, March 1997

[10] Craft, Robert, ed. *Selected Letters and Diaries of Vera and Igor Stravinsky: Dearest Bubushkin,* London: Thames and Hudson, 1985, p.44

[11] Stravinsky, Igor and Robert Craft (2), *Expositions and Developments*, London: Faber, 1962, p.82

[12] ibid., p.82

[13] Writer unknown, Another Classic Triumph For Hylton, *Melody Maker*, February 1931, p.100

[14] Stravinsky and Craft (1), op.cit., p.123

[15] Carew, op.cit., p.19

[16] Carew, op.cit., p.19

[17] At this stage of preparation for *Mavra*, Hylton was not conducting the band. Generally, the arranger would take early rehearsals, while Hylton dealt with matters of band business. Ternent in particular was an important part of the band in these situations. In: Fenton, Alasdair. *Jack's Back,* BBC Radio Blackburn, October 13th 1971, "I think the disciplinarian of them all was Billy Ternent who was the orchestra leader in fact, and the orchestrator and in fact the man behind the scenes in general... What Billy said went, and as far as rehearsals went, he was always there."

[18] This and all other cited scores, at: Lancaster University, Jack Hylton Archive

[19] Carew, op.cit., p.19

[20] Munn, Billy. Private communication, March 1997

[21] One point for which only one source has been found is that Stravinsky "kept his word" and conducted one of the band's rehearsals, just two days before the concert. They report that everything "seemed to be going smoothly". None of the other sources mention this, and surely, it would have been worth mentioning, in the circumstances. It may originally have been the idea, but Stravinsky had met them some weeks before, and was merely an onlooker and adviser on this occasion.

[22] Stravinsky and Craft (1) also mentions this in reference to Hylton. One of the chosen pieces for the concert was the *Mavra Overture*, described as having "no flavour of any sort whatever". In: Writer Unknown, BBC Concert – A Stravinsky Programme, *The Times*, January 29th 1931

[23] Herzfeld, Friedrich, *Igor Stawinsky*, Berlin: Rembrandt Verlag, 1961

[24] Piano and vocal reduction. In: Lancaster University, Jack Hylton Archive
[25] Writer Unknown, Stravinsky And Jack Hylton – Jazz Version Of Operatic Excerpt, *The Times*, January 29th 1931
[26] Rust, Brian and Sandy Forbes, *British Dance Bands On Record 1911-1945 and supplement*, 2nd rev.ed., Harrow: General Gramophone, 1989, p.442
[27] *Progres de Lyons*, Lyon, February 15th 1931
[28] Writer unknown, Another Classic Triumph For Hylton, *Melody Maker*, February 1931, p.100
[29] *Edition Musical*, op.cit.
[30] Carew, op.cit., p.20
[31] Clarke, op.cit.
[32] Jack's Mood, *Le Carnet de la Semaine*, Paris, March 11th 1931
[33] Carew, op.cit., p.20/21
[34] Clarke, op.cit.
[35] Carew, op.cit., p.20/21
[36] Writer unknown, Shades Of Grand Opera – Hylton Makes More History, *Melody Maker*, March 1931, p.217
[37] *Le Carnet de la Semaine*, op.cit.
[38] The piece was never published, as a result no doubt, of this performance and Hylton's subsequent reaction.
[39] Stravinsky and Craft (1), op.cit., p.123
[40] Stravinsky and Craft (2), op.cit., p.82
[41] White, E.W., *Stravinsky*, London: Faber, 1966, p.269
[42] *Le Carnet de la Semaine,* op.cit.
[43] Jack Hylton At The Opera, *Monde Musical*, Paris, February 28th 1931
[44] ibid.
[45] *Edition Musical*, op.cit.
[46] Jack Hylton At The Opera, *Paris Excelsior*, Paris, February 21st 1931
[47] It should be remembered, however, that *Mavra* was only ever an excursion into the world of Stravinsky, at his request and not a change of direction to which the band or the audience could relate.
[48] Clarke, op.cit.
[49] Carew, op.cit., p.21

Chapter 8

[1] Writer unknown, *Rhythm*, London, May 1931. In: *Vintage Light Music*, No.78, Spring 1994, p.2
[2] *The Daily Chronicle*, 11th August, 1931.
[3] Rust, Brian, *The Dance Bands*, Shepperton: Ian Allen, 1972, p.61
[4] Fenton, Alasdair, Jax Bax, *RSVP*, April 1966, Part 11
[5] At private engagements, the verses would become more risqué. Songwriter Leslie Sarony wrote alternatives (many of which are not suitable for print) including, for example: "There was a young girl from Madras, who had the most wonderful ass. Not round and rose pink, as some of you think, but grey with big ears and eats grass"!
[6] ibid. Part 8
[7] Broadcast To America, *Glasgow Evening News*, December 14th 1931.
[8] A Broadcasting Mystery, *The Melody Maker*, January 1932, p.21

Notes

[9] ibid.

[10] Colin, op.cit., p.92. Another source suggests that while carrying out this manoeuvre, he was also doing a 'step-dance'. In: Writer unknown, Chords, *Popular Music and Dancing Weekly*, No.2 Vol.1, October 20th 1934

[11] ibid.

[12] Hylton, Jack, This Thing Called Travel, *Rhythm*, February 1933.

[13] Room For Both, *The Daily Star*, January 12th 1933.

[14] Hylton, Jack, My Adventures in Jazzland, *Tit-Bits*, September 23rd 1933, p.13.

[15] Hylton, Jack, *A Concert Of The Music Of Duke Ellington*. At: National Jazz Archive.

[16] Panassie, Hugues, Duke Ellington at la Salle Pleyel, from *Douze Annees De Jazz, 1927-1938: Souvenirs*, Paris, 1946, p.107. Translated by Stanley Dance, 1991. In: TUCKER, Mark, ed., *The Duke Ellington Reader*, New York: OUP, 1993, p.87

[17] Rust, Brian, *The Dance Bands*, Shepperton: Ian Allen, 1972, p.62

[18] Cab Out: Jack in, *The Melody Maker*, March 24th 1934, p.1.

[19] Wareing, Tom, interviewed in Alasdair Fenton, *Jack's Back* – BBC Radio Blackburn, October 13th 1971

[20] Holloway, Stanley, *Wiv A Little Bit O' Luck*, London: Leslie Frewin, 1967, p.20-22

Chapter 9

[1] Ades, David; Bickerdyke, Percy; Holmes, Eric (July 1999). *This England's Book of British Dance Bands*. Cheltenham: This England Books.

Chapter 10

[1] Mystery U.S. Offer to Hylton, *Melody Maker*, June 9, 1934, p.1

[2] Hylton, Jack, I Don't Bear Any Ill Toward Anyone!, *Down Beat*, Vol. 2, No.11, November 1935

[3] A great deal more information on Paul Specht and his career is available online at <http://mgthomas.co.uk/Dancebands/American%20Visitors/Pages/Paul%20Specht.htm>

[4] Aeroplane Escort Of Honour Arranged To Receive Hylton On Arrival At New York, *Melody Maker*, October 5th 1935, p.1

[5] Jack Hylton's Greatest Adventure, *Melody Maker*, October 19th 1935, p.1

[6] Some reports suggest that the band travelled on the *SS Normandie*'s maiden voyage, but this occurred on May 29th 1935. The *Normandie* was the latest ship belonging Compagnie Générale Transatlantique who owned the ship on which Jack had often travelled – the *Ile De France*. The *Normandie* would break the world record for Atlantic crossings on its maiden voyage, arriving in New York in four days, three hours and fourteen minutes.

[7] Ternent, Billy, interviewed in Tony Clarke, *The Band That Jack Built* – BBC Light Programme, September 14th 1965

[8] Fenton, Alasdair, Jax Bax, *RSVP*, April 1966, Part 13

[9] *Daily News*, Chicago, January 28th 1936

Chapter 11

[1] National Programme Listings, *The Radio Times*, Issue 687, 27th November 1936, p.52

[2] Hylton At The Peak Of His Powers, *The Melody Maker*, April 3rd, 1937, p.1

[3] Brooks, Mathison, I Speak As I Find, *Rhythm*, London, December 1938, p.6

[4] Malo, June. Interview. In: Clarke, Tony, *The Band That Jack Built*, BBC Light Programme, September 14th 1965

[5] Hylton Back On The Road, *The Melody Maker*, July 2nd 1938, p.1

[6] Violinist Andre Budegary was born Ernest Lewis, and became the Hylton band's 'gypsy violinist' in 1936, where he stayed until 1939. The band felt that Ernest was not an appropriate name for such a role, so whilst on a European tour, they took half of Budapest and half of Hungary, creating 'Budegary', adding 'Andre' for extra effect! The name stuck and friends knew him as 'Andy' until his death in 2003.

[7] Brooks, Mathison, The Hyltonian Formula For Success On The Variety Stage, *The Melody Maker*, September 24th 1938, p.11

[8] < https://www.youtube.com/watch?v=dFRoNw9K8mA> Retrieved September 2014

[9] Letter from Jack Hylton to Mr H Wise, private collection.

[10] Unsourced magazine article, private collection.

[11] Hylton, Jack, *Melody Maker*, January 27th 1940

[12] Hayes, Chris, *Leader Of The Band*, Blackpool: Lancastrian Transport, 1994, p.119

[13] Fenton, Alasdair, Jax Bax, *RSVP*, April 1966, Part 22

[14] O'Malley, Pat, interviewed in Alasdair Fenton, *Jack's Back* – BBC Radio Blackburn, October 13th 1971

Chapter 13

[1] Garfield, Simon, *We Are At War: The Diaries of Five Ordinary People in Extraordinary Times*, Random House, London, 2005, p.317

[2] Hylton Rescues Philharmonic, *Daily Sketch*, July 27th 1940

[3] Malo, June, interviewed in Tony Clarke, *The Band That Jack Built* – BBC Light Programme, September 14th 1965

[4] My Weekly News, *Blackpool Gazette*, October 5th 1940

[5] Hayes, op.cit., p.130

[6] Hylton, John. Private interview, July 1998

[7] This anecdote comes courtesy of current owner Marianne Arben, who interviewed Rose in 1997.

[8] Glenn Miller Mystery Remains, *The Milwaukee Journal*, December 15th 1964

[9] Hylton, Jack, Danger! Crazy Gang At Play! *Tit-Bits*, May 4th 1945

[10] Hylton, Jack, 4000 Coupons For A Show, *The Leader*, April 1943

[11] Some sources suggest that Hylton produced *Annie Get Your Gun*. According to all other literature, Prince Littler was the producer of this long running musical. Whether Hylton had any financial input is unclear, but seems unlikely.

[12] Flanagan, Bud, Spectacular Show For A Super Showman, *TV Times*, May 27th 1965, p.8

[13] Hylton, John. Private interview, July 1998

[14] Dherbier, Yann-Price, *Audrey Hepburn: A Life In Pictures*, London: Anova Books, 2007, p.9

[15] Vedey, Julian, *Band Leaders,* London: Rockliff, 1950, p.10

[16] Goodman, Arnold, *Tell Them I'm On My Way,* London: Chapmans, 1993, p.133

[17] Willis, Ted, *Evening All*, London: Macmillan, 1991, p.103

[18] ibid.

Chapter 15

[1] Fenton, Alasdair, Jax Bax, *RSVP*, April 1966, Part 24

[2] Fight For Your Money, *Evening Standard*, December 8th 1952

[3] Manchester Guardian, quoted in full page advert for the Circus, reproduced in *The World's Fair*, January 10th 1953, p.7

[4] Balfour, John, Jack Hylton In The Lions' Den, *The Daily Sketch*, December 24th 1953

[5] Ottaway, Robert, The Indomitable Showman, *Sunday Graphic*, February 2nd 1954, p.2

[6] Jackson, Jack, interviews in: Tony Clarke, *The Band That Jack Built* – BBC Light Programme, September 14th 1965

[7] Hylton, Jack, Why I Want To Be An MP, *Daily Mirror*, February 23rd 1954, p.7

[8] Fay, Gerard, A Long Way From The "Singing Millboy" Of Bolton, *The Manchester Guardian*, February 20th 1954

[9] Logan, Pamela W., *Jack Hylton Presents*, London: BFI, 1995, p.1. The reader is referred to this excellent, detailed book for more information on Hylton's television output, of which only a brief synopsis is given here.

[10] Black, Peter. In: Logan, ibid., p.32

[11] Baily, Kenneth. In: ibid., p.57

[12] ibid., p.66

[13] Hylton, John. Private interview, July 1998

[14] Phillips, Philip, *Daily Herald*, December 22nd 1956. In: LOGAN, op.cit., p.21

[15] Willis, Ted, *Evening All*, London: Macmillan, 1991, p.103

[16] <http://robertmeyer.wordpress.com/2007/02/22/opening-night-fiasco/> Retrieved August 2014.

[17] Willis, Ted, op. cit., p.108-9

[18] Williams, John, *Miss Shirley Bassey*, London: Quercus, 2010, p.116

[19] Muir, Frank, *A Kentish Lad*, London: Random House, 2012, p.199-200

[20] Jackie Ramos, when referring to Ennis, said her father was "petrified of the woman". Private communication, August 1998

Chapter 16

[1] Jack's Juke Boxes – Records On Tap, *News Chronicle*, February 14th 1946

[2] Much of the detail comes from an unsourced PDF document, with no available author: <http://www.coin-opcommunity.co.uk/wp-content/uploads/2011/11/Jack-Hylton-and-the-first-British-jukebox.pdf> Retrieved May 2014

[3] <http://www.jukebox-world.de/Forum/Archiv/England/HawtinsMusicMaker.htm> Retrieved May 2014

[4] Hylton's Juke Box, *The Performer*, February 14th 1946

[5] Bailey, Freddie, *The Music Maker Story*, < http://www.coin-opcommunity.co.uk/blog/3568-the-music-maker-story-freddy-bailey/> Retrieved May 2014

[6] Wilson, Cecil, The House That Jack Built, *Daily Mail*, November 4th 1955, p.6

Chapter 17

[1] Lady McKay Obituary, *The Times*, May 29th 2000

[2] Willis, Ted, *Evening All*, London: Macmillan, 1991, p.107

[3] McKay, Lady Beverley. Private interview, July 1998

[4] Hylton, John. Private interview, July 1998

[5] McKay, Lady Beverley, *The View From Camelot,* unfinished and unpublished memoir, private collection, chapter 5

[6] A.P.H., *An Address For A Memorial Service To Jack Hylton.* In: Jack Hylton Archive, Lancaster University.

[7] Hylton, John. Private interview, July 1998

[8] *The Stars Shine For Jack,* un-sourced newspaper article, May 1965

[9] Passingham, Kenneth, *Daily Sketch,* January 30th 1965

[10] Lewin, David, King Of The Champagne Showmen, *Daily Mail,* January 30th 1965

Chapter 18

[1] Flanagan, Bud, Spectacular Show For A Super Showman, *TV Times,* May 27th 1965, p.8

Complete UK Discography

This is the complete discography for Jack Hylton, from the initial recordings with the Queen's Dance Orchestra in 1921, to the final recordings in March 1940, predominantly on the HMV label, but also his time working for Decca in the 1930s and other subsidiary labels.

The discography, kindly prepared for the Jack Hylton website (www.jackhylton.com) by Denis Pereyra includes recording date, recording venue and record number information. The left hand 'band code' column translates as follows:

ADO - Ariel Dance Orchestra
EDO - Embassy Dance Orchestra
GDO - Grosvenor Dance Orchestra
JH - Jack Hylton vocal, accompanied by members of orchestra
JHBLB - Jack Hylton's Brighter London Band
JHJB - Jack Hylton's Jazz Band
JHKCB - Jack Hylton's Kit-Cat Band
JHO - Jack Hylton and His Orchestra
MGDO - The "*Metro-Gnomes*" Dance Orchestra
QDO - Queen's Dance Orchestra
TR - The Rhythmagicians

For more discographical information, the reader is referred to Brian Rust and Sandy Forbes' out of print but widely regarded *British Dance Bands On Record, 1911-1945.*

Band Code	Title	Recording Date	Recording Location	Record Number
QDO	Idol of Mine	28/05/1921	Hayes, Middlesex	HMV B-1237
QDO	Turque	28/05/1921	Hayes, Middlesex	HMV B-1236
QDO	The Wind In The Trees	28/05/1921	Hayes, Middlesex	HMV B-1237
QDO	I'm Wondering If It's Love (waltz)	28/05/1921	Hayes, Middlesex	HMV B-1236
JHJB	Love Nest	08/07/1921	Hayes, Middlesex	Zonophone 2155
JHJB	Billy	08/07/1921	Hayes, Middlesex	Zonophone 2167
JHJB	Mon Homme	08/07/1921	Hayes, Middlesex	Zonophone 2155
JHJB	Wang-Wang Blues	08/07/1921	Hayes, Middlesex	Zonophone 2167
QDO	Ilo (A Voice From Mummyland)	30/08/1921	Hayes, Middlesex	HMV B-1258
QDO	So Now You Know	30/08/1921	Hayes, Middlesex	HMV B-1258
QDO	Salome	30/08/1921	Hayes, Middlesex	HMV B-1259
QDO	Campañas	30/08/1921	Hayes, Middlesex	HMV B-1262
QDO	Coal Black Mammy	04/10/1921	Hayes, Middlesex	HMV Rejected
QDO	Mooning	04/10/1921	Hayes, Middlesex	HMV Rejected
QDO	Beautiful Faces	04/10/1921	Hayes, Middlesex	HMV Rejected
QDO	A Trombone Cocktail	04/10/1921	Hayes, Middlesex	HMV B-1276
JHJB	Coal Black Mammy (take 4)	12/10/1921	Hayes, Middlesex	Zonophone 2191
QDO	Coal Black Mammy (take 5)	12/10/1921	Hayes, Middlesex	HMV B-1275
QDO	Mooning (take 4)	12/10/1921	Hayes, Middlesex	HMV B-1275
JHJB	Mooning (take 5)	12/10/1921	Hayes, Middlesex	Zonophone 2191
QDO	Counting The Days	12/10/1921	Hayes, Middlesex	HMV B-1276
JHJB	So Now You Know	18/10/1921	Hayes, Middlesex	Zonophone 2223
JHJB	T'sing	18/10/1921	Hayes, Middlesex	Zonophone 2223
JHJB	Laughing Waltz	18/10/1921	Hayes, Middlesex	Zonophone 2199
JHJB	My Mammy	18/10/1921	Hayes, Middlesex	Zonophone 2199
QDO	Circulation (waltz)	27/10/1921	Hayes, Middlesex	HMV B-1286
QDO	Gossiping (waltz)	27/10/1921	Hayes, Middlesex	HMV B-1286
QDO	Silver Star (waltz)	27/10/1921	Hayes, Middlesex	HMV B-1287
QDO	Sweet And Low (waltz)	27/10/1921	Hayes, Middlesex	HMV B-1287

Jack Hylton

QDO	Beautiful Faces	15/11/1921	Hayes, Middlesex	HMV B-1298
QDO	Why?	15/11/1921	Hayes, Middlesex	HMV B-1298
QDO	The Bull Frog Patrol	15/11/1921	Hayes, Middlesex	HMV B-1299
QDO	Come Along	15/11/1921	Hayes, Middlesex	HMV B-1299
QDO	Drifting Along With The Tide	13/02/1922	Hayes, Middlesex	HMV B-1330
QDO	J'en ai marre	13/02/1922	Hayes, Middlesex	HMV B-1330
QDO	Palais de Danse	13/02/1922	Hayes, Middlesex	HMV B-1329
QDO	True Love	02/03/1922	Hayes, Middlesex	HMV B-1342
QDO	Arabian Love	02/03/1922	Hayes, Middlesex	HMV B-1352
QDO	The Lady Of The Rose (waltz)	02/03/1922	Hayes, Middlesex	HMV B-1340
QDO	Please Do It Again	13/04/1922	Hayes, Middlesex	HMV B-1351
QDO	Little Miss Springtime	13/04/1922	Hayes, Middlesex	HMV B-1352
QDO	And Her Mother Came Too	13/04/1922	Hayes, Middlesex	HMV B-1351
QDO	Tell Tale Eyes	07/06/1922	Hayes, Middlesex	HMV B-1364
QDO	Singing	07/06/1922	Hayes, Middlesex	HMV B-1364
QDO	Hawaiian Eyes (waltz medley)	07/06/1922	Hayes, Middlesex	HMV B-1365
QDO	Tigern	27/06/1922	Hayes, Middlesex	HMV X-1536
QDO	Tidkulan	27/06/1922	Hayes, Middlesex	HMV X-1536
QDO	If Winter Comes	27/06/1922	Hayes, Middlesex	HMV B-1386
QDO	Billy	27/06/1922	Hayes, Middlesex	HMV B-1402
JHJB	Roaming	05/07/1922	Hayes, Middlesex	Zonophone 2248
JHJB	Ma!	05/07/1922	Hayes, Middlesex	Zonophone 2248
JHJB	Say It With Music	05/07/1922	Hayes, Middlesex	Zonophone 2260
JHJB	Singing	05/07/1922	Hayes, Middlesex	Zonophone Rejected
QDO	In Romany (issued as Pamela Baselow)	19/07/1922	Hayes, Middlesex	HMV C-1085
JHJB	Rosy Cheeks	19/07/1922	Hayes, Middlesex	Zonophone 2260
QDO	Evergreen Eve	19/07/1922	Hayes, Middlesex	HMV B-1386
QDO	Jenny	16/08/1922	Hayes, Middlesex	HMV B-1387
QDO	Limehouse Blues	16/08/1922	Hayes, Middlesex	HMV B-1387
QDO	Robinson Crusoe's Isle	16/08/1922	Hayes, Middlesex	HMV B-1389

Complete UK Discography

QDO	Phi-Phi	Hayes, Middlesex	15/09/1922	HMV B-1401
QDO	Honey Love	Hayes, Middlesex	15/09/1922	HMV B-1401
QDO	Pourquoi? (waltz)	Hayes, Middlesex	15/09/1922	HMV B-1402
JHJB	Singing	Hayes, Middlesex	20/09/1922	Zonophone 2284
JHJB	Stumbling	Hayes, Middlesex	20/09/1922	Zonophone 2271
JHJB	Limehouse Blues	Hayes, Middlesex	20/09/1922	Zonophone 2272
JHJB	Winter Rose	Hayes, Middlesex	20/09/1922	Zonophone 2272
JHJB	Dear Old Southland	Hayes, Middlesex	20/09/1922	Zonophone 2271
QDO	Dancing Time	Hayes, Middlesex	29/09/1922	HMV B-1403
QDO	Shufflin' Along	Hayes, Middlesex	29/09/1922	HMV B-1403
QDO	The Camel Walk	Hayes, Middlesex	06/10/1922	HMV B-1409
QDO	El Tango de Amor	Hayes, Middlesex	06/10/1922	HMV ("For Paris")
QDO	Carne de Cabaret	Hayes, Middlesex	06/10/1922	HMV ("For Paris")
JHJB	Deedle Deedle Dum	Hayes, Middlesex	06/10/1922	Zonophone 2284
QDO	Sally	Hayes, Middlesex	11/10/1922	HMV B-1409
QDO	Loving As We Do	Hayes, Middlesex	11/10/1922	HMV B-1426
QDO	Caravan	Hayes, Middlesex	06/11/1922	HMV B-1426
QDO	Uncle Sambo	Hayes, Middlesex	06/11/1922	HMV B-1425
QDO	Eleanore	Hayes, Middlesex	06/11/1922	HMV B-1425
JHJB	Wana	Hayes, Middlesex	14/11/1922	Zonophone 2298
JHJB	Kitten On The Keys	Hayes, Middlesex	14/11/1922	Zonophone 2310
EDO	Kitten On The Keys	Hayes, Middlesex	14/11/1922	Ariel 3506
JHJB	I Ain't Nobody's Darling	Hayes, Middlesex	14/11/1922	Zonophone 2298
EDO	Loving As We Do	Hayes, Middlesex	14/11/1922	Zonophone 2310
ADO	Loving As We Do	Hayes, Middlesex	14/11/1922	Ariel 3506
QDO	My Sweet Hortense	Hayes, Middlesex	22/11/1922	HMV B-1438
QDO	I Ain't Nobody's Darling	Hayes, Middlesex	22/11/1922	HMV Rejected
QDO	Someone's Losing You	Hayes, Middlesex	22/11/1922	HMV Rejected
QDO	Where The Bamboo Babies Grow	Hayes, Middlesex	22/11/1922	HMV Rejected
JHO	I Ain't Nobody's Darling	Hayes, Middlesex	20/12/1922	HMV B-1524

Jack Hylton

JHO	Oh! Star Of Eve	20/12/1922	Hayes, Middlesex	HMV B-1523
GDO	Dear Dream Rose Of Mine	20/12/1922	Hayes, Middlesex	Zonophone Rejected
JHO	Where The Bamboo Babies Grow	29/12/1922	Hayes, Middlesex	HMV B-1525
JHO	From Top To Toe	29/12/1922	Hayes, Middlesex	HMV Rejected
JHO	Who Tied The Can On The Old Dog's Tail?	29/12/1922	Hayes, Middlesex	HMV B-1524
GDO	Oh! Star Of Eve (Intro. "If Winter Comes")	09/01/1923	Hayes, Middlesex	Zonophone 2343
GDO	Hot Lips	09/01/1923	Hayes, Middlesex	Zonophone 2324
GDO	Evergreen Eve	09/01/1923	Hayes, Middlesex	Zonophone 2324
GDO	Dancing Time (Intro. "Shimmy With Me")	09/01/1923	Hayes, Middlesex	Zonophone 2343
JHO	Sheba	11/01/1923	Hayes, Middlesex	HMV B-1525
JHO	Dancing Honeymoon	11/01/1923	Hayes, Middlesex	HMV B-1523
GDO	Dear Dream Rose Of Mine	15/01/1923	Hayes, Middlesex	Zonophone 2323
GDO	Some Day Soon	15/01/1923	Hayes, Middlesex	Zonophone 2323
GDO	Gliding	15/01/1923	Hayes, Middlesex	Zonophone 2357
JHO	Russian Rose	14/02/1923	Hayes, Middlesex	HMV B-1562
GDO	Dearie, If You Knew	14/02/1923	Hayes, Middlesex	Zonophone 2357
JHO	From Top To Toe	19/02/1923	Hayes, Middlesex	HMV B-1562
JHO	Lonely	19/02/1923	Hayes, Middlesex	HMV Rejected
JHO	Tampa Bay	19/02/1923	Hayes, Middlesex	HMV B-1587
JHO	March Winds	19/02/1923	Hayes, Middlesex	HMV Rejected
JHO	Lonely	06/03/1923	Hayes, Middlesex	HMV B-1587
JHO	Greenwich Witch	06/03/1923	Hayes, Middlesex	HMV B-1588
JHO	Just Like A Thief	06/03/1923	Hayes, Middlesex	HMV B-1588
JHO	Batavia	15/03/1923	Hayes, Middlesex	HMV B-1594
JHO	En Douce	15/03/1923	Hayes, Middlesex	HMV B-1594
JHO	Eleanor	13/04/1923	Hayes, Middlesex	HMV B-1643
JHO	Lovin' Sam (The Sheik Of Alabam')	13/04/1923	Hayes, Middlesex	HMV B-1643
JHO	Shores Of Minnetonka	03/05/1923	Hayes, Middlesex	HMV B-1652
JHO	Sweetheart (I'm So Glad That I Met You)	03/05/1923	Hayes, Middlesex	HMV B-1653
JHO	Innocent Lonesome Blue Baby	03/05/1923	Hayes, Middlesex	HMV B-1653

Complete UK Discography

JHO	Singing/In Romany/Jenny	09/05/1923	Hayes, Middlesex	HMV Rejected
JHO	Everybody Loves You	06/06/1923	Hayes, Middlesex	HMV B-1667
JHO	Susannah's Squeaking Shoes	06/06/1923	Hayes, Middlesex	HMV B-1667
GDO	Fate	12/06/1923	Hayes, Middlesex	Zonophone 2356
GDO	Runnin' Wild	12/06/1923	Hayes, Middlesex	Zonophone 2370
GDO	Toot, Toot, Tootsie (Goo'bye)	12/06/1923	Hayes, Middlesex	Zonophone 2370
GDO	Just Like A Thief	12/06/1923	Hayes, Middlesex	Zonophone 2356
JHO	Someone	10/07/1923	Hayes, Middlesex	HMV B-1680
JHO	Joyce	10/07/1923	Hayes, Middlesex	HMV Rejected
JHO	Nelly Kelly, I Love You	10/07/1923	Hayes, Middlesex	HMV Rejected
JHO	Sunkist Rose	17/07/1923	Hayes, Middlesex	HMV B-1680
JHO	Honey, Dat's All (matrix Bb-3288-2)	17/07/1923	Hayes, Middlesex	HMV B-1727
JHO	Tell-Tale Twilight (waltz)	17/07/1923	Hayes, Middlesex	HMV B-1681
JHO	Have You Seen My Gal?	17/07/1923	Hayes, Middlesex	HMV B-1681
GDO	Yes! We Have No Bananas	27/08/1923	Hayes, Middlesex	Zonophone 2371
GDO	Seven And Eleven Blues	27/08/1923	Hayes, Middlesex	Zonophone 2371
GDO	When You And I Were Dancing	27/08/1923	Hayes, Middlesex	Zonophone 2384
JHO	Louisville Lou	03/09/1923	Hayes, Middlesex	HMV B-1690
JHO	Seven And Eleven Blues	03/09/1923	Hayes, Middlesex	HMV B-1701
JHO	Never Again	03/09/1923	Hayes, Middlesex	HMV B-1691
JHO	Honey, Dat's All (matrix Bb-3383-2)	03/09/1923	Hayes, Middlesex	HMV B-1727
JHO	Broadway Blues	04/09/1923	Hayes, Middlesex	HMV B-1690
JHO	Rippling Tide	04/09/1923	Hayes, Middlesex	HMV B-1692
JHO	Joyce	04/09/1923	Hayes, Middlesex	HMV B-1691
GDO	When You And I Were Dancing	10/09/1923	Hayes, Middlesex	Zonophone Rejected?
JHO	Bonnie	10/09/1923	Hayes, Middlesex	HMV B-1692
JHO	Non-Stop Dancing Craze	10/09/1923	Hayes, Middlesex	HMV B-1693
JHO	Russian Blues	10/09/1923	Hayes, Middlesex	HMV B-1693
GDO	That Red-Head Gal	10/09/1923	Hayes, Middlesex	Zonophone 2384
GDO	Saw Mill River Road	19/09/1923	Hayes, Middlesex	Zonophone 2385

Jack Hylton

QDO	Annabelle	19/09/1923	Hayes, Middlesex	Zonophone 2394
QDO	Swingin' Down The Lane	19/09/1923	Hayes, Middlesex	Zonophone 2394
GDO	Joyce	19/09/1923	Hayes, Middlesex	Zonophone 2385
JHO	House Of David Blues	19/09/1923	Hayes, Middlesex	HMV B-1702
JHO	Blue Grass Blues	19/09/1923	Hayes, Middlesex	HMV B-1702
JHO	Blue Trot Blues	19/09/1923	Hayes, Middlesex	HMV B-1701
JHO	Somewhere In Naples	22/10/1923	Hayes, Middlesex	HMV B-1726
JHO	Southern Rose	22/10/1923	Hayes, Middlesex	HMV B-1726
QDO	Who Did You Fool After All?	24/10/1923	Hayes, Middlesex	Zonophone 2395
QDO	No No Nora	24/10/1923	Hayes, Middlesex	Zonophone 2409
QDO	Love Tales	24/10/1923	Hayes, Middlesex	Zonophone 2409
QDO	My Sweetie Went Away	24/10/1923	Hayes, Middlesex	Zonophone 2395
JHO	Night Night - Bohemian Song	24/10/1923	Hayes, Middlesex	HMV B-1727
JHO	Moon Love	17/12/1923	Hayes, Middlesex	HMV B-1743
JHO	Why Did You Fool After All?	17/12/1923	Hayes, Middlesex	HMV B-1762
JHO	When You And I Were Dancing	17/12/1923	Hayes, Middlesex	HMV B-1743
JHO	Felix Kept On Walking	14/01/1924	Hayes, Middlesex	HMV B-1758
JHO	Just Keep On Dancing	14/01/1924	Hayes, Middlesex	HMV B-1762
JHO	Why Robinson Crusoe Got The Blues	14/01/1924	Hayes, Middlesex	HMV B-1758
MGDO	Cootamundra	17/01/1924	Hayes, Middlesex	Zonophone ???
MGDO	I'm Going	17/01/1924	Hayes, Middlesex	Zonophone 2527
MGDO	Wodonga	17/01/1924	Hayes, Middlesex	Zonophone ???
MGDO	Croa-Jingo-Long	17/01/1924	Hayes, Middlesex	Zonophone ???
MGDO	Kismet	17/01/1924	Hayes, Middlesex	Zonophone ???
MGDO	Aussie-Land	17/01/1924	Hayes, Middlesex	Zonophone ???
GDO	Dreamy Honolulu (waltz)	17/01/1924	Hayes, Middlesex	Zonophone 2502
JHO	Ritzi Mitzi	30/01/1924	Hayes, Middlesex	HMV B-1781
JHO	Syncopation On The Brain	30/01/1924	Hayes, Middlesex	HMV Rejected
JHO	Doo-Dah Blues	30/01/1924	Hayes, Middlesex	HMV B-1775
JHO	Syncopation On The Brain	04/02/1924	Hayes, Middlesex	HMV B-1775

Complete UK Discography

MGDO	Sleepy Seas (waltz)	04/02/1924	Hayes, Middlesex	Zonophone 2435
JHO	Askepots Bruderfœrd	04/02/1924	Hayes, Middlesex	HMV X-1951
MGDO	Down Wagga Way	04/02/1924	Hayes, Middlesex	Zonophone 2435
MGDO	Snowy River	04/02/1924	Hayes, Middlesex	Zonophone ???
JHO	Säj mej vem du umgås med	18/02/1924	Hayes, Middlesex	HMV X-1956
JHO	Om igen	18/02/1924	Hayes, Middlesex	HMV X-1956
JHO	Kirkilis Shimmy	18/02/1924	Hayes, Middlesex	HMV (Prague)
JHO	Kayz Muzika	18/02/1924	Hayes, Middlesex	HMV (Prague)
JHO	Synku, ach Synocku	18/02/1924	Hayes, Middlesex	HMV (Prague)
JHO	The Oom-Pah Trot	19/02/1924	Hayes, Middlesex	HMV B-1791
JHO	Sudanese	19/02/1924	Hayes, Middlesex	HMV B-1793
JHO	Why Worry Blues	19/02/1924	Hayes, Middlesex	HMV Rejected
JHO	Well, I Am Surprised!	13/03/1924	Hayes, Middlesex	HMV B-1791
JHO	Wembling At Wembley	13/03/1924	Hayes, Middlesex	HMV Rejected
JHO	How's Bonzo?	13/03/1924	Hayes, Middlesex	HMV B-1793
JHO	Why Worry Blues	17/03/1924	Hayes, Middlesex	HMV B-1829
JHO	Du lille Spanska fluga	17/03/1924	Hayes, Middlesex	HMV X-1957
JHO	Monna Vanna	17/03/1924	Hayes, Middlesex	HMV X-1957
JHO	Chacun sa vie	31/03/1924	Hayes, Middlesex	HMV X-1967
JHO	On dit ça	31/03/1924	Hayes, Middlesex	HMV X-1967
JHO	Quand les femmes font comme les enfants	31/03/1924	Hayes, Middlesex	HMV X-1966
JHO	Die Mädel von Java	31/03/1924	Hayes, Middlesex	HMV X-1966
JHO	Kanariefuglen	07/04/1924	Hayes, Middlesex	HMV X-1968
JHO	Kvinden er en Gåde	07/04/1924	Hayes, Middlesex	HMV X-1968
JHO	Bedstemor	07/04/1924	Hayes, Middlesex	HMV X-1969
JHO	Det skal jeg først til at lære	07/04/1924	Hayes, Middlesex	HMV X-1969
JHO	La Javanette	07/04/1924	Hayes, Middlesex	HMV X-1970
JHO	Wembling At Wembley	09/04/1924	Hayes, Middlesex	HMV B-1809
JHO	Do Shrimps Make Good Mothers?	09/04/1924	Hayes, Middlesex	HMV B-1809
JHO	It's Too Late Now	09/04/1924	Hayes, Middlesex	HMV B-1846

Jack Hylton

JHO	Riviera Rose (waltz)	09/04/1924	Hayes, Middlesex	HMV B-1808
JHO	Cara (Five-Step)	09/05/1924	Hayes, Middlesex	HMV B-1829
JHO	And That's Not All	09/05/1924	Hayes, Middlesex	HMV B-1830
JHO	Chili-Bom-Bom	09/05/1924	Hayes, Middlesex	HMV B-1830
JHO	Don't Love You	15/05/1924	Hayes, Middlesex	HMV B-1838
JHO	Let's Go To Wembley	15/05/1924	Hayes, Middlesex	HMV B-1838
JHO	Foolish Jazz Band	15/05/1924	Hayes, Middlesex	HMV (Belgium)
JHO	Zaira	15/05/1924	Hayes, Middlesex	HMV (Belgium)
JHO	Det ligger i skläten	02/07/1924	Hayes, Middlesex	HMV X-2036
JHO	Kom sum du ä'	02/07/1924	Hayes, Middlesex	HMV X-2036
JHO	Man kan aldrig fä för mycket	02/07/1924	Hayes, Middlesex	HMV X-2035
JHO	They Love It	02/07/1924	Hayes, Middlesex	HMV B-1866
JHO	Bombay Rose	02/07/1924	Hayes, Middlesex	HMV B-1866
JHO	It Ain't Gonna Rain No Mo'	07/07/1924	Hayes, Middlesex	HMV B-1878
JHO	Darlingest	07/07/1924	Hayes, Middlesex	HMV B-1878
JHO	Sappho	07/07/1924	Hayes, Middlesex	HMV B-1875
JHO	Behert dich Gott	16/07/1924	Hayes, Middlesex	HMV (Germany)
JHO	Ich mochte Träumen	16/07/1924	Hayes, Middlesex	HMV (Germany)
JHO	My Time Is Your Time	16/07/1924	Hayes, Middlesex	HMV B-1875
JHO	Sailli di Maschere	19/08/1924	Hayes, Middlesex	HMV (Italy)
JHO	Johnson One-Step	19/08/1924	Hayes, Middlesex	HMV (Italy)
JHO	It Had To Be You	19/08/1924	Hayes, Middlesex	HMV B-1887
GDO	Riley's Cowshed	15/09/1924	Hayes, Middlesex	Zonophone 2502
JHBLB	Hinkey Dinkey Parlay Voo	15/09/1924	Hayes, Middlesex	Zonophone 2492
JHBLB	What Do You Sunday, Mary?	15/09/1924	Hayes, Middlesex	Zonophone 2492
JHO	I'm Gonna Bring A Watermelon	24/09/1924	Hayes, Middlesex	HMV B-1899
JHO	When The Music Dies Away	24/09/1924	Hayes, Middlesex	HMV B-1899
JHO	The Road Hog	24/09/1924	Hayes, Middlesex	HMV B-1905
JHO	I'm Wonderful	17/10/1924	Hayes, Middlesex	HMV B-1905
JHO	Je cherche apres Titine	17/10/1924	Hayes, Middlesex	HMV B-1908

Complete UK Discography

MGDO	The World Is Mine (For I Have You)	17/10/1924	Hayes, Middlesex	Zonophone 2527
JHO	Sahara	20/11/1924	Hayes, Middlesex	HMV B-1925
JHO	Follow The Swallow	20/11/1924	Hayes, Middlesex	HMV B-1940
JHO	I Wonder What's Become Of Sally?	20/11/1924	Hayes, Middlesex	HMV B-1925
JHO	She Loves Me	23/12/1924	Hayes, Middlesex	HMV B-1940
JHO	In Between The Showers	23/12/1924	Hayes, Middlesex	HMV B-1939
JHO	The Golden West (waltz)	23/12/1924	Hayes, Middlesex	HMV B-1939
JHO	Alt kan Varkes!	14/01/1925	Hayes, Middlesex	HMV X-2151
JHO	Er der Pjank I Tagblatiken	14/01/1925	Hayes, Middlesex	HMV X-2151
JHO	Mimosa	14/01/1925	Hayes, Middlesex	HMV X-2197
JHO	Blå Pärlen	14/01/1925	Hayes, Middlesex	HMV X-2197
JHO	Opicts lov	15/01/1925	Hayes, Middlesex	HMV X-2198
JHO	Till blånende Ocean	15/01/1925	Hayes, Middlesex	HMV X-2198
JHO	In Carolina	15/01/1925	Hayes, Middlesex	HMV B-1943
JHO	Heart-Broken Rose	15/01/1925	Hayes, Middlesex	HMV B-1956
JHO	I've Got A Feeling For Ophelia	15/01/1925	Hayes, Middlesex	HMV B-1943
JHO	Eat More Fruit	29/01/1925	Hayes, Middlesex	HMV B-1959
JHO	Rose Of The Moonlight	29/01/1925	Hayes, Middlesex	HMV B-1959
JHO	When She's In Red	29/01/1925	Hayes, Middlesex	HMV B-1956
JHO	Sweet Little You	16/02/1925	Hayes, Middlesex	HMV B-1974
JHO	I Can't Stop Babying You	16/02/1925	Hayes, Middlesex	HMV B-1980
JHO	I'll Take Her Back If She Wants To Come Back	16/02/1925	Hayes, Middlesex	HMV B-1974
JHO	Red Hot Mama	20/02/1925	Hayes, Middlesex	HMV B-1969
JHO	Kongo Kate	20/02/1925	Hayes, Middlesex	HMV B-1969
JHO	In The Town Where I Was Born	20/02/1925	Hayes, Middlesex	HMV B-1980
JHO	Oh! Flo	06/03/1925	Hayes, Middlesex	HMV B-2023
JHO	Will You Remember Me?	06/03/1925	Hayes, Middlesex	HMV B-1990
JHO	Everybody Loves My Baby	06/03/1925	Hayes, Middlesex	HMV B-1990
JHO	Couldn't We Keep On Dancing?	03/04/1925	Hayes, Middlesex	HMV B-2003
JHO	The Big Tune	03/04/1925	Hayes, Middlesex	HMV B-2010

Jack Hylton

JHO	Come A Little Closer	03/04/1925	Hayes, Middlesex	HMV B-2003
JHO	Garden Of Lies	16/04/1925	Hayes, Middlesex	HMV B-2010
JHO	Dublinola	16/04/1925	Hayes, Middlesex	HMV B-2009
JHO	Leander	16/04/1925	Hayes, Middlesex	HMV B-2009
JHO	What A Life (When No-One Loves You)	22/04/1925	Hayes, Middlesex	HMV B-2023
JHO	I Know That Someone Loves Me	22/04/1925	Hayes, Middlesex	HMV B-2024
JHO	Give Me Just A Little Bit Of Love	22/04/1925	Hayes, Middlesex	HMV B-2024
JHO	Temple Bells	08/05/1925	Hayes, Middlesex	HMV B-2030
JHO	Bouquet	08/05/1925	Hayes, Middlesex	HMV B-2030
JHO	You're So Near And Yet So Far	11/05/1925	Hayes, Middlesex	HMV B-2059
JHO	No One	11/05/1925	Hayes, Middlesex	HMV B-2059
JHO	Who?	11/05/1925	Hayes, Middlesex	HMV B-2056
JHO	Yearning	26/05/1925	Hayes, Middlesex	HMV B-2056
JHO	Tell All The World (I Love You)	26/05/1925	Hayes, Middlesex	HMV B-2067
JHO	We're Back Together Again	26/05/1925	Hayes, Middlesex	HMV Rejected
JHO	We're Back Together Again	29/05/1925	Hayes, Middlesex	HMV B-2067
JHO	Don't Bring Lulu	29/05/1925	Hayes, Middlesex	HMV Rejected
JHO	The Farmer Took Another Load Away	29/05/1925	Hayes, Middlesex	HMV B-2063
JHO	No Wonder (I Love You)	29/05/1925	Hayes, Middlesex	HMV B-2064
JHO	Pango Pango Maid	12/06/1925	Hayes, Middlesex	HMV B-2063
JHO	Isn't She The Sweetest Thing?	12/06/1925	Hayes, Middlesex	HMV B-2064
JHO	Lonely And Blue	12/06/1925	Hayes, Middlesex	HMV Rejected
JHO	Ah-Ha!	24/06/1925	Hayes, Middlesex	HMV Rejected
JHO	Feelin' Kind O' Blue (first HMV electrical record)	24/06/1925	Hayes, Middlesex	HMV B-2072
JHO	Why Don't My Dreams Come True? (waltz)	24/06/1925	Hayes, Middlesex	HMV Rejected
JHO	Yes Sir, That's My Baby	30/06/1925	Hayes, Middlesex	HMV B-2110
JHO	She's Driving Me Wild	30/06/1925	Hayes, Middlesex	HMV B-2088
JHO	Who Told You?	30/06/1925	Hayes, Middlesex	HMV B-2072
JH	Ukulele Lady	09/07/1925	Hayes, Middlesex	HMV Rejected
JH	I'll See You In My Dreams	09/07/1925	Hayes, Middlesex	HMV Rejected

Complete UK Discography

JH	June Night	09/07/1925	Hayes, Middlesex	HMV Rejected
JHO	I'll See You In My Dreams	14/07/1925	Hayes, Middlesex	HMV Rejected
JHO	Sally's Come Back	14/07/1925	Hayes, Middlesex	HMV B-2146
JHO	High Street, Africa	14/07/1925	Hayes, Middlesex	HMV Rejected
JHO	In The Garden Of Tomorrow	22/07/1925	Hayes, Middlesex	HMV B-2110
JHO	Adelai	22/07/1925	Hayes, Middlesex	HMV Rejected
JHO	Babette (waltz)	22/07/1925	Hayes, Middlesex	HMV B-2088
JHO	Fantasia Orientale	22/07/1925	Hayes, Middlesex	HMV Rejected
JHO	Hylton Medley	04/09/1925	Hayes, Middlesex	HMV Rejected
JHO	Mercenary Mary	04/09/1925	Hayes, Middlesex	HMV B-2118
JHO	You Forgot To Remember (waltz)	04/09/1925	Hayes, Middlesex	HMV B-2118
JHO	The King Isn't King Any More	07/09/1925	Hayes, Middlesex	HMV Rejected
JHO	Paddlin' Madelin' Home	07/09/1925	Hayes, Middlesex	HMV Rejected
JHO	Sunny Havana	07/09/1925	Hayes, Middlesex	HMV Rejected
JHO	I'm Tired Of Everything But You	09/09/1925	Hayes, Middlesex	HMV Rejected
JHO	Sing Your Cares Away	09/09/1925	Hayes, Middlesex	HMV Rejected
JHO	Land Of Dreams Come True (waltz)	09/09/1925	Hayes, Middlesex	HMV B-2123
JHO	Stamboul	17/09/1925	Hayes, Middlesex	HMV B-2121
JHO	Chick, Chick, Chicken	17/09/1925	Hayes, Middlesex	HMV B-2121
JHO	Some Other Day, Some Other Girl	17/09/1925	Hayes, Middlesex	HMV B-2123
JHO	I'm Tired Of Everything But You	25/09/1925	Hayes, Middlesex	HMV B-2147
JHO	Honest And Truly	25/09/1925	Hayes, Middlesex	HMV B-2147
JHO	Tie A String Around Your Finger	25/09/1925	Hayes, Middlesex	HMV B-2143
JHO	Paradise	25/09/1925	Hayes, Middlesex	HMV B-2244
JHO	Hylton Medley	02/10/1925	Hayes, Middlesex	HMV B-2143
JHO	Paddlin' Madelin' Home	02/10/1925	Hayes, Middlesex	HMV B-2163
JHO	Sunny Havana	02/10/1925	Hayes, Middlesex	HMV B-2146
JHO	Mercenary Mary - Selection, Part 1	02/10/1925	Hayes, Middlesex	HMV C-1221
JHO	Mercenary Mary - Selection, Part 2	02/10/1925	Hayes, Middlesex	HMV C-1221
JHO	A Cup Of Coffee, A Sandwich And You	14/10/1925	Hayes, Middlesex	HMV B-2162

Jack Hylton

JHO	When The Bloom Is On The Heather	14/10/1925	Hayes, Middlesex	HMV B-2163
JHO	Molly	14/10/1925	Hayes, Middlesex	HMV B-2162
JHO	As The Days Go By	19/10/1925	Hayes, Middlesex	HMV B-2164
JHO	Every Sunday Afternoon	19/10/1925	Hayes, Middlesex	HMV B-2164
JHO	The Baby Looks Like Me	27/10/1925	Hayes, Middlesex	HMV B-2188
JHO	Sweet Man	27/10/1925	Hayes, Middlesex	HMV B-2189
JHO	Lillian	27/10/1925	Hayes, Middlesex	HMV B-2188
JHO	One Smile	27/10/1925	Hayes, Middlesex	HMV B-2189
JHO	Want A Little Lovin'	30/10/1925	Hayes, Middlesex	HMV B-2184
JHO	Freshie	30/10/1925	Hayes, Middlesex	HMV B-2184
JHO	His Master's Voice	30/10/1925	Hayes, Middlesex	HMV Rejected
JHO	Brown Eyes, Why Are You Blue?	11/11/1925	Hayes, Middlesex	HMV Rejected
JHO	She Showed Him This, She Showed Him That	11/11/1925	Hayes, Middlesex	HMV B-2208
JHO	My Girl's Fond Of Tulips	16/11/1925	Hayes, Middlesex	HMV B-2208
JHO	Everybody Home Is Asking For You	16/11/1925	Hayes, Middlesex	HMV B-2209
JHO	Just Around The Corner	16/11/1925	Hayes, Middlesex	HMV B-2209
JHO	I Wonder Where My Baby Is Tonight?	26/11/1925	Kingsway Hall, London	HMV Rejected
JHO	Where Does The Candlelight Go?	26/11/1925	Kingsway Hall, London	HMV Rejected
JHO	That Certain Party	26/11/1925	Kingsway Hall, London	HMV Rejected
JHO	I Wonder Where My Baby Is Tonight?	11/12/1925	Hayes, Middlesex	HMV B-2243
JHO	Where Does The Candlelight Go?	11/12/1925	Hayes, Middlesex	HMV B-2244
JHO	That Certain Party	11/12/1925	Hayes, Middlesex	HMV B-2243
JHO	Brown Eyes, Why Are You Blue?	11/12/1925	Hayes, Middlesex	HMV Rejected
JHO	Don't Wait Too Long	16/12/1925	Hayes, Middlesex	HMV B-2245
JHO	Lonesome Me	16/12/1925	Hayes, Middlesex	HMV B-2245
JHO	I'm Sitting On Top Of The World	16/12/1925	Hayes, Middlesex	HMV B-2250
JHO	Hey Hey And Hee Hee	30/12/1925	Hayes, Middlesex	HMV B-2254
JHO	Too Too	30/12/1925	Hayes, Middlesex	HMV B-2250
JHO	Close In My Arms	30/12/1925	Hayes, Middlesex	HMV B-2254
JHO	Down Paradise Way	04/01/1926	Hayes, Middlesex	HMV B-2249

Complete UK Discography

JHO	Cutie	04/01/1926	Hayes, Middlesex	HMV B-2249
JHO	I'm So Terribly In Love With You	04/01/1926	Hayes, Middlesex	HMV B-2264
JHO	Ukulele Lullaby	06/01/1926	Hayes, Middlesex	HMV B-2265
JHO	Nobody's Business	06/01/1926	Hayes, Middlesex	HMV B-2265
JHO	My Girl's Got Long Hair	06/01/1926	Hayes, Middlesex	HMV B-5016
JHO	Sleepy-Time Gal	12/01/1926	Hayes, Middlesex	HMV B-5000
JHO	Memory's Melody (waltz)	12/01/1926	Hayes, Middlesex	HMV B-2264
JHO	You Must Have A Little Bit Of Fun	12/01/1926	Hayes, Middlesex	HMV B-5000
JHO	In The Swim At Miami	15/01/1926	Hayes, Middlesex	HMV B-2258
JHO	Why Don't You Say So?	15/01/1926	Hayes, Middlesex	HMV B-5014
JHO	Along The Old Lake Trail	15/01/1926	Hayes, Middlesex	HMV B-2258
JHO	Night	11/02/1926	Hayes, Middlesex	HMV B-5012
JHO	Tin Can Fusiliers	11/02/1926	Hayes, Middlesex	HMV B-5012
JHO	Polly Put The Kettle On	11/02/1926	Hayes, Middlesex	HMV B-5014
JHO	Surabaya Maid	11/02/1926	Hayes, Middlesex	HMV B-5019
JHKCB	The Selfish Giant - Part 1	19/02/1926	Hayes, Middlesex	HMV C-1253
JHKCB	The Selfish Giant - Part 2	19/02/1926	Hayes, Middlesex	HMV C-1253
JHO	Mignonette (waltz)	19/02/1926	Hayes, Middlesex	HMV B-5016
JHO	Student Prince Serenade	25/02/1926	Hayes, Middlesex	HMV B-5023
JHO	I Love To Be In Laughterland	25/02/1926	Hayes, Middlesex	HMV B-5023
JHO	When I Said Goodbye To Maryland	25/02/1926	Hayes, Middlesex	HMV Rejected
JHO	Ukulele Baby	25/02/1926	Hayes, Middlesex	HMV B-5019
JHO	Medley of Leslie Stuart's Songs - Part 1	12/03/1926	Hayes, Middlesex	HMV B-5033
JHO	Medley of Leslie Stuart's Songs - Part 2	12/03/1926	Hayes, Middlesex	HMV B-5033
JHO	Thanks For The Buggy Ride	12/03/1926	Hayes, Middlesex	HMV B-5040
JHO	Nothing Else To Do	19/03/1926	Hayes, Middlesex	HMV B-5041
JHO	When You See That Aunt Of Mine	19/03/1926	Hayes, Middlesex	HMV B-5040
JHO	Fleur d'amour	19/03/1926	Hayes, Middlesex	HMV B-5041
JHO	Lady, Be Good - Selection, Part 1	29/03/1926	Hayes, Middlesex	HMV B-5042
JHO	Lady, Be Good - Selection, Part 2	29/03/1926	Hayes, Middlesex	HMV B-5042

Jack Hylton

JHO	Valentine	29/03/1926	Hayes, Middlesex	HMV B-5054
JHO	Behind The Clouds	09/04/1926	Hayes, Middlesex	HMV B-5044
JHO	Goodnight (I'll See You In The Morning)	09/04/1926	Hayes, Middlesex	HMV Rejected
JHO	Just A Cottage Small	09/04/1926	Hayes, Middlesex	HMV B-5044
JHO	Lady, Be Good - Selection, Part 1	14/04/1926	Hayes, Middlesex	HMV C-1261
JHO	Lady, Be Good - Selection, Part 2	14/04/1926	Hayes, Middlesex	HMV C-1261
JHO	When I Said Goodbye To Maryland	21/04/1926	Hayes, Middlesex	HMV B-5059
JHO	So Does Your Old Mandarin	21/04/1926	Hayes, Middlesex	HMV B-5054
JHO	Oh! Miss Hannah	21/04/1926	Hayes, Middlesex	HMV B-5055
JHO	Pretty Little Baby	21/04/1926	Hayes, Middlesex	HMV B-5055
JHO	I Love To Be In Laughter Land ("loud record for J.H.")	21/04/1926	Hayes, Middlesex	HMV Private Recording
JHO	When It's June Down There	23/04/1926	Hayes, Middlesex	HMV B-5056
JHO	Rose Of Samarkand	23/04/1926	Hayes, Middlesex	HMV B-5056
JHO	Oh, That Sweetie	23/04/1926	Hayes, Middlesex	HMV B-5059
JHO	Have You Forgotten Yvonne?	08/06/1926	Hayes, Middlesex	HMV B-5086
JHO	Blinky Moon Bay	08/06/1926	Hayes, Middlesex	HMV B-5086
JHO	Currants	08/06/1926	Hayes, Middlesex	HMV B-5090
JHO	Under The Ukulele Tree	11/06/1926	Hayes, Middlesex	HMV B-5087
JHO	The Pump Song	11/06/1926	Hayes, Middlesex	HMV B-5093
JHO	Tune Up The Uke	11/06/1926	Hayes, Middlesex	HMV B-5087
JHO	Lonely Acres	16/06/1926	Kingsway Hall, London	HMV B-5090
JHO	Summer Rain Brings The Roses Again	16/06/1926	Kingsway Hall, London	HMV Rejected
JHO	Jack In The Box	16/06/1926	Kingsway Hall, London	HMV B-5095
JHO	Say That You Love Me	18/06/1926	Hayes, Middlesex	HMV B-5092
JHO	Somebody's Lonely	18/06/1926	Hayes, Middlesex	HMV B-5093
JHO	So Is Your Old Lady	18/06/1926	Hayes, Middlesex	HMV B-5092
JHO	Couldn't You Care?	28/06/1926	Hayes, Middlesex	HMV B-5098
JHO	Only For You	28/06/1926	Hayes, Middlesex	HMV B-5098
JHO	I'm Taking That Baby Home	28/06/1926	Hayes, Middlesex	HMV B-5099

300

Complete UK Discography

JHO	Summer Rain Brings The Roses Again	01/07/1926	Kingsway Hall, London	HMV B-5096
JHO	In A Monastery Garden	01/07/1926	Kingsway Hall, London	HMV Rejected
JHO	Wimmin - Aah!	01/07/1926	Kingsway Hall, London	HMV B-5099
JHO	Songs Of The Fair - Part 1	13/07/1926	Hayes, Middlesex	HMV B-5106
JHO	Songs Of The Fair - Part 2	13/07/1926	Hayes, Middlesex	HMV B-5106
JHO	Blue Bonnet, You Make Me Feel Blue	13/07/1926	Hayes, Middlesex	HMV B-5113
JHO	By The Tamarisk	13/08/1926	Kingsway Hall, London	HMV B-5132
JHO	Poor Papa	13/08/1926	Kingsway Hall, London	HMV B-5110
JHO	I'd Climb The Highest Mountain	13/08/1926	Kingsway Hall, London	HMV B-5110
JHO	Do You?	17/08/1926	Hayes, Middlesex	HMV B-5113
JHO	Oh! My Bundle Of Love	17/08/1926	Hayes, Middlesex	HMV B-5112
JHO	Gentlemen Prefer Blondes	17/08/1926	Hayes, Middlesex	HMV B-5112
JHO	When The Red, Red Robin Comes Bob, Bob, Bobbin' Along	18/08/1926	Kingsway Hall, London	HMV B-5115
JHO	Don't Let Nobody	18/08/1926	Kingsway Hall, London	HMV B-5115
JHO	Ya Gotta Know How To Love	18/08/1926	Kingsway Hall, London	HMV B-5116
JHO	Am I Wasting My Time On You?	20/08/1926	Kingsway Hall, London	HMV B-5116
JHO	Sunny	20/08/1926	Kingsway Hall, London	HMV B-5129
JHO	Who?	20/08/1926	Kingsway Hall, London	HMV B-5129
JHO	Sonny Boy	16/09/1926	Small Queen's Hall, London	HMV B-5139
JHO	Just A Kiss	16/09/1926	Small Queen's Hall, London	HMV B-5131
JHO	Shake A Little Shoulder	16/09/1926	Small Queen's Hall, London	HMV B-5131
JHO	My Dream Of The Big Parade	16/09/1926	Small Queen's Hall, London	HMV B-5139
JHO	That's What I Say	16/09/1926	Small Queen's Hall, London	HMV B-5209
JHO	Two Little Bluebirds	16/09/1926	Small Queen's Hall, London	HMV B-5132
JHO	Me Too	15/10/1926	Small Queen's Hall, London	HMV B-5148
JHO	Rising Sun	15/10/1926	Small Queen's Hall, London	HMV B-5148
JHO	Lavender (waltz)	15/10/1926	Small Queen's Hall, London	HMV B-5168
JHO	Don't Forget	22/10/1926	Small Queen's Hall, London	HMV B-5159
JHO	Palace Of Dreams	22/10/1926	Small Queen's Hall, London	HMV B-5159
JHO	Who'll Mend A Broken Heart	22/10/1926	Small Queen's Hall, London	HMV B-5161

301

Jack Hylton

JHO	Swords And Sabres	27/10/1926	Small Queen's Hall, London	HMV B-5160
JHO	Babying You	27/10/1926	Small Queen's Hall, London	HMV B-5160
JHO	Because I Love You (waltz)	27/10/1926	Small Queen's Hall, London	HMV B-5161
JHO	I Couldn't Blame You	01/11/1926	Small Queen's Hall, London	HMV B-5171
JHO	Dreamily (waltz)	01/11/1926	Small Queen's Hall, London	HMV B-5171
JHO	The Hylton Minstrels - Part 1	04/11/1926	Small Queen's Hall, London	HMV C-1301
JHO	The Hylton Minstrels - Part 2	04/11/1926	Small Queen's Hall, London	HMV C-1301
JHO	Try Again Tomorrow	12/11/1926	Hayes, Middlesex	HMV B-5168
JHO	Mama's Gone Young, Papa's Gone Old	12/11/1926	Hayes, Middlesex	HMV B-5170
JHO	Alabama Stomp	12/11/1926	Hayes, Middlesex	HMV B-5170
JHO	Lay Me Down To Sleep In Carolina	12/11/1926	Hayes, Middlesex	HMV Rejected
JHO	Why Did You Leave When I Love You?	16/11/1926	Small Queen's Hall, London	HMV B-5177
JHO	Then All The World Is Mine	16/11/1926	Small Queen's Hall, London	HMV B-5188
JHO	I Must Have Forty Winks	16/11/1926	Small Queen's Hall, London	HMV B-5177
JHO	The More We Are Together	23/11/1926	Small Queen's Hall, London	HMV B-5183
JHO	I've Never Seen A Straight Banana	23/11/1926	Small Queen's Hall, London	HMV B-5197
JHO	Ukulele Dream Man	23/11/1926	Small Queen's Hall, London	HMV Rejected
JHO	The Whole Town's Talking	30/11/1926	Small Queen's Hall, London	HMV B-5186
JHO	Waiting For The Rainbow	30/11/1926	Small Queen's Hall, London	HMV B-5184
JHO	Jog, Jog, Joggin' Along	30/11/1926	Small Queen's Hall, London	HMV B-5183
JHO	Mama's Gone Young, Papa's Gone Old	30/11/1926	Small Queen's Hall, London	HMV Rejected
JHO	Mandy	09/12/1926	Small Queen's Hall, London	HMV B-5189
JHO	Hello! Bluebird	09/12/1926	Small Queen's Hall, London	HMV B-5189
JHO	Just A Little Longer	09/12/1926	Small Queen's Hall, London	HMV Rejected
JHO	The Three Bears - Part 1	30/12/1926	Small Queen's Hall, London	HMV C-1309
JHO	The Three Bears - Part 2	30/12/1926	Small Queen's Hall, London	HMV C-1309
JHO	Valse Moderne	30/12/1926	Small Queen's Hall, London	HMV Rejected
JHO	I've Never Seen A Straight Banana	31/12/1926	Small Queen's Hall, London	HMV B-5197
JHO	Andante cantabile - Part 1	31/12/1926	Small Queen's Hall, London	HMV Rejected
JHO	Andante cantabile - Part 2	31/12/1926	Small Queen's Hall, London	HMV Rejected

Complete UK Discography

JHO	Lay Me Down To Sleep In Carolina	31/12/1926	Small Queen's Hall, London	HMV Rejected
JHO	Meadow Lark	13/01/1927	Small Queen's Hall, London	HMV B-5199
JHO	Gone Again Gal	13/01/1927	Small Queen's Hall, London	HMV Rejected
JHO	Just A Little Lady	13/01/1927	Small Queen's Hall, London	HMV B-5199
JHO	Dance Suite - No. 3 (Blues) (Leighton Lucas)	18/01/1927	Small Queen's Hall, London	HMV Rejected
JHO	Dance Suite - No. 2 (Waltz) (Leighton Lucas)	18/01/1927	Small Queen's Hall, London	HMV Rejected
JHO	Dance Suite - No. 4 (Charleston) (Leighton Lucas)	18/01/1927	Small Queen's Hall, London	HMV Rejected
JHO	On The Beach At Waikiki Blues	25/01/1927	Small Queen's Hall, London	HMV B-5217
JHO	Rhythm Is The Thing	25/01/1927	Small Queen's Hall, London	HMV B-5207
JHO	Blue Eyes, Be True	25/01/1927	Small Queen's Hall, London	HMV Rejected
JHO	Just A Little Longer	26/01/1927	Small Queen's Hall, London	HMV Rejected
JHO	Valse Moderne	26/01/1927	Small Queen's Hall, London	HMV Rejected
JHO	Lay Me Down To Sleep In Carolina	26/01/1927	Small Queen's Hall, London	HMV B-5209
JHO	A New One For Two	26/01/1927	Small Queen's Hall, London	HMV B-5210
JHO	Always Some New Baby	27/01/1927	Small Queen's Hall, London	HMV B-5210
JHO	It Doesn't Matter Who She Is	27/01/1927	Small Queen's Hall, London	HMV B-5208
JHO	Blame It On The Waltz (waltz)	27/01/1927	Small Queen's Hall, London	HMV B-5211
JHO	Do The Black Bottom With Me	04/02/1927	Small Queen's Hall, London	HMV B-5217
JHO	Flat-Tyred Papa, Mama's Gonna Give You Air	04/02/1927	Small Queen's Hall, London	HMV B-5221
JHO	Dance Suite - No. 1 (Fox Trot) (Leighton Lucas)	04/02/1927	Small Queen's Hall, London	HMV Rejected
JHO	Lantern Of Love	11/02/1927	Hayes, Middlesex	HMV Rejected
JHO	Shepherd Of The Hills (take 2) (Chappie d'Amato vocal)	11/02/1927	Hayes, Middlesex	HMV B-5207
JHO	Baby	11/02/1927	Hayes, Middlesex	HMV Rejected
JHO	Shepherd Of The Hills (take 3) (Jack Hylton vocal)	02/03/1927	Small Queen's Hall, London	HMV B-5207
JHO	What Does It Matter? (waltz)	02/03/1927	Small Queen's Hall, London	HMV B-5232
JHO	Lantern Of Love	02/03/1927	Small Queen's Hall, London	HMV B-5216
JHO	Baby	02/03/1927	Small Queen's Hall, London	HMV B-5216
JHO	It All Depends On You	04/03/1927	Small Queen's Hall, London	HMV B-5232
JHO	Sing	04/03/1927	Small Queen's Hall, London	HMV B-5245
JHO	It	04/03/1927	Small Queen's Hall, London	HMV B-5235

Jack Hylton

JHO	The Desert Song (waltz)	04/03/1927	Small Queen's Hall, London	HMV B-5235
JHO	Nesting Time	21/04/1927	Small Queen's Hall, London	HMV B-5266
JHO	There's A Little White House	21/04/1927	Small Queen's Hall, London	HMV Rejected
JHO	Ting-A-Ling (waltz)	21/04/1927	Small Queen's Hall, London	HMV B-5266
JHO	Syncopated City	29/04/1927	Small Queen's Hall, London	HMV B-5264
JHO	Blue Pipes Of Pan	29/04/1927	Small Queen's Hall, London	HMV B-5264
JHO	I've Learnt A Lot	29/04/1927	Small Queen's Hall, London	HMV B-5265
JHO	Does She Love Me? Positively, Absolutely	03/05/1927	Small Queen's Hall, London	HMV B-5291
JHO	What Do I Care What Somebody Said?	03/05/1927	Small Queen's Hall, London	HMV Rejected
JHO	My Little Bunch Of Happiness	03/05/1927	Small Queen's Hall, London	HMV B-5291
JHO	Shalimar (waltz)	05/05/1927	Kensington Cinema, London	HMV B-5267
JHO	I'm Looking Over A Four-Leaf Clover	05/05/1927	Kensington Cinema, London	HMV B-5267
JHO	Da-Da-Da	03/06/1927	Small Queen's Hall, London	HMV Rejected
JHO	Crazy Words - Crazy Tune	03/06/1927	Small Queen's Hall, London	HMV Rejected
JHO	There's A Little White House	14/06/1927	Small Queen's Hall, London	HMV B-5309
JHO	Da-Da-Da	14/06/1927	Small Queen's Hall, London	HMV B-5296
JHO	Cuddle Up	16/06/1927	Small Queen's Hall, London	HMV B-5298
JHO	My Heart Stood Still (take 2)	16/06/1927	Small Queen's Hall, London	HMV B-5296
JHO	My Heart Stood Still (take ??)	30/06/1927	Small Queen's Hall, London	HMV B-5296
JHO	A Tree In The Park	30/06/1927	Small Queen's Hall, London	HMV B-5309
JHO	Maybe It's Me	19/07/1927	Small Queen's Hall, London	HMV B-5314
JHO	Following You Around	19/07/1927	Small Queen's Hall, London	Electrola EG-629
JHO	Lucky Day	19/07/1927	Small Queen's Hall, London	HMV B-5314
JHO	Clonk-er-ty-Clonk	19/07/1927	Small Queen's Hall, London	HMV B-5321
JHO	Himazas	15/08/1927	Small Queen's Hall, London	HMV B-5321
JHO	Hallelujah	15/08/1927	Small Queen's Hall, London	HMV B-5332
JHO	Sometimes I'm Happy	15/08/1927	Small Queen's Hall, London	HMV B-5332
JHO	The Girl Friend - Selection, Part 1	17/08/1927	Hayes, Middlesex	HMV B-5323
JHO	The Girl Friend - Selection, Part 2	17/08/1927	Hayes, Middlesex	HMV B-5323
JHO	I'm In Love Again	17/08/1927	Hayes, Middlesex	HMV B-5340

Complete UK Discography

JHO	When You Played The Organ And I Sang "The Rosary"	19/08/1927	Kensington Cinema, London	HMV B-5316
JHO	When Day Is Done	19/08/1927	Kensington Cinema, London	HMV B-5316
JHO	Like A Virginia Creeper	22/08/1927	Small Queen's Hall, London	HMV B-5340
JHO	Me And Jane In A 'Plane	22/08/1927	Small Queen's Hall, London	HMV B-5336
JHO	Clap Yo' Hands	22/08/1927	Small Queen's Hall, London	HMV Rejected
JHO	Anybody But You	22/08/1927	Small Queen's Hall, London	HMV B-5358
JHO	Do-Do-Do	22/08/1927	Small Queen's Hall, London	HMV Rejected
JHO	Bye-Bye, Pretty Baby	31/08/1927	Small Queen's Hall, London	HMV B-5348
JHO	Why Are There Tears In Your Eyes? (waltz)	31/08/1927	Small Queen's Hall, London	HMV B-5348
JHO	Ain't That A Grand And Glorious Feeling?	31/08/1927	Small Queen's Hall, London	HMV B-5336
JHO	Clap Yo' Hands	08/09/1927	Small Queen's Hall, London	HMV B-5346
JHO	Do-Do-Do	08/09/1927	Small Queen's Hall, London	HMV B-5346
JHO	Gonna Get A Girl	08/09/1927	Small Queen's Hall, London	HMV B-5358
JHO	Barbara	16/09/1927	Hayes, Middlesex	HMV B-5388
JHO	Here Am I, Broken Hearted	16/09/1927	Hayes, Middlesex	HMV B-5360
JHO	Dancing Tambourine	16/09/1927	Hayes, Middlesex	HMV B-5362
JHO	The Devil Is Afraid Of Music	16/09/1927	Hayes, Middlesex	HMV B-5360
JHO	Oh, Doris, Where Do Youu Live?	21/09/1927	Hayes, Middlesex	HMV B-5362
JHO	Souvenirs	21/09/1927	Hayes, Middlesex	HMV B-5356
JHO	Le-a-nore	21/09/1927	Hayes, Middlesex	HMV B-5356
JHO	Just The Same	28/09/1927	Small Queen's Hall, London	HMV Rejected
JHO	Leanora	28/09/1927	Small Queen's Hall, London	HMV B-5370
JHO	When I Met Sally	29/09/1927	Hayes, Middlesex	HMV B-5370
JHO	Pardon The Glove	29/09/1927	Hayes, Middlesex	HMV B-5378
JHO	Buffalo Rhythm	29/09/1927	Hayes, Middlesex	HMV Rejected
JHO	Creole Lullaby	04/10/1927	Hayes, Middlesex	HMV B-5388
JHO	What Do We Do On A Dew-Dew-Dewy Day?	04/10/1927	Hayes, Middlesex	HMV B-5371
JHO	What Would I Do For A Girl Like You?	04/10/1927	Hayes, Middlesex	HMV Rejected
JHO	Gentlemen Prefer Blues	04/10/1927	Hayes, Middlesex	HMV B-5371
JHO	I'm Seeking A Ladybird	13/10/1927	Small Queen's Hall, London	HMV B-5379

Jack Hylton

JHO	Are You Happy?	13/10/1927	Small Queen's Hall, London	HMV B-5387
JHO	Marvellous	13/10/1927	Small Queen's Hall, London	HMV B-5387
JHO	Buffalo Rhythm	24/10/1927	Hayes, Middlesex	HMV B-5379
JHO	Just The Same	24/10/1927	Hayes, Middlesex	HMV B-5378
JHO	Under The Moon	24/10/1927	Hayes, Middlesex	HMV Rejected
JHO	You Tell Him	24/10/1927	Hayes, Middlesex	HMV B-5393
JHO	I'm In Heaven When I See You Smile, Diane (waltz)	04/11/1927	Hayes, Middlesex	HMV B-5393
JHO	There's One Little Girl Who Loves Me	04/11/1927	Hayes, Middlesex	HMV B-5400
JHO	On The Topmost Tree In Tennessee	04/11/1927	Hayes, Middlesex	HMV B-5400
JHO	Remember (waltz)	11/11/1927	New Gallery Cinema, London	HMV B-5390
JHO	Just Once Again	11/11/1927	New Gallery Cinema, London	HMV B-5390
JHO	Les Millions d'Arlequin Serenade (waltz)	11/11/1927	New Gallery Cinema, London	HMV B-5391
JHO	Les Millions d'Arlequin Serenade (waltz)	11/11/1927	New Gallery Cinema, London	Zonophone 6049
JHO	A Persian Rosebud	11/11/1927	New Gallery Cinema, London	HMV B-5391
JHO	A Persian Rosebud	11/11/1927	New Gallery Cinema, London	Zonophone 6049
JHO	Either You Do Or You Don't	16/11/1927	Hayes, Middlesex	HMV B-5405
JHO	Just An Hour Of Love	16/11/1927	Hayes, Middlesex	HMV B-5405
JHO	The Song Is Ended (waltz)	16/11/1927	Hayes, Middlesex	HMV B-5406
JHO	Little Boy Blues	24/11/1927	Small Queen's Hall, London	HMV Rejected
JHO	Is She My Girl Friend?	24/11/1927	Small Queen's Hall, London	HMV Rejected
JHO	I'll Say To You	24/11/1927	Small Queen's Hall, London	HMV Rejected
JHO	Where Are You Now?	07/12/1927	Small Queen's Hall, London	HMV B-5406
JHO	Why Did You Say? (waltz)	07/12/1927	Small Queen's Hall, London	HMV B-5413
JHO	I'll Be Lonely	07/12/1927	Small Queen's Hall, London	HMV B-5413
JHO	Little Boy Blues	09/12/1927	Small Queen's Hall, London	HMV B-5407
JHO	Is She My Girl Friend?	09/12/1927	Small Queen's Hall, London	HMV B-5422
JHO	I'll Say To You	09/12/1927	Small Queen's Hall, London	HMV B-5407
JHO	Sing Me A Baby Song	15/12/1927	Small Queen's Hall, London	HMV B-5421
JHO	I've Got A "Yes" Girl	15/12/1927	Small Queen's Hall, London	HMV B-5421
JHR	Grieving For You	15/12/1927	Small Queen's Hall, London	HMV B-5422

Complete UK Discography

JHO	Who's That Knocking At The Door?	21/12/1927	Small Queen's Hall, London	HMV B-5426
JHO	Georgia Land	21/12/1927	Small Queen's Hall, London	HMV B-5442
JHO	In The Woodshed	21/12/1927	Small Queen's Hall, London	HMV B-5426
JHO	Heut war ich bei der Frieda	26/01/1928	Berlin, Germany	Electrola EG-782
JHO	Wir wollen so tun, als ob wir Freunde waren	26/01/1928	Berlin, Germany	Elecrola EG-781
JHO	Ja, ja, die Frau'n sing meine Schwache seite	26/01/1928	Berlin, Germany	Elecrola EG-782
JHO	Passin sie mal auf	26/01/1928	Berlin, Germany	Electrola EG-781
JHO	Sunny Skies	03/02/1928	Small Queen's Hall, London	HMV B-5453
JHO	It Don't Do Nothing But Rain	03/02/1928	Small Queen's Hall, London	HMV B-5452
JHO	One More Night	03/02/1928	Small Queen's Hall, London	HMV B-5453
JHO	Playground In The Sky	03/02/1928	Small Queen's Hall, London	HMV Rejected
JHO	I'm Going Back To Old Nebraska	03/02/1928	Small Queen's Hall, London	HMV Rejected
JHO	There's A Cradle In Caroline	03/02/1928	Small Queen's Hall, London	HMV B-5443
JHO	Janette (waltz)	14/02/1928	Small Queen's Hall, London	HMV B-5442
JHO	Sunrise (waltz)	14/02/1928	Small Queen's Hall, London	HMV Rejected
JHO	Let A Smile Be Your Umbrella	14/02/1928	Small Queen's Hall, London	HMV B-5443
JHO	Playground In The Sky	27/02/1928	Hayes, Middlesex	HMV B-5444
JHO	I'm Going Back To Old Nebraska	27/02/1928	Hayes, Middlesex	HMV B-5444
JHO	Deep Sea	27/02/1928	Hayes, Middlesex	HMV B-5450
JHO	Eastern Dreams	01/03/1928	Hayes, Middlesex	HMV Rejected
JHO	You Came Along	01/03/1928	Hayes, Middlesex	HMV B-5447
JHO	I Fell Head Over Heels In Love	01/03/1928	Hayes, Middlesex	HMV Rejected
JHO	You Can't Have My Sugar For Tea	01/03/1928	Hayes, Middlesex	HMV B-5447
JHO	Together (waltz)	02/03/1928	Hayes, Middlesex	HMV B-5451
JHO	Plenty Of Sunshine	02/03/1928	Hayes, Middlesex	HMV B-5451
JHO	Darby And Joan (waltz)	02/03/1928	Hayes, Middlesex	HMV B-5452
JHO	Sweet Suzanne (waltz)	02/03/1928	Hayes, Middlesex	HMV B-5450
JHO	Sunshine	03/05/1928	Hayes, Middlesex	HMV B-5474
JHO	Ramona (waltz)	03/05/1928	Hayes, Middlesex	HMV B-5474
JHO	I Never Dreamt (You'd Fall In Love With Me)	03/05/1928	Hayes, Middlesex	HMV B-5473

Jack Hylton

JHO	I'll See To It	Hayes, Middlesex	03/05/1928	HMV Rejected
JHO	Ça c'est Paris (6/8 One-Step)	Hayes, Middlesex	03/05/1928	HMV Rejected
JHO	Sweetheart, I'm Dreaming Of You	Hayes, Middlesex	03/05/1928	HMV B-5473
JHO	Can't Help Lovin' Dat Man	Hayes, Middlesex	09/05/1928	HMV B-5475
JHO	Ol' Man River	Hayes, Middlesex	09/05/1928	HMV B-5475
JHO	Sing Me To Sleep With A Twilight Song	London Palladium	10/05/1928	HMV B-5480
JHO	Firefly	London Palladium	10/05/1928	HMV B-5480
JHO	Spanish Rose	London Palladium	10/05/1928	HMV B-5481
JHO	The Angelus Was Ringing (waltz)	London Palladium	10/05/1928	HMV B-5481
JHO	Back To The Heather	Hayes, Middlesex	11/05/1928	HMV B-5477
JHO	Blue Eyes	Hayes, Middlesex	11/05/1928	HMV B-5477
JHO	How Long Has This Been Going On?	Hayes, Middlesex	11/05/1928	HMV B-5485
JHO	Henry's Made A Lady Out Of Lizzie	Hayes, Middlesex	11/05/1928	HMV B-5485
JHO	Borneo	Hayes, Middlesex	21/06/1928	HMV B-5500
JHO	If I Were You, Dear	Hayes, Middlesex	21/06/1928	HMV B-5503
JHO	Constantinople (6/8 One-Step)	Hayes, Middlesex	21/06/1928	HMV B-5501
JHO	Dance Of The Blue Danube	Hayes, Middlesex	22/06/1928	HMV B-5500
JHO	Tokio	Hayes, Middlesex	22/06/1928	HMV B-5513
JHO	I Want To Be Alone With Mary Brown	Hayes, Middlesex	22/06/1928	HMV B-5501
JHO	Again (waltz)	Hayes, Middlesex	22/06/1928	HMV B-5503
JHO	The Best Things In Life Are Free	Hayes, Middlesex	23/07/1928	HMV B-5507
JHO	The Varsity Drag	Hayes, Middlesex	23/07/1928	HMV B-5506
JHO	Good News	Hayes, Middlesex	24/07/1928	HMV B-5506
JHO	Lucky In Love	Hayes, Middlesex	24/07/1928	HMV B-5507
JHO	Mississippi Melody	Hayes, Middlesex	25/07/1928	HMV B-5520
JHO	Bluebird, Sing Me A Song	Hayes, Middlesex	25/07/1928	HMV B-5513
JHO	Bublitchki	Hayes, Middlesex	25/07/1928	HMV Rejected
JHO	That's My Weakness Now	Hayes, Middlesex	23/08/1928	HMV B-5520
JHO	In The Shadows (waltz)	Hayes, Middlesex	23/08/1928	HMV Rejected
JHO	My One And Only	Hayes, Middlesex	23/08/1928	HMV Rejected

Complete UK Discography

JHO	In Old Vienna	24/08/1928	Hayes, Middlesex	HMV B-5530
JHO	S Wonderful	24/08/1928	Hayes, Middlesex	HMV B-5536
JHO	Evergreen Eve (vocal - Ennis Parkes [Mrs. Jack Hylton])	24/08/1928	Hayes, Middlesex	HMV B-5548
JHO	Saskatchewan	24/08/1928	Hayes, Middlesex	HMV Rejected
JHO	Glow Worm	30/08/1928	Small Queen's Hall, London	HMV B-5525
JHO	Glow Worm	30/08/1928	Small Queen's Hall, London	Zonophone 6050
JHO	I'm Sorry (waltz)	30/08/1928	Small Queen's Hall, London	HMV B-5525
JHO	Beautiful	30/08/1928	Small Queen's Hall, London	HMV B-5529
JHO	Melodious Memories - Part 1	30/08/1928	Small Queen's Hall, London	HMV C-1575
JHO	Melodious Memories - Part 2	03/09/1928	Small Queen's Hall, London	HMV C-1575
JHO	A Room With A View	03/09/1928	Small Queen's Hall, London	HMV Rejected
JHO	In A Hidden Corner (waltz)	03/09/1928	Small Queen's Hall, London	HMV B-5529
JHO	Underneath The Blue	12/09/1928	Small Queen's Hall, London	HMV B-5539
JHO	Sweet Ukulele Maid	12/09/1928	Small Queen's Hall, London	HMV B-5539
JHO	My Inspiration Is You	12/09/1928	Small Queen's Hall, London	HMV B-5530
JHO	My One And Only	12/09/1928	Small Queen's Hall, London	HMV B-5536
JHO	Head Over Heels	12/09/1928	Small Queen's Hall, London	HMV Rejected
JHO	I Think Of What You Used To Think Of Me	19/09/1928	Small Queen's Hall, London	HMV B-5542
JHO	Ah! Sweet Mystery Of Life	19/09/1928	Small Queen's Hall, London	HMV B-5545
JHO	Rock-a-Bye Baby	19/09/1928	Small Queen's Hall, London	HMV B-5544
JHO	The Magic Violin (waltz)	21/09/1928	Small Queen's Hall, London	HMV B-5544
JHO	Sunrise (waltz)	21/09/1928	Small Queen's Hall, London	HMV B-5545
JHO	Forty-Seven Ginger-Headed Sailors	21/09/1928	Small Queen's Hall, London	HMV B-5542
JHO	A Room With A View	26/09/1928	Small Queen's Hall, London	HMV C-1577
JHO	My Inspiration Is You	26/09/1928	Small Queen's Hall, London	HMV C-1577
JHO	In The Shadows	26/09/1928	Small Queen's Hall, London	HMV B-5549
JHO	In The Shadows	26/09/1928	Small Queen's Hall, London	Zonophone 6050
JHO	Roll Away, Clouds	02/10/1928	Small Queen's Hall, London	HMV B-5546
JHO	All Mine	02/10/1928	Small Queen's Hall, London	HMV B-5547
JHO	Dreams Of Yesterday (waltz)	02/10/1928	Small Queen's Hall, London	HMV B-5546

Jack Hylton

	Title	Date	Location	Catalogue
JHO	Good Old Songs - Part 1	05/10/1928	Small Queen's Hall, London	HMV C-1592
JHO	Good Old Songs - Part 2	05/10/1928	Small Queen's Hall, London	HMV C-1592
JHO	For Old Times' Sake (waltz)	05/10/1928	Small Queen's Hall, London	HMV B-5549
JHO	Paradise Square	09/10/1928	Small Queen's Hall, London	HMV B-5547
JHO	In The Hush Of The Twilight	09/10/1928	Small Queen's Hall, London	HMV B-5548
JHO	The Song I Love	27/11/1928	Berlin, Germany	HMV B-5573
JHO	If You Want The Rainbow	27/11/1928	Berlin, Germany	HMV B-5573
JHO	A Hundred Years From Now	27/11/1928	Berlin, Germany	HMV B-5574
JHO	I Kiss Your Hand, Madame	27/11/1928	Berlin, Germany	HMV C-1616
JHO	When The White Elder Tree Blooms Again	29/11/1928	Berlin, Germany	HMV C-1616
JHO	Laughing Marionette	29/11/1928	Berlin, Germany	HMV B-5574
JHO	High Up On A Hill-Top	29/11/1928	Berlin, Germany	HMV B-5575
JHO	Considerin'	29/11/1928	Berlin, Germany	HMV B-5575
JHO	Blue Night	18/01/1929	Berlin, Germany	HMV B-5595
JHO	Oh! What A Night To Love	18/01/1929	Berlin, Germany	HMV B-5594
JHO	Where The Shy Little Violets Grow	18/01/1929	Berlin, Germany	HMV B-5594
JHO	Forget Me Not	18/01/1929	Berlin, Germany	HMV B-5610
JHO	I Don't Care	18/01/1929	Berlin, Germany	HMV B-5610
JHO	My Blackbirds Are Bluebirds Now	18/01/1929	Berlin, Germany	HMV B-5595
JHO	Oh Maiden, My Maiden	18/01/1929	Berlin, Germany	HMV B-5748
JHO	Four Words	18/01/1929	Berlin, Germany	HMV B-5748
JHO	Ich habe ihnen so viel zu sagen, sehr verehrte gnädige Frau	Jan-29	Berlin, Germany	Electrola EG-1251
JHO	Pierrot, komm' trag' mich nach Haus	Jan-29	Berlin, Germany	Electrola EG-1251
JHO	Thinking Of You	07/02/1929	Small Queen's Hall, London	HMV B-5612
JHO	Up In The Clouds	07/02/1929	Small Queen's Hall, London	HMV B-5612
JHO	All By Yourself In The Moonlight	07/02/1929	Small Queen's Hall, London	HMV C-1651
JHO	Wonderful You	12/02/1929	Small Queen's Hall, London	HMV B-5611
JHO	But I Do Say So	12/02/1929	Small Queen's Hall, London	HMV B-5611
JHO	You Made Me Love You	12/02/1929	Small Queen's Hall, London	HMV C-1651
JHO	Sarita	12/02/1929	Small Queen's Hall, London	HMV B-5607

Complete UK Discography

JHO	I Wish I Had A Talking Picture Of You	13/02/1929	Small Queen's Hall, London	HMV B-5608
JHO	I Kiss Your Hand, Madame	13/02/1929	Small Queen's Hall, London	HMV B-5602
JHO	Bogey Wail	13/02/1929	Small Queen's Hall, London	HMV B-5607
JHO	Early Ragtime Memories - Part 1	13/02/1929	Small Queen's Hall, London	HMV C-1653
JHO	Glad Feet	14/02/1929	Small Queen's Hall, London	HMV B-5615
JHO	Sally Of My Dreams	14/02/1929	Small Queen's Hall, London	HMV B-5602
JHO	I Ain't Never Been Kissed	15/02/1929	Small Queen's Hall, London	HMV B-5608
JHO	A Dicky Bird Told Me So	15/02/1929	Small Queen's Hall, London	HMV B-5615
JHO	Early Ragtime Memories - Part 2	15/02/1929	Small Queen's Hall, London	HMV C-1653
JHO	Baby	25/02/1929	Milan, Italy	HMV Rejected
JHO	Sweethearts On Parade	25/02/1929	Milan, Italy	HMV B-5619
JHO	I Must Have That Man	25/02/1929	Milan, Italy	HMV B-5617
JHO	Doin' The New Low Down	25/02/1929	Milan, Italy	HMV B-5647
JHO	Digga Digga Do	25/02/1929	Milan, Italy	HMV Rejected
JHO	My Angeline	25/02/1929	Milan, Italy	HMV B-5641
JHO	When Summer Is Gone	25/02/1929	Milan, Italy	HMV B-5619
JHO	Carolina Moon (waltz)	25/02/1929	Milan, Italy	HMV B-5617
JHO	Let's Fall In Love (Let's Do It)	26/03/1929	Small Queen's Hall, London	HMV B-5622
JHO	The Banjo (That Man Joe Plays)	26/03/1929	Small Queen's Hall, London	HMV B-5622
JHO	What Is This Thing Called Love?	26/03/1929	Small Queen's Hall, London	HMV B-5621
JHO	Looking At You	26/03/1929	Small Queen's Hall, London	HMV B-5621
JHO	House On The Hill-Top	04/04/1929	Small Queen's Hall, London	HMV B-5628
JHO	Deep Night	04/04/1929	Small Queen's Hall, London	HMV B-5638
JHO	A Love Tale Of Alsace-Lorraine	04/04/1929	Small Queen's Hall, London	HMV B-5628
JHO	Baby	04/04/1929	Small Queen's Hall, London	HMV B-5647
JHO	Sweetheart Of All My Dreams	05/04/1929	Small Queen's Hall, London	HMV B-5627
JHO	Glad Rag Doll	05/04/1929	Small Queen's Hall, London	HMV B-5627
JHO	Softly, As In A Morning Sunrise	05/04/1929	Small Queen's Hall, London	HMV Rejected
JHO	I Lift Up My Finger And Say "Tweet! Tweet!"	07/04/1929	Friends' Meeting House, London	HMV B-5629
JHO	There's A Four-Leaf Clover In My Pocket	07/04/1929	Friends' Meeting House, London	HMV B-5640

Jack Hylton

JHO	Shinaniki Da (6/8 One-Step)	07/04/1929	Friends' Meeting House, London	HMV B-5629
JHO	Down Among The Sugar Cane	07/04/1929	Friends' Meeting House, London	HMV B-5646
JHO	One Kiss (waltz)	07/04/1929	Friends' Meeting House, London	HMV B-5625
JHO	Digga Digga Do	07/04/1929	Friends' Meeting House, London	HMV B-5638
JHO	A Precious Little Thing Called Love	11/04/1929	Small Queen's Hall, London	HMV B-5630
JHO	Sleep, Baby, Sleep	11/04/1929	Small Queen's Hall, London	HMV B-5641
JHO	Softly, As In A Morning Sunrise	11/04/1929	Small Queen's Hall, London	HMV B-5625
JHO	Who Wouldn't Be Jealous Of You?	12/04/1929	Small Queen's Hall, London	HMV B-5640
JHO	Weary River	12/04/1929	Small Queen's Hall, London	HMV B-5630
JHO	My Flame Of Love (waltz)	12/04/1929	Small Queen's Hall, London	HMV B-5636
JHO	All Alone In Lover's Lane	12/04/1929	Small Queen's Hall, London	HMV B-5646
JHO	Everybody Loves You	12/04/1929	Small Queen's Hall, London	HMV B-5651
JHO	Um-Tcha-Um-Tcha Da, Da, Da	12/04/1929	Small Queen's Hall, London	HMV B-5645
JHO	Old-Time Songs - Part 1	25/04/1929	Madame Tussaud's Cinema, London	HMV C-1681
JHO	Old-Time Songs - Part 2	25/04/1929	Madame Tussaud's Cinema, London	HMV C-1681
JHO	Don't Make My Heart Your Plaything (waltz)	25/04/1929	Madame Tussaud's Cinema, London	HMV B-5649
JHO	In The Heart Of The Sunset	26/04/1929	Small Queen's Hall, London	HMV B-5636
JHO	Ever So Goosey	26/04/1929	Small Queen's Hall, London	HMV B-5649
JHO	The Wedding Of The Painted Doll	26/04/1929	Small Queen's Hall, London	HMV B-5637
JHO	My Sin	26/04/1929	Small Queen's Hall, London	HMV B-5637
JHO	My Irish Paradise (waltz)	26/04/1929	Small Queen's Hall, London	HMV B-5645
JHO	You're The Cream In My Coffee	13/05/1929	Small Queen's Hall, London	HMV B-5650
JHO	To Know You Is To Love You	13/05/1929	Small Queen's Hall, London	HMV B-5650
JHO	Don't Hold Everything	13/05/1929	Small Queen's Hall, London	HMV B-5651
JHO	The Toymaker's Dream	30/05/1929	Small Queen's Hall, London	HMV B-5656
JHO	Is Izzy Azzy Wozz?	30/05/1929	Small Queen's Hall, London	HMV B-5666
JHO	Lover, Come Back To Me	30/05/1929	Small Queen's Hall, London	HMV B-5656
JHO	Mean To Me	30/05/1929	Small Queen's Hall, London	HMV B-5657
JHO	I Wanna Go Places And Do Things	31/05/1929	Small Queen's Hall, London	HMV B-5659
JHO	My Ideal	31/05/1929	Small Queen's Hall, London	HMV B-5657

Complete UK Discography

JHO	Broadway Melody	31/05/1929	Small Queen's Hall, London	HMV B-5659
JHO	Louise	31/05/1929	Small Queen's Hall, London	HMV B-5663
JHO	Breakaway	17/06/1929	Small Queen's Hall, London	HMV B-5658
JHO	That's You, Baby	17/06/1929	Small Queen's Hall, London	HMV B-5658
JHO	Honey	17/06/1929	Small Queen's Hall, London	HMV B-5663
JHO	Little Pal	19/06/1929	Small Queen's Hall, London	HMV Rejected
JHO	Why Can't You?	19/06/1929	Small Queen's Hall, London	HMV Rejected
JHO	When I Met Connie In The Cornfield	19/06/1929	Small Queen's Hall, London	HMV B-5666
JHO	Am I Blue?	27/06/1929	Small Queen's Hall, London	HMV B-5674
JHO	Excuse Me, Lady	27/06/1929	Small Queen's Hall, London	HMV B-5674
JHO	Sarah Jane	27/06/1929	Small Queen's Hall, London	HMV B-5665
JHO	Empty Hours	27/06/1929	Small Queen's Hall, London	HMV B-5665
JHO	Bitter Sweet - Part 1	23/07/1929	Small Queen's Hall, London	HMV B-5677
JHO	Bitter Sweet - Part 1	23/07/1929	Small Queen's Hall, London	Zonophone 6014
JHO	Bitter Sweet - Part 2	23/07/1929	Small Queen's Hall, London	HMV B-5677
JHO	Bitter Sweet - Part 2	23/07/1929	Small Queen's Hall, London	Zonophone 6014
JHO	Mother Goose Parade	23/07/1929	Small Queen's Hall, London	HMV B-5685
JHO	Get Up Nice And Early In The Morning	23/07/1929	Small Queen's Hall, London	HMV B-5685
JHO	Bitter Sweet - Selection, Part 1	24/07/1929	Small Queen's Hall, London	HMV C-1727
JHO	Bitter Sweet - Selection, Part 2	24/07/1929	Small Queen's Hall, London	HMV C-1727
JHO	Through	29/08/1929	Small Queen's Hall, London	HMV B-5693
JHO	Let Me Dream In Your Arms Again (waltz)	29/08/1929	Small Queen's Hall, London	HMV B-5696
JHO	Mucking About The Garden (6/8 One-Step)	29/08/1929	Small Queen's Hall, London	HMV B-5696
JHO	My Dream Memory	29/08/1929	Small Queen's Hall, London	HMV B-5704
JHO	I'm Perfectly Satisfied	29/08/1929	Small Queen's Hall, London	HMV B-5707
JHO	You Wouldn't Fool Me, Would You?	29/08/1929	Small Queen's Hall, London	HMV B-5695
JHO	I Want To Be Bad	29/08/1929	Small Queen's Hall, London	HMV B-5695
JHO	Pagan Love Song (waltz)	29/08/1929	Small Queen's Hall, London	HMV B-5697
JHO	You're My Silver Lining Of Love	30/08/1929	Kingsway Hall, London	HMV B-5742
JHO	My Lucky Star	30/08/1929	Kingsway Hall, London	HMV Rejected

313

Jack Hylton

JHO	I'm Doing What I'm Doing For Love	30/08/1929	Kingsway Hall, London	HMV B-5693
JHO	Lovable And Sweet	30/08/1929	Kingsway Hall, London	HMV Rejected
JHO	Button Up Your Overcoat	30/08/1929	Kingsway Hall, London	HMV Rejected
JHO	This Is Heaven	30/08/1929	Kingsway Hall, London	HMV B-5697
JHO	Button Up Your Overcoat	09/09/1929	Small Queen's Hall, London	HMV B-5703
JHO	I Want To Be Bad	09/09/1929	Small Queen's Hall, London	HMV B-5695
JHO	Singin' In The Rain	09/09/1929	Small Queen's Hall, London	HMV B-5700
JHO	Orange Blossom Time	09/09/1929	Small Queen's Hall, London	HMV B-5700
JHO	Little Pal	09/09/1929	Small Queen's Hall, London	HMV B-5698
JHO	Why Can't You?	09/09/1929	Small Queen's Hall, London	HMV B-5698
JHO	My Lucky Star	17/09/1929	Small Queen's Hall, London	HMV B-5703
JHO	Come On, Baby	17/09/1929	Small Queen's Hall, London	HMV B-5708
JHO	With A Song In My Heart	17/09/1929	Small Queen's Hall, London	HMV B-5799
JHO	Love Me Or Leave Me	17/09/1929	Small Queen's Hall, London	HMV B-5702
JHO	Makin' Whoopee	17/09/1929	Small Queen's Hall, London	HMV B-5702
JHO	I'm Just In The Mood Tonight	17/09/1929	Small Queen's Hall, London	HMV B-5708
JHO	Lovable And Sweet	18/09/1929	Small Queen's Hall, London	HMV B-5704
JHO	My Song Of The Nile (waltz)	18/09/1929	Small Queen's Hall, London	HMV B-5720
JHO	If I Had My Way	18/09/1929	Small Queen's Hall, London	HMV B-5707
JHO	Dreamy Honolulu	18/09/1929	Small Queen's Hall, London	HMV B-5715
JHO	You Wanted Someone To Play With (waltz)	18/09/1929	Small Queen's Hall, London	HMV B-5730
JHO	Ain't Misbehavin' (Concert arrangement)	08/10/1929	Small Queen's Hall, London	HMV C-1779
JHO	Excuse Me, Lady	08/10/1929	Small Queen's Hall, London	HMV C-1779
JHO	Ain't Misbehavin'	08/10/1929	Small Queen's Hall, London	HMV B-5715
JHO	Old Musical Comedy Gems - Part 1	09/10/1929	Small Queen's Hall, London	HMV C-1773
JHO	Old Musical Comedy Gems - Part 2	09/10/1929	Small Queen's Hall, London	HMV C-1773
JHO	Good Old Dances - Part 1	09/10/1929	Small Queen's Hall, London	HMV Rejected
JHO	Good Old Dances - Part 2	09/10/1929	Small Queen's Hall, London	HMV Rejected
JHO	Good Old Dances - Part 1	15/10/1929	Small Queen's Hall, London	HMV C-1784
JHO	Good Old Dances - Part 2	15/10/1929	Small Queen's Hall, London	HMV C-1784

Complete UK Discography

JHO	If You Were Mine	15/10/1929	Small Queen's Hall, London	HMV B-5720
JHO	More Old Songs - Part 1	15/10/1929	Small Queen's Hall, London	HMV C-1783
JHO	More Old Songs - Part 2	15/10/1929	Small Queen's Hall, London	HMV C-1783
JHO	Stepping Out	15/10/1929	Small Queen's Hall, London	HMV B-5727
JHO	Lonesome Little Doll	15/10/1929	Small Queen's Hall, London	HMV B-5727
JHO	Tip-Toe Through The Tulips	24/10/1929	Small Queen's Hall, London	HMV B-5722
JHO	Yours Sincerely	24/10/1929	Small Queen's Hall, London	HMV B-5728
JHO	Moscow (6/8 One-Step)	24/10/1929	Small Queen's Hall, London	HMV B-5728
JHO	If I Had A Talking Picture Of You	24/10/1929	Small Queen's Hall, London	HMV Rejected
JHO	Parisienne Doll	25/10/1929	Small Queen's Hall, London	HMV B-5730
JHO	Painting The Clouds With Sunshine	25/10/1929	Small Queen's Hall, London	HMV B-5722
JHO	Tondeleyo	25/10/1929	Small Queen's Hall, London	HMV B-5721
JHO	Turn On The Heat	25/10/1929	Small Queen's Hall, London	HMV B-5741
JHO	Memories Of Paris - Part 1 (Padilla)	30/10/1929	Small Queen's Hall, London	HMV B-3314
JHO	Memories Of Paris - Part 2 (Yvain)	30/10/1929	Small Queen's Hall, London	HMV B-3273
JHO	Memories Of Paris - Part 3 (Moretti)	30/10/1929	Small Queen's Hall, London	HMV B-3314
JHO	Memories Of Paris - Part 4 (Christine)	30/10/1929	Small Queen's Hall, London	HMV B-3273
JHO	She's Such A Comfort To Me	04/11/1929	Small Queen's Hall, London	HMV B-5736
JHO	The Thought Never Entered My Head	04/11/1929	Small Queen's Hall, London	HMV B-5736
JHO	My Wife Is On A Diet	04/11/1929	Small Queen's Hall, London	HMV B-5721
JHO	Love	04/11/1929	Small Queen's Hall, London	HMV B-5735
JHO	The Kinkajou	08/11/1929	Small Queen's Hall, London	HMV B-5733
JHO	High And Low	08/11/1929	Small Queen's Hall, London	HMV B-5772
JHO	Who Cares?	08/11/1929	Small Queen's Hall, London	HMV B-5735
JHO	Rio Rita	08/11/1929	Small Queen's Hall, London	HMV B-5733
JHO	If I Had A Talking Picture Of You	21/11/1929	Small Queen's Hall, London	HMV B-5741
JHO	Jollity Farm	21/11/1929	Small Queen's Hall, London	HMV B-5744
JHO	Piccolo Pete	21/11/1929	Small Queen's Hall, London	HMV B-5742
JHO	On Her Doorstep Last Night	21/11/1929	Small Queen's Hall, London	HMV B-5744
JHO	Hang On To Me	03/01/1930	Small Queen's Hall, London	HMV B-5759

315

Jack Hylton

JHO	Just You - Just Me	Small Queen's Hall, London	03/01/1930	HMV B-5759
JHO	I May Be Wrong	Small Queen's Hall, London	03/01/1930	HMV B-5760
JHO	Bunkey-Doodle-I-Doh (6/8 One-Step)	Small Queen's Hall, London	03/01/1930	HMV B-5760
JHO	The World's Greatest Sweetheart Is You	Small Queen's Hall, London	10/01/1930	HMV B-5765
JHO	Tiger Rag	Small Queen's Hall, London	10/01/1930	HMV B-5789
JHO	Limehouse Blues	Small Queen's Hall, London	10/01/1930	HMV B-5789
JHO	Marianne	Small Queen's Hall, London	10/01/1930	HMV B-5764
JHO	When The Organ Played At Twilight (waltz)	Madame Tussaud's Cinema, London	13/01/1930	HMV B-5763
JHO	Ain't It Great To Be Home Again?	Madame Tussaud's Cinema, London	13/01/1930	HMV Rejected
JHO	I Don't Want Your Kisses	Madame Tussaud's Cinema, London	13/01/1930	HMV B-5765
JHO	Give Yourself A Pat On The Back (6/8 One-Step)	Small Queen's Hall, London	17/01/1930	HMV B-5763
JHO	Say, Sadie	Small Queen's Hall, London	17/01/1930	HMV B-5768
JHO	Somebody Mighty Like You	Small Queen's Hall, London	17/01/1930	HMV B-5764
JHO	Speaking Of Kentucky Days	Small Queen's Hall, London	17/01/1930	HMV B-5786
JHO	I'm Like A Sailor	Small Queen's Hall, London	22/01/1930	HMV B-5772
JHO	Nobody's Using It Now	Small Queen's Hall, London	22/01/1930	HMV B-5769
JHO	The Kerb Step	Small Queen's Hall, London	22/01/1930	HMV B-5768
JHO	Dream Lover (waltz)	Small Queen's Hall, London	22/01/1930	HMV Rejected
JHO	We're Uncomfortable	Kingsway Hall, London	27/01/1930	HMV B-5783
JHO	Fancy You Falling For Me	Kingsway Hall, London	27/01/1930	HMV B-5777
JHO	Maggie's Cold	Kingsway Hall, London	27/01/1930	HMV B-5778
JHO	My Dream Lover (waltz)	Small Queen's Hall, London	30/01/1930	HMV B-5769
JHO	Happy Days Are Here Again	Small Queen's Hall, London	30/01/1930	HMV B-5771
JHO	Lucky Me - Lovable You	Small Queen's Hall, London	30/01/1930	HMV B-5771
JHO	Singin' In The Bathtub	Small Queen's Hall, London	30/01/1930	HMV B-5788
JHO	Medley of Chappell Ballads - Part 1	Kingsway Hall, London	07/02/1930	HMV C-1846
JHO	Medley of Chappell Ballads - Part 2	Kingsway Hall, London	07/02/1930	HMV C-1846
JHO	Body And Soul	Kingsway Hall, London	07/02/1930	HMV B-5777
JHO	Dance Of The Raindrops	Kingsway Hall, London	07/02/1930	HMV B-5778
JHO	Punch And Judy Show	Small Queen's Hall, London	14/02/1930	HMV B-5786

Complete UK Discography

JHO	Jack O' Lanterns	14/02/1930	Small Queen's Hall, London	HMV B-5795
JHO	That Wonderful Something Is Love	14/02/1930	Small Queen's Hall, London	HMV B-5792
JHO	Chant Of The Jungle	14/02/1930	Small Queen's Hall, London	HMV B-5792
JHO	It's An Old Spanish Custom	14/02/1930	Small Queen's Hall, London	HMV B-5783
JHO	H'lo Baby	14/02/1930	Small Queen's Hall, London	HMV B-5788
JHO	Share Your Lips, Cherie, With Me	14/02/1930	Small Queen's Hall, London	HMV B-5851
JHO	Prelude in G minor, Op. 23, No. 5 (Rachmaninoff)	19/02/1930	Kingsway Hall, London	HMV C-1864
JHO	Prelude in C sharp minor, Op. 3, No. 2 (Rachmaninoff)	19/02/1930	Kingsway Hall, London	HMV C-1864
JHO	With A Song In My Heart	25/02/1930	Small Queen's Hall, London	HMV B-5799
JHO	Body And Soul	25/02/1930	Small Queen's Hall, London	HMV C-1855
JHO	Far Away	25/02/1930	Small Queen's Hall, London	HMV B-5787
JHO	Wind In The Willows	26/02/1930	Small Queen's Hall, London	HMV B-5795
JHO	Indispensible You	26/02/1930	Small Queen's Hall, London	HMV B-5787
JHO	Moanin' Low	26/02/1930	Small Queen's Hall, London	HMV B-5952
JHO	Can't We Be Friends?	26/02/1930	Small Queen's Hall, London	HMV B-5952
JHO	Xylophone Stampede	06/03/1930	Small Queen's Hall, London	HMV B-5809
JHO	Why?	06/03/1930	Small Queen's Hall, London	HMV B-5839
JHO	The Sunshine Of Marseilles	06/03/1930	Small Queen's Hall, London	HMV B-5798
JHO	Molly (waltz)	06/03/1930	Small Queen's Hall, London	HMV B-5798
JHO	Boosey Ballads - Part 1	07/03/1930	Small Queen's Hall, London	HMV C-1866
JHO	With A Song In My Heart	07/03/1930	Small Queen's Hall, London	HMV C-1855
JHO	Just As We Used To Do (waltz)	07/03/1930	Small Queen's Hall, London	HMV B-5799
JHO	Vamp Of Baghdad	13/03/1930	Madame Tussaud's Cinema, London	HMV B-5809
JHO	Boosey Ballads - Part 2	13/03/1930	Madame Tussaud's Cinema, London	HMV C-1866
JHO	Tommies' War Time Memories	13/03/1930	Madame Tussaud's Cinema, London	HMV C-1888
JHO	Songs Of The Officers' Mess	13/03/1930	Madame Tussaud's Cinema, London	HMV C-1888
JHO	Jag är törstig efter kyssar	14/03/1930	Small Queen's Hall, London	HMV X-3396
JHO	Fast det bara är en liten bit	14/03/1930	Small Queen's Hall, London	HMV X-3396
JHO	Cross Your Fingers	14/03/1930	Small Queen's Hall, London	HMV B-5839
JHO	Vielles Chansons Françaises - Part 1	14/03/1930	Small Queen's Hall, London	HMV K-5904

Jack Hylton

JHO	Vielles Chansons Françaises - Part 2	14/03/1930	Small Queen's Hall, London	HMV K-5904
JHO	Song Of The Dawn	09/05/1930	Berlin, Germany	HMV B-5838
JHO	Happy Feet	09/05/1930	Berlin, Germany	HMV B-5843
JHO	It Happened In Monterey (waltz)	09/05/1930	Berlin, Germany	HMV B-5838
JHO	Why Was I Born?	09/05/1930	Berlin, Germany	HMV Rejected
JHO	Ragamuffin Romeo	10/05/1930	Berlin, Germany	HMV B-5843
JHO	Handsome Gigolo	10/05/1930	Berlin, Germany	HMV C-1970
JHO	They All Fall In Love	10/05/1930	Berlin, Germany	HMV B-5841
JHO	A Cottage For Sale	13/05/1930	Berlin, Germany	HMV B-5841
JHO	Lazy Lou'siana Moon (waltz)	13/05/1930	Berlin, Germany	HMV B-5840
JHO	Watchung My Dreams Go By	13/05/1930	Berlin, Germany	HMV B-5846
JHO	Oh! What A Silly Place To Kiss A Girl	13/05/1930	Berlin, Germany	HMV B-5836
JHO	Ro-Ro-Rollin' Along	13/05/1930	Berlin, Germany	HMV B-5840
JHO	Thine Is My Whole Heart	21/05/1930	Berlin, Germany	HMV C-1970
JHO	Herr Lehmann, was macht die Fraulein Gemahlin in Marienbad?	21/05/1930	Berlin, Germany	Electrola EG-1996
JHO	Stein Song (6/8 One-Step)	02/06/1930	Small Queen's Hall, London	HMV B-5844
JHO	Amy	02/06/1930	Small Queen's Hall, London	HMV B-5836
JHO	When You're Smiling	02/06/1930	Small Queen's Hall, London	HMV B-5852
JHO	Under A Texas Moon	03/06/1930	Small Queen's Hall, London	HMV B-5846
JHO	Here Comes Emily Brown	03/06/1930	Small Queen's Hall, London	HMV B-5850
JHO	On The Sunny Side Of The Street	03/06/1930	Small Queen's Hall, London	HMV B-5844
JHO	Cheer Up And Smile	06/06/1930	Small Queen's Hall, London	HMV B-5850
JHO	Doin' The Derby	06/06/1930	Small Queen's Hall, London	HMV B-5851
JHO	You Taught Me All I Know	06/06/1930	Small Queen's Hall, London	HMV B-5864
JHO	Falling In Love Again (waltz)	06/06/1930	Small Queen's Hall, London	HMV B-5864
JHO	When I Passed The Old Church Door (waltz)	16/06/1930	Kingsway Hall, London	HMV B-5845
JHO	Meet Me In My Dreams Tonight (waltz)	16/06/1930	Kingsway Hall, London	HMV B-5852
JHO	Ain't It Great To Be Home Again? (waltz)	16/06/1930	Kingsway Hall, London	HMV B-5845
JHO	Harmonica Harry	16/07/1930	Glasgow, Scotland	HMV B-5875
JHO	When It's Springtime In The Rockies (waltz)	16/07/1930	Glasgow, Scotland	HMV B-5873

Complete UK Discography

JHO	Around The Corner (6/8 One-Step)	16/07/1930	Glasgow, Scotland	HMV B-5873
JHO	Scottish Medley	16/07/1930	Glasgow, Scotland	HMV B-5872
JHO	One Night Alone With You	16/07/1930	Glasgow, Scotland	HMV B-5871
JHO	Fine Alpine Milkman	16/07/1930	Glasgow, Scotland	HMV B-5874
JHO	A Quiet Little Corner	16/07/1930	Glasgow, Scotland	HMV B-5871
JHO	I Don't Wanna Go Home	16/07/1930	Glasgow, Scotland	HMV B-5874
JHO	The Chum Song	16/07/1930	Glasgow, Scotland	HMV B-5872
JHO	Suppose	17/07/1930	Glasgow, Scotland	HMV B-5978
JHO	Rose Of Spain	17/07/1930	Glasgow, Scotland	HMV B-5950
JHO	Honolulu Moon (waltz)	17/07/1930	Glasgow, Scotland	HMV B-5950
JHO	The King's Horses	17/07/1930	Glasgow, Scotland	HMV B-5875
JHO	Song Of Swanee	17/07/1930	Glasgow, Scotland	HMV B-5881
JHO	Our Jack's Back	17/07/1930	Glasgow, Scotland	HMV B-5887
JHO	Sam Sat With Sophie On The Sofa	17/07/1930	Glasgow, Scotland	HMV B-5881
JHO	If Your Kisses Can't Hold The Man You Love	27/08/1930	Small Queen's Hall, London	HMV B-5891
JHO	Without A Song	27/08/1930	Small Queen's Hall, London	HMV B-5879
JHO	Great Day	27/08/1930	Small Queen's Hall, London	HMV B-5879
JHO	The First Week-End In June	27/08/1930	Small Queen's Hall, London	HMV Rejected
JHO	Little White Lies	28/08/1930	Small Queen's Hall, London	HMV B-5887
JHO	Without My Gal	28/08/1930	Small Queen's Hall, London	HMV B-5883
JHO	What A Perfect Night For Love	28/08/1930	Small Queen's Hall, London	HMV B-5883
JHO	Tid-dle-id-dle-um-pum!	29/08/1930	Small Queen's Hall, London	HMV B-5897
JHO	Under The Sweetheart Tree	29/08/1930	Small Queen's Hall, London	HMV B-5897
JHO	The Pick Up	29/08/1930	Small Queen's Hall, London	HMV B-5882
JHO	My Future Just Passed	29/08/1930	Small Queen's Hall, London	HMV B-5882
JHO	The First Week-End In June	09/09/1930	Small Queen's Hall, London	HMV B-5891
JHO	I Owe You	09/09/1930	Small Queen's Hall, London	HMV B-5900
JHO	After Your Kiss	09/09/1930	Small Queen's Hall, London	HMV B-5898
JHO	That's Where The South Begins	09/09/1930	Small Queen's Hall, London	HMV B-5899
JHO	There's A Good Time Coming (6/8 One-Step)	10/09/1930	Small Queen's Hall, London	HMV B-5892

319

Jack Hylton

	Title	Date	Location	Catalogue
JHO	That Night In Venice	10/09/1930	Small Queen's Hall, London	HMV B-5890
JHO	Dancing With Tears In My Eyes (waltz)	10/09/1930	Small Queen's Hall, London	HMV B-5899
JHO	Over The Garden Wall	10/09/1930	Small Queen's Hall, London	HMV B-5892
JHO	In A Japanese Garden	12/09/1930	Small Queen's Hall, London	HMV B-5900
JHO	A Californian Serenade	12/09/1930	Small Queen's Hall, London	HMV B-5890
JHO	Adeline	12/09/1930	Small Queen's Hall, London	HMV B-5889
JHO	Absence Makes The Heart Grow Fonder	12/09/1930	Small Queen's Hall, London	HMV B-5899
JHO	Don't Tell Her What Happened To Me	12/09/1930	Small Queen's Hall, London	HMV B-5898
JHO	Confessin'	14/10/1930	Small Queen's Hall, London	HMV B-5910
JHO	Swingin' In A Hammock	14/10/1930	Small Queen's Hall, London	HMV B-5910
JHO	Tomorrow Is Another Day	14/10/1930	Small Queen's Hall, London	HMV B-5912
JHO	Cupid On The Cake	17/10/1930	Small Queen's Hall, London	HMV B-5929
JHO	Rollin' Down The River	17/10/1930	Small Queen's Hall, London	HMV B-5912
JHO	I'd Like To Find The Guy That Wrote The Stein Song (6/8 One-Step)	17/10/1930	Small Queen's Hall, London	HMV B-5922
JHO	Somewhere In Old Wyoming (waltz)	17/10/1930	Small Queen's Hall, London	HMV B-5917
JHO	Soldier On The Shelf	21/10/1930	Small Queen's Hall, London	HMV B-5917
JHO	It's A Great Life	21/10/1930	Small Queen's Hall, London	HMV B-5933
JHO	Drinking Songs - Part 1	21/10/1930	Small Queen's Hall, London	HMV C-2074
JHO	Drinking Songs - Part 2	21/10/1930	Small Queen's Hall, London	HMV C-2074
JHO	Memories Of Sullivan - Part 1	22/10/1930	Kingsway Hall, London	HMV C-2073
JHO	Memories Of Sullivan - Part 2	22/10/1930	Kingsway Hall, London	HMV C-2073
JHO	The Smoking Concert - Part 1	23/10/1930	Small Queen's Hall, London	HMV C-2079
JHO	The Smoking Concert - Part 2	23/10/1930	Small Queen's Hall, London	HMV C-2079
JHO	I Am The Words, You Are The Melody	23/10/1930	Small Queen's Hall, London	HMV B-5928
JHO	More Melodious Memories - Part 1	24/10/1930	Small Queen's Hall, London	HMV C-2095
JHO	More Melodious Memories - Part 2	24/10/1930	Small Queen's Hall, London	HMV C-2095
JHO	Still More Old Songs - Part 1	24/10/1930	Small Queen's Hall, London	HMV C-2082
JHO	Still More Old Songs - Part 2	27/10/1930	Small Queen's Hall, London	HMV C-2082
JHO	Gorgonzola (6/8 One-Step)	27/10/1930	Small Queen's Hall, London	HMV B-5922
JHO	There's Something About An Old-Fashioned Girl	27/10/1930	Small Queen's Hall, London	HMV B-5928

Complete UK Discography

JHO	My Ideal	Small Queen's Hall, London	27/10/1930	HMV B-5933
JHO	Never Swat A Fly	Small Queen's Hall, London	28/10/1930	HMV B-5943
JHO	Sing Something Simple	Small Queen's Hall, London	28/10/1930	HMV B-5943
JHO	Tap Your Feet	Small Queen's Hall, London	28/10/1930	HMV B-5939
JHO	Stick 'Em Up	Small Queen's Hall, London	28/10/1930	HMV B-5929
JHO	Let's Be Sentimental	Small Queen's Hall, London	28/10/1930	HMV B-5923
JHO	Dancing On The Ceiling	Small Queen's Hall, London	30/10/1930	HMV B-5923
JHO	Talkie Hits Medley - Part 1	Small Queen's Hall, London	30/10/1930	HMV B-5926
JHO	Talkie Hits Medley - Part 2	Small Queen's Hall, London	30/10/1930	HMV B-5926
JHO	Eton Boating Song (waltz)	Small Queen's Hall, London	31/10/1930	HMV Rejected
JHO	Nippy - Selection, Part 1	Small Queen's Hall, London	31/10/1930	HMV B-5927
JHO	Nippy - Selection, Part 2	Small Queen's Hall, London	31/10/1930	HMV B-5927
JHO	Beyond The Blue Horizon	Small Queen's Hall, London	31/10/1930	HMV B-5924
JHO	Give Me A Moment, Please (waltz)	Small Queen's Hall, London	31/10/1930	HMV B-5924
JHO	Maurice Chevalier Medley - Part 1	Paris, France	28/11/1930	HMV B-3686
JHO	Maurice Chevalier Medley - Part 2	Paris, France	28/11/1930	HMV B-3686
JHO	Go Home And Tell Your Mother	Paris, France	28/11/1930	HMV B-5939
JHO	Maurice Chevalier Medley - Part 3	Paris, France	28/11/1930	HMV K-3065
JHO	Maurice Chevalier Medley - Part 4	Paris, France	28/11/1930	HMV K-3065
JHO	Singing A Song To The Stars	Small Queen's Hall, London	21/12/1930	HMV Rejected
JHO	Under The Roofs Of Paris (waltz)	Small Queen's Hall, London	21/12/1930	HMV B-5949
JHO	Sing (A Happy Little Thing)	Small Queen's Hall, London	21/12/1930	HMV Rejected
JHO	Here Comes The Sun	Small Queen's Hall, London	21/12/1930	HMV B-5948
JHO	Singing A Song To The Stars	Small Queen's Hall, London	05/01/1931	HMV B-5949
JHO	Sing (A Happy Little Thing)	Small Queen's Hall, London	05/01/1931	HMV B-5948
JHO	I'm Yours	Small Queen's Hall, London	05/01/1931	HMV B-5964
JHO	Sweet Jennie Lee	Small Queen's Hall, London	14/01/1931	HMV B-5962
JHO	If You Can't Sing, Whistle	Small Queen's Hall, London	14/01/1931	HMV B-5962
JHO	Sitting On A Five-Barred Gate	Small Queen's Hall, London	14/01/1931	HMV B-5961
JHO	Oh Donna Clara (tango)	Small Queen's Hall, London	14/01/1931	HMV B-5963

Jack Hylton

JHO	I Don't Want To Dream	14/01/1931	Small Queen's Hall, London	HMV B-5963
JHO	Always In All Ways	16/01/1931	Small Queen's Hall, London	HMV B-5964
JHO	Baby's Birthday Party	16/01/1931	Small Queen's Hall, London	HMV B-5966
JHO	We All Go Oo-Ha-Ha Together	16/01/1931	Small Queen's Hall, London	HMV B-5961
JHO	Reaching For The Moon (waltz)	16/01/1931	Small Queen's Hall, London	HMV B-5985
JHO	Wedding Bells Are Ringing For Sally (waltz)	16/01/1931	Small Queen's Hall, London	HMV B-5976
JHO	Song Of The Drum	28/01/1931	Small Queen's Hall, London	HMV B-5970
JHO	Between The Devil And The Deep Blue Sea	28/01/1931	Small Queen's Hall, London	HMV B-5966
JHO	It's Not You	30/01/1931	Small Queen's Hall, London	HMV B-5971
JHO	There's Always Tomorrow	30/01/1931	Small Queen's Hall, London	HMV B-5971
JHO	Within My Heart	30/01/1931	Small Queen's Hall, London	HMV B-5970
JHO	The Little Things In Life	30/01/1931	Small Queen's Hall, London	HMV B-5972
JHO	Shamrock Land - Part 1	02/02/1931	Small Queen's Hall, London	HMV C-2172
JHO	Shamrock Land - Part 2	02/02/1931	Small Queen's Hall, London	HMV C-2172
JHO	Don't Forget Me In Your Dreams	02/02/1931	Small Queen's Hall, London	HMV B-5988
JHO	Cheerful Little Earful	03/02/1931	Small Queen's Hall, London	HMV B-5972
JHO	Choo-Choo	03/02/1931	Small Queen's Hall, London	HMV B-5973
JHO	Topsy-Turvy Talk	03/02/1931	Small Queen's Hall, London	HMV B-5973
JHO	Songs I Heard At Mother's Knee	11/02/1931	Friends' Meeting House, London	HMV B-5986
JHO	I'm Alone Because I Love You (waltz)	11/02/1931	Friends' Meeting House, London	HMV B-5986
JHO	The Silver-Toned Chimes Of The Angelus (waltz)	11/02/1931	Friends' Meeting House, London	HMV B-5978
JHO	Clowning The Blues Away	11/02/1931	Friends' Meeting House, London	HMV B-5976
JHO	Say Yes	13/02/1931	Small Queen's Hall, London	HMV B-5988
JHO	99 Out Of A Hundred (6/8 One-Step)	13/02/1931	Small Queen's Hall, London	HMV B-5987
JHO	The Wedding Of The Garden Insects	13/02/1931	Small Queen's Hall, London	HMV B-5995
JHO	She's A Very Good Friend Of Mine (6/8 One-Step)	13/02/1931	Small Queen's Hall, London	HMV B-5985
JHO	Betty Co-ed (6/8 One-Step)	13/02/1931	Small Queen's Hall, London	HMV B-5987
JHO	Ten Cents A Dance	03/03/1931	Milan, Italy	HMV B-5991
JHO	I Haven't Heard A Single Word From Baby	03/03/1931	Milan, Italy	HMV B-5991
JHO	Your Eyes	03/03/1931	Milan, Italy	HMV B-5997

Complete UK Discography

JHO	Hurt	09/03/1931	Berlin, Germany	HMV B-5995
JHO	I Lost My Gal Again	09/03/1931	Berlin, Germany	HMV B-5996
JHO	Hello, Beautiful!	09/03/1931	Berlin, Germany	HMV B-5994
JHO	Egyptian-Ella	11/03/1931	Berlin, Germany	HMV B-5996
JHO	The One-Man Band	11/03/1931	Berlin, Germany	HMV B-5994
JHO	O Dorothea	11/03/1931	Berlin, Germany	HMV Rejected
JHO	It Would Be Wonderful	11/03/1931	Berlin, Germany	HMV B-5997
JHO	Without Love	09/04/1931	Berlin, Germany	HMV B-6003
JHO	Nos Bons Vieux Airs - Part 1	09/04/1931	Paris, France	HMV K-6230
JHO	Nos Bons Vieux Airs - Part 2	09/04/1931	Paris, France	HMV K-6230
JHO	Potpourri de vielles chansons - Part 1	09/04/1931	Paris, France	HMV K-6378
JHO	Potpourri de vielles chansons - Part 2	09/04/1931	Paris, France	HMV K-6378
JHO	Francaise	09/04/1931	Paris, France	HMV Rejected
JHO	Lonesome Lover	11/04/1931	Paris, France	HMV B-6004
JHO	Got The Bench, Got The Park	11/04/1931	Paris, France	HMV B-6013
JHO	River, Stay 'Way From My Door	11/04/1931	Paris, France	HMV B-6004
JHO	White Horse Inn - Selection, Part 1	13/04/1931	Paris, France	HMV B-6006
JHO	Hurt	13/04/1931	Paris, France	HMV B-5995
JHO	White Horse Inn - Selection, Part 2	13/04/1931	Paris, France	HMV B-6006
JHO	Thank Your Father	13/04/1931	Paris, France	HMV B-6003
JHO	Let's Get Friendly	04/05/1931	Small Queen's Hall, London	HMV B-6012
JHO	Bubbling Over With Love	04/05/1931	Small Queen's Hall, London	HMV B-6012
JHO	Girl Of A Million Dreams	04/05/1931	Small Queen's Hall, London	HMV B-6013
JHO	When I Take My Sugar To Tea	04/05/1931	Small Queen's Hall, London	HMV B-6016
JHO	Bweavin' On De Window	06/05/1931	Small Queen's Hall, London	HMV Rejected
JHO	When The Guards Are On Parade	06/05/1931	Small Queen's Hall, London	HMV B-6015
JHO	City Lights	06/05/1931	Small Queen's Hall, London	HMV B-6025
JHO	Oh! Rosalita (tango)	06/05/1931	Small Queen's Hall, London	HMV B-6015
JHO	By The River Sainte Marie	06/05/1931	Small Queen's Hall, London	HMV B-6016
JHO	Pretty Kitty Kelly (waltz)	02/06/1931	Empire Theater, Glasgow, Scotland	HMV B-6026

Jack Hylton

JHO	My Brother Makes The Noises For The Talkies	02/06/1931	Empire Theater, Glasgow, Scotland	HMV B-6024
JHO	My Brother Makes The Noises For The Talkies	02/06/1931	Empire Theater, Glasgow, Scotland	Zonophone 6012
JHO	Fourteen Rollicking Sailors	02/06/1931	Empire Theater, Glasgow, Scotland	HMV B-6024
JHO	Fourteen Rollicking Sailors	02/06/1931	Empire Theater, Glasgow, Scotland	Zonophone 6012
JHO	When The Moon Comes Over The Mountain (waltz)	02/06/1931	Empire Theater, Glasgow, Scotland	HMV B-6027
JHO	Bweavin' On De Window	02/06/1931	Empire Theater, Glasgow, Scotland	HMV B-6027
JHO	Scottish Hikers' Song	02/06/1931	Empire Theater, Glasgow, Scotland	HMV B-6026
JHO	Bell-Bottom Trousers	02/06/1931	Empire Theater, Glasgow, Scotland	HMV B-6025
JHO	Wedding Of The Rose	16/06/1931	Small Queen's Hall, London	HMV B-3790
JHO	Come To Me	16/06/1931	Small Queen's Hall, London	HMV B-6036
JHO	Lucerne (waltz)	16/06/1931	Small Queen's Hall, London	HMV B-6037
JHO	The Grasshoppers' Dance	16/06/1931	Small Queen's Hall, London	HMV B-3790
JHO	Springtime Reminds Me Of You (waltz)	16/06/1931	Small Queen's Hall, London	HMV B-6046
JHO	Springtime Reminds Me Of You (waltz)	16/06/1931	Small Queen's Hall, London	Zonophone 6045
JHO	If You Haven't Got Love	18/06/1931	Small Queen's Hall, London	HMV B-6036
JHO	Little Sweetheart Of The Prairie (waltz)	18/06/1931	Small Queen's Hall, London	HMV B-6043
JHO	Little Sweetheart Of The Prairie (waltz)	18/06/1931	Small Queen's Hall, London	Zonophone 6042
JHO	Life	18/06/1931	Small Queen's Hall, London	HMV B-6037
JHO	Yet	18/06/1931	Small Queen's Hall, London	HMV B-6043
JHO	Yet	18/06/1931	Small Queen's Hall, London	Zonophone 6042
JHO	If You're Really And Truly In Love	26/06/1931	Small Queen's Hall, London	HMV B-6041
JHO	We're All Good Pals At Last (6/8 One-Step)	26/06/1931	Small Queen's Hall, London	HMV B-6042
JHO	Try	26/06/1931	Small Queen's Hall, London	HMV B-6042
JHO	We're All Alone (waltz)	26/06/1931	Small Queen's Hall, London	HMV B-6041
JHO	Love For Sale	02/07/1931	Small Queen's Hall, London	HMV B-6046
JHO	Love For Sale	02/07/1931	Small Queen's Hall, London	Zonophone 6045
JHO	Trees	02/07/1931	Small Queen's Hall, London	HMV B-6048
JHO	Trees	02/07/1931	Small Queen's Hall, London	Zonophone 6044
JHO	O Cara Mia	02/07/1931	Small Queen's Hall, London	HMV B-6045
JHO	O Cara Mia	02/07/1931	Small Queen's Hall, London	Zonophone 6051

Complete UK Discography

JHO	Oh! Glory	02/07/1931	Small Queen's Hall, London	HMV B-6045
JHO	Oh! Glory	02/07/1931	Small Queen's Hall, London	Zonophone 6051
JHO	The Match Parade	02/07/1931	Small Queen's Hall, London	HMV B-6048
JHO	The Match Parade	02/07/1931	Small Queen's Hall, London	Zonophone 6044
JHO	Pardon, Madame	22/07/1931	Small Queen's Hall, London	HMV B-6053
JHO	Good-Night	22/07/1931	Small Queen's Hall, London	HMV B-6053
JHO	Viktoria And Her Hussar - Selection, Part 1	22/07/1931	Small Queen's Hall, London	HMV B-6054
JHO	Viktoria And Her Hussar - Selection, Part 2	22/07/1931	Small Queen's Hall, London	HMV B-6054
JHO	Put Your Loving Arms Around Me (waltz)	22/07/1931	Small Queen's Hall, London	HMV B-6060
JHO	Put Your Loving Arms Around Me (waltz)	22/07/1931	Small Queen's Hall, London	Zonophone 6015
JHO	Sitting At A Table Laid For Two	25/08/1931	Friends' Meeting House, London	HMV Rejected
JHO	You Do Something To Me	25/08/1931	Friends' Meeting House, London	HMV Rejected
JHO	That Certain Thing	25/08/1931	Friends' Meeting House, London	HMV Rejected
JHO	Rocky Mountain Lullaby (waltz)	25/08/1931	Friends' Meeting House, London	HMV Rejected
JHO	Little Old Church In The Valley (waltz)	26/08/1931	Friends' Meeting House, London	HMV Rejected
JHO	Waltzes From Vienna - Selection, Part 1	26/08/1931	Friends' Meeting House, London	HMV Rejected
JHO	Waltzes From Vienna - Selection, Part 2	26/08/1931	Friends' Meeting House, London	HMV Rejected
JHO	Ain't That The Way It Goes?	26/08/1931	Friends' Meeting House, London	HMV Rejected
JHO	Would You Take Me Back Again? (waltz)	26/08/1931	Friends' Meeting House, London	HMV Rejected
JHO	Today I Feel So Happy	26/08/1931	Friends' Meeting House, London	HMV Rejected
JHO	Sitting At A Table Laid For Two	07/09/1931	Small Queen's Hall, London	HMV B-6070
JHO	Sitting At A Table Laid For Two	07/09/1931	Small Queen's Hall, London	Zonophone 6043
JHO	Today I Feel So Happy	07/09/1931	Small Queen's Hall, London	HMV B-6070
JHO	Today I Feel So Happy	07/09/1931	Small Queen's Hall, London	Zonophone 6043
JHO	Rocky Mountain Lullaby (waltz)	07/09/1931	Small Queen's Hall, London	HMV B-6060
JHO	Rocky Mountain Lullaby (waltz)	07/09/1931	Small Queen's Hall, London	Zonophone 6015
JHO	Little Old Church In The Valley (waltz)	07/09/1931	Small Queen's Hall, London	HMV B-6059
JHO	Little Old Church In The Valley (waltz)	07/09/1931	Small Queen's Hall, London	Zonophone 6046
JHO	Ain't That The Way It Goes?	07/09/1931	Small Queen's Hall, London	HMV B-6059
JHO	Ain't That The Way It Goes?	07/09/1931	Small Queen's Hall, London	Zonophone 6046

Jack Hylton

	Title	Date	Location	Issue
JHO	Jolly Good Company (6/8 One-Step)	07/09/1931	Small Queen's Hall, London	HMV B-6069
JHO	The Changing Of The Guard (6/8 One-Step)	10/09/1931	Abbey Road, St. John's Wood, London	HMV Rejected
JHO	Waltzes From Vienna - Selection, Part 1	10/09/1931	Abbey Road, St. John's Wood, London	HMV Rejected
JHO	Waltzes From Vienna - Selection, Part 2	10/09/1931	Abbey Road, St. John's Wood, London	HMV Rejected
JHO	You Do Something To Me	10/09/1931	Abbey Road, St. John's Wood, London	HMV Rejected
JHO	Would You Take Me Back Again? (waltz)	10/09/1931	Abbey Road, St. John's Wood, London	HMV Rejected
JHO	Time Alone Will Tell	10/09/1931	Abbey Road, St. John's Wood, London	HMV Rejected
JHO	Time Alone Will Tell (take 4)	11/09/1931	Abbey Road, St. John's Wood, London	HMV B-6064
JHO	Time Alone Will Tell (take 4)	11/09/1931	Abbey Road, St. John's Wood, London	Zonophone 6013
JHO	Love Is Like That	11/09/1931	Abbey Road, St. John's Wood, London	HMV Rejected
JHO	I Believe In You (take 2)	11/09/1931	Abbey Road, St. John's Wood, London	HMV B-6064
JHO	I Believe In You (take 2)	11/09/1931	Abbey Road, St. John's Wood, London	Zonophone 6013
JHO	You Are My Heart's Delight	11/09/1931	Abbey Road, St. John's Wood, London	HMV Rejected
JHO	You Were My Salvation	11/09/1931	Abbey Road, St. John's Wood, London	HMV B-6074
JHO	You Were My Salvation	11/09/1931	Abbey Road, St. John's Wood, London	Zonophone 6047
JHO	Goodnight, Sweetheart	14/09/1931	Abbey Road, St. John's Wood, London	HMV Rejected
JHO	Time On My Hands	14/09/1931	Abbey Road, St. John's Wood, London	HMV Rejected
JHO	When The Circus Comes To Town	14/09/1931	Abbey Road, St. John's Wood, London	HMV B-6076
JHO	The Changing Of The Guard (6/8 One-Step)	21/09/1931	Small Queen's Hall, London	HMV B-6071
JHO	Waltzes From Vienna - Selection, Part 1	21/09/1931	Small Queen's Hall, London	HMV B-6063
JHO	Waltzes From Vienna - Selection, Part 2	21/09/1931	Small Queen's Hall, London	HMV B-6063
JHO	Would You Take Me Back Again? (waltz)	21/09/1931	Small Queen's Hall, London	HMV B-6069
JHO	Time Alone Will Tell (take 5)	21/09/1931	Small Queen's Hall, London	HMV B-6064
JHO	Time Alone Will Tell (take 5)	21/09/1931	Small Queen's Hall, London	Zonophone 6013
JHO	I Believe In You (take 6)	21/09/1931	Small Queen's Hall, London	HMV B-6064
JHO	I Believe In You (take 6)	21/09/1931	Small Queen's Hall, London	Zonophone 6013
JHO	Love Is Like That	22/09/1931	Small Queen's Hall, London	HMV B-6074
JHO	Love Is Like That	22/09/1931	Small Queen's Hall, London	Zonophone 6047
JHO	You Are My Heart's Delight	22/09/1931	Small Queen's Hall, London	HMV B-6071
JHO	Goodnight, Sweetheart	22/09/1931	Small Queen's Hall, London	HMV C-2283

Complete UK Discography

JHO	Negro Spiritual Medley - Part 1	24/09/1931	Small Queen's Hall, London	HMV C-2287
JHO	Negro Spiritual Medley - Part 2	24/09/1931	Small Queen's Hall, London	HMV C-2287
JHO	When It's Night-Time In Nevada (waltz)	25/09/1931	Kingsway Hall, London	HMV B-6083
JHO	Looking For You	25/09/1931	Kingsway Hall, London	HMV B-6081
JHO	My Sunshine Is You	25/09/1931	Small Queen's Hall, London	HMV C-2283
JHO	Song Of Happiness	25/09/1931	Small Queen's Hall, London	HMV B-6076
JHO	What's Gonna Happen To Me?	25/09/1931	Small Queen's Hall, London	HMV B-6081
JHO	Cherie, c'est vous	07/10/1931	Kingsway Hall, London	HMV B-6083
JHO	Over The Blue	07/10/1931	Kingsway Hall, London	HMV B-6085
JHO	Over The Blue	07/10/1931	Kingsway Hall, London	Zonophone 5996
JHO	Neath The Spell Of Monte Carlo	07/10/1931	Kingsway Hall, London	HMV B-6085
JHO	Neath The Spell Of Monte Carlo	07/10/1931	Kingsway Hall, London	Zonophone 5996
JHO	You've Got That Thing	07/10/1931	Kingsway Hall, London	HMV Rejected
JHO	Song Of Happiness	07/10/1931	Kingsway Hall, London	HMV B-6076
JHO	Guilty	09/10/1931	Kingsway Hall, London	Zonophone 5992
JHO	The Birthday Of A Kiss	09/10/1931	Kingsway Hall, London	Zonophone 5998
JHO	This Is The Missus	09/10/1931	Kingsway Hall, London	Zonophone 5995
JHO	Dreaming Of You	09/10/1931	Kingsway Hall, London	Zonophone 5998
JHO	Life Is Just A Bowl Of Cherries	14/10/1931	Kingsway Hall, London	Zonophone 5995
JHO	Got A Date With An Angel	14/10/1931	Kingsway Hall, London	Zonophone 5993
JHO	On A Cold And Frosty Morning	14/10/1931	Kingsway Hall, London	Zonophone 5994
JHO	Life's Desire	14/10/1931	Kingsway Hall, London	Zonophone 5994
JHO	For The Love Of Mike	15/10/1931	Kingsway Hall, London	Zonophone 5993
JHO	The Smoking Concert, No. 2 - Part 2	15/10/1931	Kingsway Hall, London	HMV C-2306
JHO	The Smoking Concert, No. 2 - Part 1	16/10/1931	Kingsway Hall, London	HMV C-2306
JHO	Further Old Songs - Part 1	16/10/1931	Kingsway Hall, London	HMV C-2307
JHO	Further Old Songs - Part 2	16/10/1931	Kingsway Hall, London	HMV C-2303
JHO	Old-Time Sea Songs - Part 1	16/10/1931	Kingsway Hall, London	HMV C-2303
JHO	Old-Time Sea Songs - Part 2	16/10/1931	Kingsway Hall, London	HMV C-2307
JHO	Rhymes - Part 1	16/10/1931	Kingsway Hall, London	Zonophone 5997

327

Jack Hylton

JHO	The Wooden Rocking Horse	16/10/1931	Kingsway Hall, London	Zonophone 5992
JHO	Rhymes - Part 2	27/10/1931	Kingsway Hall, London	Zonophone 5997
JHO	Nevertheless	02/11/1931	London	Decca F-2664
JHO	You're My Decline And Fall	02/11/1931	London	Decca F-2664
JHO	Tom Thumb's Drum	02/11/1931	London	Decca F-2672
JHO	Just One More Chance	02/11/1931	London	Decca Rejected
JHO	My Sunshine Is You	02/11/1931	London	Decca Rejected
JHO	For The Sake Of Days Gone By (waltz)	02/11/1931	London	Decca F-2666
JHO	Heartaches	02/11/1931	London	Decca F-2665
JHO	El Relicario (3/4 One-Step)	03/11/1931	London	Decca F-2678
JHO	Me!	03/11/1931	London	Decca F-2684
JHO	Oh, What A Night	03/11/1931	London	Decca F-2672
JHO	For You (waltz)	03/11/1931	London	Decca F-2685
JHO	Close Your Eyes	03/11/1931	London	Decca F-2665
JHO	Cavalcade - Selection, Part 1	04/11/1931	London	Decca K-619
JHO	The Chocolate Soldier - Selection	04/11/1931	London	Decca K-620
JHO	Carry On (6/8 One-Step)	04/11/1931	London	Decca F-2666
JHO	The Merry Widow - Selection	05/11/1931	London	Decca K-620
JHO	Time Alone Will Tell	05/11/1931	London	Decca K-618
JHO	Cavalcade - Selection, Part 2	05/11/1931	London	Decca K-619
JHO	Rhymes - Part 1	05/11/1931	London	Decca F-2679
JHO	Rhymes - Part 2	05/11/1931	London	Decca F-2679
JHO	Ça c'est Paris (6/8 One-Step)	06/11/1931	London	Decca F-2678
JHO	When It's Sleepy-Time Down South	06/11/1931	London	Decca F-2681
JHO	Just One More Chance	10/11/1931	London	Decca K-618
JHO	I Don't Know Why	10/11/1931	London	Decca F-2684
JHO	Rio de Janeiro (3/4 One-Step)	10/11/1931	London	Decca F-2685
JHO	Old-Time Favourites - Part 1 (take 2)	10/11/1931	London	Decca K-624
JHO	Old-Time Favourites - Part 1 (take 3)	11/11/1931	London	Decca Rejected
JHO	My Sunshine Is You	11/11/1931	London	Decca K-622

Complete UK Discography

JHO	Goodnight, Sweetheart	11/11/1931	London	Decca K-622
JHO	Running Round The Trees	11/11/1931	London	Decca F-2700
JHO	Sea Songs - Part 1	11/11/1931	London	Decca K-625
JHO	Sea Songs - Part 2	11/11/1931	London	Decca K-625
JHO	Three Little Times	12/11/1931	London	Decca F-2681
JHO	I'll Always Be Dreaming Of You	12/11/1931	London	Decca F-2699
JHO	When The Music Is Playing	12/11/1931	London	Decca F-2698
JHO	Old-Time Favourites - Part 2	13/11/1931	London	Decca K-624
JHO	A Smoking Concert - Part 1	13/11/1931	London	Decca K-623
JHO	Under The Spell Of The Waltz (waltz)	13/11/1931	London	Decca F-2699
JHO	A Smoking Concert - Part 2	13/11/1931	London	Decca K-623
JHO	Just Once For All Time	13/11/1931	London	Decca F-2698
JHO	Joey The Clown	13/11/1931	London	Decca F-2700
JHO	Pantomime Hits - Part 1 (labelled as Peter Yorke and His Band)	20/11/1931	London	Decca F-2702
JHO	Pantomime Hits - Part 2 (labelled as Peter Yorke and His Band)	20/11/1931	London	Decca F-2702
JHO	More Pantomime Hits - Part 1 (labelled as Peter Yorke and His Band)	20/11/1931	London	Decca F-2703
JHO	More Pantomime Hits - Part 2 (labelled as Peter Yorke and His Band)	20/11/1931	London	Decca F-2703
JHO	Life Is Just A Bowl Of Cherries	01/12/1931	London	Decca F-2701
JHO	Song Of Happiness	01/12/1931	London	Decca F-2701
JHO	Cavalcade - Selection, Part 1	14/12/1931	London	Decca F-2729
JHO	Cavalcade - Selection, Part 2	14/12/1931	London	Decca F-2729
JHO	Resolutions for 1932	16/12/1931	London	Decca F-2753
JHO	Live, Laugh and Love (waltz)	16/12/1931	London	Decca F-2751
JHO	I Wanna Be Loved By You	16/12/1931	London	Decca F-2758
JHO	Today I Feel So Happy	17/12/1931	London	Decca F-2751
JHO	I Apologise	17/12/1931	London	Decca F-2756
JHO	Meet Me Tonight In The Cowshed	17/12/1931	London	Decca F-2754
JHO	Eleven More Months And Ten More Days - Part 1	17/12/1931	London	Decca F-2752
JHO	Eleven More Months And Ten More Days - Part 2	17/12/1931	London	Decca F-2752
JHO	Put Your Little Arms Around Me	17/12/1931	London	Decca F-2769

Jack Hylton

JHO	Consolation	17/12/1931	London	Decca F-2756
JHO	Yodle-Odle	17/12/1931	London	Decca F-2754
JHO	The Cough-Drop Shop	18/12/1931	London	Decca F-2753
JHO	Love Came Into My Heart	18/12/1931	London	Decca F-2784
JHO	Tonight Or Never	18/12/1931	London	Decca F-2784
JHO	Cuban Love Song	18/12/1931	London	Decca F-2769
JHO	It's Great To Be In Love	21/12/1931	London	Decca F-2758
JHO	Lies	21/12/1931	London	Decca F-2771
JHO	Sweet And Lovely	21/12/1931	London	Decca K-633
JHO	Sentenced For Life	21/12/1931	London	Decca F-2767
JHO	Sunshine And Roses	21/12/1931	London	Decca F-2768
JHO	I Found You	21/12/1931	London	Decca K-633
JHO	Flame Of Desire	21/12/1931	London	Decca Rejected
JHO	More Rhymes - Part 1	21/12/1931	London	Decca F-2750
JHO	More Rhymes - Part 2	21/12/1931	London	Decca F-2750
JHO	You're Blasé	22/12/1999	London	Decca F-2757
JHO	A Faded Summer Love	22/12/1999	London	Decca F-2767
JHO	Starlight Serenade	22/12/1999	London	Decca F-2771
JHO	Mona Lisa	22/12/1999	London	Decca F-2757
JHO	Flame Of Desire	13/01/1932	London	Decca F-2768
JHO	My Mystery Girl	13/01/1932	London	Decca F-2788
JHO	Colonel Bogey	13/01/1932	London	Decca F-2785
JHO	The Changing Of The Guard (6/8 One-Step)	13/01/1932	London	Decca F-2785
JHO	That's My Desire	13/01/1932	London	Decca F-2788
JHO	Dancing In The Dark	15/01/1932	London	Decca F-2786
JHO	Helen - Selection	15/01/1932	London	Decca F-2786
JHO	By The Fireside	15/01/1932	London	Decca F-2802
JHO	One Of Us Was Wrong	15/01/1932	London	Decca F-2802
JHO	Let's All Sing Like One O' Clock (6/8 One-Step)	15/01/1932	London	Decca F-2795
JHO	Home	26/01/1932	London	Decca F-2796

Complete UK Discography

JHO	All Of Me	26/01/1932	London	Decca F-2814
JHO	One More Kiss, Then Goodnight	26/01/1932	London	Decca F-2797
JHO	Once Aboard The Lugger	26/01/1932	London	Decca F-2795
JHO	My Heart Is Bluer Than Your Eyes (waltz)	30/01/1932	London	Decca F-2796
JHO	Just Friends	30/01/1932	London	Decca F-2797
JHO	He Played His Ukulele As The Ship Went Down - Part 1	30/01/1932	London	Decca F-2798
JHO	He Played His Ukulele As The Ship Went Down - Part 2	30/01/1932	London	Decca F-2798
JHO	Open Up Dem Pearly Gates	08/02/1932	London	Decca F-2824
JHO	By The Sycamore Tree	08/02/1932	London	Decca F-2845
JHO	Now's The Time To Fall In Love	08/02/1932	London	Decca F-2823
JHO	In The Bushes At The Bottom Of The Garden	08/02/1932	London	Decca F-2896
JHO	You Try Somebody Else	08/02/1932	London	Decca F-2823
JHO	In The Jailhouse Now	08/02/1932	London	Decca F-2824
JHO	The Whistling Waltz	08/02/1932	London	Decca F-2847
JHO	Save The Last Dance For Me (waltz)	08/02/1932	London	Decca F-2814
JHO	Sweetheart In My Dreams Tonight	09/02/1932	London	Decca F-2847
JHO	When The Rest Of The Crowd Goes Home (waltz)	09/02/1932	London	Decca F-2845
JHO	Goopy Geer	09/02/1932	London	Decca F-2876
JHO	Ever Since I Kissed Her On The Volga	09/02/1932	London	Decca F-2876
JHO	Hello, Twins!	09/02/1932	London	Decca F-2846
JHO	The King Was In The Counting-House	09/02/1932	London	Decca F-2846
JHO	Too Late	03/03/1932	London	Decca F-2883
JHO	Now That You're Gone	03/03/1932	London	Decca F-2883
JHO	Who's Your Little Who-Zis?	03/03/1932	London	Decca F-2904
JHO	Perry Werry Winkle	03/03/1932	London	Decca F-2896
JHO	With Love In My Heart	03/03/1932	London	Decca F-2904
JHO	Dick Turpin's Ride To York - Part 1	29/03/1932	London	Decca F-2894
JHO	Dick Turpin's Ride To York - Part 2	29/03/1932	London	Decca F-2894
JHO	Back Again To Happy-Go-Lucky Days (6/8 One-Step)	29/03/1932	London	Decca F-2917
JHO	Old Man Bluebeard	01/04/1932	London	Decca F-2917

Jack Hylton

JHO	Auf Wiedersehen, My Dear	20/04/1932	London	Decca F-2983
JHO	Rain On The Roof	20/04/1932	London	Decca F-2939
JHO	With All My Love And Kisses	20/04/1932	London	Decca F-2938
JHO	Where The Blue Of The Night (Meets The Gold Of The Day) (waltz)	20/04/1932	London	Decca F-2939
JHO	Rhythm Like This	20/04/1932	London	Decca F-2958
JHO	Snuggled On Your Shoulder	28/04/1932	London	Decca F-2959
JHO	Five Minutes To Twelve (waltz)	28/04/1932	London	Decca F-2959
JHO	How Long Will It Last?	28/04/1932	London	Decca F-2984
JHO	Just Humming Along	28/04/1932	London	Decca F-2949
JHO	Lonely Little Silhouette	28/04/1932	London	Decca F-2949
JHO	One Hour With You	28/04/1932	London	Decca F-2960
JHO	You	30/04/1932	London	Decca K-664
JHO	I Give My Heart	30/04/1932	London	Decca F-2958
JHO	By The Fireside	30/04/1932	London	Decca K-660
JHO	Goodnight, Vienna - Selection, Part 1	30/04/1932	London	Decca K-666
JHO	Goodnight, Vienna - Selection, Part 2	30/04/1932	London	Decca K-666
JHO	You Said It	30/04/1932	London	Decca F-3039
JHO	Paradise	02/05/1932	London	Decca K-660
JHO	Lawd, You Made The Night Too Long	02/05/1932	London	Decca K-664
JHO	What Would You Do?	02/05/1932	London	Decca F-2960
JHO	Lawd, You Made The Night Too Long	02/05/1932	London	Decca F-2984
JHO	Nursery Masquerade	31/05/1932	London	Decca F-3000
JHO	I Love A Parade (6/8 One-Step)	31/05/1932	London	Decca F-3000
JHO	Paradise (waltz)	31/05/1932	London	Decca F-3030
JHO	Dream Sweetheart	31/05/1932	London	Decca Rejected
JHO	The Derby Of 1932 - Part 1	03/06/1932	London	Decca F-3027
JHO	The Derby Of 1932 - Part 2	03/06/1932	London	Decca F-3027
JHO	Dream Sweetheart	17/06/1932	London	Decca F-3030
JHO	Sing, Brothers	17/06/1932	London	Decca Rejected
JHO	Hoch, Caroline	17/06/1932	London	Decca Rejected

Complete UK Discography

JHO	When Work Is Through	17/06/1932	London	Decca F-3039
JHO	Sing, Brothers	23/06/1932	London	Decca F-3033
JHO	Hoch, Caroline	23/06/1932	London	Decca F-3033
JHO	Little Anna Gramm	23/06/1932	London	Decca F-3040
JHO	You're Taking A Chance With Me	23/06/1932	London	Decca F-3040
JHO	I Want To Cling To Ivy	01/07/1932	London	Decca F-3050
JHO	The Flies Crawled Up The window	01/07/1932	London	Decca F-3050
JHO	Do-De-O-Do	01/07/1932	London	Decca F-3079
JHO	Chinese Blues	01/07/1932	London	Decca F-3079
JHO	A Bungalow, A Piccolo And You	29/07/1932	London	Decca F-3070
JHO	Underneath The Arches	29/07/1932	London	Decca F-3070
JHO	Pagan Moon (waltz)	29/07/1932	London	Decca F-3092
JHO	Little Spanish Villa By The Sea	29/07/1932	London	Decca F-3092
JHO	The Daily Herald Switch Medley - Part 1	29/07/1932	London	Decca F-3075
JHO	The Daily Herald Switch Medley - Part 2	29/07/1932	London	Decca F-3075
JHO	Brave Jim	24/08/1932	London	Decca F-3108
JHO	When The Band Goes Marching By (6/8 One-Step)	24/08/1932	London	Decca F-3108
JHO	A Great Big Bunch Of You	24/08/1932	London	Decca F-3109
JHO	The Clouds Will Soon Roll By	24/08/1932	London	Decca F-3109
JHO	Happy-Go-Lucky You (And Broken-Hearted Me)	24/08/1932	London	Decca F-3111
JHO	They All Start Whistling Mary	24/08/1932	London	Decca F-3111
JHO	Wrap Your Arms Around Me	07/09/1932	London	Decca F-3161
JHO	There's Another Trumpet Playing In The Sky	07/09/1932	London	Decca F-3147
JHO	Marching Along Together (6/8 One-Step)	07/09/1932	London	Decca F-3148
JHO	She Was Only Somebody's Daughter	07/09/1932	London	Decca F-3148
JHO	Then We'll Have Some More	07/09/1932	London	Decca F-3147
JHO	Masquerade (waltz)	23/09/1932	London	Decca F-3161
JHO	We Just Couldn't Say Goodbye	23/09/1932	London	Decca F-3183
JHO	In A Shanty In Old Shanty Town	23/09/1932	London	Decca F-3183
JHO	Sweet Sixteen And Never Been Kissed	23/09/1932	London	Decca F-3227

Jack Hylton

JHO	Song Of The Bells (waltz)	28/09/1932	London	Decca Rejected
JHO	Listen To The German Band	28/09/1932	London	Decca Rejected
JHO	Mad About The Boy	28/09/1932	London	Decca Rejected
JHO	The Younger Generation	28/09/1932	London	Decca Rejected
JHO	Silver Hair And Heart Of Gold (waltz)	28/09/1932	London	Decca Rejected
JHO	Special record of a Strauss waltz for Sonia Henie	28/09/1932	London	Decca Special
JHO	Special record for Sonia Henie (details unknown)	28/09/1932	London	Decca Special
JHO	Listen To The German Band	03/10/1932	London	Decca F-3204
JHO	Mad About The Boy	03/10/1932	London	Decca F-3185
JHO	The Younger Generation	03/10/1932	London	Decca F-3185
JHO	Silver Hair And Heart Of Gold (waltz)	03/10/1932	London	Decca F-3221
JHO	Song Of The Bells (waltz)	04/10/1932	London	Decca F-3221
JHO	Love Is The Sweetest Thing	04/10/1932	London	Decca F-3253
JHO	After Tonight We Say Goodbye	04/10/1932	London	Decca F-3215
JHO	How Are You?	04/10/1932	London	Decca F-3204
JHO	Someday We'll Meet Again	04/10/1932	London	Decca F-3238
JHO	A Bed-Time Story	05/10/1932	London	Decca F-3223
JHO	St. Louis Blues	05/10/1932	London	Decca F-3239
JHO	Same Old Moon (waltz)	05/10/1932	London	Decca F-3216
JHO	Goodbye Blues	05/10/1932	London	Decca F-3216
JHO	Mad About The Boy	12/10/1932	London	Decca Rejected
JHO	Goodbye Blues	12/10/1932	London	Decca Rejected
JHO	The Baked Potato Man	12/10/1932	London	Decca F-3222
JHO	Bird Of Love Divine	12/10/1932	London	Decca Rejected
JHO	I Hear You Calling Me	12/10/1932	London	Decca Rejected
JHO	Hylton Stomp	12/10/1932	London	Decca F-3239
JHO	I'm Bloomin' Well Glad To Be Alive	12/10/1932	London	Decca Rejected
JHO	Pal Of My Dreams	12/10/1932	London	Decca F-3227
JHO	Marry Me	12/10/1932	London	Decca F-3215
JHO	Yes, Mr. Brown	12/10/1932	London	Decca F-3285

Complete UK Discography

JHO	Round The Bend Of The Road	12/10/1932	London	Decca F-3253
JHO	Where Is This Lady?	12/10/1932	London	Decca F-3224
JHO	Say It Isn't So	12/10/1932	London	Decca F-3240
JHO	You, Just You	13/10/1932	London	Decca F-3213
JHO	Rock Your Cares Away	13/10/1932	London	Decca F-3223
JHO	On A Dreamy Afternoon	13/10/1932	London	Decca F-3240
JHO	Don't Say Goodbye	13/10/1932	London	Decca F-3213
JHO	The Old Kitchen Kettle	13/10/1932	London	Decca F-3222
JHO	Tell Me Tonight	13/10/1932	London	Decca F-3224
JHO	I Told My Baby With The Ukulele (issued as George Formby)	13/10/1932	London	Decca F-3219
JHO	Sweet Muchacha (rumba)	13/10/1932	London	Decca F-3238
JHO	If You Don't Want The Goods (issued as George Formby)	13/10/1932	London	Decca F-3219
JHO	The Yo Yo Men Of England - Part 1	13/10/1932	London	Decca Rejected
JHO	The Yo Yo Men Of England - Part 2	13/10/1932	London	Decca Rejected
JHO	Underneath The Arches (issued as Master David Kidd)	13/10/1932	London	Decca F-3217
JHO	Song Of The Bells (waltz)(issued as Master David Kidd)	13/10/1932	London	Decca F-3217
JHO	Der alte Schwede	Nov-32	Berlin, Germany	Decca F-40303
JHO	O wie schöne ist ein Feiertag	Nov-32	Berlin, Germany	Decca F-40304
JHO	Sag mit mir wenn du ausgehst	Nov-32	Berlin, Germany	Decca F-40303
JHO	Sag mit mir wenn du ausgehst	Nov-32	Berlin, Germany	Decca F-40312
JHO	Wenn ich einmal traurig bin	Nov-32	Berlin, Germany	Decca F-40304
JHO	Wenn ich einmal traurig bin	Nov-32	Berlin, Germany	Decca F-40312
JHO	Wenn ich einmal traurig bin	Nov-32	Berlin, Germany	Decca F-3285
JHO	Frau Wirtin empfangt Jack Hylton and His Boys - Part 1	Nov-32	Berlin, Germany	Decca F-40305
JHO	Frau Wirtin empfangt Jack Hylton and His Boys - Part 2	Nov-32	Berlin, Germany	Decca F-40305
JHO	Just A Little Home For The Old Folks	05/01/1933	Chelsea Town Hall, London	Decca F-3395
JHO	Standing On The Corner	05/01/1933	Chelsea Town Hall, London	Decca F-3409
JHO	Old Father Thames	05/01/1933	Chelsea Town Hall, London	Decca F-3425
JHO	I'll Never Have To Dream Again	05/01/1933	Chelsea Town Hall, London	Decca F-3395
JHO	Pu-leeze! Mr. Hemingway	05/01/1933	Chelsea Town Hall, London	Decca F-3409

335

Jack Hylton

	Title	Date		Label
JHO	Try A Little Tenderness	18/01/1933	London	Decca F-3440
JHO	Take Me Away From The River	18/01/1933	London	Decca F-3425
JHO	Sweethearts Of Yesterday - Part 1	18/01/1933	London	Decca F-3426
JHO	Sweethearts Of Yesterday - Part 2	18/01/1933	London	Decca F-3426
JHO	Play, Fiddle, Play	19/01/1933	London	Decca F-3440
JHO	Fit As A Fiddle	19/01/1933	London	Decca F-3424
JHO	Fit As A Fiddle	19/01/1933	London	Mayfair G-329
JHO	I'm Sure Of Everything But You	19/01/1933	London	Decca F-3424
JHO	A Boy And Girl Were Dancing (waltz)	19/01/1933	London	Decca F-3427
JHO	Puss! Puss! Puss!	19/01/1933	London	Decca F-3427
JHO	Why Don't Women Like Me? (issued as George Formby)	29/01/1933	London	Decca F-3524
JHO	Running Round The Fountains In Trafalgar Square (George Formby)	29/01/1933	London	Decca F-3524
JHO	Sitting On The Ice At The Ice-Rink (issued as George Formby)	29/01/1933	London	Decca F-3458
JHO	Levi's Monkey Mike (issued as George Formby)	29/01/1933	London	Decca F-3458
JHO	Can't We Meet Again	06/02/1933	London	Decca F-3459
JHO	I'm Playing With Fire	06/02/1933	London	Decca F-3475
JHO	Do You Know?	06/02/1933	London	Decca F-3445
JHO	Sunny Madeira	06/02/1933	London	Decca F-3489
JHO	Sunny Madeira	06/02/1933	London	Mayfair G-321
TR	Sunny Madeira	06/02/1933	London	Panachord 25519
JHO	I Wish I Knew A Bigger Word Than Love	09/02/1933	London	Decca F-3475
JHO	Pickaninnies' Heaven	09/02/1933	London	Decca F-3516
JHO	There's Something About A Soldier (take 2)	09/02/1933	London	Decca F-3476
JHO	Have You Ever Been Lonely?	09/02/1933	London	Decca F-3476
JHO	There's Something About A Soldier (take 4)	17/02/1933	London	Decca F-3476
JHO	Jolly Old Ma, Jolly Old Pa	17/02/1933	London	Decca F-3490
JHO	I Want To Go Home	17/02/1933	London	Decca F-3484
JHO	I May Never Pass Your Way Again	17/02/1933	London	Decca F-3484
JHO	I Love To Yodel	17/02/1933	London	Decca F-3445
JHO	Let Bygones Be Bygones	17/02/1933	London	Decca F-3489

Complete UK Discography

JHO	Let Bygones Be Bygones	17/02/1933	London	Mayfair G-321
TR	Let Bygones Be Bygones	17/02/1933	London	Panachord 25519
JHO	My Darling	17/02/1933	London	Decca F-3490
JHO	Farewell To Arms	14/03/1933	London	Decca F-3515
JHO	Moon Song (That Wasn't Meant For Me)	14/03/1933	London	Decca F-3516
JHO	Hallelujah! I'm A Tramp	14/03/1933	London	Decca F-3573
JHO	The Lord Mayor's Show	14/03/1933	London	Decca F-3519
JHO	Her Name Is Mary	14/03/1933	London	Decca F-3515
JHO	If You Believe	22/03/1933	London	Decca Rejected
JHO	Put A Little Springtime In The Winter Of Their Lives	22/03/1933	London	Decca F-3519
JHO	That's My Home	22/03/1933	London	Decca F-3520
JHO	That's My Home	22/03/1933	London	Mayfair G-332
TR	That's My Home	22/03/1933	London	Panachord 25521
JHO	Sitting In The Dark	22/03/1933	London	Decca F-3520
JHO	What A Lady Josephine Must Have Been	23/03/1933	London	Decca F-3548
JHO	Stay On The Right Side Of The Road	23/03/1933	London	Decca F-3528
JHO	Pop Gun	23/03/1933	London	Decca F-3526
JHO	They All Do The Rumba (rumba)	23/03/1933	London	Decca Rejected
JHO	Waltzing In A Dream (waltz)	23/03/1933	London	Decca Rejected
JHO	I Sigh For You, Rio Rita	23/03/1933	London	Decca F-3527
JHO	I Sigh For You, Rio Rita	23/03/1933	London	Panachord 25525
JHO	My Wishing Song	23/03/1933	London	Decca Rejected
JHO	They All Do The Rumba (rumba)	06/04/1933	London	Decca F-3527
JHO	Waltzing In A Dream (waltz)	06/04/1933	London	Decca F-3526
JHO	My Wishing Song	06/04/1933	London	Decca F-3528
JHO	Hyde Park Corner (6/8 One-Step)	06/04/1933	London	Decca F-3548
JHO	Hyde Park Corner (6/8 One-Step)	06/04/1933	London	Mayfair G-332
JHO	Hyde Park Corner (6/8 One-Step)	06/04/1933	London	Panachord 25521
JHO	It's The Band (6/8 One-Step)	06/04/1933	London	Decca F-3549
JHO	It's The Band (6/8 One-Step)	06/04/1933	London	Panachord 25525

Jack Hylton

	Title	Date	Location	Catalogue
JHO	If You Believe	12/04/1933	London	Decca Rejected
JHO	Rock-a-Bye Moon (waltz)	12/04/1933	London	Decca Rejected
JHO	Little Miss Muffet	12/04/1933	London	Decca Rejected
JHO	We'll Always Be Friends	12/04/1933	London	Decca Rejected
JHO	The Jubilee Song	12/04/1933	London	Decca F-3540
JHO	Sure And Steadfast	12/04/1933	London	Decca Rejected
JHO	This Is The Rhythm For Me	12/04/1933	London	Decca F-3549
JHO	Rock-a-Bye Moon (waltz)	21/04/1933	London	Decca F-3569
JHO	We'll Always Be Friends	21/04/1933	London	Decca F-3568
JHO	The Song Is You	21/04/1933	London	Decca F-3545
JHO	And Love Was Born	21/04/1933	London	Decca F-3545
JHO	I've Told Every Little Star	21/04/1933	London	Decca F-3544
JHO	We Belong Together	21/04/1933	London	Decca F-3544
JHO	If You Believe	25/04/1933	London	Decca F-3568
JHO	Little Miss Muffet	25/04/1933	London	Decca F-3567
JHO	I'm One Of The Lads Of Valencia (waltz)	25/04/1933	London	Decca Rejected
JHO	Wear A Great Big Smile	25/04/1933	London	Decca F-3569
JHO	Out In The Open	25/04/1933	London	Decca F-3567
JHO	In Every Nook And Corner You Are Missing	25/04/1933	London	Decca Rejected
JHO	You've Got Me Crying Again	11/05/1933	London	Decca F-3572
JHO	Stormy Weather	11/05/1933	London	Decca F-3572
JHO	You Are Too Beautiful	11/05/1933	London	Decca F-3573
JHO	How Do You Do, Honolulu	11/05/1933	London	Decca F-3614
JHO	You're Mine, You	30/06/1933	London	Decca F-3600
JHO	You're Mine, You	30/06/1933	London	Mayfair G-355
JHO	Dancing Butterfly	30/06/1933	London	Decca F-3613
JHO	Dancing Butterfly	30/06/1933	London	Mayfair G-358
JHO	Hold Me	30/06/1933	London	Decca F-3600
JHO	Hold Me	30/06/1933	London	Mayfair G-355
JHO	Having A Good Time, Wish You Were Here	30/06/1933	London	Decca F-3613

Complete UK Discography

JHO	I Can't Remember (waltz)	30/06/1933	London	Decca F-3614
JHO	I Can't Remember (waltz)	30/06/1933	London	Mayfair G-358
JHO	Daily Herald Competition Record - Part 1	05/07/1933	London	Decca F-3616
JHO	Daily Herald Competition Record - Part 2	05/07/1933	London	Decca F-3616
JHO	42nd Street - Selection, Part 1	05/07/1933	London	Decca F-3619
JHO	42nd Street - Selection, Part 2	05/07/1933	London	Decca F-3619
JHO	The Gold-Diggers' Song (We're In The Money)	28/07/1933	London	Decca F-3672
JHO	Learn To Croon	28/07/1933	London	Decca F-3633
JHO	Learn To Croon	28/07/1933	London	Mayfair G-359
JHO	Moonstruck	28/07/1933	London	Decca F-3633
JHO	Moonstruck	28/07/1933	London	Mayfair G-359
JHO	Si Petite (waltz)	28/07/1933	London	Decca Rejected
JHO	Pettin' In The Park	28/07/1933	London	Decca F-3673
JHO	Shadow Waltz (waltz)	28/07/1933	London	Decca F-3672
JHO	I've Got To Sing A Torch Song	28/07/1933	London	Decca F-3673
JHO	Black And Blue Rhythm	28/07/1933	London	Decca Rejected
JHO	Some Of These Days	28/07/1933	London	Decca Rejected
JHO	Don't Blame Me	13/09/1933	London	Decca F-3659
JHO	Lazybones	13/09/1933	London	Decca F-3659
JHO	In The Valley Of The Moon (waltz)	13/09/1933	London	Decca F-3658
JHO	Sweetheart Darlin'	13/09/1933	London	Decca F-3658
JHO	With You And Me Here	13/09/1933	London	Decca F-3670
JHO	You're An Old Smoothie	13/09/1933	London	Decca Rejected
JHO	Tick Tock	13/09/1933	London	Decca Rejected
JHO	The Wedding Of Mr. Mickey Mouse	14/09/1933	London	Decca Rejected
JHO	The Grasshopper's Dance	14/09/1933	London	Decca F-3662
JHO	The Wedding Of The Rose	14/09/1933	London	Decca F-3662
JHO	Poème (Fibich)(take 1)	14/09/1933	London	Decca K-708
JHO	Praeludium (Järnefelt)(take 2)	14/09/1933	London	Decca K-708
JHO	Negro Spiritual Medley - Part 1	14/09/1933	London	Decca Rejected

Jack Hylton

JHO	Negro Spiritual Medley - Part 2	14/09/1933	London	Decca Rejected
JHO	Drinking Songs - Part 1	14/09/1933	London	Decca K-709
JHO	Drinking Songs - Part 2	14/09/1933	London	Decca K-709
JHO	Trouble In Paradise	16/09/1933	London	Decca F-3663
JHO	Happy As The Day Is Long	16/09/1933	London	Decca Rejected
JHO	I Like To Go Back In The Evening	16/09/1933	London	Decca Rejected
JHO	Reflections In The Water (waltz)	16/09/1933	London	Decca Rejected
JHO	Black And Blue Rhythm	16/09/1933	London	Decca Rejected
JHO	Some Of These Days	16/09/1933	London	Decca F-3767
JHO	Poème (Fibich)(take 4)	26/09/1933	London	Decca K-708?
JHO	Praeludium (Järnefelt)(take 3 or 4)	26/09/1933	London	Decca Rejected
JHO	Trouble In Paradise	26/09/1933	London	Decca Rejected
JHO	I Like To Go Back In The Evening	26/09/1933	London	Decca Rejected
JHO	Reflections In The Water (waltz)	26/09/1933	London	Decca F-3671
JHO	Black And Blue Rhythm	26/09/1933	London	Decca F-3767
JHO	You're An Old Smoothie	27/09/1933	London	Decca Rejected
JHO	Tick Tock	27/09/1933	London	Decca F-3669
JHO	Some Of These Days	27/09/1933	London	Decca Rejected
JHO	The Merry Widow (waltz)	27/09/1933	London	Decca Rejected
JHO	Night And Day	27/09/1933	London	Decca F-3698
JHO	You're An Old Smoothie	06/10/1933	London	Decca F-3670
JHO	The Wedding Of Mr. Mickey Mouse	06/10/1933	London	Decca F-3669
JHO	Happy As The Day Is Long	06/10/1933	London	Decca F-3671
JHO	I Like To Go Back In The Evening	06/10/1933	London	Decca F-3663
JHO	It's The Talk Of The Town	06/10/1933	London	Decca F-3687
JHO	The Last Round-Up	06/10/1933	London	Decca F-3687
JHO	After You	20/10/1933	London	Decca F-3698
JHO	Old-Fashioned Sweetheart	20/10/1933	London	Decca F-3713
JHO	Aunt Sally - Selection, Part 1	20/10/1933	London	Decca F-3718
JHO	Aunt Sally - Selection, Part 2	20/10/1933	London	Decca F-3718

Complete UK Discography

JHO	Yvonne (waltz)	20/10/1933	London	Decca F-3714
JHO	A Couple Of Pals (6/8 One-Step)	20/10/1933	London	Decca F-3713
JHO	He Was A Handsome Young Soldier (6/8 One-Step)	20/10/1933	London	Decca F-3715
JHO	Hand In Hand	20/10/1933	London	Decca F-3714
JHO	One-Horse Town	20/10/1933	London	Decca F-3808
JHO	Did My Heart Beat, Did I Fall In Love?	20/10/1933	London	Decca F-3715
JHO	Sousa Marches - Medley, Part 1	24/10/1933	London	Decca F-5216
JHO	Sousa Marches - Medley, Part 2	24/10/1933	London	Decca F-5216
JHO	Swingy Little Thingy	24/10/1933	London	Decca F-3808
JHO	Too Much Harmony - Selection, Part 2	24/10/1933	London	Decca F-3774
JHO	There's A Home In Wyoming	24/10/1933	London	Decca F-3743
JHO	Too Much Harmony - Selection, Part 1	24/10/1933	London	Decca F-3774
JHO	Musical Comedies - Medley, Part 1	25/10/1933	London	Decca K-711
JHO	Musical Comedies - Medley, Part 2	25/10/1933	London	Decca K-711
JHO	Gilbert And Sullivan Medley - Part 1	25/10/1933	London	Decca K-712
JHO	Gilbert And Sullivan Medley - Part 2	25/10/1933	London	Decca K-712
JHO	Rhapsody In Blue - Part 1	18/11/1933	London	Decca F-3763
JHO	Ellingtonia	18/11/1933	London	Decca F-3764
JHO	Rhapsody In Blue - Part 2	18/11/1933	London	Decca F-3763
JHO	Dinah (A Band That Money Can't Buy)	18/11/1933	London	Decca F-3764
JHO	Tain't	18/11/1933	London	Decca F-3743
JHO	La-Di-Da-Di-Da	18/11/1933	London	Decca F-3780
JHO	Honeymoon Hotel	18/11/1933	London	Decca F-3806
JHO	By A Waterfall	18/11/1933	London	Decca F-3806
JHO	What Is The Use Of It Now?	18/11/1933	London	Decca F-3807
JHO	I'm Hitching My Wagon To You	18/11/1933	London	Decca F-3780
JHO	My Song Goes Round The World	18/11/1933	London	Decca F-3807
JHO	The Glow Worm Idyll	28/11/1933	London	Decca F-3857
JHO	Down South	28/11/1933	London	Decca F-3857
JHO	Kasmiri Song	28/11/1933	London	Decca F-3829

Jack Hylton

JHO	Temple Bells	28/11/1933	London	Decca F-3829
JHO	Life Begins At Oxford Circus	12/03/1935	London	HMV Rejected
JHO	Put On An Old Pair Of Shoes	12/03/1935	London	HMV Rejected
JHO	I Believe In Miracles	12/03/1935	London	HMV Rejected
JHO	She Wore A Little Jacket Of Blue	15/03/1935	London	HMV Rejected
JHO	Put On An Old Pair Of Shoes	15/03/1935	London	HMV Rejected
JHO	I Believe In Miracles	15/03/1935	London	HMV Rejected
JHO	Life Begins At Oxford Circus	20/03/1935	London	HMV BD-142
JHO	Put On An Old Pair Of Shoes	20/03/1935	London	HMV BD-142
JHO	I Believe In Miracles	20/03/1935	London	HMV BD-143
JHO	She Wore A Little Jacket Of Blue	20/03/1935	London	HMV BD-143
JHO	My Dance	13/04/1935	London	HMV BD-150
JHO	So Red The Rose	13/04/1935	London	HMV BD-149
JHO	Far Away In Shanty Town	13/04/1935	London	HMV BD-150
JHO	If The Moon Turns Green	13/04/1935	London	HMV BD-149
JHO	Life Begins Again	13/04/1935	London	HMV BD-157
JHO	Chinatown, My Chinatown	26/04/1935	London	HMV Unissued
JHO	Gentlemen! The King	26/04/1935	London	HMV BD-157
JHO	Jubilee Cavalcade - Part 1	26/04/1935	London	HMV C-2744
JHO	Jubilee Cavalcade - Part 2	26/04/1935	London	HMV C-2744
JHO	Solitude	26/04/1935	London	HMV BD-5035
JHO	The Girl With The Dreamy Eyes	11/05/1935	London	HMV BD-164
JHO	Orchids To My Lady	11/05/1935	London	HMV BD-164
JHO	Zing! Went The Strings Of My Heart	11/05/1935	London	HMV BD-163
JHO	Olga Pullofski; The Beautiful Spy (waltz)	11/05/1935	London	HMV BD-163
JHO	Anything Goes - Selection, Part 1	06/06/1935	London	HMV C-2757
JHO	Anything Goes - Selection, Part 2	06/06/1935	London	HMV C-2757
JHO	Anything Goes	06/06/1935	London	HMV BD-172
JHO	You're The Top	06/06/1935	London	HMV BD-172
JHO	Give A Broken Heart A Break	04/07/1935	London	HMV BD-198

Complete UK Discography

JHO	I Won't Dance	04/07/1935	London	HMV BD-200
JHO	Lovely To Look At	04/07/1935	London	HMV BD-200
JHO	Chasing Shadows	04/07/1935	London	HMV BD-197
JHO	Jump On The Wagon	04/07/1935	London	HMV BD-198
JHO	Kiss Me Goodnight	04/07/1935	London	HMV BD-197
JHO	Love Me Forever (waltz)	15/07/1935	London	HMV BD-203
JHO	Footloose And Fancy Free	15/07/1935	London	HMV BD-204
JHO	I'll Never Say "Never Again" Again	15/07/1935	London	HMV BD-204
JHO	South American Joe (rumba)	15/07/1935	London	HMV BD-203
JHO	She's A Latin From Manhattan	26/08/1935	London	HMV BD-212
JHO	About A Quarter To Nine	26/08/1935	London	HMV BD-212
JHO	Weather Man	26/08/1935	London	HMV BD-216
JHO	In The Middle Of A Kiss	26/08/1935	London	HMV BD-215
JHO	Every Single Little Tingle Of My Heart	28/08/1935	London	HMV BD-216
JHO	Lovely Liza Lee	28/08/1935	London	HMV BD-214
JHO	Nothing Lives Longer Than Love (waltz)	28/08/1935	London	HMV BD-215
JHO	Lonely Villa	28/08/1935	London	HMV BD-236
JHO	Where The Arches Used To Be	28/08/1935	London	HMV BD-214
JHO	Car Of Dreams	27/09/1935	London	HMV BD-296
JHO	You Give Me Ideas	27/09/1935	London	HMV BD-235
JHO	When The Rain Comes Rolling Down	27/09/1935	London	HMV BD-236
JHO	Song Of The 'Cello	27/09/1935	London	HMV BD-235
JHO	Schoolboy Howlers, Part 1	04/12/1935	London	HMV BD-5005
JHO	Schoolboy Howlers, Part 2	04/12/1935	London	HMV BD-5005
JHO	Everything Stops For Tea	04/12/1935	London	HMV BD-5006
JHO	When The Guardsman Started Crooning On Parade	04/12/1935	London	HMV BD-5006
JHO	Lights Out	02/01/1936	Chicago, IL. USA	HMV BD-5030
JHO	The Music Goes 'Round And Around	02/01/1936	Chicago, IL. USA	HMV BD-5030
JHO	Eeny Meeny Miney Mo	02/01/1936	Chicago, IL. USA	HMV BD-5035
JHO	A Little Bit Independent	02/01/1936	Chicago, IL. USA	HMV Rejected

Jack Hylton

JHO	She Shall Have Music	HMV BD-5017	03/01/1936	London
JHO	Doin' The Runaround	HMV BD-5017	03/01/1936	London
JHO	My First Thrill	HMV BD-5018	03/01/1936	London
JHO	May All Your Troubles Be Little Ones	HMV BD-5018	03/01/1936	London
JHO	Sailing Along On A Carpet Of Clouds	HMV BD-5024	19/01/1936	London
JHO	Moanin' Minnie	HMV BD-5024	19/01/1936	London
JHO	Why Did She Fall For The Leader Of The Band? (6/8 One-Step)	HMV BD-5023	19/01/1936	London
JHO	The Darling Of The Guards	HMV BD-5023	19/01/1936	London
JHO	Swing	HMV BD-5034	14/02/1936	London
JHO	Hypnotised	HMV BD-5034	14/02/1936	London
JHO	This'll Make You Whistle	HMV BD-5037	14/02/1936	London
JHO	There Isn't Any Limit To My Love	HMV BD-5037	14/02/1936	London
JHO	Fancy Meeting You	HMV BD-5054	28/03/1936	London
JHO	Yours Truly Is Truly Yours	HMV BD-5054	28/03/1936	London
JHO	He Went In Like A Lion	HMV BD-5055	28/03/1936	London
JHO	When H'I Was H'Out in H'India	HMV BD-5055	28/03/1936	London
JHO	Tiger Rag	HMV BD-5128	24/08/1936	London
JHO	Sweet Sue	HMV C-2856	24/08/1936	London
JHO	Grinzing	HMV C-2856	25/08/1936	London
JHO	Free (Isn't It The Way It Ought To Be?)	HMV BD-5102	25/08/1936	London
JHO	The Fleet's In Port Again	HMV BD-5102	25/08/1936	London
JHO	Knock, Knock, Who's There?	HMV BD-5103	25/08/1936	London
JHO	Did I Remember?	HMV BD-5103	25/08/1936	London
JHO	Rose Room	HMV BD-5128	25/08/1936	London
JHO	Does Your Heart Beat For Me?	HMV BD-5119	07/10/1936	London
JHO	You've Got The Wrong Rumba	HMV BD-5119	07/10/1936	London
JHO	Drop In Next Time You're Passing	HMV BD-5118	07/10/1936	London
JHO	Unbelievable	HMV BD-5118	07/10/1936	London
JHO	Sing, Baby, Sing	HMV BD-5127	17/10/1936	London
JHO	You Turned The Tables On Me	HMV BD-5127	17/10/1936	London

Complete UK Discography

JHO	Just Say Aloha	17/10/1936	London	HMV BD-5136
JHO	Little Audrey	17/10/1936	London	HMV Rejected
JHO	Organ Grinder's Swing	05/11/1936	London	HMV BD-5137
JHO	Midnight Blue	05/11/1936	London	HMV BD-5137
JHO	I'm In A Dancing Mood	05/11/1936	London	HMV BD-5136
JHO	Cabin On The Hilltop	05/11/1936	London	HMV BD-5144
JHO	Mendel's Son's Swing Song	05/11/1936	London	HMV BD-5144
JHO	Bolero (Ravel)	13/11/1936	London	HMV BD-393
JHO	Vienna, City Of My Dreams	13/11/1936	London	HMV BD-393
JHO	Goodbye	13/11/1936	London	HMV BD-394
JHO	Rockin' Chair	13/11/1936	London	HMV BD-394
JHO	Jack Hylton Throws A Party - Part 1	16/11/1936	London	HMV C-2883
JHO	Jack Hylton Throws A Party - Part 2	16/11/1936	London	HMV C-2883
JHO	Did You Mean It?	01/12/1936	London	HMV BD-5142
JHO	Have You Forgotten So Soon? (waltz)	01/12/1936	London	HMV BD-5142
JHO	Goodbye, Little Dream, Goodbye	01/12/1936	London	HMV BD-5143
JHO	When A Woman Smiles	01/12/1936	London	HMV BD-5143
JHO	At The Balalaika	10/01/1937	London	HMV BD-5165
JHO	Pennies From Heaven	10/01/1937	London	HMV BD-5166
JHO	On Your Toes	10/01/1937	London	HMV BD-5164
JHO	There's A Small Hotel	10/01/1937	London	HMV BD-5164
JHO	One, Two, Button Your Shoe	10/01/1937	London	HMV BD-5166
JHO	Delyse (waltz)	10/01/1937	London	HMV BD-5165
JHO	Timber	10/01/1937	London	HMV BD-5167
JHO	Goodnight, My Love	10/01/1937	London	HMV BD-5167
JHO	Making Up A Song	06/04/1937	London	HMV BD-5201
JHO	Swing Is In The Air	06/04/1937	London	HMV BD-5200
JHO	Red, White And Blue	06/04/1937	London	HMV BD-5200
JHO	Boo-Hoo	06/04/1937	London	HMV BD-5201
JHO	That Song In My Heart	23/04/1937	London	HMV BD-5208

Jack Hylton

JHO	The Dart Song	23/04/1937	London	HMV BD-5207
JHO	The Love Bug Will Bite You	23/04/1937	London	HMV BD-5207
JHO	With A Twinkle In Your Eye	23/04/1937	London	HMV BD-5208
JHO	September In The Rain	07/05/1937	London	HMV BD-5216
JHO	Gangway	07/05/1937	London	HMV BD-5255
JHO	Melody For Two	07/05/1937	London	HMV BD-5216
JHO	Moon Or No Moon	07/05/1937	London	HMV Rejected
JHO	When You Gotta Sing, You Gotta Sing	13/05/1937	London	HMV BD-5256
JHO	Lord And Lady Whoozis	13/05/1937	London	HMV BD-5256
JHO	Love Live Forever And Rule My Heart (waltz)	13/05/1937	London	HMV BD-5217
JHO	Girls Were Made To Love And Kiss (waltz)	13/05/1937	London	HMV Rejected
JHO	Moon Or No Moon	31/05/1937	London	HMV BD-5255
JHO	Girls Were Made To Love And Kiss (waltz)	31/05/1937	London	HMV BD-5217
JHO	Music, Maestro, Please	20/09/1938	London	HMV BD-5407
JHO	A-Tisket, A-Tasket	20/09/1938	London	HMV BD-5407
JHO	Ride, Tenderfoot, Ride	20/09/1938	London	HMV BD-5408
JHO	When You Dream About Hawaii	20/09/1938	London	HMV BD-5408
JHO	Watermelon Fete	27/09/1938	London	HMV BD-603
JHO	Down South	27/09/1938	London	HMV BD-603
JHO	The Whistler And His Dog	27/09/1938	London	HMV BD-620
JHO	Colonel Bogey	27/09/1938	London	HMV BD-620
JHO	Neil Gwynne Suite (German) No. 1 : Country Dance	03/10/1938	London	HMV BD-604
JHO	Neil Gwynne Suite (German) No. 2 : Pastoral Dance	03/10/1938	London	HMV BD-604
JHO	Neil Gwynne Suite (German) No. 3 : Merrymakers' Dance	03/10/1938	London	HMV BD-606
JHO	Neil Gwynne Suite (German) No. 4 : Morris Dance	03/10/1938	London	HMV BD-606
JHO	Alexander's Ragtime Band	10/10/1938	London	HMV BD-5413
JHO	Now It Can Be Told	10/10/1938	London	HMV BD-5413
JHO	When The Circus Comes To Town	10/10/1938	London	HMV BD-5417
JHO	What Goes On Here In My Heart?	10/10/1938	London	HMV BD-5417
JHO	Cinderella Sweetheart (waltz)	10/11/1938	London	HMV BD-5426

Complete UK Discography

JHO	Change Partners	10/11/1938	London	HMV BD-5425
JHO	Rhythm Is The Alphabet	10/11/1938	London	HMV BD-5426
JHO	I Used To Be Colour Blind	10/11/1938	London	HMV BD-5425
JHO	The Old Sow	10/11/1938	London	HMV Rejected
JHO	The Bassoon	10/11/1938	London	HMV BD-635
JHO	Stop Beatin' Round The Mulberry Bush	02/12/1938	London	HMV BD-5440
JHO	All Ashore	02/12/1938	London	HMV BD-5440
JHO	Love Makes The World Go Around	02/12/1938	London	HMV BD-5439
JHO	The Chestnut Tree	02/12/1938	London	HMV BD-5439
JHO	Ya Got Something There	02/12/1938	London	HMV BD-635
JHO	Blue Skies Are Round The Corner	13/12/1938	London	HMV BD-5446
JHO	I'm Singing A Song For The Old Folks	13/12/1938	London	HMV BD-5446
JHO	Don't Let That Moon Get Away	13/12/1938	London	HMV BD-5445
JHO	Why Doesn't Somebody Tell Me These Things?	13/12/1938	London	HMV BD-5445
JHO	There's A New Apple Tree	06/01/1939	London	HMV BD-5451
JHO	Day After Day	06/01/1939	London	HMV BD-5451
JHO	Ferdinand The Bull (waltz)	06/01/1939	London	HMV BD-5450
JHO	The Umbrella Man (waltz)	06/01/1939	London	HMV BD-5450
JHO	Nice People	31/01/1939	London	HMV BD-5455
JHO	I Shall Always Remember You Smiling (waltz)	31/01/1939	London	HMV BD-5456
JHO	Sha-Sha	31/01/1939	London	HMV BD-5456
JHO	You Must Have Been A Beautiful Baby	31/01/1939	London	HMV BD-5455
JHO	Gotta Get Some Shut-Eye	08/03/1939	London	HMV BD-5466
JHO	Say It With A Kiss	08/03/1939	London	HMV BD-5465
JHO	Jeepers Creepers	08/03/1939	London	HMV BD-5465
JHO	I Go For That	08/03/1939	London	HMV BD-5466
JHO	I Can't Get You Out Of My Mind	14/04/1939	London	HMV BD-5475
JHO	Hold Tight	14/04/1939	London	HMV BD-5475
JHO	The Masquerade Is Over	14/04/1939	London	HMV BD-5474
JHO	Hurry Home	14/04/1939	London	HMV BD-5474

Jack Hylton

JHO	Poor Contrary Mary	04/05/1939	London	HMV BD-5483
JHO	Gypsy Tears	04/05/1939	London	HMV BD-5484
JHO	Chopsticks	04/05/1939	London	HMV BD-5484
JHO	Apple Blossom Time	04/05/1939	London	HMV BD-5483
JHO	Youth Take A Bow - Part 1	04/05/1939	London	HMV C-3103
JHO	Youth Take A Bow - Part 2	04/05/1939	London	HMV C-3103
JHO	The Handsome Territorial	25/05/1939	London	HMV BD-5489
JHO	Wishing (Will Make It So)	25/05/1939	London	HMV BD-5492
JHO	Summer Sweetheart	25/05/1939	London	HMV BD-5499
JHO	Sing, My Heart	25/05/1939	London	HMV BD-5492
JHO	Beer Barrel Polka	25/05/1939	London	HMV BD-5490
JHO	The Birthday Of The Little Princess	26/05/1939	London	HMV BD-5491
JHO	Three Little Fishies	26/05/1939	London	HMV BD-5491
JHO	Deep Purple	26/05/1939	London	HMV BD-5489
JHO	Goosey Goosey	26/05/1939	London	HMV BD-5490
JHO	My Melancholy Baby	26/05/1939	London	HMV BD-5550
JHO	Darktown Strutter's Ball	26/05/1939	London	HMV BD-5550
JHO	You Grow Sweeter As The Years Go By	29/06/1939	London	HMV BD-5500
JHO	The Shabby Old Cabby (waltz)	29/06/1939	London	HMV Rejected
JHO	Our Love	29/06/1939	London	HMV BD-5500
JHO	Sing A Song Of Sunbeams	29/06/1939	London	HMV BD-5503
JHO	That Sly Old Gentleman (From Featherbed Lane)	29/06/1939	London	HMV BD-5503
JHO	Boomps-A-Daisy	29/06/1939	London	HMV BD-5499
JHO	Stairway To The Stars	24/07/1939	London	HMV BD-5513
JHO	My Prayer	24/07/1939	London	HMV BD-5508
JHO	Dance Hits Of The Day - Part 1	24/07/1939	London	HMV BD-5509
JHO	Wish Me Luck	24/07/1939	London	HMV BD-5508
JHO	Dance Hits Of The Day - Part 2	24/07/1939	London	HMV BD-5509
JHO	Sunrise Serenade	24/07/1939	London	HMV BD-5513
JHO	White Sails	14/09/1939	London	HMV BD-5518

JHO	I Poured My Heart Into A Song	14/09/1939	London	HMV BD-5517
JHO	The Girl Who Loves A Sailor	14/09/1939	London	HMV BD-5523
JHO	An Old Fashioned Song Is Always New	14/09/1939	London	HMV BD-5517
JHO	Moon Love	14/09/1939	London	HMV BD-5518
JHO	Run, Rabbit, Run	14/09/1939	London	HMV BD-5523
JHO	Bon Voyage, Cherie	09/10/1939	London	HMV BD-5526
JHO	Good Luck Until We Meet Again	09/10/1939	London	HMV BD-5525
JHO	Love Never Grows Old (waltz)	09/10/1939	London	HMV BD-5526
JHO	The Daughter of Madamoiselle From Armentieres	09/10/1939	London	HMV BD-5525
JHO	I'll Remember	06/11/1939	London	HMV BD-5537
JHO	Lords Of The Air	06/11/1939	London	HMV BD-5537
JHO	If A Grey-Haired Lady Says "How's Your Father?"	06/11/1939	London	HMV BD-5528
JHO	Ridin' Home	06/11/1939	London	HMV BD-5528
JHO	Day In, Day Out	06/11/1939	London	HMV BD-5539
JHO	Blue Orchids	06/11/1939	London	HMV BD-5539
JHO	A Mother's Prayer At Twilight	08/11/1939	London	HMV BD-5530
JHO	Most Gentlemen Don't Like Love	08/11/1939	London	HMV BD-5538
JHO	Crash! Bang! I Want To Go Home	08/11/1939	London	HMV BD-766
JHO	Oh, Ain't It Grand To Be In The Navy?	08/11/1939	London	HMV BD-765
JHO	The Hole In The wall	08/11/1939	London	HMV BD-765
JHO	Willow, Tit Willow	08/11/1939	London	HMV BD-766
JHO	Have You Met Miss Jones?	08/11/1939	London	HMV BD-5529
JHO	Al Clear - Medley	10/11/1939	London	HMV BD-783
JHO	Black Velvet - Medley	10/11/1939	London	HMV BD-783
JHO	Get Out Of Town	10/11/1939	London	HMV BD-5529
JHO	My Heart Belongs To Daddy	10/11/1939	London	HMV Rejected
JHO	Goodbye, Sally	10/11/1939	London	HMV BD-5530
JHO	My Heart Belongs To Daddy	17/11/1939	London	HMV BD-5538
JHO	Heaven Will Be Heavenly	17/11/1939	London	HMV BD-802
JHO	My Heart Belongs To Daddy	17/11/1939	London	HMV BD-785

Jack Hylton

JHO	Most Gentlemen Don't Like Love	17/11/1939	London	HMV BD-785
JHO	Follow The White Line (Arthur Askey)	28/11/1939	London	HMV BD-781
JHO	I'll Remember (Arthur Askey)	28/11/1939	London	HMV BD-788
JHO	I'm Sending A Letter To Santa Claus (Arthur Askey)	28/11/1939	London	HMV BD-788
JHO	F. D. R. Jones (Arthur Askey)	28/11/1939	London	HMV BD-781
JHO	We'll Meet Again	29/11/1939	London	HMV BD-5540
JHO	Somewhere In France With You	29/11/1939	London	HMV BD-5540
JHO	I Hear A Dream	29/11/1939	London	HMV BD-5541
JHO	Faithful Forever	29/11/1939	London	HMV BD-5541
JHO	The Organ Grinder Grinds All Day	01/12/1939	London	HMV BD-5548
JHO	Fare Thee Well	01/12/1939	London	HMV BD-5547
JHO	Goodnight, Children, Everywhere	01/12/1939	London	HMV BD-5547
JHO	Haw Haw	01/12/1939	London	HMV BD-5549
JHO	You've Done Something To My Heart	02/12/1939	London	HMV BD-5544
JHO	Drift	02/12/1939	London	HMV BD-5544
JHO	All Through A Glass Of Champagne (waltz)	02/12/1939	London	HMV BD-5548
JHO	Little Boy Bubbles	02/12/1939	London	HMV BD-5549
JHO	Bella Bambina	21/12/1939	London	HMV BD-5552
JHO	Grandma's Parcel	21/12/1939	London	HMV BD-5553
JHO	Scatterbrain	21/12/1939	London	HMV BD-5555
JHO	Where Or When	21/12/1939	London	HMV BD-5556
JHO	So Deep Is The Night	22/12/1939	London	HMV BD-5554
JHO	Over The Rainbow	22/12/1939	London	HMV BD-5552
JHO	Good Morning	22/12/1939	London	HMV BD-5556
JHO	Oh, Johnny	22/12/1939	London	HMV BD-5555
JHO	Are You Havin' Any Fun?	22/12/1939	London	HMV BD-5554
JHO	Boom	22/12/1939	London	HMV BD-5553
JHO	The Only One Who's Difficult Is You	23/12/1939	London	HMV BD-5558
JHO	Heaven Will Be Heavenly	23/12/1939	London	HMV BD-5557
JHO	Roadhouse Revels	23/12/1939	London	HMV BD-5557

Complete UK Discography

JHO	Melody Maker	23/12/1939	London	HMV BD-5558
JHO	There'll Never Be Another You	01/02/1940	London	HMV BD-5563
JHO	Rosita	01/02/1940	London	HMV BD-5562
JHO	Let The People Sing	01/02/1940	London	HMV BD-5562
JHO	Lilacs In The Rain	01/02/1940	London	HMV BD-5561
JHO	In An 18th Century Drawing-Room	01/02/1940	London	HMV BD-5561
JHO	Neath The Shanty Town Moon	01/02/1940	London	HMV BD-5563
JHO	You Never Miss The Old Faces	01/02/1940	London	HMV BD-5564
JHO	It's A Lovely Day Tomorrow	01/02/1940	London	HMV BD-5564
JHO	Moonlight Avenue	06/03/1940	London	HMV BD-5571
JHO	A Little Rain Must Fall	06/03/1940	London	HMV BD-5571
JHO	Give A Little Whistle	06/03/1940	London	HMV BD-5570
JHO	Little Wooden Head	06/03/1940	London	HMV BD-5570

Jack Hylton

Bibliography

Books and Articles

Ades, David; Bickerdyke, Percy; Holmes, Eric, *This England's Book Of British Dance Bands*. Cheltenham: This England Books, 1999

Beardsley, Robert & Leech-Wilkinson, Daniel, *A Brief History Of Recording To Ca. 1950*, <http://www.charm.rhul.ac.uk/history/p20_4_1.html>

Bickerdyke, Percy And Arthur Jackson, Dance Band Days: Jack Hylton, *This England*, Winter, 1992

Briggs, Asa, *The History Of Broadcasting In The United Kingdom: Volume I: The Birth Of Broadcasting*, Oxford: OUP, 1995

Carew, Les, How Are The Mighty..?, *Nostalgia*, Vol.10 No.40, October 1990

Chapman, Gary, Welcome To The Cabaret, *The Jazz Age*, <http://www. jazzage-club.com/cabaret/welcome-to-the-cabaret/>

Chilton, John, *Who's Who Of British Jazz: 2nd Edition*, London: Bloomsbury Publishing, June 2004.

Colin, Sid, *And The Bands Played On*, London: Elm Tree Books, 1977

Craft, Robert, Ed. *Selected Letters And Diaries Of Vera And Igor Stravinsky: Dearest Bubushkin*, London: Thames And Hudson, 1985

Dherbier, Yann-Price, *Audrey Hepburn: A Life In Pictures*, London: Anova Books, 2007

Dregni, Michael, *Django: The Life and Music of a Gypsy Legend*, Oxford: OUP, 2006

Faint, Peter, *Jack Hylton, His Life in Music*, unpublished MPhil thesis, University of Lancaster, 1999

Fenton, Alasdair, Jax Bax, *RSVP*, April 1966

Garfield, Simon, *We Are At War: The Diaries of Five Ordinary People in Extraordinary Times*, Random House, London, 2005

Godbolt, Jim, *A History Of Jazz In Britain 1919-50*, Northway Publications, 2005

Goodman, Arnold, *Tell Them I'm On My Way*, London: Chapmans, 1993

Hayes, Chris, *Leader Of The Band*, Blackpool: Lancastrian Transport, 1994

Holloway, Stanley, *Wiv A Little Bit O' Luck*, London: Frewin, 1967

Jackson, Jeffrey H., *Making Jazz French: Music and Modern Life in Interwar Paris*, Durham, North Carolina: Duke University Press, July 2003

Jack Hylton

Kernfeld, Barry, Ed. *The New Grove Dictionary Of Jazz*, London: Macmillan, 1988

Kershaw, Baz (et al) *The Cambridge History Of British Theatre, Volume 3*, Cambridge University Press, 2004

Kilburn, Michael, *London's Theatres*, London: New Holland Publishers, 2002

Kirkwood, Pat, *The Time Of My Life*, Robert Hale Ltd., 1999

Laurence, Dan H., Ed., *Shaw's Music – The Complete Music Criticism Of Bernard Shaw, Volume 3*. London: The Bodley Head, 1989

Lipton Farris, Celia, *My Three Lives*, Irc Promotions, Inc., 2008

Logan, Pamela W., *Jack Hylton Presents*, London: BFI, 1995

Lubenow, William C., *Liberal Intellectuals And Public Culture In Modern Britain, 1815-1914: Making Words Flesh*, Boydell & Brewer, 2010

Lynn, Vera, *Vocal Refrain*, London: W.H.Allen, 1975

Mccarthy, Albert, *The Dance Band Era*, London: Hamlyn, 1971

Martland, Peter, *Recording History The British Record Industry 1888-1931*. Plymouth: Scarecrow Press, 2013

Mellor, Geoff J., *The Northern Music Hall*, Newcastle-Upon-Tyne: Frank Graham, 1970

Muir, Frank, *A Kentish Lad*, London: Random House, 2012,

Owen, Maureen, *The Crazy Gang – A Personal Reminiscence*, London: Weidenfeld And Nicolson, 1986

Parker, John, *Who's Who In The Theatre: A Biographical Record of the Contemporary Stage, Twelfth Edition*, London: Pitman, 1956

Parsonage, Catherine, *The Evolution Of Jazz In Britain 1880-1935*, London: Ashgate, 2005

Parsonage, Catherine, A Critical Reassessment Of The Reception Of Early Jazz In Britain. *Popular Music*, 22(3), 2003

Pertwee, Bill, *Pertwee's Promenades and Pierrots*, London: Westbridge Books, 1979

Riesenfeld, Hugo, "New Forms For Old Noises", *League Of Composers Review [Modern Music]* 1 (June 1924)

Rust, Brian, *The Dance Bands*, Shepperton: Ian Allen, 1972

Rust, Brian And Sandy Forbes, *British Dance Bands On Record, 1911-1945 and Supplement, 2nd Rev. Ed.*, Harrow: General Gramophone, 1989

Rust, Brian, *Fascinating Rhythm*, Baldock: Egon, 1990

Bibliography

Schuller, Gunther, *Early Jazz: Its Roots And Musical Development*, New York: OUP, 1968

Stravinsky, Igor And Robert Craft, *Expositions And Developments*, London: Faber, 1962

Stravinsky, Igor And Robert Craft, *Selected Correspondence Volume II*, London: Faber, 1984

Taruskin, Richard, *Stravinsky And The Russian Traditions Volume II*, Oxford: OUP, 1996

Tracy, Sheila, *Talking Swing*, Edinburgh: Mainstream, 1997

Tucker, Mark, Ed., *The Duke Ellington Reader*, New York: OUP, 1993

Vedey, Julian, *Band Leaders*, London: Rockliff, 1950

Walker, Ted, The "Queen's" Dance Orchestra, *Storyville 15*, London: Storyville Publications And Co. February-March 1968

White, E.W., *Stravinsky*, London: Faber, 1966

Whitehouse, Edmund, *London Lights: A History Of West End Musicals*, Cheltenham: This England Books, 2005

Williams, John, *Miss Shirley Bassey*, London: Quercus, 2010

Willis, Ted, *Evening All*, London: Macmillan, 1991

Radio Programmes

Clarke, Tony, *The Band That Jack Built*, BBC Light Programme, September 14th, 1965

Dell, Alan, *The Golden Age Of British Dance Bands*, BBC Radio Two, 1972

Fenton, Alasdair, *Jack's Back*, BBC Radio Blackburn, October 13th, 1971

Race, Steve, *The Jack Hylton Story*, BBC Radio Two, February/March 1994

Richards, Jeffrey, *Salvaging Jack Hylton*, August 7th, 2004

Personal Correspondence

Drew, Malcolm. Private Correspondence, February 1998

Fenton, Alasdair. Private Correspondence, April 1998

Hylton, John. Private Interviews, 1998 & 2014

McKay, Lady Beverley. Private Interview, July 1998

Munn, Billy. Private Interview, March 1997

Jack Hylton

Ramos, Jackie. Private Interview, August 1998

Archives

Jack Hylton Archive, Lancaster University, Lancaster

National Jazz Archive, Loughton Central Library, Traps Hill, Loughton, Essex

Jack Hylton Archive, V&A Museum, London

The National Archives, Kew, Richmond

EMI Archive Trust, Hayes, Middlesex

Index

Index

I

J

K

L

M

Index

Index

CPSIA information can be obtained at www.ICGtesting.com
Printed in the USA
BVOW08*1154230716

456620BV00004B/13/P